D0862442

This is a textbook designed for senior undergraduate courses in monetary economics, advanced macroeconomics, or macroeconomic policy. Students will feel comfortable with this material if they have completed an intermediate course in macroeconomics, relying on one of the more demanding texts in this field. The prime focus of the book is on the role of money in the macroeconomy and on the place of monetary policy as an instrument for controlling inflation and unemployment. There are only three important macrovariables that are featured: the rate of inflation, the interest rate, and output or income. Behavioral relationships in the goods, money, and labor markets determine these variables, using only the now common *IS–LM–AS* model. The model is not ideological, but opposing views of the efficacy of stabilization policy are allowed to confront each other. There is a great deal of emphasis on relating the theoretical propositions to recent Canadian and U.S. macroeconomic performance. To expose students to diversity of experience, both countries receive equal treatment, one to serve as an example of a closed economy and the other as an example of an open economy.

The book relies mostly on verbal and diagrammatical exposition; equations are used to show why and how curves shift in the diagrams. Also, numerical examples are provided in "boxes" at appropriate places in the text, and exercises are given at the end of most chapters. A booklet containing answers to these exercises is available to instructors on request to the author.

Martin F. J. Prachowny is professor of economics at Queen's University, where he has taught since 1967. He is the author of four previous books (most recently *Macroeconomic Analysis for Small Open Economies*), and is a member of the American Economic Association, the Canadian Economic Association, and the Royal Economic Society.

MONEY IN THE MACROECONOMY

Money in the macroeconomy

Martin F. J. Prachowny
Professor of Economics
Queen's University

Cambridge University Press
Cambridge
London New York New Rochelle
Melbourne Sydney

Published by the Press Syndicate of the University of Cambridge
The Pitt Building, Trumpington Street, Cambridge CB2 1RP
32 East 57th Street, New York, NY 10022, USA
10 Stamford Road, Oakleigh, Melbourne 3166, Australia

First published 1985

Printed in the United States of America

Library of Congress Cataloging in Publication Data

Prachowny, Martin F. J.

Money in the macroeconomy.

Includes bibliographies and index.

1. Monetary policy. 2. Macroeconomics. I. Title.
HG230.3.P7 1985 339.5'3 85-12795

British Library Cataloguing in Publication Data

Prachowny, Martin F. J.

Money in the macroeconomy.

1. Money – Mathematical models
2. Macroeconomics – Mathematical models
I. Title
332.4 HG221.3

ISBN 0 521 30613 2 hard covers
ISBN 0 521 31594 8 paperback

Contents

Charts, figures, and tables

Charts

Figures

Tables

Preface

This textbook is intended to serve courses in monetary economics, advanced macroeconomics, or macroeconomic policy. Students will feel comfortable with this material if they have completed an intermediate course in macroeconomics relying on one of the more demanding textbooks in this field.

The book focuses primarily on the role of money in the macroeconomy and on the place of monetary policy as an instrument for controlling inflation and unemployment. From beginning to end there is only one macroeconomic model that the student must understand: the now common *IS–LM–AS* model. The three behavioral relationships in this model determine the three important variables in the macroeconomy: the rate of inflation, the interest rate, and income or output.

Although there is great temptation to take sides on the ideological issues in macroeconomics, the *IS–LM–AS* model is a middle-of-the-road approach that allows both monetarist and institutionalist views of the world to be incorporated. In fact, these views are allowed to confront each other, especially in Chapters 3 and 4, but no winner can be declared in this debate. This may be frustrating to an undergraduate student who expects only indisputable facts in a textbook, but controversy cannot be avoided, because macroeconomics now relies so heavily on unobservable variables such as expected inflation and the natural rate of unemployment. If we cannot measure these variables with any confidence, then we cannot verify or reject competing hypotheses that involve behavioral relationships among these and other variables, and we cannot conclude that empirical evidence favors one side or the other.

The book is designed for both American and Canadian students. In economics we learn from diversity; from that perspective it is useful to compare the monetary experience of Canada and that of the United States since 1975, not only because one is an "open" economy and the other is "closed" but also, and more important, because they have tried to reach similar goals, with essentially similar methods but not always with uniform results. Data from both countries will be presented and applied to the theoretical and policy issues that arise from the analysis. Only those events through the end of 1982 are treated in these applied sections of the book; by the time these sections are read, the discussion may appear somewhat "dated," but the role of empirical evidence here is to test the model, not to provide definitive judgments on the latest developments and policies.

It is customary for writers of textbooks to apologize for the heavy use of difficult mathematics. No such apology is necessary here, because the exposition is mainly verbal and diagrammatic. Some equations are used, but their manipulation requires only high-school algebra, and they help the student to understand how and why curves shift. Calculus is used in only two minor instances. However, natural logs are an important feature of the *IS–LM–AS* model, because they make it easier to explain inflation in equilibrium; an appendix to Chapter 2, where they first appear, explains the use of logs in simple terms and with illustrations. As a further aid to understanding abstract theory, numerical examples are provided in "boxes" at appropriate places in the text, and exercises are given at the ends of most chapters. Finally, to avoid confusion regarding what each symbol means, a complete list of definitions of symbols is provided.

A final word of advice. An economics textbook is not bedtime reading. A student should not expect to *understand* the material in this book without manipulating the equations and curves over and over again, without making copious notes in the margins and figures, and without working through each argument carefully.

After three years of writing this book I am no longer certain that I can remember all those who made the process less difficult or more pleasant or both, and so this is, at best, an incomplete list of my acknowledgments. First, I would like to thank all my mentors in monetary economics, especially the late Warren Smith of the University of Michigan, whose enthusiasm for the subject remains infectious to this day. Next, my colleague Neil Bruce should be credited with creating the elegant simplicity of the open-economy model in Chapter 9. Further, I would like to extend my gratitude to Christopher Holling, who kindly provided some econometric results for use in Chapter 5. My debates with Murray Frank on macroeconomic ideology led me to take a more even-handed approach than I might have otherwise. Also, anonymous editorial readers fortunately caused me to rethink some of the more muddled material in earlier drafts of the manuscript. My wife, Marguerite Prachowny, not just "le chef de cuisine'' in our household, made indispensable editorial contributions for which the reader will certainly be grateful, as am I. Last, my students in Economics 322 at Queen's University stimulated me to try the herculean task of making monetary economics both fascinating and rigorous. Even though I may not have succeeded, to them this book is dedicated.

Martin F. J. Prachowny

Kingston, Ontario

List of symbols

a_0	natural log of exogenous expenditures in the *IS* curve
a_1	interest elasticity of investment in the *IS* curve
a_2	income elasticity of the demand for money in the *LM* curve
a_3	interest (semi)elasticity of the demand for money in the *LM* curve
a_4	price elasticity of output in the *AS* curve
a_5	price elasticity of demand for home goods in the open-economy *IS* curve
$b_0 \ldots b_{15}$	parameters in the behavioral relationships underlying the *IS–LM–AS* model
b_g, b_m, b_s	coefficients capturing the pervasiveness of previous shocks to goods, money, and labor markets
C_b, C_p	currency held by the banks and by the public
$c_0 \ldots c_9$	contrived coefficients required to calculate rational expectations
D_b, D_p	demand and time deposits held by the public at commercial banks
D_t	deposits of the commercial banks at the central bank
e_d, e_t	reserve ratios for demand and time deposits
f	indexation factor
G_1, G_2	individual commodities
g	coefficient of adjustment in money holdings
h	weight attached to home goods in the consumption bundle of an open economy
h^*	weight attached to home goods in the consumption bundle of the foreign economy
I	natural log of investment and government expenditures (and exports in an open economy)

i	interest rate, sometimes the natural log of the interest rate
i_B, i_K	rate of return to bonds and equities
i^*	foreign interest rate
J	per-unit cost of exchanging money and bonds
j	coefficient of adaptive expectations
K	natural log of capital-stock services
k	natural log of the money multiplier
L	natural log of units of labor supplied
M	nominal money balances
m	natural log of nominal money balances
m_b	natural log of monetary base
μ	growth rate of nominal money balances
$\mu 1$, $\mu 2$, $\mu 3$	growth rate of M1, M2, and M3
μ_b	growth rate of the monetary base
μ_s, μ_r	growth rate of central bank holdings of government securities and international reserves
N	natural log of units of labor demanded
n	number of goods or time periods
P	price level
P_1, P_2	price of individual goods
p	natural log of the price level
p^*	natural log of foreign price level
p_c	natural log of domestic Consumer Price Index
p_c^*	natural log of foreign Consumer Price Index
π	inflation rate
π^*	foreign inflation rate
π_c	rate of increase of consumer prices
π_c^*	rate of increase of foreign consumer prices
π^e	expected rate of inflation
π_o^e, π_n^e	expected rate of inflation in old and new labor contracts
π^{*e}	expected rate of inflation in the rest of the world
π_c^e	expected rate of increase of consumer prices
Q	real income or output
q_c, q_t, q_e	currency ratio, time deposit ratio, and excess reserve ratio
r	natural log of exchange rate
r^e	natural log of expected exchange rate
ρ	rate of change of exchange rate
ρ^e	expected rate of change of the exchange rate
S	natural log of saving and taxes (and imports in an open economy)
s	proportion of government securities in the monetary base

t	natural log of the terms of trade
t_e	natural log of equilibrium terms of trade
u	unemployment rate
V	income velocity of money
v	natural log of income velocity of money
w	natural log of nominal wage rate
ω	rate of change of nominal wage rate
ω_o, ω_n	rate of change of nominal wage rate specified in old and new labor contracts
x_b	monetary-base shock
x_g	goods-market shock
x_{i^*}	foreign interest-rate shock
x_k	money-multiplier shock
x_m	money-market shock
x_{π^*}	foreign inflation-rate shock
x_s	supply shock
Y	nominal income
y	natural log of real income or output
y_e	natural log of equilibrium income
y^d	natural log of output demanded
y^s	natural log of output supplied
z_g, z_m, z_s	new components of shocks to goods, money, and labor markets

CHAPTER 1

The roles of money and monetary policy in the macroeconomy

1.1 INTRODUCTION

"Money is what makes the world go 'round," as the old saying has it; but would an absence of money stop the world in its tracks? Probably not. Barter trade, in which people search out one another in an attempt to exchange things they do not want for things they do, would still enable us to survive, but barter trade requires a *double coincidence of wants*: Two people with exactly opposite requirements must find each other. This is time-consuming and wasteful of resources. It might not be easy for a candlestick maker who wants to exchange a surplus candle for a loaf of bread to find a baker who wants to trade bread for a candle and then to negotiate an acceptable exchange ratio between these two goods. This process would have to be repeated many times over as the candlestick maker tries to exchange his output for all the other goods and services that satisfy his wants. Market activity, which processes their transactions, uses up real resources that do not directly satisfy these wants; it is therefore desirable to minimize the costs of these activities. Perhaps "specialists" would appear who would help buyers and sellers to find each other and to consummate their transactions. But these markets would be rather small and thin, and specialists could not earn enough to justify their activities. In essence, barter trade fragments markets. In an economy with n goods there would have to be $n(n - 1)/2$ markets; as n became larger, the number of markets would increase even faster.

EXAMPLE

For three goods, candles, bread, and wine, there would have to be three markets: candles exchanging for bread, candles for wine, and bread for wine. Adding one more good, sausages, would add the requirement for three more markets: sausages for candles, bread, and wine.

The contrivance of money reduces or eliminates much of this activity and allows the resources thus saved to be used in more productive ways. The candlestick maker would no longer have to find a baker; he would merely sell his wares in one market and buy his needs in another, using money as the medium of exchange. The requirement of a double coincidence of wants is eliminated. The existence of money saves resource costs of market activity in three ways:

1. It reduces the number of markets. (For n goods there will now be only n markets, one for each good, with money acting as the common denominator in these markets.)
2. It allows the producers of goods and services to devote all their energies to production, rather than dissipating some energy in market activities.
3. Money is more efficient than a market specialist, because money, especially fiat money such as dollar bills, checks, and entries in savings accounts, can be produced at virtually zero cost.

A monetary economy is therefore more efficient than a nonmonetary economy: With the same resources and technology, more goods and services can be produced, simply because transactions with money are cheaper than transactions without money. It is the ability of money to "lubricate" the economy that makes it important, not any ability to satisfy our wants directly.

1.2 THE STUDY OF MONETARY ECONOMICS

It is easy to see that money plays an important and pervasive role in any economy, and hence monetary economics is a broad area. Monetary economics breaks down into two major branches, much the same as in other areas of applied economics: (1) the microeconomic aspect of money, which concerns the characteristics of money; (2) the macroeconomic aspect of money, which concerns the optimum quantity of money. This book does not take an encyclopedic approach to monetary economics; it concentrates on money in the macroeconomy. However, a brief discussion of the issues involved in the other major branch is necessary to set the stage for the rest of the book. Two questions are often asked in monetary economics:

1. What distinguishes money from other things?
2. Why do we want to have it if it provides no direct satisfaction of wants?

Money differs from the other *n* goods in the economy because it is better than any of them as (1) a medium of exchange, (2) a unit of account, and (3) a store of value. To lend some substance to this statement, consider dollar bills as prime examples of money and a loaf of bread as a typical commodity. The assertion is that although bread satisfies certain primitive needs, it does not have good characteristics for use as money; conversely, dollar bills are not very nourishing, but they are better money than is bread. Let us compare dollar bills and loaves of bread in terms of the previously listed characteristics. First, as shown earlier, it is resource-saving to exchange one item for money and then money for another item rather than try to make the exchange directly; hence money serves as a medium of exchange, and dollar bills perform that function better than does a loaf of bread, if for no other reason than that they are easier to carry. Second, we need a reliable unit of account just as we need measurement standards, such as miles, pounds, and gallons. A dollar bill is a well-defined unit of account, but loaves of bread may vary in weight and size and therefore require verification each time they are used.[1] Third, we need to be able to transform present income into future spending, because we do not always spend exactly what we earn in a given period; dollar bills are more durable than bread for this purpose. This is not to argue that dollar bills are the best money in all circumstances or to show that bread is the worst money, but merely to make the general point that money is different from other goods and services and plays a specialized role in the economy.

Because of its special characteristics, money is treated differently in determining an optimal allocation of resources. As a general proposition, we can say that any increase in the availability of goods and services improves our welfare, but regarding money all we can assert is that some is better than none. Individuals are assumed to maximize a utility function, subject to a production or budget constraint. For the simple economy that contains only two goods, G_1 and G_2, Figure 1-1 depicts the optimizing process diagrammatically. Faced by a production-possibility frontier of AB and given an indifference map, of which IC_0 is just one curve, equilibrium is achieved at E_0, where the slope of the indifference curve (MRS or marginal rate of substitution) equals the slope of the production-possibility frontier (MRT or marginal rate of transformation). The optimal

[1] Gold used to circulate in the form of coins in an earlier period, but the temptation to "sweat" coins – shaking them around in a bag to remove small particles – was so great that they had to be inspected carefully each time they were received to ensure that they had full value; no wonder gold coins are no longer used as money!

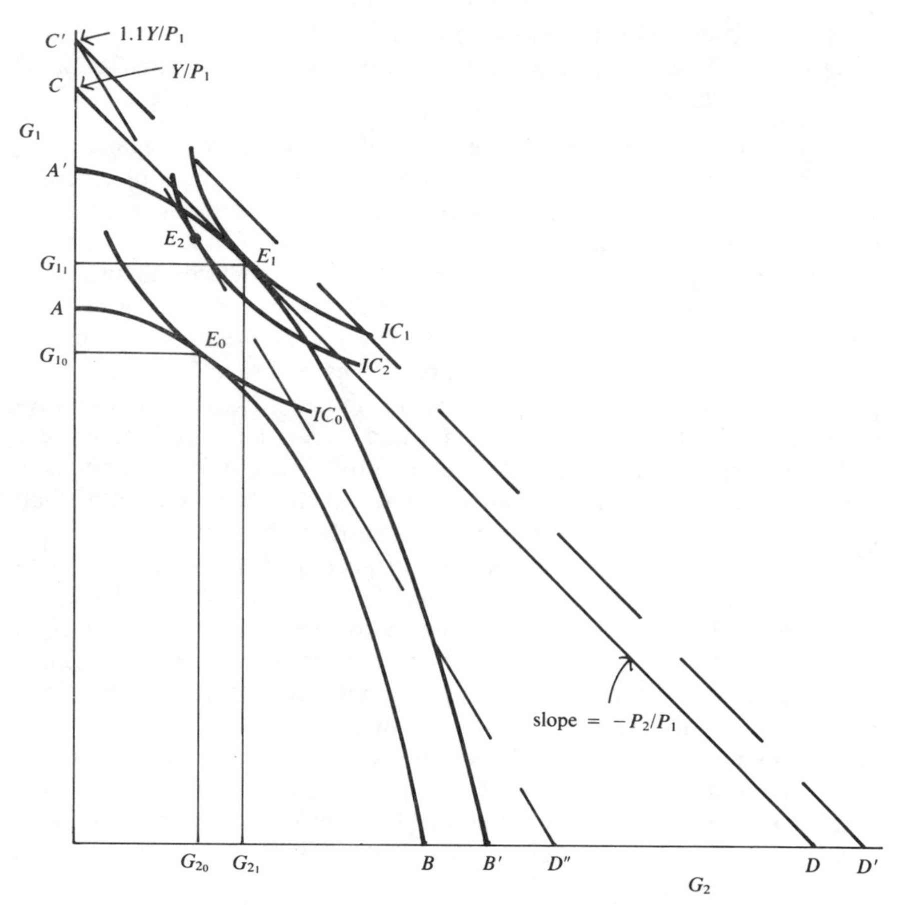

Figure 1-1 Resource allocation, with and without money.

quantities of the two goods are G_{1_0} and G_{2_0}. A change in technology or resource availability affects the location of the production-possibility curve, and a change in tastes affects the location of the indifference map. Either of these events will lead to predictable changes in the optimal quantities of the two goods.

On the other hand, how do we decide on the optimal amount of money? Money cannot be put directly into the utility function because it does not satisfy wants in the same way as G_1 and G_2. Instead, from the previous discussion, we know that money increases the efficiency of the economy, allowing the production-possibility frontier to shift from AB to $A'B'$, enabling the representative individual to move to E_1 on a higher indifference curve, IC_1. Now, with the existence of money, the budget line $Y = P_1G_1 + P_2G_2$, where Y is nominal income and P_1 and P_2 are prices denominated in money, can be rewritten as $G_1 = Y/P_1 - (P_2/P_1)G_2$ and drawn in Figure 1-1 as the line CD, with slope $-P_2/P_1$ and vertical intercept Y/P_1.

The improvement in welfare in moving from a nonmonetary economy at E_0 to a monetary economy at E_1 is self-evident, but the optimal quantity of money to achieve this result is not. All we can do is to assert that there must be a limit to the improvement available from the process of monetizing the economy. In other words, increasing the quantity of money from zero increases the efficiency of the economy up to a point, but after that point is reached, money should be neutral and should not influence our welfare. This property of the *neutrality of money* is important in monetary economics. Its role in the economy can be explored by a mental experiment. Assume that we have reached the highest production-possibility curve that the existence of money allows and now increase the quantity of money by 10% overnight. This is achieved by giving everyone 1.1 times as much money income as before and is depicted by moving to the dashed budget line $C'D'$, where the vertical intercept is $1.1Y/P_1$. People will try to spend their new-found wealth, but the economy is still constrained by the production-possibility curve $A'B'$. As a result, P_1 and P_2 will rise until they are 10% higher than their original values. Only then will the budget line return to its original location, CD, with the same equilibrium at E_1. Hence, the neutrality of money means that *real* magnitudes such as G_1, G_2 and the relative price P_2/P_1 are unaffected by the quantity of money, which only influences *nominal* variables such as Y, P_1, and P_2 in the same proportion.

This is the outcome we would expect in a frictionless economy; however, it is not the only possibility. Consider the same experiment of raising Y by 10%, but this time P_1 will be held constant for some period of time because it is an administered price that can be changed only by legislation. Now the adjustment will differ because $1.1Y/P_1$ is fixed, and the budget line must be anchored at C'. There will still be a rise in P_2, and in the process the budget line will rotate to $C'D''$, with a new tangency to the highest indifference curve, IC_2, at E_2. In this case the economy must operate inside the production-possibility curve if firms produce only that amount that can be sold to customers, implying that some resources are left unemployed. In this experiment, money is definitely not neutral, and its quantity does affect the economy's welfare. The difference in outcomes created by the increase in the amount of money in the economy by 10% is very much the result of the alternative assumptions about frictions in the economy. Frictions can lead to unemployment, and changing the quantity of money therefore brings about changes in the extent of unemployment. We have now made the transition from the microeconomics of money, which is concerned with the benefits of a "price tag economy" over a barter economy, to the macroeconomics of money, which raises questions about how price tags respond to changes in the quantity of money.[2]

1.3 THE IMPORTANCE OF THE QUANTITY OF MONEY

It is now evident that the quantity of money in an economy is important for two reasons:

1. It determines nominal quantities such as prices, and therefore changes in the quantity of money influence the rate of change of prices.
2. In case of frictions existing in the economy, it also determines real quantities such as output and employment.

Both of these are related to the traditional macroeconomic concerns of inflation and unemployment. In this section it is useful to explore in greater detail the effects that changes in the quantity of money have on these important variables.

1.3.1 MONEY AND INFLATION

In macroeconomics, in contrast to microeconomics, interest centers on the determination of absolute prices much more than on relative prices. For that reason, in the two-good economy, the ratio P_2/P_1 will be taken as fixed in the face of changes in the quantity of money. Also, we concentrate on a *price level*, which represents a weighted average of P_1 and P_2, and on a *composite good*, which aggregates the amount of G_1 and G_2 produced in the economy. The price level is usually measured as the price of a "basket of goods," but because relative prices are assumed to remain constant, P_1 and P_2 must move together, and therefore it is easier to identify the price level, P, with either P_1 or P_2. Let us choose P_1 for this purpose. Then the aggregation of G_1 and G_2 is achieved by defining the composite good, Q, as $G_1 + (P_2/P_1)G_2$, which allows us to add candles and bread by using the relative price to translate bread into candles; therefore, Q is measured in the same units as candles. Taking the previously defined budget constraint and substituting the definitions of P and Q, we have

$$(1.1) \quad Y = P_1G_1 + P_2G_2 = P(P_1G_1 + P_2G_2)/P_1$$
$$= P[G_1 + (P_2/P_1)G_2] = PQ$$

[2] The late Arthur Okun coined the descriptive term *price tag economy*.

so that nominal income is the product of the price level and the quantity of the composite good.

EXAMPLE

> Let P_1 = \$2.00, P_2 = \$1.50, G_1 = 20 pounds, and G_2 = 50 gallons. Note that G_1 and G_2 are measured in different units. First, Y = \$115. Next, $P = 2$ (index number) and $Q = 20 + (1.5/2)50 = 57.5$ pounds. Last, we can calculate Y again, this time from P and Q, so that $Y = 2 \times 57.5$ = \$115.

The next step is to relate the quantity of money, M, which is a stock existing at a point in time, to nominal income, Y, which is a flow per unit of time. This is done through the concept of *velocity*, which is defined as the number of times each dollar is used to make transactions during the period of time under consideration. The velocity of money is a measure similar to the speed of a car, that is, miles per hour. Hence,

$$V = Y/M \tag{1.2}$$

where V is a pure number since both Y and M are measured in dollars.

EXAMPLE CONTINUES

> Let M be \$50. If \$115 worth of transactions are made during a period, then $V = 115/50 = 2.3$. That is, each dollar is used 2.3 times per period.

Combining equations (1.1) and (1.2) yields

$$MV = PQ \tag{1.3}$$

which is often called the *equation of exchange*, because both sides of the equation measure the value of goods and services exchanged in the economy: the left side in terms of money and the right side in terms of goods. If V is considered to be an institutionally determined constant based on the transactions technology that exists at that time, and if Q is a particular combination of G_1 and G_2 on the production-possibility curve that is impervious to changes in the quantity of money, then equation (1.3) shows how M and P are related. In general, a given percentage increase in M gives rise to the same percentage increase in P.

EXAMPLE CONTINUES

> Let there be a 10% increase in M; thus, the new value of $M = 1.1 \times \$50 = \$55$. Since V is still equal to 2.3 and $Q = 57.5$, P must rise from 2 to 2.2, an increase of 10%.

Thus, even in a frictionless economy, the quantity of money plays an important role: It is the sole determinant of the rate of inflation. Furthermore, changing the growth rate of the money supply should have predictable effects on the rate of inflation.

The term *inflation* is often misused. Inflation does not mean a one-time increase in the price level; instead, it means that prices rise continuously. Inflation does not mean that the price of any one good is rising; instead, it means that the price level is rising. Lower inflation does not mean that the price level is falling; instead, it means that the price level is rising at a slower rate.

1.3.2 MONEY AND OUTPUT OR EMPLOYMENT

Although equation (1.3) is an identity that is true at all times and under all circumstances, the one-for-one relationship between M and P derived earlier represents only one of many possibilities and is likely to be achieved only in a frictionless, stationary economy. However, as in physics, economic relationships are often characterized by frictions. Frictions come from many sources, but their general effect is that they prevent instantaneous reestablishment of equilibrium in a market if some exogenous event has created a situation of disequilibrium.

Let us return to the equation of exchange to explore an alternative relationship, this time holding P constant because friction of some kind prevents both P_1 and P_2 from changing to preserve equilibrium in the market for G_1 and G_2. Now let V fall exogenously by 10%. If M is given and P remains constant, the decline in V must be reflected in an equiproportionate change in Q, as well as equiproportionate changes in G_1 and G_2 individually.

EXAMPLE CONTINUES

> V decreases from 2.3 to 2.07. If $M = \$50$, then MV will now be \$103.50; since $P = 2$, then $Q = 51.75$, which is also a drop of 10%

from its previous value of 57.5. Finally, since P_2/P_1 remains at .75, the drop in Q must be shared equally between G_1 and G_2; G_1 falls from 20 to 18, and G_2 from 50 to 45.

Now the economy is operating inside the production-possibility curve; more could be produced, but demand for the composite good has declined. Such a situation would not be economically desirable, because we would observe some resources being unemployed; their extra output could be used to satisfy our wants, which are limitless. In this light, can the quantity of money be changed to restore the previous position of equilibrium on the production-possibility curve with the full employment of all resources? The answer is yes in this case. If V declines by 10%, all that need be done to keep PQ constant is to increase the quantity of money by 10%, since this will hold MV constant. In other words, changing the quantity of money in a world that has some frictions can overcome the effects of exogenous changes on output. If we cannot eliminate the frictions, at least we can manipulate the quantity of money to maintain equilibrium in the economy.

Why is equilibrium "good" and disequilibrium "bad"? One might think that the term *equilibrium* is not a normative concept but purely a descriptive one, implying simply that supply equals demand. But since a supply curve shows how suppliers want to react when prices change and a demand curve shows how demanders want to adjust their purchases when prices rise or fall, only in equilibrium are both groups satisfied; in disequilibrium, one or both groups will be dissatisfied. Thus, equilibrium is desirable in its own right.

This point requires further clarification. In Figure 1-2, a simple demand-and-supply diagram is drawn. At this stage it does not matter what commodity is represented by the price–quantity relationships in the supply and demand curves. Any point on the demand curve indicates an optimal position for the consumer of that commodity, given his or her income and prices of all other goods. The same optimality holds true for all positions on the supply curve for the producers of this commodity. Only the point E_0 allows both groups to reach their optimum simultaneously. At P_0, demanders and suppliers are content to make exchanges equal to P_0E_0. Any other price–quantity combination is inferior for one or both participants in the market. Consider, for example, a price such as P_1. This is a position of excess supply. It is not obvious that any transactions will take place at this price, but if they do, the quantity exchanged will be at E_2 which is the lesser of two quantities: the amount demanded, E_2, and the amount supplied, E_1. In this case, suppliers of E_1E_2 will be unhappy since they cannot get rid of this quantity. Lowering the price from P_1 to

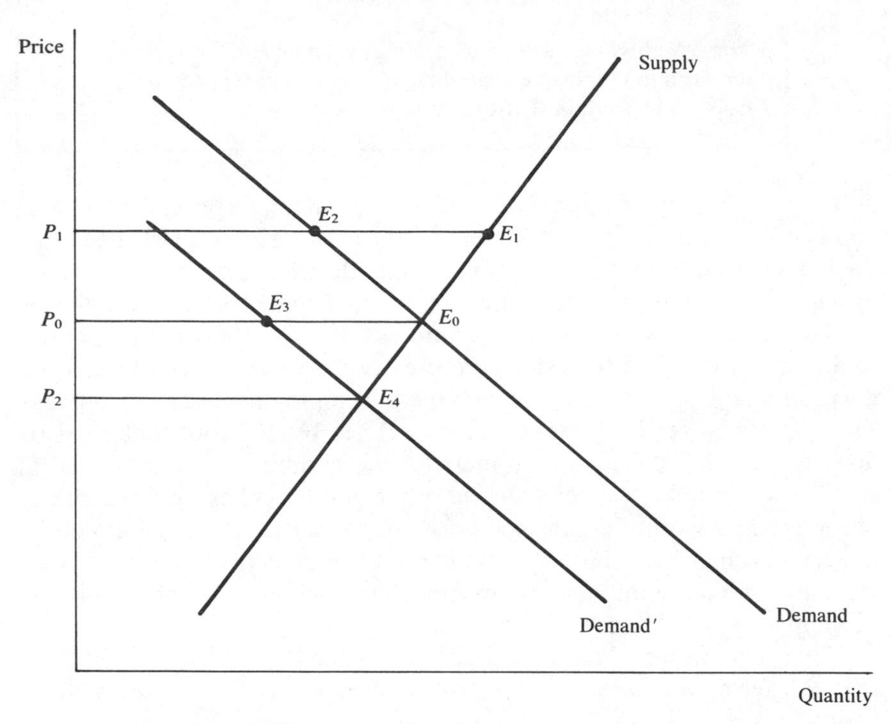

Figure 1-2 Equilibrium and disequilibrium in a market.

P_0 would make both suppliers and demanders better off. Alternatively, at any price below P_0 there is excess demand, and if transactions take place, only the quantity supplied at that price would be exchanged. Now an increase in the price would improve the welfare of both groups. Hence there are powerful forces pulling a market to equilibrium and there is a strong association between equilibrium and welfare maximization. At the same time, there are frictions that prevent instantaneous achievement of equilibrium, and thus disequilibrium may last for some period of time.

In a macroeconomy there are three groups of markets: (1) the market for goods and services; (2) the market for assets, of which money is the most prominent; and (3) the market for factors of production, with labor receiving primary attention. All these markets have some frictions, but they are likely to be most significant in the labor market. The reason for this is that transactions in this market are based on *contracts*, in which employees and employers establish an implicit or explicit relationship of some duration, the conditions of which are set out at the beginning of the term of the contract. There are two main lines of argument that favor contractual transactions over spot transactions in the labor market:

1. They are the only satisfactory way of dealing with deferred benefits such as vacation pay and pensions.
2. They save on transactions costs of establishing such a relationship since these costs tend to be fixed.

Examples of such costs are those of obtaining reliable information about the employee by the employer and vice versa and the costs of negotiating union contracts, including the threats of strikes and lockouts; being of a fixed nature, the less frequently they are incurred, the better. However, the existence of contracts creates frictions in the labor market and raises the possibility of disequilibrium prevailing for some time.[3]

Returning to Figure 1-2, now interpreted as the labor market with the quantity axis measuring the number of hours supplied and demanded in the market and the price axis the wage rate per hour, suppose that at the beginning of the period workers and employers agree to a wage rate of P_0 based on the marginal product of labor on the demand curve equaling the marginal disutility of work on the supply curve at E_0, and leading to P_0E_0 hours of work as the planned exchange. Then it becomes known that the demand curve for labor has really shifted downward because of an unexpected decline in the marginal product of labor at every level of employment. The new equilibrium would now be found at E_4 with the wage declining to P_2 and the quantity of work to P_2E_4. But the contract still stipulates P_0 as the wage rate, even in the new circumstances, which now produces excess supply as firms are likely to move to E_3, laying off workers to the extent of E_0E_3. In this situation, there is an incentive to renegotiate the contract to eliminate this disequilibrium, but there is also a disincentive because of the transactions costs involved in the negotiating process. If the costs of unemployment are less than the costs of negotiating, the contract will remain in force and the labor market will exhibit disequilibrium until the contract expires. Alternatively, if the costs of unemployment exceed the costs of negotiating a new contract, the old contract will be abrogated by mutual consent and the economy will move fairly quickly from E_0 to E_4. Therefore, the importance of frictions in the labor market depend on such factors as the size of the disturbance, the extent of disequilibrium, the length of contracts, and the cost of negotiating new ones. Frictions can also exist in goods and asset markets, but they are likely to be of lesser relative importance because traditional attachments between buyers and sellers are not as significant in these markets, and therefore spot transactions are more advantageous than contractual transactions.

In summary, a macroeconomy in which all markets are in equilibrium has achieved a certain kind of optimality. This does not mean that every-

[3] Okun also coined the term *invisible handshake* to describe implicit contracts.

one is satisfied with the income distribution, with the division between the private and public sectors or with a host of other economic conditions, nor does it mean that all other kinds of distortions have been eliminated. In that sense, one should not identify equilibrium with Pareto optimality, the "bliss point" of the economy. Nevertheless, economists tend to claim that equilibrium is "good" and disequilibrium is "bad" because only at the point where supply equals demand are the frustrations of unsatisfied buyers or sellers eliminated. An economy faced with the necessity of moving from one equilibrium to another after some exogenous event may not be able to reach the new equilibrium in an instant because of the existence of frictions. Since the quantity of money can be used to overcome frictions that cannot be eliminated and to restore equilibrium, who should control this important macroeconomic variable? We now turn to an answer to this crucial question.

1.3.3 MONEY AND MONETARY POLICY

The amount of money in an economy cannot be left to market forces. Whatever one's view about the appropriate role of the public sector relative to the private sector, the determination of the money supply must be left to the government as the decision maker in the public sector. Since money represents command over goods and services, competitive market determination of the money supply would be impossible. Everyone would want to issue money with which to buy the things that they want. Since this is essentially a costless process, especially relative to "earning" the money through work, everyone would prefer printing money to working. The result would be an infinite supply of money and no goods and services on which to spend the money; prices would also rise to infinity and money would become useless. Money is made useful by its scarcity relative to goods and services over which it has purchasing power. Therefore, we need to have a monopoly in the production of money, and that monopoly must rest with the government as the protector of the public interest.[4]

It is true that in most countries a large part of the quantity of money is not issued directly by governments through its central bank in the form of currency or coin. In fact, most of what is used as money is a liability of the private banking system in the form of various checking and savings accounts that households and firms maintain at banks. But this does not mean that the supply of money is really in private hands after all. The central bank controls the size of the privately supplied quantity of money through reserve requirements and other banking legislation. Therefore, the government influences the quantity of money in the economy in an indirect and admittedly imperfect manner. How should the government

[4] However, these issues are debated once more in Section 12.3.

use this influence? There is little controversy over the proposition that the government should exercise monetary policy in such a way as to maximize the country's welfare, but there is considerable dispute among economists as to how this is best achieved.

The choice that has to be made by policy makers is between manipulating the quantity of money to influence the price level, P, and adjusting the money supply to change the amount of the composite good, Q. If there are no frictions present in the economy, then Q is impervious to changes in M and the quantity of money can be geared to the determination of the price level. But in this situation there are no welfare implications involved in this choice. Since the price level is irrelevant to the well-being of the economy, it is essentially an arbitrary and meaningless decision. However, if there are frictions in the economy, especially in the labor market, it would appear self-evident that M should be manipulated to keep Q at a point on the production-possibility curve, a quantity that is often called *full-employment output*. Instead, even in this environment, there is a seemingly unresolvable conflict about the optimal target for monetary policy.

On the one hand, there is a group of economists, often labeled as Keynesian but better described as interventionist, who argue that the private sector cannot maintain equilibrium in the economy without help from the public sector through the provision of the right amount of M. Therefore, their policy advice is to increase the supply of money whenever Q falls below its full-employment level and, for symmetry, to lower the money supply if Q has a tendency to move above the production-possibility curve.[5] In other words, monetary policy becomes stabilization policy; it is used to "fine-tune" the economy through active intervention in the money market to maintain equilibrium in the labor market in the face of exogenous events that have a tendency to create disequilibrium.

On the other side of the debate are the noninterventionist economists (often called monetarists) who argue in favor of a stable and predictable path for the money supply and against the central bank reacting to changes in Q. They tend to downplay the importance of frictions. Instead, they believe that the self-equilibrating forces are powerful and operate quickly to eliminate frictions. The basis of their stand against intervention is that attempts at fine-tuning the economy introduce frictions rather than overcome them. This argument goes as follows:

> Labor-market contracts attempt to achieve and maintain equilibrium for the duration of the contract because this is in everyone's interest.

[5] Overfull employment is possible if the capital stock is worked harder than is optimal in the long run and if excess demand in the labor market is allowed to prevail for some time.

In order to maximize the possibility of equilibrium, both sides have to have information about future developments, including the expected change in the price level during the contract.

The best indicator of the price level is the money supply, and therefore predictability of this variable enables workers and firms to make agreements that contain more useful information and that are therefore better than if the money supply were unpredictable.

If the central bank, however, uses the money supply to respond to deviations of Q from equilibrium, then M essentially becomes unpredictable and cannot be used for forming expectations about the future price level. By taking away an important source of useful information, the central bank forces the participants in the labor market to look for alternative and more expensive sources of information resulting in higher costs of negotiating contracts or to make alternative contractual arrangements, such as cost-of-living allowances, that make the real wage constant ex post, but introduce a new rigidity or friction if this variable has to change during the contract to maintain labor-market equilibrium.

Therefore, the differences between the two sides seem to hinge on the role of frictions in the economy and the contribution that monetary policy makes to creating them or overcoming them. The debate is therefore about empirical issues: What and how large are the transactions costs that create frictions in an economy, and what is the best way to minimize them? The conflicting views are not easily reconciled, but they raise important issues about the success of stabilization policy. Thus the next three chapters are devoted to a presentation of macroeconomic theory and the role of monetary policy as a stabilization instrument. First, Chapter 2 spells out the basic long-run version of the macroeconomic model, in which by definition there is no role for stabilization policy. Then Chapters 3 and 4 present the two schools of thought on this issue and show the differences in the conclusions that can be drawn about the effectiveness of stabilization policy.

1.4 COMPARATIVE EXPERIENCE WITH RECENT MONETARY POLICY

Because both sides realize that empirical evidence will ultimately make or break the hold that they have on "received theory," much of the debate concerns the way in which recent events are to be interpreted. The dispute is usually in terms of whether events are consistent with the monetarist or the Keynesian version of the macro model. Unfortunately, one example is usually taken to be conclusive evidence, one way or the other. Yet it is diversity of experience that helps us to detect general trends. If a particular behavioral relationship holds up under different institutional arrangements, then it is more powerful than one that is limited to a certain set of circumstances. In criticizing recent theorizing about labor-market arrangements, Robert Gordon of Northwestern University makes a point that is relevant beyond its particular target:

> American economists, whose theoretical ingenuity is matched by their institutional chauvinism, have not succeeded in developing an adequate economic explanation of labour-market arrangements; their theories . . . are mainly based on elements that do not differ across nations and thus have little potential for explaining why the degree of wage flexibility is much greater in some places than in others. It seems remarkable that the modern American literature on labour-market contracts contains no mention of cross-country differences in the extent of wage flexibility, much less any explanation of these differences.[6]

In the light of this persuasive argument, one must resist the temptation to cite examples only for one's own country. To overcome this chauvinistic tendency and to strive for generality, this book will lay equal stress on U.S. and Canadian monetary experience, not only because one is essentially a closed economy and the other open, but also because they have different traditions and institutions in the monetary sector, leading one to expect different outcomes from similar experiments. But how different? The smaller are the differences, the greater is the generality of the conclusion to be derived from the results of the experiment, the greater are the differences, the weaker are the conclusions.

Although it is not possible to spread the net wider to even more countries in the rest of the book, at least in this chapter it is useful to describe briefly what has happened in other places, stressing both similarities and differences. First the similarities. Sometime during the early 1970s, central banks in many of the important industrialized countries converted from Keynesianism to monetarism. In other words, they gave up attempts to fine-tune the economy and tried to generate constant and predictable growth rates of certain monetary aggregates. It was not necessarily a complete conversion: Fine-tuning was deemphasized but not eliminated. Also, growth rates of money were not held completely constant: Over a fairly long time horizon they were to be lowered in an attempt to reduce the inflation rate, which at that time was at historical highs in most of these countries; over a very short time period the money supply would be allowed to deviate from a fixed target or move within an acceptable target range. The goal was medium-term constancy and predictability. The latter characteristic was a novelty. Central banks were not accus-

[6] R. J. Gordon, "Why U.S. Wages and Employment Behaviour Differs From That in Britain and Japan," *Economic Journal*, 92, March 1982, pp. 13–14.

tomed to making announcements about their intentions, but they realized that part of the monetarist strategy is that knowledge of future central bank activity is useful information because it allows participants to make better contracts.

Now for the differences. In an article in the *Federal Reserve Bulletin*, Karen H. Johnson discusses the experience with monetary targets of six countries: Canada, France, Germany, Japan, Switzerland, and the United Kingdom. Leaving out Canada for later detailed analysis, a description of the diversity of experience of the other five countries can be gleaned from Johnson's article. First, countries started to target money growth rates at different times: Germany in December 1974, Switzerland in 1975, the United Kingdom in July 1976, and France in December 1976, whereas Japan has never adopted official targets, but instead has short-term forecasts. Second, they adopted different monetary aggregates for their targets: Germany selected a composite target, the United Kingdom a broad aggregate called M3, France a somewhat narrower aggregate M2, Switzerland M1, whereas Japan's forecasts are for M2 plus certificates of deposit.[7] In the beginning, all the countries announced their targets in terms of a single figure, but in later years all the central banks except that of Switzerland changed to a target range. Finally, they differed in their views as to what constituted a "miss" and in their reaction to one: In France, M2 was above its target much of the time; for Germany and Switzerland, there was a period of being above target (early) and a period of being below target (later); the United Kingdom allowed deviations for exceptional events such as civil service strikes.

In drawing conclusions from these episodes, Johnson declares:

> Over the past decade a wide variety of targeting or forecasting procedures have been used by the six major foreign industrial countries discussed in this article. Indeed, no two of them have used the same procedure. Nevertheless, most of these countries have found it necessary to make adjustments in their particular form of monetary control as economic events have unfolded over the past several years.
>
> The adoption of monetary targeting has not eliminated the problem of dealing with conflicting or ambiguous information with respect to monetary conditions. . . . Regulatory change, financial innovation, and structural shifts of many kinds all have the potential to distort the effects of a given target for money growth from those expected and intended. Foreign experience suggests that the ability to respond flexibly to disturbances of these kinds is an essential aspect of the implementation of targets for monetary aggregates.[8]

[7] Definitions of monetary aggregates also differ among countries. In general, the higher the number attached to "M," the more assets are included in the definition; hence M2 is broader than M1. In Section 5.4, the various aggregates in use in Canada and the United States are defined precisely.

[8] K. H. Johnson, "Foreign Experience with Targets for Money Growth," *Federal Reserve Bulletin*, 69, October 1983, pp. 753–4.

1.5. SUMMARY

This chapter has set the stage for the rest of the book by introducing the importance of money to the functioning of a modern economy. Several conclusions can be summarized here:

1. A monetary economy is more efficient than a barter economy since the existence of money pushes the production possibility curve outward.
2. However, there is a limit to these gains so that more money does not always produce greater efficiency.
3. The quantity of money, as opposed to its mere existence, belongs to those issues considered in the macroeconomic aspects of money.
4. In a frictionless economy, increasing the quantity of money increases the price level in the same proportion.
5. In an economy with frictions created by unavoidable transactions costs, changing the quantity of money affects both prices and quantities.
6. In a friction-prone economy, there is considerable debate as to whether the central bank should use its potential ability to influence real variables through monetary policy, with prointerventionist economists arguing that stabilization policy is able to overcome frictions while antiinterventionist economists maintain that attempts at fine-tuning the economy create new frictions where none existed before.
7. Since 1975, many central banks have adopted a monetarist strategy to money-supply determination in which they forced themselves to keep money growth along a preannounced path, but there was considerable diversity in the way in which this strategy was implemented; understanding this diversity is as important as the common characteristics of either interventionism or antiinterventionism.

FURTHER READING

Friedman, M., "The Role of Monetary Policy," *American Economic Review*, 58, March 1968, pp. 1–17. Despite the author's reputation as a Monetarist, this is not an exposition of an extreme position.

Johnson, K. H., "Foreign Experience with Targets for Money Growth," *Federal Reserve Bulletin*, 69, October 1983, pp. 745–54. A comparison of monetary targeting procedures in six major countries.

Marshall, A., *Money, Credit, and Commerce*, London, Macmillan, 1924, pp. 38–50. Reprinted in R. W. Clower (editor), *Monetary Theory*, Harmondsworth, Penguin, 1969, pp. 80–93. A classic treatment of the functions of money and the role of the quantity of money.

CHAPTER 2

A model of the macroeconomy

2.1 INTRODUCTION

Three "rates" dominate discussions of macroeconomic issues: (1) the inflation rate, (2) the interest rate, and (3) the unemployment rate. In order to understand what can and cannot be done about them it is necessary to have at hand a model of the macroeconomy that can explain movements in these variables. Without the discipline of such a model it is easy to become confused by uninformed opinions and misleading observations. Only with such a model is it possible to comprehend why expanding the money supply is likely to increase the interest rate rather than decrease it, as is often suggested, and why it is virtually impossible to fulfill the politician's promise of "full" employment in a market-oriented economy.

The macroeconomic model to be presented in this chapter is not complicated. In fact, any student who has mastered an intermediate course in macroeconomics has learned the basic ingredients of the model. The *IS–LM–AS* curves are the only ones that will be used. The basic purpose of the model is to describe in a fairly general way the behavior observed in certain important markets in the economy. In microeconomics we are interested in markets for specific commodities, and the distinction between apples and oranges may be important in that context, but in macroeconomics we take a broader perspective where apples and oranges are just two of many commodities, all lumped together in one aggregate. For the economy as a whole the important markets are (1) goods and services, (2) assets, and (3) labor. It is the demand-and-supply relationships in these markets that provide us with the *IS–LM–AS* curves. From the goods market we derive the *IS* curve, which shows combinations of income and the interest rate that keep aggregate demand for goods and services equal to their supply. In the asset markets, equilibrium is maintained along the *LM* curve, which is again a locus of points in income–interest-rate space. Finally, the labor market provides us with the aggregate supply curve via a production function. The *AS* curve is a relationship between output or income and the rate of inflation.

In this chapter the economy that we will be dealing with is a closed one in the sense that international transactions are assumed to be absent. The closed economy is only the first important step; later, in Chapter 9, an open economy that buys and sells in international goods and asset markets will be introduced. In this way, the complications are introduced one at a time.

2.2 THE BUILDING BLOCKS OF THE MODEL

Since the student is expected to be familiar with the details of the construction of the *IS–LM–AS* model, only the general characteristics of the model will be dealt with here. Because there are a number of variables, such as the inflation rate, that are expressed as "rates of change," it is more convenient to work with natural logs than with the original units of account, and the student who is not familiar with this technique should look quickly through the Appendix to the chapter. Once the use of natural logs is mastered, it is straightforward and uncomplicated to apply them to the model. In fact, they make it much easier to understand how a continuing *increase* in the price level (i.e., inflation) is consistent with an equilibrium *level* of output.

2.2.1 THE *IS* CURVE

Equilibrium aggregate demand in the goods market is attained when unintended inventory accumulation or decumulation is absent. This requires that planned saving equal intended investment or, in a more complicated version of the economy, that ex ante saving plus taxes equal ex ante investment plus government expenditures. (Remember that imports and exports, which in an open economy would respectively subtract from and add to domestic aggregate demand, are assumed to be absent.) Saving and taxes are positively related to the level of income, investment expenditures are determined partly by income and partly by the real interest rate, while government expenditures are treated as being exogenous to the model (i.e., they are presumed to be determined by the legislative process). Therefore, defining S as the natural log (from now on written as ln) of saving plus taxes, I as ln of investment plus government expenditures, y as ln of income, and $i - \pi^e$ as the real interest rate, all per unit of time, we obtain two relationships as follows:

$$S = b_0 + b_1 y \tag{2.1}$$

$$I = b_2 + b_3 y - b_4(i - \pi^e) \tag{2.2}$$

Although these equations must be familiar to the student, a number of characteristics contained in the symbols are worth mentioning. The constant b_1 is the *elasticity* of saving plus taxes with respect to income and should not be interpreted as the sum of the marginal propensities to save and to tax. Therefore, b_1 need not be less than one. The use of natural logs gives rise to elasticities, since the change in S required by a change in y involves *proportionate* changes, not *absolute* changes. The elasticity b_1 is equal to the marginal propensity to save and to tax divided by the average propensity to save and to tax, both of which must be less than one. This makes it possible for the elasticity to exceed unity when the marginal propensity is larger than the average propensity. Similarly, b_3 is the income elasticity of investment expenditures. Also, b_2 contains the exogenous government expenditures, while b_0 represents any autonomously determined taxes and saving. Finally, b_4 is the interest elasticity of investment expenditures. Since investment and the interest rate are negatively related, there is a minus sign in front of b_4, which itself is positive, as are all other constants in equations (2.1) and (2.2).

Investment depends on its profitability, which is defined as revenues minus costs. One of the most important elements in the cost of investment projects is that associated with borrowing the funds necessary for the project. Even retained earnings are internal borrowings and can be treated similarly to borrowing from a bank, selling bonds, or issuing stocks. These costs are equal to the prevailing interest rate times the size of the borrowed funds. The higher the interest rate, the greater is the cost of borrowing and the lower is the profitability of planned investment expenditures, suggesting a negative relationship between investment expenditures and the interest rate.

THE NOMINAL VERSUS THE REAL INTEREST RATE

Investment expenditures are related to the *real* interest rate, not to the *nominal* interest rate. This distinction is important. Confusion about these terms has led to unnecessary debate about the role of monetary policy in a number of emotional issues such as mortgage interest rates. A nominal rate of 15% may be very attractive to home buyers under some circumstances, while 10% may be very unattractive under other circumstances, depending on what expectations people hold about the future inflation rate. The reason for subtracting the expected inflation rate from the nominal interest rate is that individual behavior in making expenditure decisions involves looking at real variables, not nominal variables. If all prices doubled over a period of time, fundamental decisions would not change. Quantities purchased would remain the same; only their nominal value would double.

The real interest rate is expressed as the nominal interest rate, i, minus the expected inflation rate, π^e. Since the payoff on current investment expenditures lies in the future, the real cost of repaying borrowed funds depends on both the nominal interest payments and the expected change in the price level between now and the time that income is generated by the investment goods and concurrently the time that repayment of the loan must be made. To put the matter more concretely, consider a loan of one dollar that requires a repayment of $\$(1 + i)$ at the end of one year. The purchasing power of this amount will deteriorate over time if inflation is present. For instance, if inflation is at the rate of 10%, the real cost of the interest payments is also reduced by 10%. This reduction in purchasing power is measured by the price level at the beginning of the year divided by the future price level, or $p_{-1} - p^e$, where p_{-1} is the ln of the price level at the start of the year and p^e is the ln of the price level expected to prevail at the end of the year. Notice that with p^e we are dealing with a variable that is not known at the present time and therefore must be estimated on the basis of whatever information is at hand at the time that expectations are formed; for that reason a superscript "e" identifies a variable for which an expected value is required. From this discussion we can see that the real cost (expressed in natural logs) of borrowing one dollar is $\ln(1 + i) + p_{-1} - p^e$. This expression can then be rewritten as $i - \pi^e$, since $\ln(1 + i)$ is approximately equal to i, when it is written as a fraction, according to property 5 of natural logs in the Appendix, and by definition, $p^e - p_{-1} = \pi^e$.

EXAMPLE

If the interest rate is 10%, $\ln(1 + i) = .0953$; if the price level is expected to rise from 100 to 107 during a year, $p_{-1} = 4.605$ and $p^e = 4.673$; therefore, $\pi^e = .068$ or 7%. In this example the real interest rate is then .027 or 3% per annum.

After the fact, the real interest rate may or may not indicate the true real cost of borrowing funds for investment expenditures, depending on whether the forecast for inflation was correct or not. While the investor knows the nominal interest cost at the beginning of the period, he does not know the rate of inflation that will prevail, and there may be a difference between expected and realized inflation. The ex post real interest rate would be $i - \pi$, where $\pi = p - p_{-1}$ is the rate of inflation actually experienced, but since it cannot be observed at the time that the decision is made, it is not a very useful piece of information.

Does a high nominal interest rate imply a high cost of borrowing? We can now see that the answer depends on the expected rate of inflation. If prices are expected to rise very little, the real interest rate will be high compared to a situation where prices are expected to rise steeply. In fact, a "high" nominal interest rate may involve a negative real interest rate if $\pi^e > i$, in which case the stimulus to invest may have no bounds since the income from such investment expenditures rises faster than the cost of the borrowed funds.

Since π^e cannot be observed directly we cannot measure the real interest rate. From time to time there is a ferocious debate about whether monetary policy is "tight" or "easy." One of the major reasons for the lack of agreement is that we have many opinions about the expected rate of inflation. Throughout this book expectations about future events play a pivotal role in the performance of the economy, but one of the frustrating features of macroeconomics is that a lot of subjective evaluation is involved with no "right" or "wrong" answer to the question "What is the expected rate of inflation for the next month or for the next year?"

DETERMINATION OF AGGREGATE DEMAND

Saving and taxes remove spending power from the stream of aggregate demand, whereas government expenditures and investment add to it. When they exactly offset each other, aggregate demand for goods and services is constant. Therefore, $S = I$ is an equilibrium condition from which we derive the *IS* curve. Setting equations (2.1) and (2.2) equal to each other allows us to find those values of y and $i - \pi^e$ that satisfy this equilibrium condition:

$$y = a_0 - a_1(i - \pi^e) \tag{2.3}$$

where $a_0 = (b_2 - b_0)/(b_1 - b_3)$ and $a_1 = b_4/(b_1 - b_3)$. Equation (2.3) is the *IS* curve of the model. To appreciate fully its place in macroeconomic analysis, it is important to understand its derivation from equations (2.1) and (2.2). In the denominator of both a_0 and a_1 there appears $b_1 - b_3$, the difference between two positive numbers. In order to have the *IS* curve as a negatively sloped line in Figure 2-1, this difference must be unambiguously positive. This in turn implies that the income elasticity of saving plus taxes must exceed the income elasticity of investment. In the simple Keynesian model of income determination this same requirement was put forward as the savings function being steeper than the investment function to guarantee a stable equilibrium; or put another way, it is necessary that the marginal propensity to save (MPS) is greater than the marginal propensity to invest (MPI). This is essentially the same requirement as $b_1 > b_3$ since both b_1 and b_3 are ratios of marginal propensities to average propensities, and the average propensities to save and to invest will be equal when $S = I$. The numerator of a_0 also contains the difference between two positive numbers, b_2 and b_0, which represent the autonomous components of investment, government expenditures, saving, and taxes. For the *IS* curve to be in the first quadrant with only positive values for y and i, we must restrict a_0 to be positive, which in turn means that $b_2 > b_0$.

Since an increase in government expenditures is treated as an exogenous event, it is captured by a rise in b_2, which is then translated into an increase in a_0. The change in a_0 is related to the change in b_2 by $1/(b_1 - b_3)$ which is the Keynesian multiplier. On the other hand, an increase in lump-sum taxes involves a higher b_0 and through a similar multiplier process reduces a_0. For these reasons a_0 will be identified with fiscal policy: An increase in a_0 represents expansionary fiscal policy through a reduction in taxes or an increase in government purchases or both, while a reduction in a_0 is associated with contractionary fiscal policy.

Figure 2-1 shows the *IS* curve with y measured on the horizontal axis and i, not $i - \pi^e$, on the vertical axis. Therefore, points on the *IS* curve represent constant aggregate demand only for a given rate of expected inflation. Its horizontal intercept is $a_0 + a_1\pi^e$, its vertical intercept is $a_0/a_1 + \pi^e$, and its slope is $-1/a_1$. An increase in a_0 shifts the *IS* curve upwards and to the right. An increase in π^e has the same effect, and it should be noted carefully for later reference that the vertical displacement of the *IS* curve is exactly equal to the increase in π^e.

If points on the *IS* curve represent equilibrium in the market for goods and services, what can we say about points to the left or to the right of the *IS* curve? Consider a point such as *B* in Figure 2-1 and compare it to point *A*, which is on the *IS* curve. Now *B* has a higher interest rate than *A* but the same income. Thus at *B* saving and taxes are higher than investment plus government expenditures, and therefore demand for the existing output is deficient. For this reason, all points to the right of the *IS* curve are designated as excess-supply points, requiring a fall in output to reestablish equilibrium at *C*. Excess supply is identified with involuntary inventory accumulation as output produced exceeds output demanded. Similarly, points to the left of the *IS* curve indicate excess demand, since $I > S$. Excess demand is indicated by inventory reductions. From this argument it can be seen that the interest rate and income must

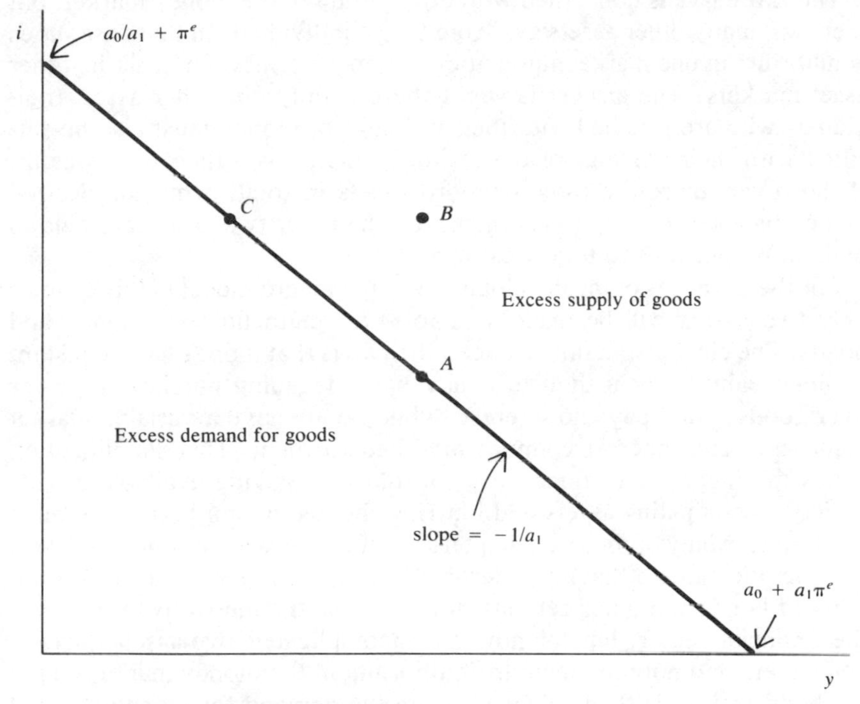

Figure 2-1 The IS curve.

move in opposite directions to keep total demand for goods and services constant.

2.2.2 THE *LM* CURVE

Whereas the *IS* curve deals with the market for goods and services as flows per period of time, the *LM* curve deals with asset markets as stocks at a point in time, but this is not an inconsistency in the model because flow equilibrium characterizes the former and stock equilibrium is essential to the latter. Nevertheless, there is a connection between the stocks and flows that is often misleading: Saving is a flow determined by the difference between income and expenditures, but accumulated savings from the past is a stock that is allocated to the various assets available in the economy. It is for this reason that a statement such as "to save money" is inappropriate; it is more accurate to say that (1) an individual saves part of his or her income and (2) the resulting addition to his or her wealth is held in the form of money. There are two decisions involved in this process, and they must be analytically separated.

The *LM* curve is concerned with equilibrium in the money market, but there are many other assets available to the individual. In that case, does equilibrium in one market automatically imply equilibrium in all the other asset markets? The answer is yes if there is only *one* other asset. Individuals who are satisfied with their holdings of money must also be satisfied with their holdings of the residual asset, given their total wealth. If, however, there are three or more assets in total, achieving desired money balances does not guarantee that the other two assets are held in optimal proportions to total wealth.

For the purposes of the development of the macro model in this chapter only two assets will be made available to wealth holders: money and bonds. The chief distinction between the two is that money has a constant nominal value – even though it may have declining purchasing power over goods – and pays no interest, while bonds have a variable market value and have interest coupons attached to them. This simplification belies the ingenuity of financial institutions in making available a wide variety of competing assets and blurring the distinction between money and bonds. Many of the later chapters in this book will be concerned with the complications of having different "kinds" of money, the substitutability of bonds and other debt instruments, and the innovative process in the financial sector, but for now an uncomplicated two-asset model is convenient and not too fanciful. Equilibrium in the money market *and* in the bond market is then achieved when the demand for money is equal to its supply.

THE DEMAND FOR MONEY

In an inflationary environment the first important distinction to make is between *nominal* money balances and *real* money balances. The latter are obtained by dividing the former by a price index to capture the purchasing power of money holdings. The demand for money is a demand for real money balances, and behavioral predictions are made for this variable. If all prices doubled but nothing else changed, demand for real money balances will remain unaltered; all that happens is that people will want to hold twice as much in nominal balances.

In an elementary course in macroeconomics, students are introduced to three separate "demands" for money: (1) transactions demand, (2) precautionary demand, and (3) speculative demand. Although Chapter 5 will delve into these more carefully, for now a composite demand for money depends positively on income and negatively on the interest rate so that

$$m - p = a_2 y - a_3 i \tag{2.4}$$

where m is the natural log of the stock of nominal money. According to property 3 of natural logs in the Appendix, the ratio of two numbers can be represented by the difference in their natural logs. Therefore $m - p$ represents the demand for real money balances. The two constants in equation (2.4) are both positive. The first, a_2, is the income elasticity of the demand for money and a_3 is the interest semielasticity since the interest rate is not expressed in natural logs. Again it should be noted that the a's are elasticities and not marginal propensities. An increase in real income will lead to higher real money balances being demanded, basically for transactions purposes. If institutionalized habits such as the pay period are changed, the demand-for-money function will also be affected. Being paid twice as often, for instance, does not change the level of income, although it does change the relationship between the flow of income and the stock of money, thus lowering a_2. An increase in the nominal interest rate will lower the demand for real money balances according to equation (2.4). Here we have a connection between a nominal variable and a real variable. Why is real money demand not a function of the real interest rate in an inflationary environment? The answer is that neither money nor bonds, the only two assets in which wealth can be held, provide any protection against inflation. They are denominated in dollars, and the purchasing power of both falls equally for any given rate of inflation. Therefore, the opportunity cost of holding money is the interest income forgone by not holding bonds, namely the nominal interest rate. If banks were to pay implicit interest on money balances equal to the inflation rate in the form of free services, the opportunity cost of holding money would be the real interest rate. More on this topic in Chapter 5.

THE SUPPLY OF MONEY

Equation (2.4) represents the demand for money, but it can be converted into an equilibrium condition for the money market if the left side is redefined as the supply of real money. The supply of money is associated with the activities of the central bank and the commercial banks. Because of the importance of the role of the central bank in the money-supply process, monetary policy is one of the two major stabilization instruments. However, the central bank has a direct influence only on the *nominal* money supply so that as a first approximation m can be treated as an exogenous variable, whereas p will be an endogenous variable. To make matters more complicated, when inflation prevails the central bank does not concern itself as much with the level of the money supply as with its growth rate. In many countries monetary-policy targets are stated in terms of an acceptable range for the growth rates of various definitions of the money supply because central banks know that a given stock of money will become inadequate for transactions purposes with the mere passage of time as rising prices erode its purchasing power. To incorporate the requirement that monetary policy controls the growth rate of the nominal money supply we can link levels and changes in levels from one period to the next by

$$\mu - \pi = m - p - (m - p)_{-1} \tag{2.5}$$

where μ is the exogenously determined growth rate of the money supply and π is the inflation rate during a specific period. According to property 4 of natural logs, the change in the real money supply from the last period (indicated by the subscript -1) to the present period [$(m - p)$ without a time subscript] is measured by the growth rate of real money balances, $\mu - \pi$, which in turn can be decomposed into the difference between μ and π by property 3. If $\mu > \pi$, then real money balances are growing over time as the central bank is "pumping" money into the economy faster than it is being "drained" by the loss of purchasing power. If $\mu = \pi$, then nominal money balances are rising with time but real money balances are constant.

EXAMPLE

> Assume $m_{-1} = 5.298$ (or the nominal stock of money is equal to \$200 billion at the end of the last period), and $m = 5.394$ (\$220 billion); the price level rises from 100 to 107 or $p_{-1} = 4.605$ and $p = 4.673$. This means that $\mu = 5.394 - 5.298 = .096$ or close to 10% and that $\pi = 4.673 - 4.605 = .068$ or 7%. Finally, we can calculate $\mu - \pi = .095 - .068 = .028$ or 3%.

We are now ready to formulate the equation for the *LM* curve where supply and demand in the money market are equal. The equation is derived by substituting (2.5) into (2.4) to arrive at

$$\mu - \pi = a_2 y - a_3 i - (m - p)_{-1} \tag{2.6}$$

The *LM* curve is drawn in Figure 2-2. However, it will not remain in place unless $\mu = \pi$. If that condition is satisfied, we are back to equation (2.4), which is consistent with any rate of inflation as long as real money balances remain constant. The slope of the *LM* curve is a_2/a_3 which is positive; its intercept on the horizontal axis is $(m - p)/a_2$ and its vertical intercept is $-(m - p)/a_3$, which is always negative. Starting from this position, if μ increases and therefore becomes larger than π, $m - p$ will be increasing through time and the *LM* curve will move steadily down

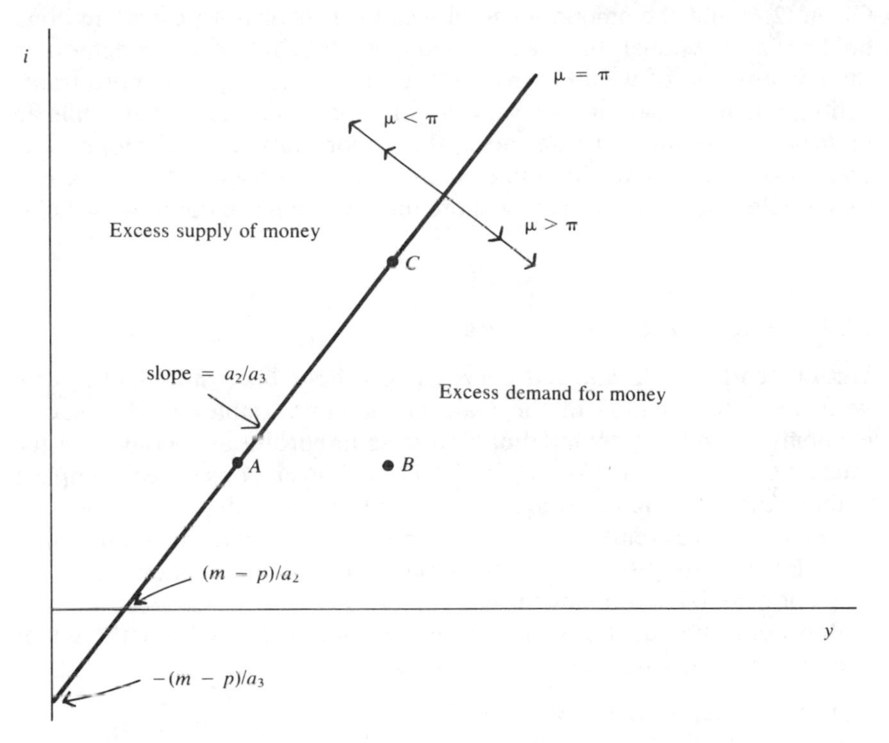

Figure 2-2 The *LM* curve.

and to the right. This is a continuous movement and does not produce the same result as a once-and-for-all increase in the real money supply without the passage of time.

Points on either side of the *LM* curve imply something about the nature of disequilibrium in the money market. Starting from a point such as *A* on the *LM* curve, an increase in income would move the economy to *B*. Here there is excess demand for money since transactions requirements are higher. The existing real money balances can only be consistent with this higher income if the interest rate rises to a point such as *C*. Conversely, any point to the left of *LM* signifies excess supply of real money balances.

THE BOND MARKET

As indicated earlier, the demand and supply conditions in the bond market do not provide any additional information about asset-market equilibrium given that money and bonds are the only two assets available. Total real wealth is the sum of real money balances and real bond holdings.

Given (2.4) and the amount of total wealth, it is easy to calculate bond holdings as a residual. In essence, income and the interest rate determine the *composition* of wealth. An increase in income requires more transactions balances and forces a shift out of bonds and into money while an increase in the interest rate raises the opportunity cost of money and creates an incentive to shift out of money and into bonds. An increase in total wealth, however, will allow more money and more bonds to be held.

2.2.3 THE *IS–LM* FRAMEWORK

Until recently the *IS* and *LM* curves would have been sufficient to deal with the determination of the main economic variables in the macroeconomy, y and i. Now inflation is just as important as income and the interest rate, and the *IS–LM* model is no longer considered complete without the addition of an aggregate-supply relationship. However, the *IS* and *LM* curves remain an important part of the augmented model since they describe fully the aggregate-demand side of the economy and the place of stabilization policy in that model.

Repeating the equations for the equilibrium conditions for the goods markets and asset markets

$$(2.3) \qquad y = a_0 - a_1(i - \pi^e)$$

$$(2.6) \qquad \mu - \pi = a_2 y - a_3 i - (m - p)_{-1}$$

we can see that they jointly determine y and i if π^e is exogenous in (2.3) and if $\mu = \pi$ in (2.6). Therefore, the inflation rate and its expectation are not yet endogenous variables. Given these assumptions, the *IS* and *LM* curves are drawn in Figure 2-3. In fact, two *IS* curves are drawn in the diagram, one for $\pi^e = 0$ and the other for the current value of π^e, the vertical distance between them being π^e. This procedure allows us to read both the nominal and real interest rates on the vertical axis. Equilibrium in the goods and asset markets is achieved simultaneously when $IS(\pi^e)$ and LM intersect because y_0 and i_0 satisfy both markets at the same time. Subtracting π^e from i_0 at E_0 moves us to A, where the vertical distance is $i - \pi^e$. In the absence of inflationary expectations, there would be only the $IS(\pi^e = 0)$ curve and equilibrium would be at E_1. Compared to E_0, the real interest rate would be higher and the nominal interest rate would be lower until they coincide.

The diagram also shows indirectly other variables of interest. Once y and i are determined, and given π^e, S and I can be calculated. Also, given real wealth and real money balances, $(m - p)$, bond holdings can be

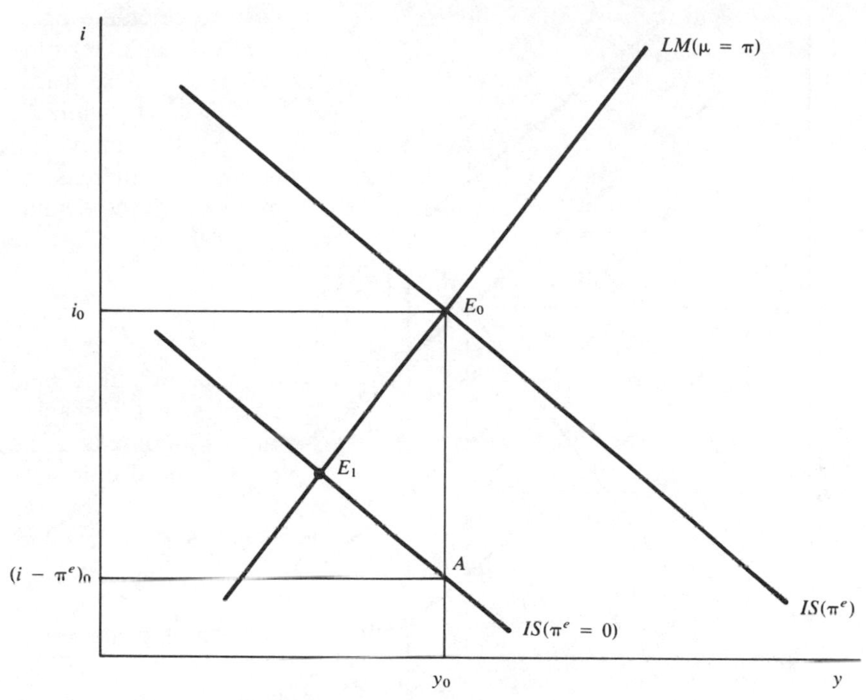

Figure 2-3 Equilibrium in the *IS–LM* framework.

determined residually. Furthermore, given m, y, and i, the price level, p, can also be calculated.

While it is too early for a full discussion of policy analysis, the two major instruments of macroeconomic policy, fiscal and monetary policies, are incorporated into the *IS* and *LM* curves. Fiscal policy is captured in the term a_0 in the *IS* curve with an increase in government expenditures or a decrease in lump-sum taxes increasing the size of a_0.[1] This shifts both *IS* curves upward equally in Figure 2-4 as long as π^e has not changed. A new equilibrium is reached at E_1, where we observe higher income, a higher nominal interest rate, and a higher real interest rate. The increased government demand for goods and services can only be accommodated by a decline in investment spending, which is achieved by raising the real interest rate. The nominal interest rate must rise since real money balances are unchanged and transactions requirements are now higher. The real interest rate follows suit because inflationary expectations are assumed to have remained constant.

[1] A change in the income-tax rate is treated as an exercise.

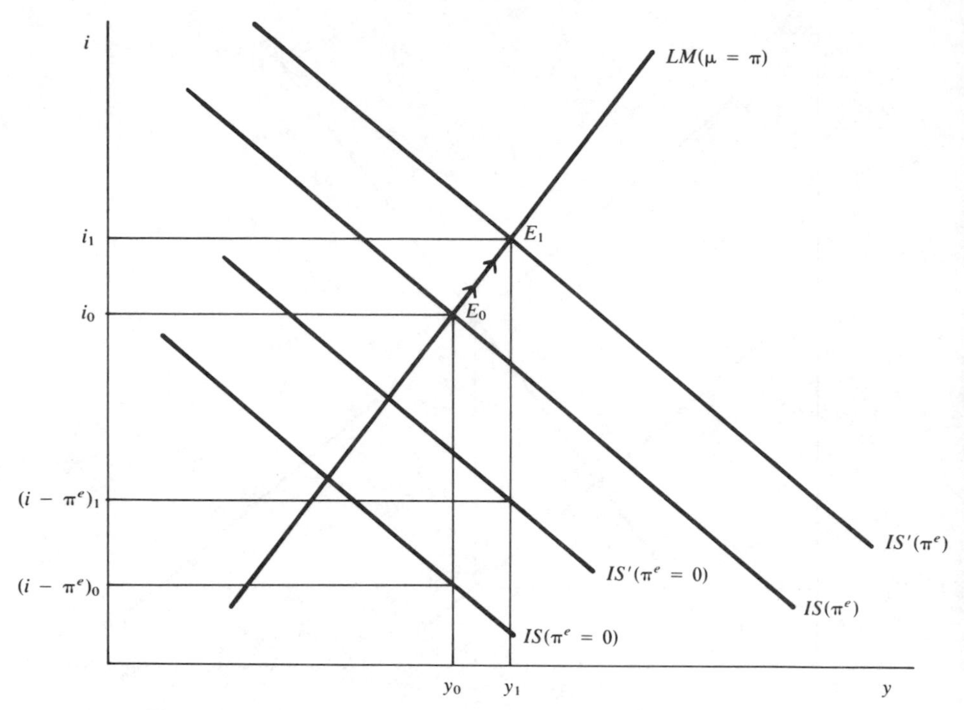

Figure 2-4 Fiscal policy – an increase in a_0.

An alternative is expansionary monetary policy, which involves having μ increase to μ_1 so that $\mu > \pi$ for some period of time, allowing $m - p$ to grow. Afterward LM has moved to LM' in Figure 2-5, where $\mu_1 = \pi_1$ and y is higher but i and $i - \pi^e$ are both lower. The increased real money balances reduce both the nominal and real interest rates, stimulating investment and increasing aggregate demand. In the end, the extra money is partly allocated to transactions balances and partly to speculative balances. It is worth emphasizing that in an inflationary setting the central bank is concerned about μ, not m. If we had an economy where inflation as a continuing process is absent, m would be the logical variable that the central bank would try to control. An increase in m would shift the LM curve once and for all to the right and lower the nominal interest rate, which is now identical to the real interest rate since $\pi^e = 0$. Therefore, the model can accommodate situations with inflation, in which case equation (2.6) is appropriate, and conditions without inflation, where equation (2.4) is relevant.

Nevertheless, both of these policy experiments can be misleading if we keep π^e constant in the face of changes in the actual inflation rate. Therefore Figures 2-4 and 2-5 should be used only to show how macro policies

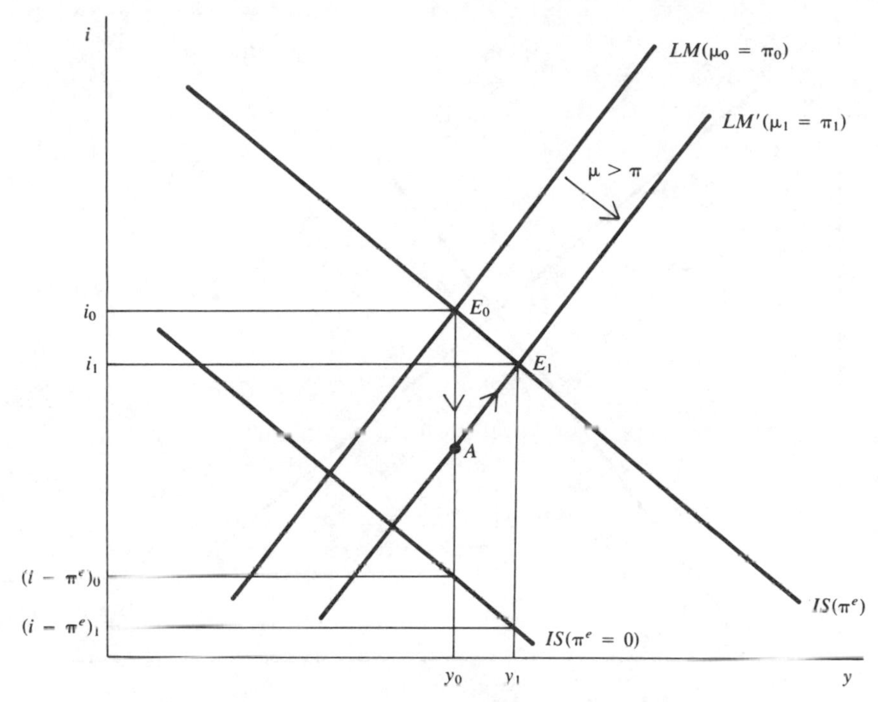

Figure 2-5 Monetary policy – an increase in μ.

are incorporated into the model and not to show their final effect on the economy. That comes later.

DYNAMICS IN THE *IS–LM* MODEL

The economy does not move instantaneously from one equilibrium to another when a change is required. In fact, it is the economy's inability to adapt to exogenous shocks without friction that is cited as the basis for stabilization-policy initiatives. But before we can deal with such issues we need to understand the path taken by the economy when it is disturbed from its initial equilibrium. For this we need to look at the dynamics of adjustment, that is, the evolution of y and i during the adjustment from one equilibrium to another. In many circumstances, we are only interested in comparative statics results where we compare initial and final values of y and i after an exogenous change in the economy, but at other times the intervening period of disequilibrium is important too, and we want more detailed information, namely the path that y and i take as the economy proceeds from one equilibrium to another.

If the *IS* curve shifts upward as in Figure 2-4, E_1 becomes the new

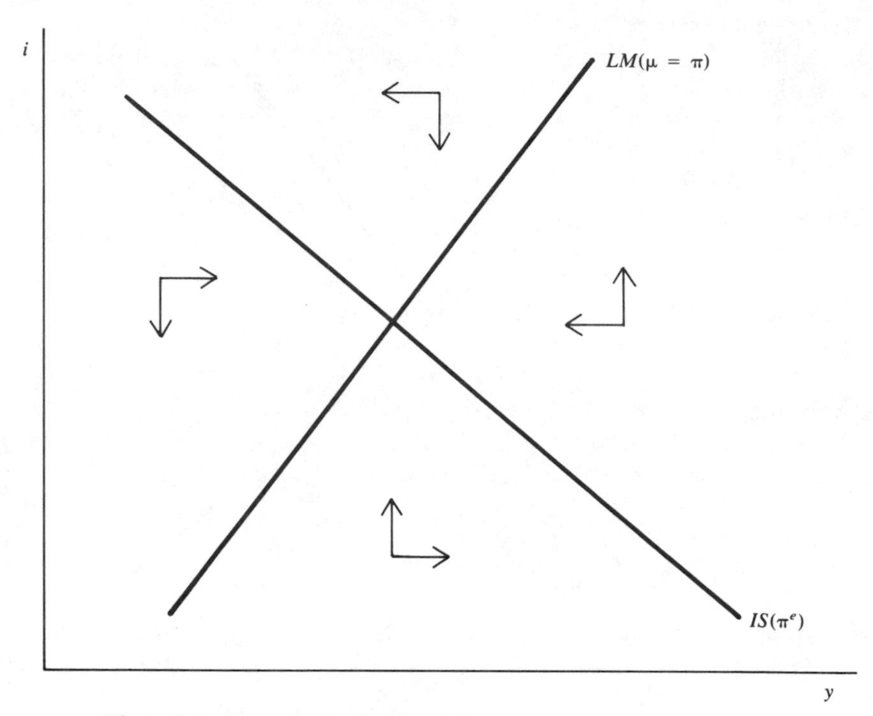

Figure 2-6 Dynamics in the *IS–LM* framework.

equilibrium position to which y and i must adjust and E_0 becomes a position of disequilibrium. Similarly, in Figure 2-5, after a shift of the *LM* curve, y will rise and i will fall as the economy moves from E_0 to E_1. The path taken from E_0 to E_1 in either case depends on a number of other assumptions about the adjustment process. The first two deal with allocating adjustment variables to specific markets.

1. Income and output rise when there is excess demand for goods and services. The signal to increase output comes from involuntary inventory decumulation when demand for current production exceeds its availability. Conversely, output is reduced when firms find their inventories climbing unintentionally. The horizontal arrows in Figure 2-6 depict this adjustment, moving to the right from any position to the left of the *IS* curve and moving to the left from any position to the right of *IS*.

2. The interest rate rises when there is excess demand in the money market. Since the interest rate is considered to be the relative price between money and bonds, it responds to eliminate disequilibrium in these markets simultaneously. If there is excess demand in the money market, as there would be at any point below the *LM* curve, the interest rate rises,

whereas excess supply in the money market is represented by points above the *LM* curve and requires a fall in the interest rate. The vertical arrows in Figure 2-6 show these movements. Alternatively, the price of bonds falls when there is excess supply in the bond market. Since the interest rate and the price of bonds move in opposite directions and since excess supply of bonds goes along with excess demand for money, both approaches give the same result.

Reversing this allocation would not make much sense. It would be difficult to argue that the interest rate, an asset-market relative price, should adjust to cope with disequilibrium in the goods market or to find reasons for output adjustment when only asset markets are out of equilibrium.

Returning to Figure 2-4, we can see that E_0 is a position of excess demand in the goods market but that the money market remains in equilibrium. According to the arrows in Figure 2-6, this causes an initial increase in y, but i remains constant. However, as soon as the economy moves to the right of E_0 there is now excess demand for money and the interest rate will have a tendency to rise as well. Consequently, the adjustment from E_0 to E_1 will require both y and i to rise. But we have not yet established whether horizontal movements dominate vertical movements or vice versa at any stage of the adjustment. We therefore need to make one more assumption about the *relative* speeds of adjustment of income and the interest rate.

3. The adjustment of the interest rate is much faster than the adjustment of income and output. From differences in the nature of the markets and the signals that operate in them, it is clear that bond prices and interest rates can change very quickly in response to new developments, whereas the output response may take weeks or even months because of lags in inventory information. In fact, if the adjustment in the money market becomes close to instantaneous, we would never observe any combination of y and i that was off the *LM* curve. In that case the adjustment path can be predicted even more precisely. In Figure 2-4, the adjustment from E_0 to E_1 would be entirely along the *LM* curve, with y and i rising continuously. In Figure 2-5, on the other hand, E_0 represents a position of excess supply of money which would be immediately eliminated by a fall in the interest rate before any adjustment in output can take place. Thus the economy is temporarily at A. After this, both y and i rise as we move along the new *LM* curve to E_1. The important implication of this process is that the initial adjustment of the interest rate is too large to be consistent with the new equilibrium. The "overshooting" of the final target must then be corrected by a partial reversal in the movement of the interest rate. This volatility of the interest rate in response to policy or other

exogenous changes is a feature of the rapid adjustment in the asset market and causes it to bear a disproportionate share of the total adjustment that must take place.

One dimension of the adjustment process has not been discussed, namely the time that it takes for the economy to reach a new equilibrium. The length of adjustment is a hotly debated issue between neoclassical economists who tend to believe in a fast, self-equilibrating mechanism and Keynesians who advocate policy intervention because the economy can be trapped for long periods of time in disequilibrium. In these circumstances, assumptions about the speed of adjustment are far from innocuous, and their implications will receive much more attention at various stages of the book.

2.2.4 THE AGGREGATE-DEMAND CURVE

The *IS–LM* framework determines the interest rate and income, but only if the inflation rate is taken as exogenous. Moreover, the level of income is not yet related to capacity constraints that come from the aggregate-supply relationship. But the *IS* and *LM* curves together provide us with the aggregate-demand curve. From them we can derive an important demand-side relationship between the inflation rate and output or income. Just like any other demand curve, quantity demanded decreases as price increases; the only differences are that we are dealing not with any specific commodity but instead with commodities in general and instead of a price level we have an inflation rate determining demand.

To derive the *AD* curve first rewrite the *IS* curve as

$$(2.3') \quad i = a_0/a_1 - y/a_1 + \pi^e$$

and then substitute this expression into the *LM* curve of equation (2.6)

$$(2.6') \quad \mu - \pi = a_2 y - a_3(a_0/a_1 - y/a_1 + \pi^e) - (m - p)_{-1}$$

which after rearrangement becomes the *AD* curve

$$(2.7) \quad \pi = \mu + (m - p)_{-1} - (a_2 + a_3/a_1)y^d + a_3 a_0/a_1 + a_3\pi^e$$

where the superscript d is added to y to enable us to treat it as the ln of output demanded and to distinguish it from y^s, which later refers to aggregate supply. The *AD* curve is drawn in Figure 2-7, where the inflation rate is on the vertical axis and income is on the horizontal axis. The vertical intercept is $\mu + (m - p)_{-1} + a_3 a_0/a_1 + a_3\pi^e$ and the slope of the *AD* curve is $-(a_2 + a_3/a_1)$, which is negative. Thus the *AD* curve represents an inverse relationship between y and π. Why does the demand

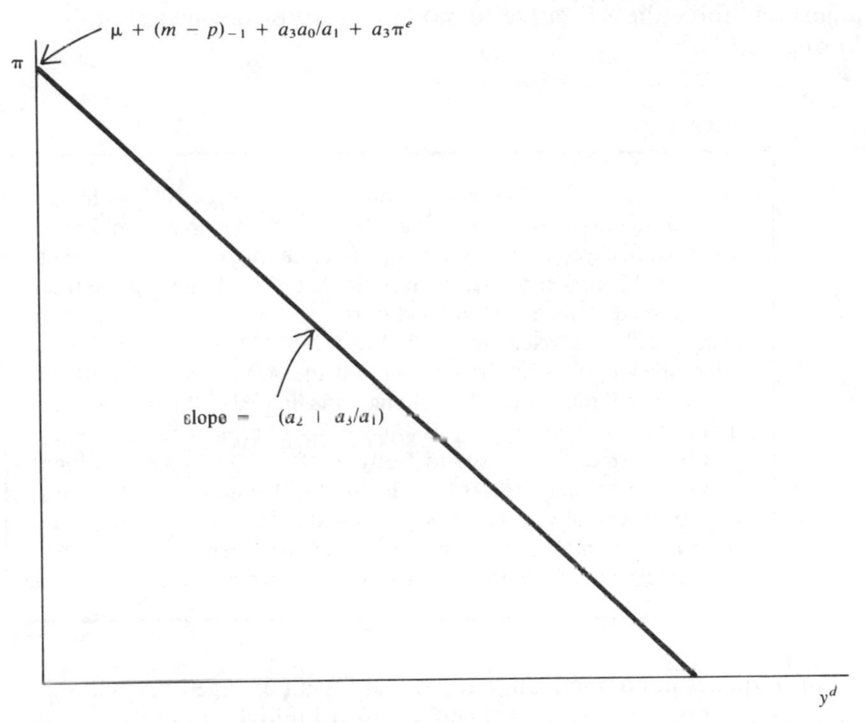

Figure 2-7 The aggregate-demand curve.

for goods and services decline after an increase in π? By looking at equation (2.6) we can see that an increase in π reduces the real quantity of money in the economy creating excess demand in the money market. In turn, this causes the nominal interest rate to rise. With π^e held constant the real interest rate also rises, choking off some investment expenditures and thereby reducing aggregate demand. Therefore, as we move up along the *AD* curve, the real interest rate must be rising.

There are two other important characteristics of the *AD* curve: (1) the effects of policy changes on its position and (2) the continuing adjustment arising from the presence of $(m - p)_{-1}$ in the vertical intercept. In our earlier discussion we saw that a_0 was associated with fiscal policy and μ was the monetary policy instrument. An increase in either variable will shift the *AD* curve upward, in the former case by a_3/a_1 and in the latter case on a one-for-one basis. These are, however, the first-round effects only. Since $(m - p)_{-1}$ also determines the intercept of the *AD* curve, subsequent changes in the real money supply must also be taken into account. As long as μ and π are not equal, $(m - p)_{-1}$ will continue to adjust and force the *AD* curve to move upward or downward in the following period.

EXAMPLE

> Assume that $m = 5.298$, $p = 0$, and $\mu = \pi = .10$, or 10%, initially. Then μ increases to .15, shifting *AD* upward. We do not yet know what happens to π without an aggregate-supply curve to intersect with the *AD* curve, but let us assume that $\pi = .12$ during the first period of adjustment. At the end of the first period the real money supply will have risen from 5.298 to $5.298 + .15 - .12 = 5.301$, which means that for the next period the *AD* curve will shift up again, even though the policy change was limited to the first period. Then in the second period, assume $\pi = .13$ after which $(m - p)$ will rise further from 5.301 to $5.301 + .15 - .13 = 5.303$, which allows *AD* to shift upward again for the beginning of the third period. Eventually, μ and π will coincide at .15 and $(m - p)$ will remain constant over time, but it remains true that policy changes have lingering effects that need to be taken into account.

For purposes of comparison, a once-and-for-all change in a_0 has somewhat different results. Again *AD* shifts upward initially, and the inflation rate rises, but since μ has not been changed, $(m - p)_{-1}$ will now be smaller and *AD* starts shifting back down again until its previous position is reestablished, where $\mu = \pi$ and $(m - p)$ is constant.

So far expected inflation has been treated as exogenously determined. An increase in π^e, from whatever source, will also force the *AD* curve to shift upward by the amount a_3, which represents the interest elasticity of the demand for money. Why does this parameter appear here, since π^e is in the *IS* curve, not in the *LM* curve? Higher inflationary expectations increase the nominal interest rate to the same extent, according to equation (2.3′) if y and a_0 are given. This reduces the demand for real money balances by a_3; given μ, the only way that this can be achieved is through an increase in π.

An increase in π^e will shift the *AD* curve upward by a_3 times the change in π^e. At any given level of income this would also increase π by a_3. In that way expected inflation pushes actual inflation, but there must be some constraint on this self-fulfilling prophecy; otherwise π and π^e would chase each other upward or downward without reference to μ and the real money supply would either disappear or reach infinity. If $0 < a_3 < 1$, the process is self-limiting.

EXAMPLE

> If $a_3 = .25$ and π^e rises by 1%, then π rises by .25%. In turn, this should lead to π^e rising and shifting *AD* upward to that extent. Then π rises by another .06%, and so on. The process comes to an end when π and π^e have risen by $1/(1 - .25) = 1.33\%$.

Keep in mind however, that this is a mental experiment where π^e rose exogenously; π being higher than μ cannot be maintained indefinitely, but the limit on a_3 remains valid.[2]

For all of these shifts in the *AD* curve it has been the vertical intercept that has been analyzed, because it will be found later that its economic interpretation is more meaningful than that of its horizontal intercept.

2.2.5 THE AGGREGATE-SUPPLY CURVE

The *AD* curve by itself cannot determine output and the inflation rate. To complete the model we also need the aggregate-supply curve. Although emphasis on the aggregate-supply relationship is relatively new, the older Keynesian model did not neglect it entirely; it merely contained an assumption that minimized its role. In the 1950s and 1960s when the price level was virtually constant but output fluctuated through a number of business cycles, it was taken for granted that until the economy reached "full" employment there would be no pressure on prices as demand determined output and income through the *IS–LM* framework. This assumption has become unrealistic in the 1970s and 1980s, and in these circumstances the *AS* curve is more complicated. However, its derivation is relatively straightforward and its usefulness is quite general, allowing us to incorporate a number of competing assumptions about behavior in the labor market, which is the crucial market for the *AS* curve, with the Keynesian and neoclassical predictions treated as polar cases.

The derivation of the *AS* curve, which shows combinations of y and π that satisfy the requirements of the labor market, has two steps:

1. The production function for the economy relates total output to factor inputs.
2. Factor-market supply-and-demand relationships relate factor inputs to the inflation rate.

[2] See Chapter 5 for theoretical and empirical arguments about the value of a_3.

THE PRODUCTION FUNCTION

Treating all output as being a homogeneous entity we can use a single production function for the entire economy that determines total output on the basis of the various factor inputs, the principal ones being labor and capital. The production function can now be written as

$$(2.8) \quad y^s = b_5 + b_6N + b_7K$$

where y^s is now interpreted as the natural log of total output supplied to the economy, N is the ln of total labor services, and K is the ln of capital services in the production process. The b's are all positive parameters. Here b_6 is the elasticity of output with respect to the labor input, and b_7 is the elasticity of output with respect to the capital input; b_5 represents a productivity factor and indicates how y could increase even if N and K were constant. Restrictions could be imposed on this production function. For example, it may be argued that empirical evidence suggests that a doubling of both inputs always doubles output, in which case $b_6 + b_7 = 1$.

EXAMPLE

It is observed that when N and K are zero, so is y; therefore, $b_5 = 0$. It is further observed that when the labor input is 50 hours and the capital input is 100 hours, output is 60 units; therefore, $N = 3.912$, $K = 4.605$, and $y^s = 4.094$. If $b_6 + b_7 = 1$, then from equation (2.8), $4.094 = 0 + b_6(3.912) + (1 - b_6)(4.605)$ and $b_6 = .737$, while $b_7 = .263$.

There is an important time dimension that must be assigned to the production function. A macro model that deals with policy issues has a fairly short time horizon. For such purposes it is useful to distinguish between fixed and variable factors of production, as Alfred Marshall suggested. Of the two factors in equation (2.8), K will be treated as the fixed factor that remains constant throughout the analysis and N is the variable factor that firms can hire or fire as demand for their output rises or falls. Of course, this distinction is too sharp to be completely relevant to everyday experience. A significant element of the labor force in any firm, such as management personnel, can really be treated as a fixed factor. On the other hand, investment expenditures above those required for depreciation add to the capital stock existing at the beginning of any period and therefore K is not really a constant. The important question is: How long does it take to translate an investment decision into additional productive

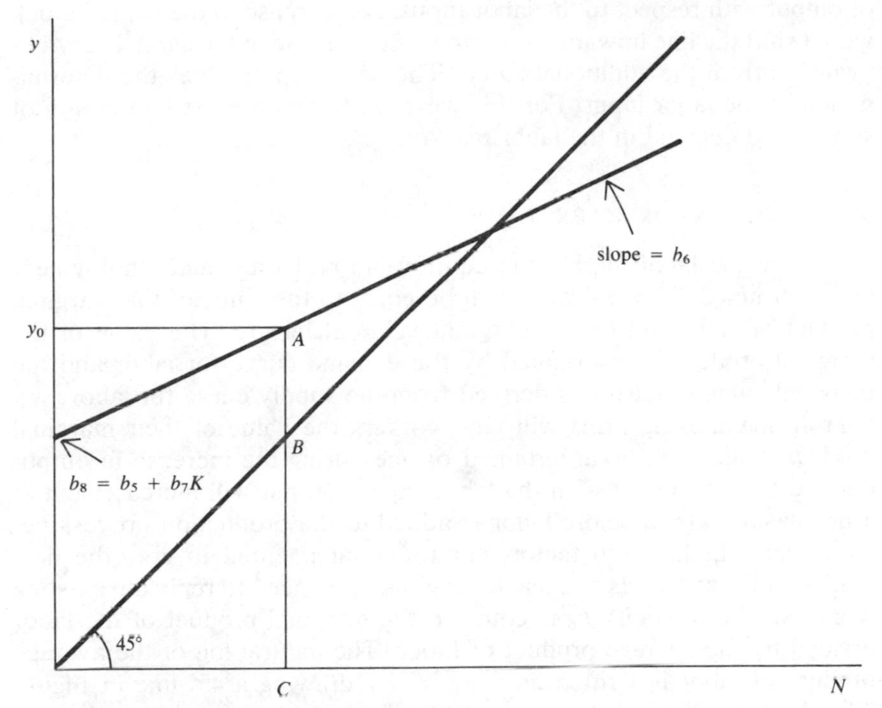

Figure 2-8 The production function.

capital services? The answer depends very much on the specific characteristics of the capital equipment involved, but for many capital goods this time horizon is longer than the typical period for which stabilization policy is relevant. Nevertheless, the reader should remember that this assumption accounts for many of the policy results that follow, and if indeed the capital stock responds to macroeconomic policy, the outcome for the economy would be substantially different. Returning to equation (2.8), since K is constant, the production function can be simplified to

(2.8′) $y^s = b_8 + b_6N$

where $b_8 = b_5 + b_7K$.

EXAMPLE CONTINUES

$$b_8 = 0 + .263(4.605) = 1.211.$$

This relationship between y^s and N is shown as the straight line in Figure 2-8. The vertical intercept is b_8 and the slope is b_6, which is the elasticity of output with respect to the labor input. An increase in the capital stock would shift the line upward by b_7 times the increase in the capital services available from the additional stock. The next step involves the determination of the labor input. For this we need to explore the interaction of supply and demand in the labor market.

THE LABOR MARKET

In the labor market the equilibrium real wage and employment are determined. The real wage will be equal to the value of the marginal product of labor and to the marginal value of leisure. The value of the marginal product is determined by the demand curve for labor and the marginal value of leisure is derived from the supply curve for labor.

Profit-maximizing firms will pay workers the value of their marginal product, which can be ascertained by measuring the increase in output derived from an increase in the labor input. Output will increase, but at a decreasing rate, as more labor is added to the production process because capital, the fixed factor, cannot be augmented to give the new workers the extra tools and machinery that they need to replicate existing workers. The elasticity b_6 is equal to the marginal product of the labor divided by the average product of labor. The natural log of the average product of labor is written as $y - N$. By drawing a 45° line in Figure 2-8, along which $y = N$, the vertical distance between the production function and the 45° line measures $y - N$. For instance, at C on the horizontal axis, $y = AC$, $N = BC$, and thus $y - N = AB$. As long as $b_6 < 1$, this distance falls as N increases. Thus marginal product and the real wage fall with increased employment. This relationship presents us with the demand curve for labor, which can be written as

$$N = b_9 - b_{10}(w - p) \tag{2.9}$$

where $(w - p)$ is the natural log of the real wage, obtained by dividing the nominal wage by a price index or, in terms of natural logs, subtracting p from w, the natural log of the nominal wage. Now b_9 is a positive constant, and b_{10} is the elasticity of labor demand with respect to the real wage. It is also positive, since there is a minus sign in front of it. Written this way, it can be easily seen that a given decrease in w or the same increase in p will have the same effect on the real wage and employment. On the other hand, equal increases in w and p will leave the real wage unchanged and have no effect on firms' demand for labor.

In an environment where wages and prices are always rising but not necessarily in the same proportion we want to write the demand relationship in terms of inflation rates. Writing equation (2.9) for the previous period, that is, relating N_{-1} to $(w - p)_{-1}$ and subtracting from (2.9), produces

$$(2.9') \quad N - N_{-1} = b_{10}[w - w_{-1} - (p - p_{-1})]$$

or

$$(2.9'') \quad N = N_{-1} - b_{10}(\omega - \pi)$$

where ω is the rate of change of nominal wages. From this perspective, the demand for labor rises if $\omega < \pi$ since the real wage would be falling over time. Only if $\omega = \pi$ is the real wage constant and $N = N_{-1}$.

EXAMPLE

The nominal wage rises from \$10 to \$12 an hour or $w_{-1} = 2.303$ and $w = 2.485$. If $\pi = .068$ as in the previous example, $\omega - \pi = 2.485 - 2.303 - .068 = .114$ or 11%.

Work generates income, which in turn allows individuals to buy goods and services to satisfy their needs. But more work means less leisure, which also satisfies basic human wants. An increase in the wage rate makes work more attractive and leisure less desirable. That is the substitution effect of a change in relative prices. At the same time the higher wage allows workers to earn the same income with less work effort. This is the income effect. Assuming that the substitution effect always overpowers any adverse income effect on work effort, the supply of labor will respond positively to an increase in the real wage. The nominal wage by itself is not an important consideration to the worker since he or she is trying to measure the purchasing power of work effort and not merely the dollar income that it generates. For instance, an equal increase in both nominal wages and prices leaves unchanged the goods and services that an hour of work will command and therefore leaves workers at the same level of welfare and unwilling to change their previous work–leisure decision. In other words, workers do not suffer from "money illusion." The supply curve of labor is the relationship between work effort by workers and the real wage and is written as

$$(2.10) \quad L = b_{11} + b_{12}(w - p)$$

where L is ln of the units of labor supplied by workers to all firms collectively. Here b_{11} is a positive constant and b_{12} is the elasticity of labor

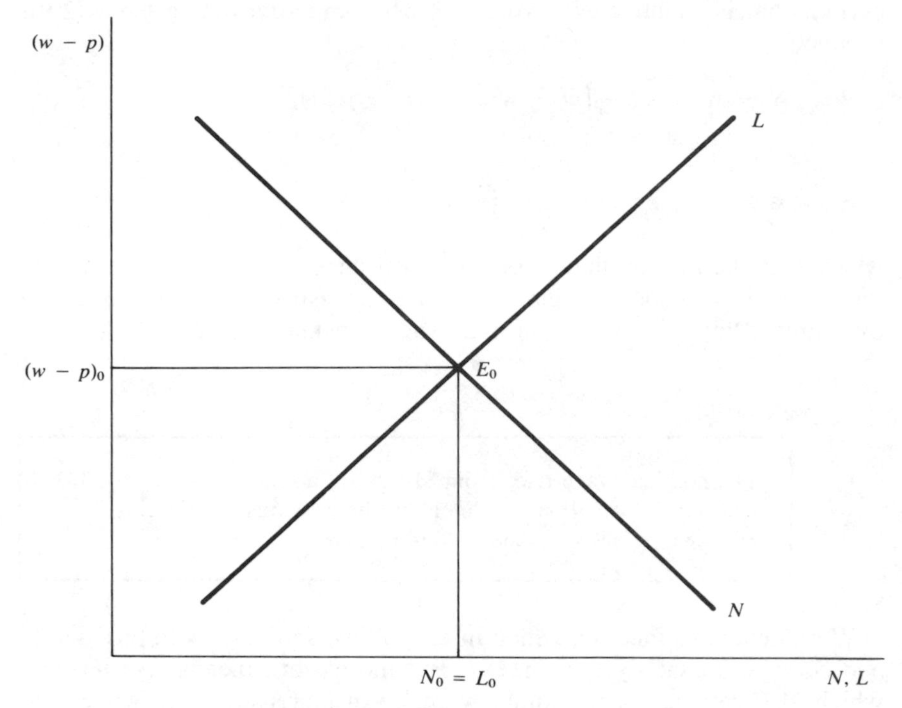

Figure 2-9 Equilibrium in the labor market.

supply with respect to the real wage and is also positive.[3] Performing the same transformation as for the demand curve, we can obtain a relationship between labor supply and rates of change of nominal wages and prices:

$$(2.10') \quad L = L_{-1} + b_{12}(\omega - \pi)$$

Equilibrium in the labor market is depicted by $N = L$ and also by $\omega = \pi$. If this latter condition were not fulfilled, N and L would move in opposite directions over time, making it impossible to maintain an initial equality. Equations (2.9) and (2.10) are drawn in Figure 2-9, where $(w - p)$, the real wage, is measured on the vertical axis. Their intersection is at E_0, which simultaneously determines both the equilibrium level of N_0 (or L_0) and the constant real wage, $(w - p)_0$. If we observe that $\omega > \pi$,

[3] The empirical evidence on this elasticity being positive is not strong. That is, a possibility exists that negative income effects are stronger than the positive substitution effect. For a full discussion, see J. T. Addison and W. S. Siebert, *The Market for Labor: An Analytical Treatment*, Santa Monica, Goodyear, 1979, chap. 4. Nevertheless, the supply curve of labor could be vertical or even backward-bending as long as it is steeper than the demand curve without changing much of the subsequent discussion.

$(w - p)$ will be increasing over time, causing ever-increasing excess supply in the labor market, requiring that the relationship between ω and π must be reversed to reattain equilibrium.

Even though the labor market is in equilibrium, there is no guarantee that the economy is at "full" employment. In fact, Milton Friedman has labeled the unemployment that does exist when the real wage remains constant as the "natural rate of unemployment." How can unemployment be consistent with equilibrium in the labor market? It arises from a lack of complete homogeneity in the aggregate called "labor." Demand for labor consists of *satisfied* demand, in the sense that firms have hired the workers that they want, plus *unsatisfied* demand, in the form of vacancies that they have not been able to fill. On the supply side of the market, there are those who are *employed* and those who are still looking for work and therefore definitionally *unemployed*. Since satisfied demand and satisfied supply are the same thing, equilibrium in the labor market implies that the number of vacancies must equal the number of unemployed. If labor markets were homogeneous, those who are unemployed would be able to find and fill the vacancies that exist and unemployment would disappear. For instance, in New Zealand, where labor markets are fairly homogeneous, the unemployment rate rarely rises above 1%, but in North America, with its geographic dispersion and segmented labor markets, the unemployment rate rarely falls below 5%. The natural rate of unemployment is largely a matter of "square pegs and round holes." Vacancies may exist in one part of the country and the unemployed in another with the costs of moving, both economic and emotional, being too high to overcome the problem. Or vacancies may exist for skilled workers with the unemployed being largely unskilled, requiring long periods of training to eliminate the discrepancy.

If vacancies are a constant proportion of total demand for labor, say 5%, we can distinguish between *demand for labor* and *employment* quite easily. We can find the quantity demanded at equilibrium, as in Figure 2-9, at N_0 and then take 95% of that to measure employment.

There is another kind of unemployment that prevails in equilibrium, but it is *voluntary*. Looking back at the supply curve for labor, we can see that workers are choosing between work and leisure on the basis of the real wage. To the extent that they are not working 24 hours a day, seven days a week, they are at least partially unemployed. This is a free choice, and eliminating this "unemployment" through macroeconomic policy would be tantamount to slavery. Those captured by the natural rate of unemployment, on the other hand, are involuntarily unemployed. They are those who want to work at the going wage but cannot find work for which they are suitable. They require training or mobility before they can fill existing job vacancies.

THE DERIVATION OF "NATURAL RATE OUTPUT"

Having established a link between output and labor input and having derived equilibrium conditions for the labor market, we can determine that level of output and income that is consistent with equilibrium in the labor market. This is called *natural rate output* or *equilibrium output* or *potential output*, the natural log of which is labeled as y_e. It is an *economically* desirable level of output because it satisfies both worker–consumers and firms. It is not the role of stabilization policy to maximize y_e, but to keep actual output as close to it as possible.

From the production function of equation (2.8′), we obtain

$$(2.11) \quad y_e = b_8 + b_6 N_e$$

where N_e represents the ln of the level of employment that is consistent with equilibrium in the labor market, or N_0 in Figure 2-9. Going back to Figure 2-8, N_e is marked on the horizontal axis, say at C, and then y_e can be read from the vertical axis at AC. If either the supply curve or the demand curve in Figure 2-9 were to shift, we would have a new equilibrium in the labor market and through equation (2.11) a new level of equilibrium output. For instance, consider an exogenous increase in the productivity of labor such that every worker produces more output than before. This is captured by an increase in the parameter b_6 to b_6'. Diagrammatically, equation (2.8′) becomes steeper as drawn in the upper portion of Figure 2-10. This higher productivity at every level of employment is translated into a higher real wage so that in the lower portion of Figure 2-10 the demand curve for labor shifts upward to N'. At the new equilibrium, E_1, both employment and the real wage have risen. Now y^s increases for two reasons in this instance:

1. The increase in b_6 causes existing workers to produce more output (y^s rises to the intermediate position of $y^{s\prime}$).
2. The higher equilibrium level of employment allows output to increase from $y^{s\prime}$ to y_1^s.

However, y_e does not respond to the inflation rate and therefore in Figure 2-11 the AS curve is drawn as a vertical line with a horizontal intercept at y_e. This is an important element in the model and deserves greater attention. Both N_e and the required real wage that gives rise to it are consistent with *any* rate of inflation π as long as ω and π are equal. If ω and π are not equal, we do not observe N_e nor y_e since the real wage is changing over time. There is still an aggregate supply curve for these circumstances, and this AS curve will be taken up next, but it remains true that y_e and π are unrelated.

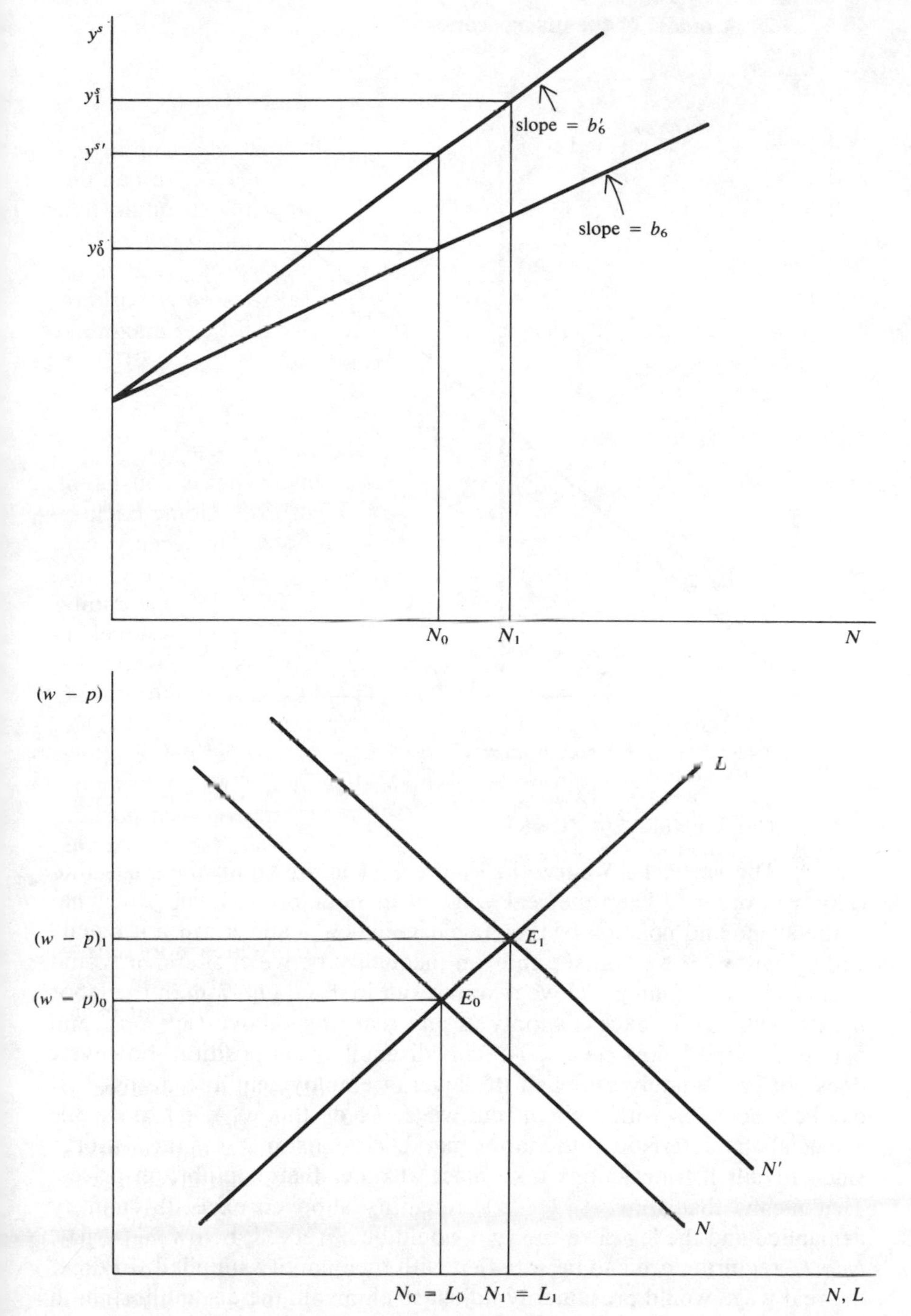

Figure 2-10 An increase in labor productivity.

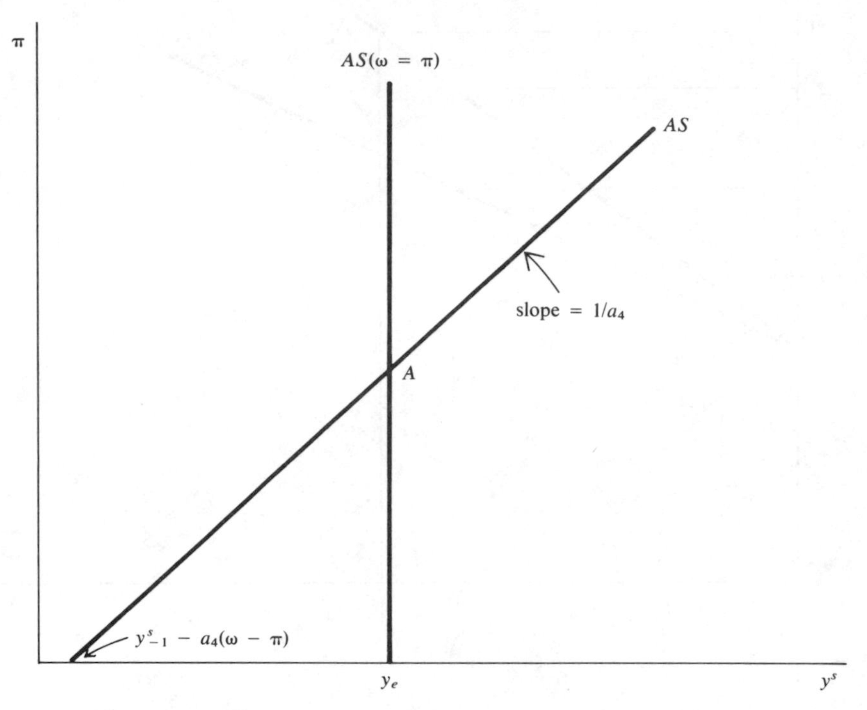

Figure 2-11 The aggregate-supply curve.

THE GENERAL *AS* CURVE

The vertical *AS* curve in Figure 2-11 is drawn on the basis that $\omega = \pi$ in order to keep the real wage at its equilibrium level. But what is the shape and position of the *AS* curve when ω and π are not equal? From Figure 2-9 we can see that an inequality between ω and π would mean a rising or falling real wage and result in disequilibrium in the labor market with either excess supply at any real wage above $(w - p)_0$ and excess demand below $(w - p)_0$. This disequilibrium position, however, does not immediately establish the level of employment and output that can be associated with a given real wage. To do this we need to invoke a special characteristic of the labor market. In most markets the "short" side prevails if transactions take place at other than equilibrium prices. That means that above $(w - p)_0$, quantity supplied exceeds quantity demanded and the lesser of the two would be observed; below $(w - p)_0$, $N > L$, requiring firms to be satisfied with the quantity supplied. In time, the real wage would presumably adjust to eliminate the disequilibrium in the labor market, but we need to know what are the quantities exchanged in the market before equilibrium is reestablished. The labor market differs from other markets in that the *demand* side of the market usually prevails in disequilibrium. In most union contracts, wages, fringe benefits, and even working conditions may be specified in great detail, but it is rare for such a contract to mention the level of employment. It is typical for the firm's management to retain the right to adjust the labor force in response to changing conditions. When firms experience increased demand they can require, within limits, overtime work, they can hire extra workers, or they can even introduce another complete shift to get the additional labor input that is needed. On the other hand, when demand for the product falls off, firms can use "short hours," lay off workers temporarily, or even fire them outright. Thus, as a general rule, firms can operate on their demand schedule for labor, but workers will only be on their supply curve in equilibrium. Because of this institutional setting, the combinations of the real wage and employment that we observe are likely to be those on the demand curve with the two variables moving in opposite directions.

Once the real wage is set, the corresponding point on the demand curve is more profitable than any other level of employment. To the right of the demand curve, marginal product of labor is less than the real wage, and firms can increase profits by reducing employment, which raises the marginal product of the remaining workers; to the left of the demand curve, marginal product exceeds the real wage and increasing the use of labor also increases profits.

This discussion can also be related to the vacancy-unemployment situation in the labor market. In equilibrium, we saw earlier, the number of vacancies equaled the number of unemployed and the resulting unemployment rate was referred to as the "natural rate." In disequilibrium the economy departs from the natural rate. With excess demand for labor, vacancies fall relative to the number of unemployed as extra workers are hired and the unemployment rate falls below the natural rate. This may involve filling some of the "round holes" with "square pegs," with the consequence that the marginal product of labor falls, but firms are prepared to accept this if $\omega < \pi$ and the real wage is falling. When there is excess supply in the labor market, vacancies are fewer than the number of unemployed and the unemployment rate rises above the natural rate. In this case there are some round holes and some round pegs available, but temporarily they cannot find each other.

In summary, there are two kinds of *involuntary* unemployment: (1) *structural* unemployment, which is equal to the number of unemployed at the natural rate; and (2) *disequilibrium* unemployment, which is the difference between vacancies and the total number of unemployed. The first is always positive but the second may be positive, negative, or zero. In practice it is difficult to separate these two concepts since we cannot

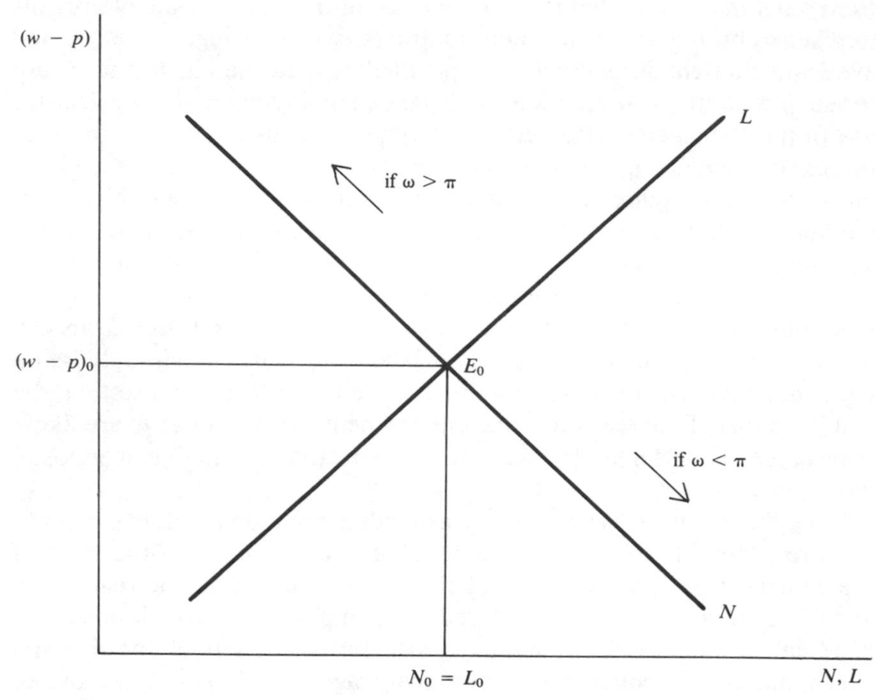

Figure 2-12 The real wage and employment.

observe directly the natural rate of unemployment, but analytically the distinction is important for policy purposes. To reduce the structural element in unemployment it is necessary to increase the homogeneity of the labor force; to eliminate disequilibrium unemployment the government would have to find ways to increase the flexibility of the real wage.

In Figure 2-12 we can relate ω and π on the one hand and N on the other. Starting from equilibrium, where $N = L$, if $\omega > \pi$, N will be falling over time as the real wage rises. This is shown by the arrows alongside the N curve. Conversely, if $\omega < \pi$, the real wage is falling and firms will want to move down and to the right along their demand curve. Above E_0 on the demand curve, workers are unwillingly unemployed since they want to work more at rising real wages, while below E_0 on the demand curve they are involuntarily made to work more than they want. These situations are unlikely to last as the excess demand or supply puts pressure on the real wage, but for some period of time workers acknowledge the right of management to dictate the level of employment.

It is not always the case that the real wage and employment are inversely related. In some instances $(w - p)$ and N can move together. Consider again an increase in the productivity of workers. We saw earlier that this produced an upward shift in the demand curve for labor and resulted in both higher employment and an increased real wage. More important for macroeconomic theory, there is evidence that productivity per person-hour and output have moved together during business cycles in the 1970s. In a recession, productivity fell and it rose in a boom period. This cannot be consistent with movements along a labor-demand curve. One oft-repeated explanation of this empirical evidence is that employment remained more stable than output that required that employees work harder at business-cycle peaks and were allowed to have "leisure on the job" in the troughs. If that is so, then counting the number of people who are employed or even the number of person-hours may be an inaccurate measure of the total labor input. If it were possible to redefine existing measures of employment to capture the intensity of work as well as its quantity, we would probably observe that productivity falls as employment and output rise and vice versa, which would be consistent with movements along a demand curve for labor.[4]

When the demand curve remains in place, it provides us with the link between output and changes in the real wage. First, transpose equation (2.8′) for one period back. This is written as

$$(2.8'') \quad y^s_{-1} = b_8 + b_6 N_{-1}$$

Then subtracting from (2.8′) and substituting (2.9″) produces

$$y^s - y^s_{-1} = b_6(N - N_{-1}) = -b_6 b_{10}(\omega - \pi)$$

or

$$(2.12) \quad y^s = y^s_{-1} - a_4(\omega - \pi)$$

where $a_4 = b_6 b_{10} > 0$.

Equation (2.12) is the general *AS* curve and can be plotted in Figure 2-11, along with the vertical *AS* curve, which is relevant for an economy in equilibrium. Given y^s_{-1} and ω, it shows a positive relationship between y^s and π; it has a slope of $1/a_4$. An increase in π with ω held constant begins to lower the real wage and causes firms to increase employment and output. On the other hand, an increase in ω shifts the *AS* curve to the left as can be seen from its horizontal intercept $y^s_{-1} - a_4\omega$. Furthermore, the *AS* curve has dynamic properties just like the *AD* curve because of the presence of y^s_{-1} in the horizontal intercept. Starting from *A* in Figure 2-11, if ω rises above π, the *AS* curve will shift to the left and it is possible

[4] Robert Gordon argues that the procyclical behavior of real wages in the 1970s can be explained by the prevalence of "supply shocks" compared to earlier cycles, which were dominated by "demand shocks." The differences between these shocks will be taken up in Chapter 3. See R. J. Gordon, *Macroeconomics*, third edition, Boston, Little, Brown, 1984, pp. 226–9.

that y will fall, although this cannot be determined unambiguously without an *AD* curve to intersect the new *AS* curve. Then the lower level of output for this period shifts the *AS* curve to the left in the next period and further adjustment would be necessary.

NOMINAL WAGE DETERMINATION

The last step in the process of deriving the *AS* curve involves the determination of ω, the rate of change of nominal wages. Again a special characteristic of the labor market is involved. The labor market is distinguished from most other markets by not being a "spot" market where purchases and sales are made for current use. Whether or not a union contract exists, employment involves a longer-term commitment. This commitment is not absolutely binding on either the firm or the worker, but a tacit agreement is in force that sets the nominal wage for some time into the future. If a spot market were the rule in labor transactions, it would mean that workers and management would be renegotiating the wage every day or even every hour as new developments occurred in the labor market. The costs of this process are sufficiently high and the uncertainty is sufficiently annoying to both parties that a "fixed" wage for some period of time is accepted by both parties. This does not mean that the length of time for which wages are constant is institutionally rigid. The recent acceleration of inflation and the uncertainty about its trend have made long-term wage contracts dangerous for both workers and firms. As a result, contract length has been considerably shortened to minimize the length of time for which both sides are exposed to unexpected changes in the inflation rate. Another adjustment in wage bargaining that has occurred is the widespread use of cost-of-living-adjustment clauses that entail negotiating about the real wage instead of the nominal wage.

As a general proposition, the nominal wage, or in an inflationary setting its rate of change, will be set so as to maintain equilibrium in the labor market since workers want to be on their labor-supply curve and firms want to be on their demand curve, making E_0 in Figure 2-9 the only point that satisfies both parties. This requires a constant real wage that can be guaranteed by setting ω equal to π. But since ω is set for a *future* period, π cannot yet be observed, and π^e, the expected inflation rate, will have to be used instead. This requirement can be written as

$$\omega = \pi^e \tag{2.13}$$

The determination of wages is a complex process where emotional issues are just as important as economic ones and in specific circumstances equation (2.13) is wide of the mark, but for now we will accept it as a first approximation. However, there are two general sets of circumstances where equation (2.13) would not hold:

1. when the marginal product of workers is increasing over time so that the real wage should also rise, and this requires that $\omega > \pi^e$; and
2. if the bargaining is taking place at a time when the labor market is not in equilibrium and ω will diverge from π^e to allow the real wage to rise or fall to reestablish equilibrium.

For the present, in order to keep the analysis as uncomplicated as possible, the absence of both of these circumstances will be assumed. In that case, equation (2.13) can be substituted into the *AS* curve of equation (2.12), but also y_e can be substituted for y_{-1} when the economy starts from equilibrium. Thus the final version of the *AS* curve is

$$(2.14) \quad y^s = y_e - a_4(\pi^e - \pi)$$

remembering that other provisions can be made for the determination of ω and that the economy could currently be at a position other than equilibrium, in which case equation (2.12) should be used as the *AS* curve.

Equation (2.14) captures both the long-run and short-run properties of the *AS* curve. If the long run is identified with equilibrium, the vertical *AS* curve of Figure 2-11 is obtained if $\pi^e = \pi$ or, in other words, if inflationary expectations are fulfilled. On the other hand, if π^e does not coincide with π, as could occur in the short run, then the last term in (2.14) is either positive or negative and y^s exceeds or falls short of y_e. Equation (2.14) is still the positively sloped line in Figure 2-11, except that now the horizontal intercept is $y_e - a_4\pi^e$. For equation (2.14) the vertical intercept is now economically more meaningful as can be seen by rewriting the *AS* curve as

$$(2.14') \quad \pi = (1/a_4)(y^s - y_e) + \pi^e$$

An increase in π^e will shift the *AS* curve upward by the full extent of the increase in π^e.

This completes the discussion of the various building blocks of the macroeconomic model, and we are now ready to take a look at its structure.

2.3 THE COMPLETE SYSTEM

The macroeconomic model consists of the *IS*, *LM*, and *AS* equations, which are repeated here as

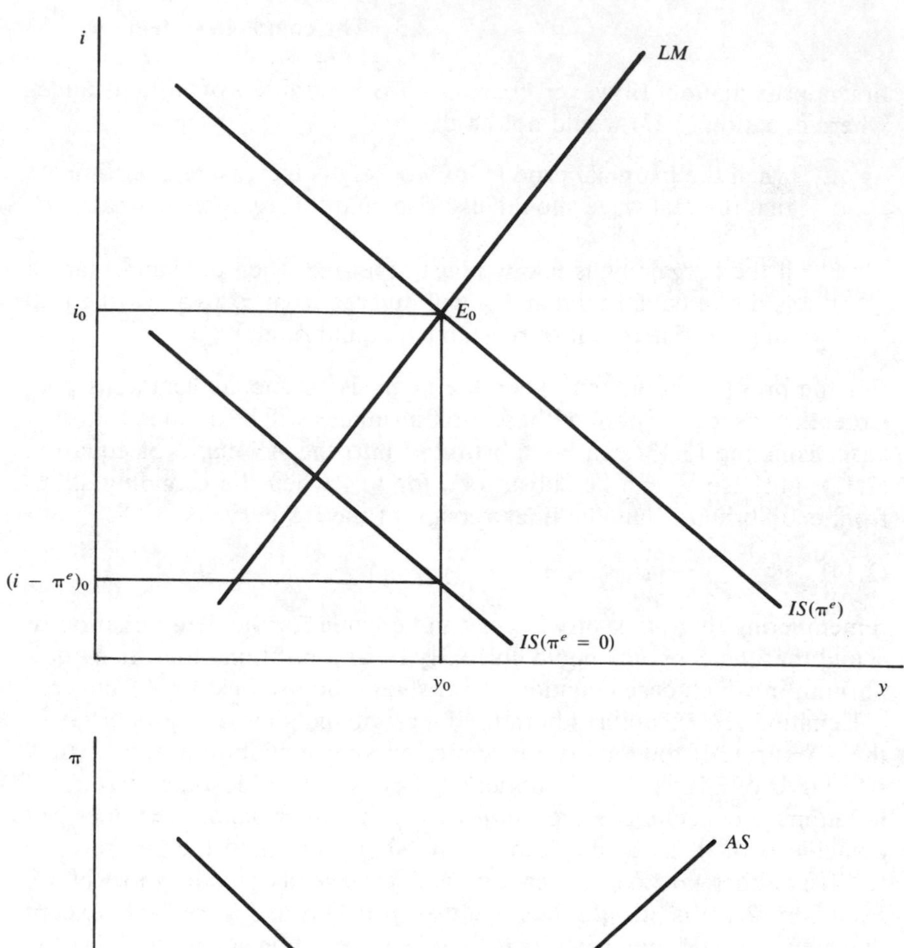

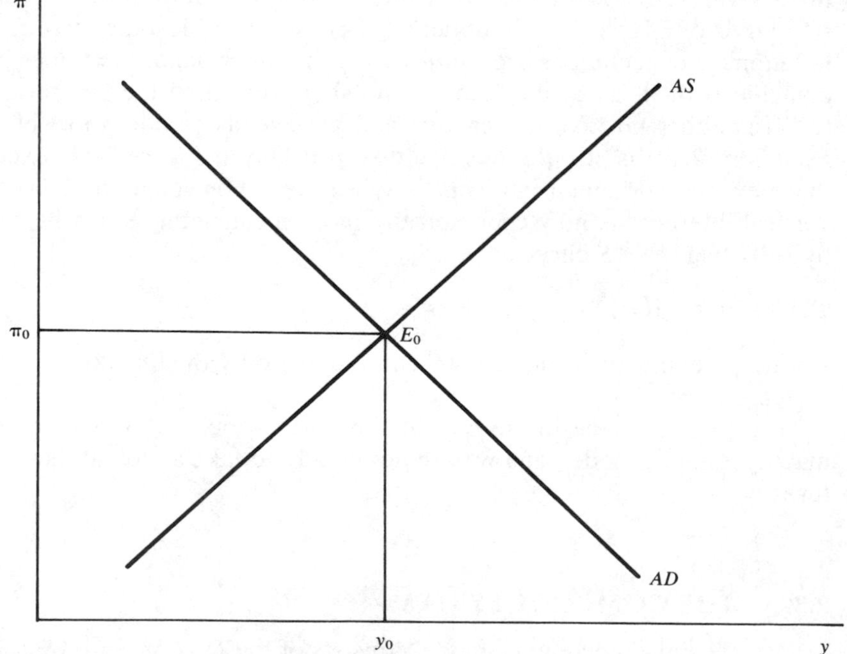

Figure 2-13 The complete system.

(2.3) $y^d = a_0 - a_1(i - \pi^e)$

(2.6) $\mu - \pi = a_2 y^d - a_3 i - (m - p)_{-1}$

(2.14) $y^s = y_e - a_4(\pi^e - \pi)$

The only additional information that we need to close the system is that output demanded as determined by the *IS–LM* equations equals output supplied as derived from the *AS* curve. This requirement can be written as

(2.15) $y = y^d = y^s$

where y^d is the relevant variable in the *AD* curve which is obtained by collapsing the *IS–LM* equations into

(2.7) $\pi = \mu + (m - p)_{-1} - (a_2 + a_3/a_1)y^d + a_3 a_0/a_1 + a_3\pi^e$

This system is very flexible. If we want to determine all three important macroeconomic variables, y, i, and π, we use equations (2.3), (2.6), and (2.14) together with our information about μ, $(m - p)_{-1}$, π^e, and y_e, the parameters a_0 through a_4, and the equilibrium condition of equation (2.15). If, on the other hand, we are content to calculate y and π, we need only use equations (2.7) and (2.14) together with (2.15). Nevertheless, these two ways of looking at the economy do not present different views; they are really the same, with the former having somewhat more detail than the latter. This must be so since the *AD* curve is just another way of writing the combined *IS–LM* curves.

The complete system is depicted in Figure 2-13. The upper portion is the *IS–LM* framework and is similar to Figure 2-3. The lower portion combines the *AD* and *AS* curves of Figure 2-7 and Figure 2-11. Because of the connection between the *IS–LM* curves and the *AD* curve, the equilibrium level of income in the upper portion of the diagram cannot differ from that in the lower portion.

The intersection of $IS(\pi^e)$ and *LM* determines y and i, and from $IS(\pi^e = 0)$ we can read $i - \pi^e$. Then from the intersection of *AD* and *AS*, we can derive the equilibrium values of π and y. More important, we can determine the changes in y, i, and π that occur if policy changes can shift one or more of the *IS–LM–AS* curves, and a discussion of these effects will occupy a large portion of this book.

2.4 LONG-RUN EQUILIBRIUM

If left to its own resources for a period of time, the economy would settle down at a particular combination of y, i, and π and would replicate itself year after year. We do not observe such a situation very often, if at all, since there are always new events occurring that start a fresh round of adjustment before the previous one is completed. Nevertheless, this concept of *long-run equilibrium* is useful for analyzing the path that y, i, and π *would* take if sufficient time were to elapse. How long does it take to reach long-run equilibrium? No precise answer can be given in terms of months or years, especially since there is much dispute about what contributes to the speed of adjustment in the economy when presented with an exogenous event. Keynesians feel that the adjustment process is slow and that long-run equilibrium is a distant goal, whereas neoclassical economists believe that the economy has the ability to adjust quickly and that the long run is easily reached. Both sides believe in equilibrium, but their notions of what constitutes equilibrium differ. To accommodate both positions in the macroeconomic model we can introduce another version of equilibrium, namely *short-run equilibrium*, more aptly called *temporary equilibrium* in that the economy can be observed to be in this position for some short period of time before it continues its adjustment process to the long run.

We can define these concepts of equilibrium more precisely in terms of certain characteristics of the model. Short-run equilibrium requires only the previously stated mechanism of closing the system, namely

$$(2.15) \quad y = y^d = y^s$$

while long-run equilibrium requires, in addition, that

$$(2.16) \quad \pi^e = \pi$$

From these requirements we can see that the goods market is in a position of rest under both concepts of equilibrium. If output demanded did not conform to output supplied, there would be involuntary inventory adjustments and further changes in output and income would occur. This process is assumed to be completed every time we observe an economy in short-run equilibrium. Equation (2.15) also indirectly requires the asset markets to be in equilibrium at all times, since the position of the *AD* curve would not remain constant if μ or $(m - p)_{-1}$ were changing over time. However, the labor market may not be in equilibrium in the short run, although it must be in the long run. Only if equation (2.16) is satisfied is the real wage constant at the level required to set supply equal to demand in the labor market. When expectations about inflation are fulfilled, there is no incentive to make further adjustments, and the economy can settle down to a stationary state; if π^e and π do not coincide, this will not be known until the end of the current period, during which no adjustment takes place, but after which a new estimate of π^e will be made.

Expectations about the future rate of inflation play a vital role in the macroeconomy but π^e cannot be observed directly and we can therefore never be sure how it is determined or how it adjusts to new circumstances. It is this unobservability of π^e that makes macroeconomics both frustrating and exciting. All the other variables in our macroeconomic model can be measured – some more accurately than others – but π^e remains elusive. We could take a poll, asking a random selection of people for their estimate of π^e. But opinion polls are fragile things to interpret, and since expected inflation is a more important variable for some economic decisions than for others, it is not clear how one can get a meaningful index of expected inflation. Alternatively, we might perhaps infer π^e from current wage settlements. If, for instance, we observe $\omega = 12\%$, we might be entitled to believe that π^e is also 12% according to equation (2.13). But as we saw earlier, there are times when ω and π^e need not coincide, and unless we can pinpoint the change in labor productivity, the extent by which ω can diverge from π^e cannot be calculated.

Despite the fact that π^e remains a state of mind we can insist that long-run equilibrium is only achieved when $\pi = \pi^e$. A situation where π is not equal to π^e is an error message that informs individuals that they made a mistake in the past and that π^e needs correction. When equation (2.16) is satisfied however, individuals are happy with their previous decisions and are ready to repeat them unless new events come along that break the existing pattern.

The last major task in this chapter is to explore the characteristics of long-run equilibrium, leaving for Chapters 3 and 4 a discussion of the series of short runs as the economy evolves to a new long-run equilibrium. If $\pi = \pi^e$, the macroeconomic model of equations (2.3), (2.6), and (2.14) becomes simpler still. First of all, the *AS* curve becomes $y^s = y_e$ and is drawn as the vertical line in Figure 2-14. Because it is vertical, the *AS* curve determines income and output without reference to the *AD* curve. Second, given y, the *IS* curve can be rewritten as $i = (a_0 - y_e)/a_1 + \pi$. Next, for the *LM* curve to remain in place means that $\mu = \pi$, which suggests that equation (2.4) becomes relevant and that $\mu = \pi = \pi^e$. Then substituting in the *LM* curve allows us to solve for the real money supply. Finally, the real interest rate is determined by $i - \pi^e = (a_0 - y_e)/a_1$.

There are a number of important implications of this long-run structure of the economy. First, the solutions for y, π, and i are determined sequentially, not simultaneously. Output and income are determined only by the *AS* curve, the inflation rate is equal to the given growth rate of the money supply, and the interest rate is determined by the location of the *IS* curve. In the lower portion of Figure 2-14, the *AD* curve plays a limited role; it intersects with the *AS* curve at a vertical distance of $\mu =$

π. To summarize, the long-run values of y, π, and i are given by

(2.17) $y = y^s = y_e$ [from *AS* and (2.16)]

(2.18) $\pi = \mu = \pi^e$ [from *LM* and (2.16)]

(2.19) $i = (a_0 - y_e)/a_1 + \mu$ [from *IS*, *AS* and (2.18)]

All the variables on the right side of these equations are exogenous, and they uniquely determine the three variables of greatest interest to any discussion of macroeconomic performance.

Second, this structure must be interpreted in a way that may be unfamiliar to a student who has been exposed only to the *IS–LM* framework. As a case in point, aggregate-demand policies in the form of fiscal or monetary policy, although they affect the location of the *IS* or *LM* curves, do not influence the level of income. No matter what happens in the upper portion of Figure 2-14, output remains at y_e as dictated by the *AS* curve. Since the real wage remains constant in the long run, the labor input into the production process remains unaltered, and together with a fixed capital stock, y_e is the only possible output from the production function. Demand for that output will automatically materialize. As we shall see later, from a long-run perspective, policy influences on output and income have to come through the *AS* curve, hence the term *supply-side policies*.

Another instance of required reinterpretation is the connection between monetary policy and interest rates. From the *IS–LM* model it would appear that expansionary monetary policy, by shifting the *LM* curve down and to the right as in Figure 2-15, would lower both the nominal and the real interest rate. However, in the full, long-run *IS–LM–AS* model, expansionary monetary policy through an increase in μ will *increase* the nominal interest rate and leave the real interest rate unchanged. After an increase in μ to μ_1 the *LM* curve starts shifting downward to a position such as *LM*′, but in the end it must be in a higher position than it started. How does this happen? Leaving out all the intermediate steps, we know that π^e must rise to equal the new μ (to π_1^e) since in the long run μ and π will be equal again. This causes the *IS* curve to shift upward. This effect of monetary policy on the *IS* curve complicates the picture but makes it a more accurate reflection of the current facts. Because y cannot change from y_e, the new equilibrium requires an intersection of *IS*′ and *LM*″ at E_1. For this to happen, the *LM* curve must alter its original "travel plans." To move upward, we must have a period in which $\pi > \mu$ so that the real money supply is shrinking over time. In the new equilibrium, there is a smaller real money supply and a constant level of y. From equation (2.4) and our knowledge of the dynamics in the asset markets we know that the interest rate must rise. In fact, since *IS* shifts upward by π^e, which is equal to the change in μ, the interest rate must also rise by this amount.

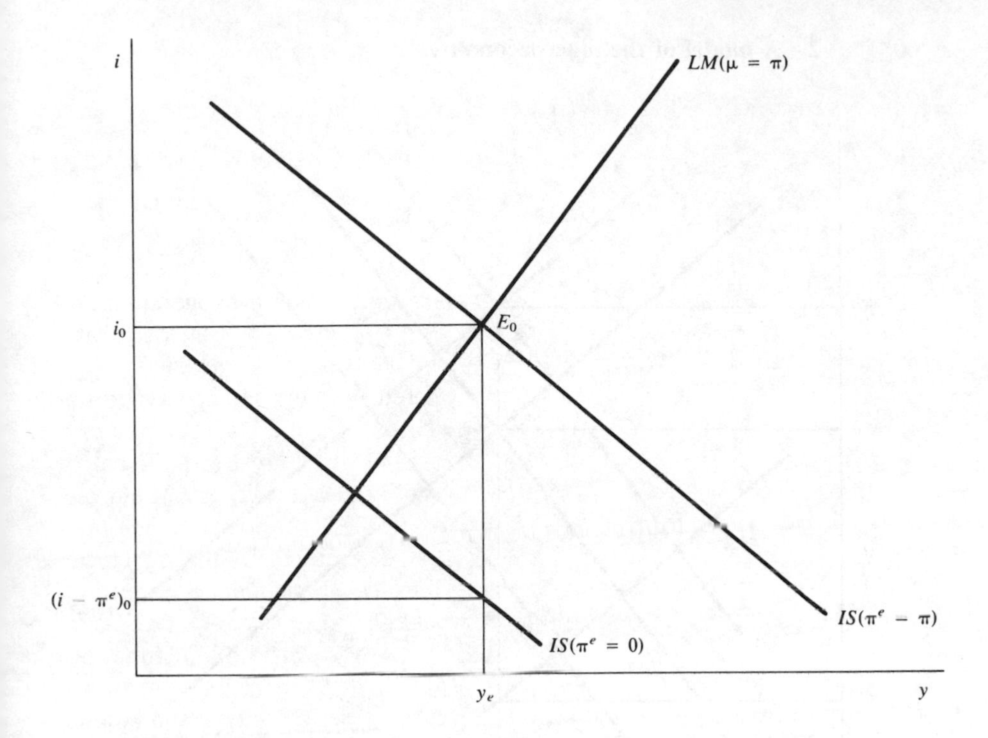

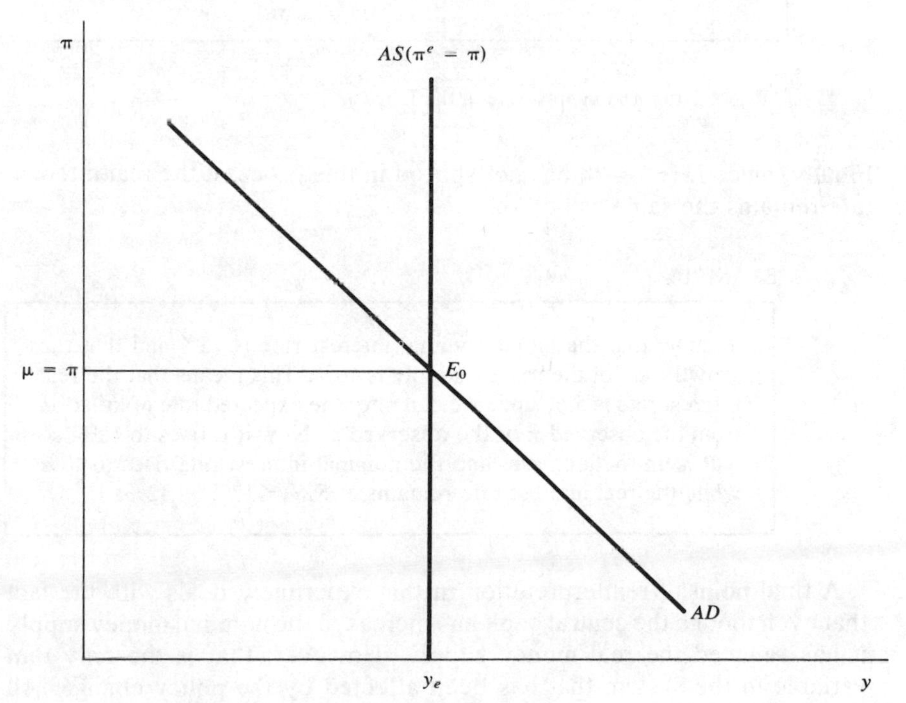

Figure 2-14 Long-run equilibrium.

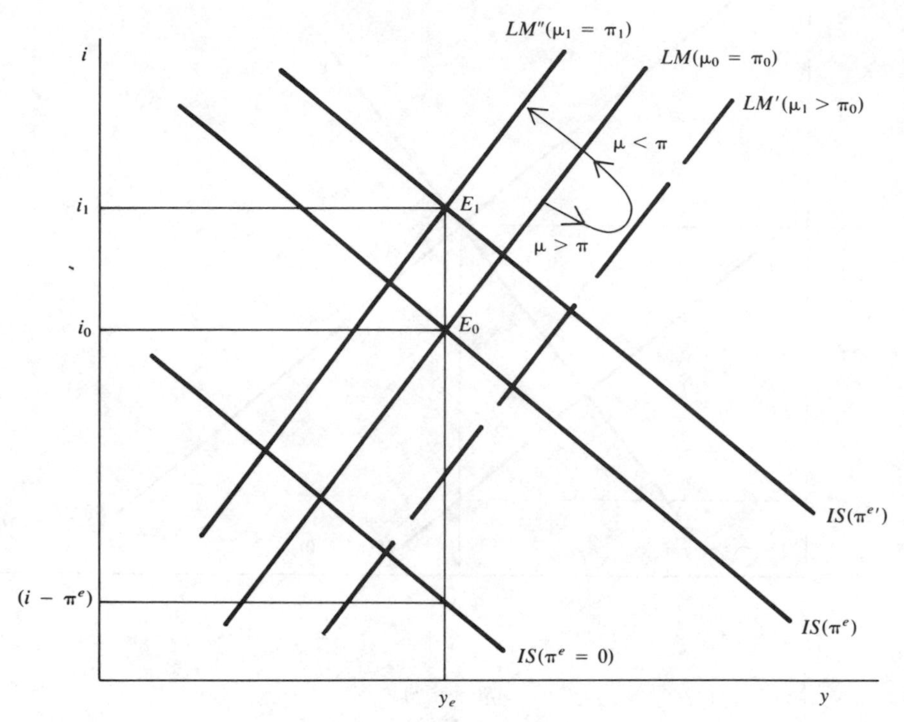

Figure 2-15 The interest rate in the long run.

Finally, since $IS(\pi^e = 0)$ has not shifted in this process, the real interest rate remains the same as before.

EXAMPLE

> Assume that the initial nominal interest rate is 15% and that the growth rate of the money supply is 10%. This means that the real interest rate is 5%, since we can infer the expected rate of inflation from the observed π or the observed μ. Now if μ rises to 12%, so will π^e in the long run, and the nominal interest rate rises to 17% while the real interest rate remains at 5% = 17% − 12%.

A final point of reinterpretation in this experiment deals with the fact that even though the central bank has increased the nominal money supply it has reduced the real money supply. However, that is the only *real* variable in the system that has been affected by the policy change. All the other real variables, y_e, S, I, $i - \pi^e$, N, and L (as well as the natural

Table 2-1. *Growth rates of money supply, prices, output, and interest rates, various countries, 1971–80*

Country	Compound annual growth rate (%) of: money supply[a] (1)	prices[b] (2)	output[c] (3)	Short-term interest rates, 1980 (%) (4)
Belgium	7.9	7.2	3.0	14.06
Canada	10.1	9.3	3.6	13.12
France	11.0	9.8	3.5	12.18
Germany	8.9	4.9	2.8	9.45
Italy	18.6	15.6	3.3	17.50
Japan	12.5	7.4	4.9	11.45
Netherlands	9.3	8.1	2.7	10.60
Switzerland	4.4	4.7	1.0	5.79
United Kingdom	12.8	14.4	1.7	16.59
United States	6.6	7.1	3.1	11.49

[a] The money supply is generally "narrowly" defined.
[b] Prices are measured by the implicit GNP deflator.
[c] Output is measured by gross national product, except for France, Italy, and the United Kingdom, where gross domestic product is used.
Sources: (1)–(3), Federal Reserve Bank of St. Louis, *International Economic Conditions: Annual Data, 1962–1981*; (4), *Federal Reserve Bulletin*, December 1981, tables 3.27 and 1.35, line 6.

rate of unemployment), have remained the same as in the initial position. These variables may be higher or lower during successive short-run equilibria, but comparing only two long-run equilibrium points, they do not change.

2.4.1 EMPIRICAL EVIDENCE

If we look at the evidence over the long run, such as the decade of the 1970s, we find that, on average, countries with high rates of monetary expansion also had correspondingly high rates of inflation and high interest rates. In Table 2-1, it can be seen that a country like Switzerland that kept μ at a fairly low level also had much lower inflation and interest rates than most other countries, while the United Kingdom had both μ and π at a much higher level. These differences occurred despite the fact that Switzerland was likely to be affected much more by the OPEC oil-price increases in 1973 and 1979 than the United Kingdom, which by this time could rely, at least partially, on its own North Sea oil. This points to the fact that in the long run, inflation is a monetary phenomenon and is not influenced by structural changes or "real shocks" to the system. This does not mean, however, that we can always expect to observe that

$\mu = \pi$ exactly. For one thing, we know that other variables were not held constant during the 1970s. To the extent that real income grew through capital accumulation or increases in the labor force, the transactions demand for money would also grow by π plus the growth rate of y [columns (2) and (3) in Table 2-1] and require μ to be greater than π to allow $(m - p)$ to rise. Furthermore, the interest rate rose sharply during the decade of the 1970s, making money holding less attractive relative to bonds, suggesting that $(m - p)$ should be lower. These are conflicting effects on the required relationship between μ and π and we cannot tell which is the stronger in any one country. Finally, because of financial developments in many countries in this period the growth rate of M1 that is reported in Table 2-1 may have become less relevant as new types of money became more attractive to individuals and firms. This requires a shift in the demand function for money, which is not taken into account in our discussion of long-run equilibrium, but will receive much more attention in Chapter 5.

2.5 THE LONG-RUN EFFECTS OF A SUPPLY SHOCK

To understand better the long-run characteristics of the macro model, it is useful to postulate some exogenous shock to the system that has lasting real and nominal repercussions. From the previous discussion of expansionary monetary policy it is obvious that this can only be accomplished by some event that affects the location of the long-run *AS* curve. In the long run the horizontal intercept of the *AS* curve is determined by equilibrium employment. Now consider an increase in the supply of labor at every wage rate, as might occur after a tax cut on wage income, since the after-tax wage would now be higher and make work more attractive. This shifts the *L* curve down and to the right in panel (a) of Figure 2-16, leading to a lower $(w - p)$ and to a higher level of N.[5] In Figure 2-16(b) the increased labor input is translated into higher equilibrium output by a shift to the right of the vertical *AS* curve and y increases to y_{e_1}. If the *AD* curve did not shift, the inflation rate would fall to π_1. However, since μ has not changed, π must remain as before and *AD* will shift to the right to intersect *AS'* at E_1. The *LM* curve is also affected by this exogenous event. To determine desired real money balances we can substitute (2.19) into the *LM* curve of equation (2.4) to obtain

$$m - p = (a_2 + a_3/a_1)y - a_3a_0/a_1 - a_3\mu \tag{2.20}$$

[5] Even though the pretax real wage, $(w - p)$, is lower, it is likely that the after-tax real wage is higher, but this is not shown in the diagram.

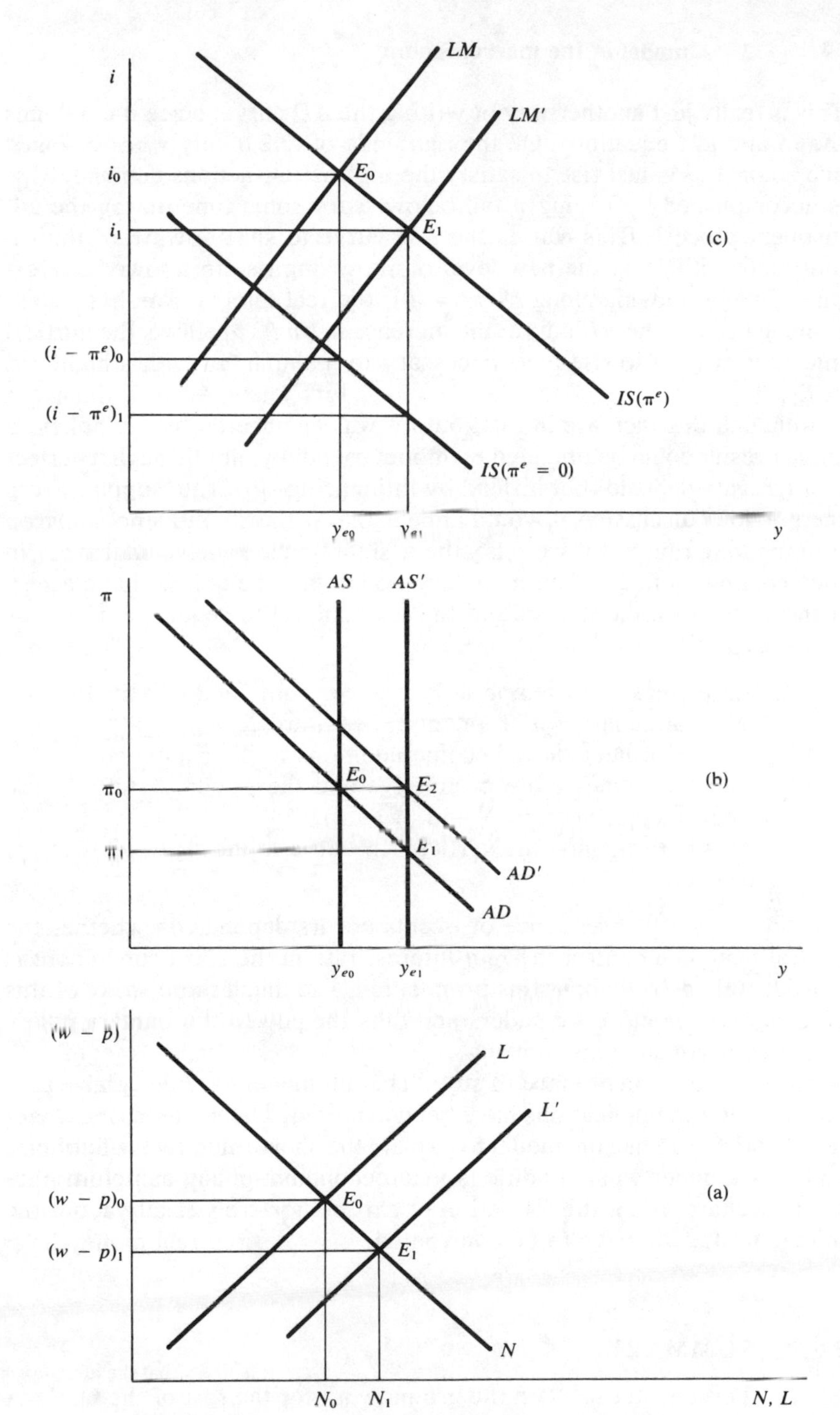

Figure 2-16 The long-run effects of a supply shock.

This is really just another way of writing the *AD* curve, since it combines the *IS* and *LM* equations. On the right side of (2.20) only y has changed and so $(m - p)$ must rise to satisfy the higher transactions demand. This is accomplished by having π fall below μ for some time during the adjustment process. This causes the *LM* curve to shift downward until it intersects with *IS* at the new level of y_e, giving rise to a lower interest rate. Finally, moving along $IS(\pi^e = 0)$, the real interest rate has fallen. Coming back to the *AD* curve, the increase in $(m - p)$ allows the vertical intercept of (2.7) to rise as is necessary to maintain π_0 with a higher y_e at E_2.

Although this increase in total output was engineered by tax policy, a similar result could be obtained by monetary policy, not through its effect on aggregate demand, but instead by influencing aggregate supply. From the previous discussion it would appear that μ has its influence only on π in the long run, but if we relax the assumption that the capital stock in the economy is fixed, then monetary policy may be able to have a permanent effect on the real side of the economy. The sequence of events would be as follows:

1. An increase in μ temporarily reduces both i and $i - \pi^e$, thereby stimulating larger investment expenditures.
2. Sooner or later these become additions to the capital stock.
3. Labor becomes more productive and the N curve shifts to the right, increasing both N and $(w - p)$.
4. This in turn shifts the vertical *AS* curve to the right, allowing y_e to rise.

Whether or not this sequence of events occurs depends on whether the central bank can control the *real* interest rate in the short run. There is considerable debate about this proposition, and much more study of this issue is needed before we understand fully the power of monetary policy as a macroeconomic instrument.

This is a convenient place to stop. The full model has been elaborated and its long-run implications have been explored. The next step, in Chapters 3 and 4, is to use the model to explain the short-run effects of policies and to ask under what conditions macroeconomic policy can contribute to our welfare. Also, the formation of expectations, especially about the inflation rate, will have to be confronted.

2.6 SUMMARY

This chapter has laid the groundwork for the rest of the book. A simple but comprehensive model of macroeconomic behavior has been developed and analyzed. It has some important characteristics that are worth repeating:

1. It attempts to explain the most significant variables in the economy: income, the interest rate, and the inflation rate.
2. It incorporates the most important markets: goods, assets, and labor.
3. It uses the now familiar *IS–LM–AS* framework.
4. It distinguishes between the short-run equilibrium where only aggregate demand equals aggregate supply and the long run where, in addition, inflationary expectations are fulfilled.
5. It distinguishes between nominal and real economic magnitudes and the effect that exogenous changes can have on these two categories of variables.
6. It incorporates, in a very general way, both fiscal and monetary policy instruments.
7. It has dynamic features, allowing for continuing adjustment in the economy following a one-time change in an exogenous variable.
8. Its most important feature is that it does not take sides in the debate between Keynesians and neoclassical macroeconomists. At this stage it is relatively neutral; later, explicit assumptions favored by the two sides can be incorporated into the model and predictions can be compared, enabling the student to make his or her own value judgments about the relative merits of the two approaches.

EXERCISES

1. In equation (2.1), assume that S is also sensitive to the interest rate. What should be the sign of the parameter attached to the interest rate? Derive a new version of equation (2.3) and explain the result.
2. An increase in the capital stock increases the marginal product of all existing workers. Incorporate such a change into the macroeconomic model and predict the effects on y, i, and π.
3. Assume an increase in the income tax rate. Show how this influences equation (2.1) and the slope and position of the *IS* curve.
4. Consider the following numerical version of the *IS–LM–AS* model:

$$y = 4 - 33.4(i - \pi^e)$$

$$m - p = .75y - .25i$$

$$y = y_e - 7(\pi^e - \pi)$$

Initial conditions are $p = 0$, $\pi^e = .10$, $(m - p) = 1.71$, and $y_e = 2.33$.

(a) Calculate μ.

(b) Derive the *AD* curve and indicate its vertical intercept and slope.

(c) Calculate y, i, and π in long-run equilibrium and take antilogs, where necessary, to obtain the actual values of these variables.

(d) Calculate new long-run values of all variables for $y_e = 2.15$.

FURTHER READING

Addison, J. T., and W. S. Siebert, *The Market for Labor: An Analytical Treatment*, Santa Monica, Calif., Goodyear, 1979. Demand and supply relations in the labor market are discussed in chapters 3 and 4.

Dornbusch, R., and S. Fischer, *Macroeconomics*, third edition, New York, McGraw-Hill, 1984, or R. Dornbusch, S. Fischer, and G. Sparks, *Macroeconomics: Second Canadian Edition*, Toronto, McGraw-Hill Ryerson, 1985. Chapter 13 in the former and chapter 15 in the latter develop a macroeconomic model similar to the one presented here.

McDonald, I. M., and R. Solow, "Wage Bargaining and Employment," *American Economic Review*, 71, December 1981, pp. 896–908. Discusses the efficiency of bargains between unions and firms.

APPENDIX TO CHAPTER 2: THE USE OF NATURAL LOGARITHMS

Any positive number can be converted to natural logs, with $e = 2.71828$ as its base. The number 1 becomes 0, 10 converts to 2.302, and 100 becomes 4.605. In the days before pocket calculators it was a time-consuming chore to calculate logs; now it is simplicity and ease itself. To find the natural log of a number (often written as ln) you merely enter the number on the keyboard and push the "ln" button. To reverse the procedure – that is, to take antilogs – you push the "e^x" button. Some care must be taken as to which button to push, since calculators also have a second set of logs, with base 10, often labeled "log." The macroeconomic model in this chapter is based on the use of *natural logs*; it will not work with base-10 logs.

There are five important characteristics of natural logs that are useful for economic analysis. These properties are listed below, together with an example. The student is urged to work out a number of examples to gain familiarity with these concepts.

1. *Scale:* Both the original number and its natural log increase together, but the natural log increases more slowly. Example: $\ln 10 = 2.302$,

whereas ln 100 = 4.605. The increase from 10 to 100 is tenfold, whereas the natural log only doubles.

2. *Multiplication*: Consider any two variables, x and y: $\ln(xy) = \ln x + \ln y$. In words, the natural log of a product is the *sum* of the two logs. If $x = 5$ and $y = 6$, $xy = 30$, and $\ln(xy) = 3.401$; alternatively, $\ln x = 1.609$ and $\ln y = 1.792$, so that $\ln x + \ln y = 3.401$.

3. *Division*: For the same variables, x and y, $\ln(x/y) = \ln x - \ln y$, or the natural log of a ratio is the *difference* between their logs. Again, assume $x = 5$ and $y = 6$. Their ratio is .833 and the log of that number is $-.182$. (Numbers between 0 and 1 have negative natural logs. Negative numbers have no natural logs.) The same result is obtained by $\ln x - \ln y = 1.609 - 1.792 = -.183$.

4. *Rates of change*: The rate of change of any variable x is defined as $(x - x_{-1})/x_{-1}$, where the subscript -1 refers to the value of x in the previous period. The absolute change in x is given by $x - x_{-1}$. The *rate of change* is determined by the *absolute change* in the natural logs, or $\ln x - \ln x_{-1}$. Example: $x_{-1} = 100$ and $x = 110$; then the rate of change is $(110 - 100)/100 = .10$ or 10%. A faster way of making this calculation is ln 100 = 4.605, whereas ln 110 = 4.700 and their difference is .095. This points to the fact that the difference in the natural logs is only approximately correct; the larger is the change, the greater is the discrepancy. Try $x = 100.5$ and $x_{-1} = 100$.

Using base-10 logs will not work for calculating rates of change in this way. Log 100 = 2 whereas log 110 = 2.041, suggesting a growth rate of only 4%.

5. *Interest rate*: After one period \$1 is worth \$$(1 + i)$ if the interest rate is i. Now $\ln(1 + i) = i$, that is, the value of a \$1 bond after one year, written in natural logs, is equal to the interest rate. It is for this reason that interest rate variables in the *IS* and *LM* curves are *not* in natural logs. Assume that the interest rate is 12%, written as .12. Here $\ln(1 + .12) = .113$, which is close to .12. Again, the larger the interest rate, the less reliable is this rule. Try $i = .04$.

These properties of natural logs have not been derived rigorously from first principles, but in this book we are only interested in using them to simplify the economic analysis, and practice with them will be rewarded by an understanding of how inflation rates, and not just price levels, can be introduced into the macroeconomic model.

CHAPTER 3

The new classical model

THE CASE AGAINST STABILIZATION POLICY

3.1 INTRODUCTION

Until recently, the *IS–LM* model with a positively sloped *AS* curve (often called the Phillips curve) would have sufficed for a thorough analysis of stabilization policy. The effect of monetary policy or fiscal policy on income, the interest rate, and the inflation rate could be calculated and a number of related issues, such as the budgetary effects of policy changes, could be discussed in great detail. But during the past decade or so, some fundamental questions about this framework have been raised that make the macroeconomist's life much more complicated, such as:

1. What is the goal of macroeconomic policy in the face of a self-equilibrating economy? and
2. What advantage does the government have over private individuals in dealing with an economy that is operating temporarily in disequilibrium?

New classical and Keynesian-oriented economists would provide different answers to these questions, but they would not disagree about the long-run version of the *IS–LM–AS* model and the effect of macroeconomic policies on the equilibrium position of the economy.

It is appropriate at this point to look at the names of various schools of thought in macroeconomics. The model in Chapter 2 is often called the *neoclassical model* because its focus is long-run equilibrium where output is supply-constrained and not demand-determined. The *new classical model,* to be developed in this chapter, has many of the same antecedents and present-day adherents; however, its main purpose is to show that there is little room for policy intervention even in the short run, contrary to the *Keynesian model*. This distinction between neoclassical and new classical models is hardly illuminating, but the names have become part of the jargon and cannot be avoided.

It is generally agreed among interventionist and noninterventionist macroeconomists alike that government manipulation of the aggregate-demand curve is largely ineffective in the long run; lasting measures to increase output must deal with productivity, capital formation, and labor force participation, namely "supply-side" factors, but some Keynesians would argue that aggregate-demand policies can influence aggregate supply. It is further agreed that monetary policy does have a great deal of influence on the one important nominal variable in the economy, the inflation rate. Neither side would argue against the need for restrictive monetary policy as the only way to lower the inflation rate permanently. Both of these propositions are accepted and are entirely consistent with the model of Chapter 2, but they are only the starting point for an up-to-date analysis of macroeconomic policy in the current environment.

The dispute, then, is about additional characteristics of the economy relevant for short-run model building. These features are (1) the role of random events in the economy and (2) the information-processing system used by individuals to form expectations about the future rate of inflation. Depending on how stochastic variables and inflationary expectations are incorporated into the model, it is possible to get diametrically opposed answers to the previous questions.

In this chapter the new classical position on uncertainty and expectations formation, based on the contributions of Robert Barro, Robert Lucas, Thomas Sargent, and Neil Wallace, among others, will be added to the model, and the role of stabilization policy in this environment will become extremely limited. Then, in the next chapter, a more institutional approach to these issues will be introduced and the role of stabilization policy once again expands. In this sense, the present chapter deals with the case against active stabilization policy, whereas Chapter 4 presents the case for stabilization policy. While debating rules give priority to the argument *for* a proposition, it makes more sense to reverse the order in this case since the new classical model is now considered as "received theory" and is therefore somewhat easier to explain.

To complete the new classical model of the macroeconomy it is necessary to incorporate variables representing uncertainty and to formulate a "rational" expectations process, tasks to which we now turn.

3.2 INTRODUCING UNCERTAINTY IN THE MODEL

Since the macroeconomic goal of y_e has been identified with an equilibrium position for the economy, it would appear that stabilization policy is an empty issue. Once the economy reaches equilibrium, with or without government intervention, it has reached its optimal point and no further improvement is possible. One may argue that, for political reasons, a government may want to disturb this equilibrium with expansionary policy to reduce, even temporarily, an uncomfortably high rate of unemployment associated with equilibrium. That may be the case and it will be explored in Section 3.6, but it is not the main emphasis of stabilization policy whose intention it is to overcome existing departures from equilibrium. But even that task becomes redundant if these departures are predictable. For instance, assume that at the beginning of a period it is established that consumer expenditures will be lower than previously by a known amount. This event would shift the *IS* curve downward, but before we can calculate the effects of this change we must be aware that there are other adjustments as well. Since the event is known beforehand, its effect on the inflation rate can be predicted precisely and incorporated into the expected rate of inflation, leaving the equality between expected and actual inflation undisturbed, and, dictated by the aggregate-supply curve, output remains at the equilibrium level. There will be a lower real interest rate that allows investment expenditures to replace the reduced consumption expenditures in the total demand for goods and services. Stabilization policy has no role to play in this environment since private individuals were able to make a complete adjustment to this exogenous change without any assistance from the government.

The complications for macroeconomic policy arise from uncertainty about the future. If, in the previous example, the consumers' intentions were not known economywide until after they were observed, a reduction in their expenditures would not be offset by increased investment purchases since the expected rate of inflation would not fall, as in the previous case. At least the possibility now appears that government demand for goods and services would be needed to maintain total aggregate demand at its equilibrium level. The debate concerns whether the government's activities are likely to reduce instability in the economy or to add to it. From this perspective, interpretations of uncertainty about future events play a crucial role in determining a place for government activity in the macroeconomy.

The version of the macroeconomic model developed in Chapter 2 does not contain elements of uncertainty and is therefore lacking an important ingredient for a coherent discussion of policy issues. However, this situation can be remedied. Uncertainty is everywhere and its existence will be introduced into all three markets in the macroeconomy: goods and services, assets, and labor. This is done by adding a stochastic variable to each of the *IS*, *LM*, and *AS* equations. A stochastic variable represents a random draw from a probability distribution that is known beforehand. For instance, the outcome of the toss of a die is unknown, but we can

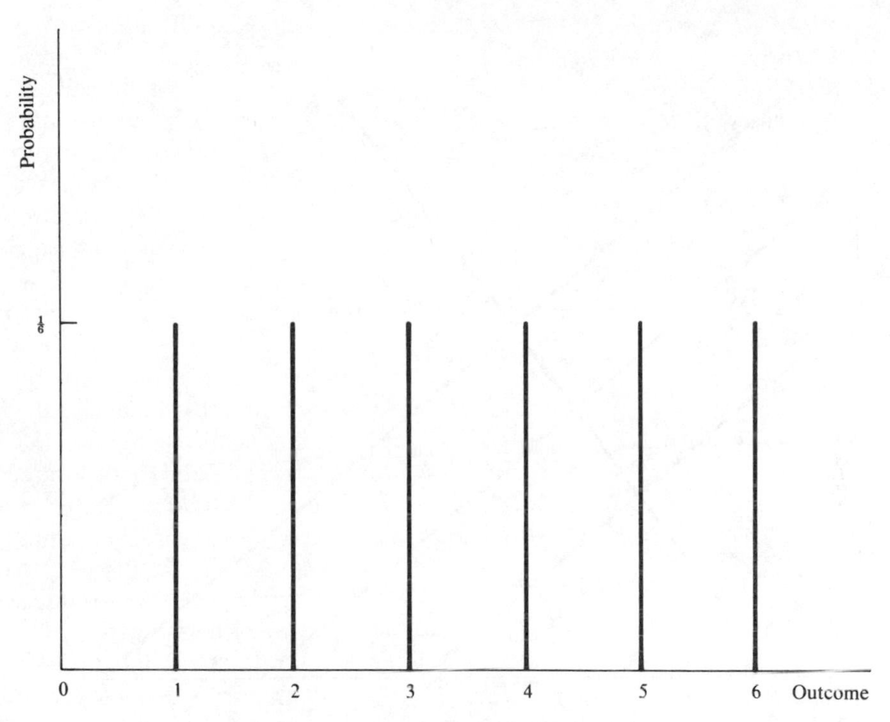

Figure 3-1 Probability distribution of the toss of a die.

be certain that it must be a number between 1 and 6; we also know that each number has an equal chance of turning up. From this information, we can draw a probability distribution for the toss of a die as shown in Figure 3-1. It reveals that each of 1, 2, 3, 4, 5, and 6 has a one-sixth chance of appearing. Stochastic variables in the economy are assumed to have similar properties; we do not know the outcome, but we know the probability distribution from which they are drawn. For instance, consumption expenditures are largely predictable on the basis of known income, but some randomness continues to exist. This does not mean that consumers are making capricious decisions about their expenditures, but rather that it is impossible to capture all the factors that determine everyone's consumption expenditures. All we can do is hope that these missing factors are random and relatively unimportant.

These random elements are literally added to the existing model, which can now be written as follows:

$$y = a_0 - a_1(i - \pi^e) + x_g \tag{3.1}$$

$$\mu - \pi + x_m = a_2 y - a_3 i - (m - p)_{-1} \tag{3.2}$$

$$y = y_e - a_4(\pi^e - \pi - x_s) + x_s \tag{3.3}$$

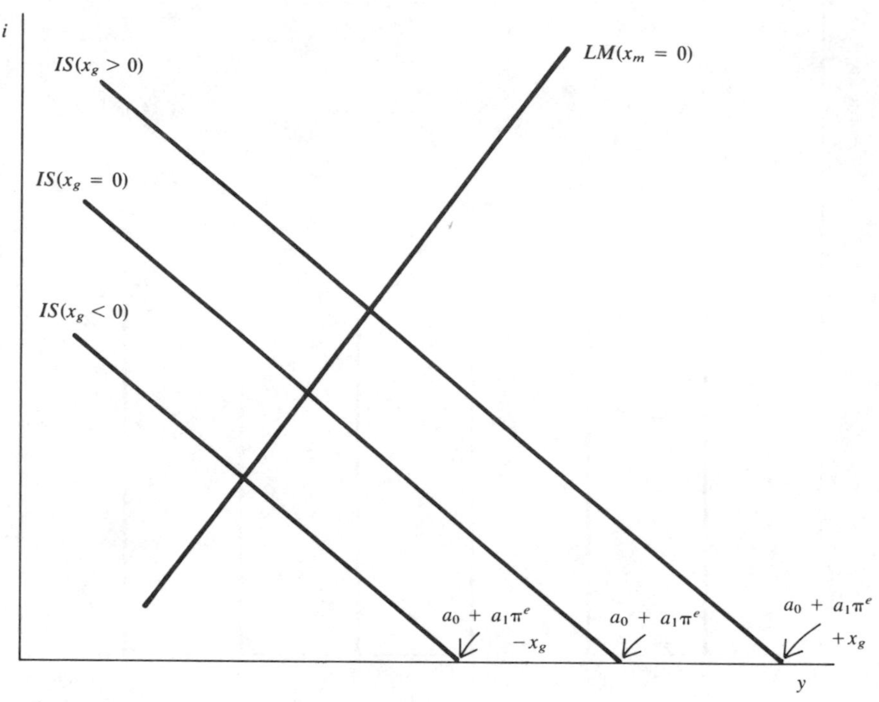

Figure 3-2 The stochastic *IS* curve.

Previously defined variables are y = income or output, i = interest rate, π^e = expected inflation, μ = growth rate of the money supply, π = inflation rate, $(m - p)_{-1}$ = real money supply at the end of the previous period, and y_e = equilibrium output. Here y, y_e, and $(m - p)_{-1}$ are defined as the natural logs of their actual values. The a's are positive parameters and can be interpreted as elasticities with respect to the variable to which they are attached.

Now the new variables are x_g, x_m, and x_s, the stochastic variables, one to each equation. They are associated with unexpected "shocks" to the economy. They are also expressed as natural logs. When the economy is in full equilibrium, shocks must be absent by definition and each x is equal to zero. This means that the antilog of each x is 1, leaving the *IS*, *LM* or *AS* equations influenced only by the deterministic elements of the model. Thus the expected value of each x is zero. This is written as $E[x] = 0$. But we know from past experience that x's have been positive or negative. For instance, if x_g is positive it can be interpreted as a "shock" that causes an unexpected increase in aggregate demand and shifts the *IS* curve upward and to the right, as shown in Figure 3-2. The value of x_g adds to the horizontal intercept of the deterministic *IS* curve for which $x_g = 0$. Alternatively, a negative x_g subtracts from the existing demand and shifts the *IS* curve to the left. Although we do not know the direction and extent of the shift in the *IS* curve for the current period, we do know all the past shocks that have occurred. This information can be summarized by a measure called the *standard deviation*. It is calculated from

$$\text{(3.4)} \qquad \text{s.d.} = [\text{sum}(x_{g_i})^2/n]^{1/2}$$

where $x_{g_i} = x_{g_1} \ldots x_{g_n}$ represents all n of the previously observed shocks to the *IS* curve. In other words, we square each of the x_g's, sum them up, divide by the total number of observations, and take the square root.

EXAMPLE

Let $-1, 3, -2, -1$, and 1 be five observations of x_g; their s.d. is equal to $[(1 + 9 + 4 + 1 + 1)/5]^{.5} = 1.79$.

With our information about $E[x_g]$ and s.d. we can draw its probability distribution in Figure 3-3. It does not need to have the same shape as the distribution for the toss of the die, but its characteristics are generally the same. In the case of x_g, the larger the absolute value of x_g, the less likely its occurrence. The distribution is also drawn symmetrical about $E[x_g] = 0$. Furthermore, for a "normal" distribution, two-thirds of all outcomes lie within one standard deviation of the mean (the shaded area in the diagram), 95% lie within two s.d.'s, and three s.d.'s exhaust all but 3 out of 1,000 possibilities, virtually the entire area under the bell-shaped curve.

Having identified x_g with demand shocks in the *IS* curve, we need to make comparable economic interpretations of x_m and x_s. In equilibrium, $x_m = 0$, but an unexpected increase in the growth rate of the money supply means that $x_m > 0$. This would tend to increase $(m - p)$ over time and have the effect of shifting the *LM* curve to the right, period after period, until π catches up. A deviation of x_m from zero is labeled a "monetary shock." Finally, x_s is associated with a "supply shock." If $x_s > 0$, then output can expand beyond y_e even if π and π^e remain equal to each other. This may arise from an unexpected increase in labor productivity, as discussed in Section 2.5.

Unlike the other shocks, x_s appears twice in equation (3.3). The reason for this is that x_s has two separate effects on y: (1) The existing labor force becomes more productive and adds x_s to output, and (2) the marginal

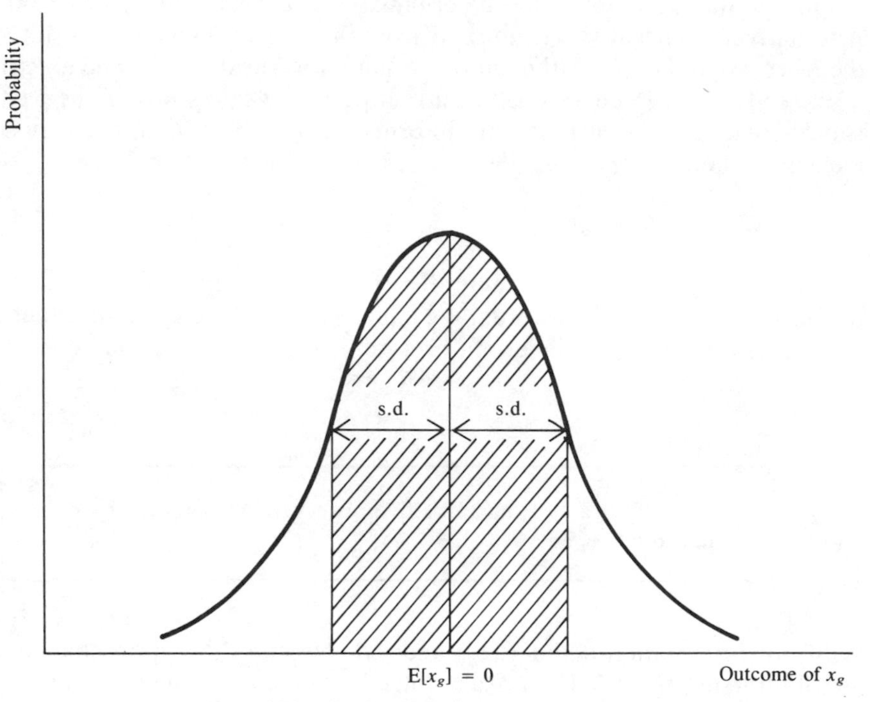

Figure 3-3 Probability distribution of x_g.

product of labor increases, as measured by $\omega - \pi - x_s$.[1] This causes firms to add workers to their labor force by the value of b_{10}, the parameter in the demand equation (2.9) in Chapter 2, who in turn produce more output by the value of b_6 in the production function of equation (2.8); a_4 is then defined as $b_6 b_{10}$, so that output expands a further $a_4 x_s$ for a total of $(1 + a_4)x_s$. In this model, the demand curve for labor is stochastic but the supply curve is not. If the work–leisure decision had a random element, we would have to use another x to play this role.

The stochastic version of the *AD* curve is derived by substituting the *IS* curve of equation (3.1) into the *LM* curve of equation (3.2) and is written as

(3.5) $$\pi = \mu + (m - p)_{-1} - (a_2 + a_3/a_1)y + a_3 a_0/a_1 + a_3\pi^e + x_m + (a_3/a_1)x_g$$

[1] From Chapter 2, the natural log of the marginal product of labor is equal to the real wage, $(w - p)$, where w and p are the natural logs of nominal wage and the price level; since $\ln MP_1 = \ln MP_0 + x_s$, $w_1 - p_1 = w_0 - p_0 + x_s$, and $\omega = w_1 - w_0$, $\pi = p_1 - p_0$.

The values for x_g, x_m, and x_s are not directly observable, even after the fact because our data do not distinguish between anticipated and unexpected events. For instance, if the growth rate of the money supply for a given year is measured at 10%, it is unlikely that the central bank would be able to indicate that 8% was expected and 2% was unintended. However, we can extract information about the x's by observing π, y, and i. The *IS–LM–AS* curves of equations (3.1), (3.2), and (3.3) are drawn in Figure 3-4, initially with all x's equal to zero. Now each x will be allowed to take on a positive value that will change π, y, and i, but the combination of these changes will be unique for each x. Start with $x_g > 0$. This shifts the *IS* curve up to *IS'* and also the *AD* curve to *AD'*. The new short-run equilibrium is observed at E_1 with y_1, π_1, and i_1. Now consider a positive x_m. For this event the *LM* curve shifts to *LM'* and the *AD* curve again moves to *AD'*. At E_2, we observe y_1, π_1, but i_2. Thus a goods-market shock can be differentiated from a money-market shock by what happens to the interest rate. Finally, assume that $x_s > 0$. This shock shifts the *AS* curve down and to the right, leading to E_3, where y_1, π_3, and i_2 prevail. Now x_s and x_m can be distinguished by the reaction of the inflation rate. It should be noted that the *LM* curve will have to shift to *LM'* because $\pi > \mu$ for some period of time. In all cases y rose to y_1, but negative shocks would lead to a reduction in income. There is, of course, the possibility that more than one x is nonzero in any one period, in which case information extraction becomes more complicated but not impossible. We know that in general π, y, and i depend on all the x's and solving equations (3.1), (3.2), and (3.3) for the x's with π, y, and i treated as exogenous variables would show how the observed changes in π, y and i would give rise to certain values for the x's. However, in order to do this we would have to have accurate estimates for all the a's as well as the other variables in the system.

3.3 FORMING EXPECTATIONS ABOUT INFLATION

In the previous discussion about the effects of a reduction in consumption expenditures, the distinction between a predicted change and an unexpected event was paramount. In the former case the effect of lower consumption expenditures could be incorporated into π^e, but in the latter case this could not be done. As a result, with predictable events, $\pi^e = \pi$ and $y = y_e$, but if the event occurs without warning, π^e need not equal π, and y need not coincide with y_e, so that the economy may now diverge from its equilibrium position. This suggests an important role for π^e and the process by which it is determined in the performance of the macroeconomy.

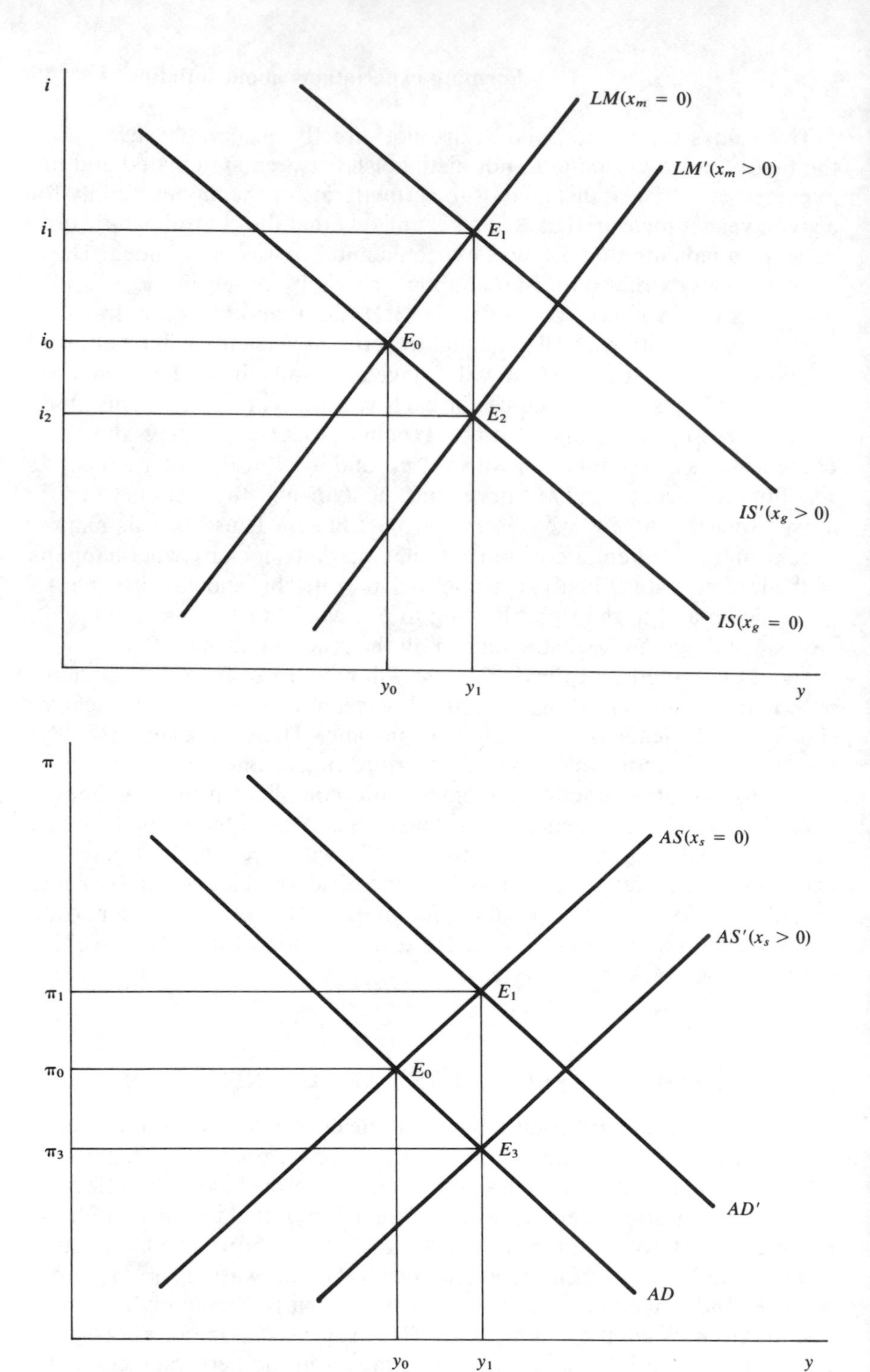

Figure 3-4 Information extraction for different random shocks.

How are expectations about inflation formed? Since we cannot observe *expected* variables, we are forced to theorize about this process without being able to verify it explicitly. However, individuals can be expected to be economically rational about this process, which means that they should make optimal forecasts of inflation based on their knowledge of the macroeconomic model and conditioned on the efficient use of all available information. Hence, this process is called *rational expectations*.

If forming expectations is merely information processing, what information do individuals have and how do they use it? First, they know the *IS–LM–AS* model and the role of the inflation rate in it. For instance, individuals can be presumed to know that a decrease in consumption expenditures will cause a temporary decline in the inflation rate and that an increase in μ will cause a permanent increase in the inflation rate. If they observe either event, they would want to incorporate its effect in their prediction of the inflation rate for the next period. Second, they have certain information about the current performance of the economy and policies in force at the moment that they would use in forecasting inflation.

This procedure can be formalized in the following way. First we need to solve the *IS–LM–AS* model to obtain the determinants of the inflation rate. This involves finding the solutions for y, i, and π simultaneously in equations (3.1), (3.2), and (3.3) in terms of all the exogenous variables in the system. An alternative way to proceed is to substitute the *AS* curve of equation (3.3) into the *AD* curve of equation (3.5) to obtain an expression for π with only exogenous variables on the right side. Either way, the solution for π is

$$\begin{aligned}(3.6)\quad \pi = {} & [1/(a_1 + a_3a_4 + a_1a_2a_4)] \\ & \times [a_1(\mu + \{m - p\}_{-1} + x_m) \\ & + a_3(a_0 + x_g) - (a_1a_2 + a_3)(y_e + \{1 + a_4\}x_s) \\ & + (a_1a_3 + a_3a_4 + a_1a_2a_4)\pi^e]\end{aligned}$$

Each individual now knows what causes inflation and to what extent. For instance, a decrease in consumption expenditures is captured by a fall in a_0; multiplying by the known value of $a_3/[a_1 + a_3a_4 + a_1a_2a_4]$ allows us to calculate the effect on π. Similarly, an *exogenous* increase in π^e increases π by $[a_1a_3 + a_3a_4 + a_1a_2a_4]/[a_1 + a_3a_4 + a_1a_2a_4]$. To ensure that π does not rise more than π^e we can impose a limit of $0 < a_3 < 1$ on the parameter a_3; otherwise, we would end up with an explosive cycle of inflation merely through the expectations process without an accompanying increase in μ.[2]

[2] See Section 2.2.4 for a fuller discussion of this point.

But even more important is the fact that π^e should not be treated as an *exogenous* variable. If a_0 changes and π responds, why would π^e remain at its previous level? If it did, we may not be using all the information we have at hand. To get out of this vicious cycle of π determining π^e and vice versa, we need to preserve the structure of equation (3.6) but to eliminate π^e from it. Without π^e in equation (3.6), the parameters attached to the other variables in the equation would no longer be the same, since the underlying model now treats π^e as an endogenous variable, rather than as an exogenous variable as before. To cope with this vexing problem, we "invent" an equation similar to (3.6), but without π^e in it, which means that π and the other exogenous variables are connected by what are known as *undetermined coefficients*. This equation is written as

$$(3.7) \quad \pi = c_0\mu + c_1(m - p)_{-1} + c_2x_m + c_3a_0 + c_4x_g + c_5y_e + c_6x_s$$

where the c's are not yet identified. Nevertheless, equation (3.7) also represents a way of determining inflation.

Next, π^e is the mathematical expectation of π from this equation. Therefore,

$$(3.8) \quad \pi^e = \mathrm{E}[\pi] = c_0\mu + c_1(m - p)_{-1} + c_3a_0 + c_5y_e$$

The terms c_2x_m, c_4x_g, and c_6x_s have been eliminated, since the expected value of the x's is zero, and therefore these variables cannot influence expected inflation, although the subsequent occurrence of nonzero x's will affect actual inflation.

Now equation (3.8) includes all the factors that can influence expected inflation and it can be substituted back into equation (3.6) to eliminate π^e from the list of exogenous variables. This produces

$$\begin{aligned}(3.9) \quad \pi = {} & [1/(a_1 + a_3a_4 + a_1a_2a_4)] \\ & \times [(a_1 + c_0\{a_1a_3 + a_3a_4 + a_1a_2a_4\})\mu \\ & + (a_1 + c_1\{a_1a_3 + a_3a_4 + a_1a_2a_4\})(m - p)_{-1} \\ & + a_1x_m + (a_3 + c_3\{a_1a_3 + a_3a_4 + a_1a_2a_4\})a_0 + a_3x_g \\ & + (c_5\{a_1a_3 + a_3a_4 + a_1a_2a_4\} - \{a_1a_2 + a_3\})y_e \\ & - (a_1a_2 + a_3)(1 + a_4)x_s]\end{aligned}$$

By a careful comparison it can be seen that equation (3.9) has exactly the same variables on the right side as equation (3.7), the one that each individual invents who forms expectations about π^e. Since they both come from the very same *IS–LM–AS* model of equations (3.1), (3.2), and (3.3), the coefficients attached to each variable must be the same. With this information we can now solve for the undetermined coefficients, the c's in equation (3.7), by setting them equal to the corresponding coefficient in (3.9) and solving for the c's. Thus

$$c_0 = [a_1 + c_0(a_1a_3 + a_3a_4 + a_1a_2a_4)]/[a_1 + a_3a_4 + a_1a_2a_4]$$

which simplifies to

$$c_0 = 1/(1 - a_3)$$

which is positive because it was shown earlier that $a_3 < 1$. Next,

$$c_1 = [a_1 + c_1(a_1a_3 + a_3a_4 + a_1a_2a_4)]/[a_1 + a_3a_4 + a_1a_2a_4]$$

which again simplifies to

$$c_1 = 1/(1 - a_3) > 0$$

Then

$$c_2 = a_1/[a_1 + a_3a_4 + a_1a_2a_4] > 0$$

In a similar fashion the other coefficients are determined to be

$$c_3 = a_3/[a_1(1 - a_3)] > 0$$

$$c_4 = a_3/[a_1 + a_3a_4 + a_1a_2a_4] > 0$$

$$c_5 = -[a_1a_2 + a_3]/[a_1(1 - a_3)] < 0$$

$$c_6 = -[(a_1a_2 + a_3)(1 + a_4)]/[a_1 + a_3a_4 + a_1a_2a_4] < 0$$

We have now come full circle. The undetermined coefficients are now determined and we can get rid of the c's in equation (3.7), which now represents the structural relationship for the inflation rate, including the role of expected inflation, but without having π^e as a variable on the right side. By substituting for the c's in equation (3.7) we arrive at

$$\begin{aligned}(3.10)\quad \pi = {} & [1/(1 - a_3)][\mu + (m - p)_{-1}] \\ & + [a_1/(a_1 + a_3a_4 + a_1a_2a_4)]x_m + [a_3/a_1(1 - a_3)]a_0 \\ & + [a_3/(a_1 + a_3a_4 + a_1a_2a_4)]x_g \\ & - [(a_1a_2 + a_3)/(a_1\{1 - a_3\})]y_e \\ & - [(a_1a_2 + a_3)(1 + a_4)/(a_1 + a_3a_4 + a_1a_2a_4)]x_s\end{aligned}$$

The last step in completing the model involves forming expectations about inflation from equation (3.10). Thus

$$\begin{aligned}(3.11)\quad \pi^e = E[\pi] = {} & [1/(1 - a_3)][\mu + (m - p)_{-1}] \\ & + [a_3/(a_1\{1 - a_3\})]a_0 - [(a_1a_2 + a_3)/(a_1\{1 - a_3\})]y_e\end{aligned}$$

Equation (3.11) only differs from (3.10) since $E[x_m] = E[x_g] = E[x_s] = 0$. This completes the process by which expectations about inflation are formed by rational individuals who use all the information available to them in order to minimize the indesirable effects of errors in π^e. It is a complicated and conceptually difficult procedure, but it is one that each student must understand; otherwise, how could we be sure that all agents in the economy would be rational in forming π^e?

3.4 POLICY INEFFECTIVENESS IN THE NEW CLASSICAL MODEL

We are now in a position to apply the new classical model to the problems of stabilization policy. It will become clear that with this particular structure of the economy, the government is unable either to maintain equilibrium in the economy when it is presented with an unexpected shock or to reduce deliberately the unemployment rate below the natural rate, even temporarily. In other words, there is no room for either *accommodating* or *activist* policies. On the other hand, antiinflation policy becomes more appealing because it does not force the economy to go through the "wringer" in an effort to eliminate inflationary expectations. What this amounts to is that deliberate monetary or fiscal policy measures have no effect on real variables such as output or employment, but have their full impact on nominal variables such as the inflation rate. This is known as *policy neutrality*. Another way of viewing the new classical model is that long-run results, discussed in Chapter 2, are achieved in the short run as well; there is no meaningful distinction between these two time horizons.

From the *AS* curve of equation (3.3) it can be seen that there are two sources of change for y: (1) a deviation of π from π^e and (2) a nonzero x_s. To see what policy can and cannot do we need only focus on these two sources. Substituting equations (3.10) and (3.11) into (3.3) allows us to find the effect of various exogenous changes on y when expected inflation is permitted to adapt to the changes as well.

$$(3.12)\quad y = y_e + [a_4/(a_1 + a_3a_4 + a_1a_2a_4)] \times [a_1x_m + a_3x_g - (a_1a_2 + a_3)(1 + a_4)x_s] + (1 + a_4)x_s$$

According to equation (3.12), y deviates from y_e only when x_m, x_g, or x_s take on positive or negative values. In equation (3.12) x_s appears twice, once with a minus sign and once with a plus sign, indicating an ambiguous effect on y. On the one hand, $x_s > 0$ increases output directly through higher marginal product of labor; on the other hand, it also reduces π below π^e, which causes firms to reduce output.

It is evident now that it is the *difference* between π^e and π that has an impact on income and output. To detect this difference we must compare equations (3.10) and (3.11). There are two important observations from this comparison: (1) A change in a predictable exogenous variable such as μ, a_0 or y_e has exactly the same effect on π and on π^e, and (2) random events such as x_g, x_m, or x_s affect π but not π^e. The difference between π^e and π represents the error that people make in predicting inflation. With rational expectations these errors are not eliminated. New classical economists do not ascribe superhuman qualities of *perfect foresight* to economic decision makers; they do, however, insist that errors that are made should be random ones since there are strong incentives to eliminate systematic ones. Therefore predictable policies such as changes in μ or a_0 will not affect y, while unpredictable shocks will change income but since policy makers cannot anticipate them, they cannot overcome them. This is the essence of policy impotence in the new classical model, a detailed analysis of which now follows.

3.4.1 SHORT-RUN EFFECTS OF POLICY CHANGES AND RANDOM SHOCKS

Let us first consider an economy operating at equilibrium when the government decides to reduce unemployment below its natural rate. It uses monetary policy as its instrument and therefore increases μ, the rate of growth of the nominal money supply, to μ_1. In Figure 3-5, this is shown as a downward movement of the *LM* curve to *LM'* as $\mu > \pi$. From equation (3.5) it seems that *AD* shifts up by the increase in μ to *AD'* and, given the positively sloped short-run *AS* curve, it would appear that y should increase, which in turn would reduce unemployment. However, since everyone in the economy is aware of the policy and knows how the inflation rate will be affected by this move, the expected rate of inflation is adjusted to the new environment, shifting the *AD* curve upward even more. Hence we need to measure the combined effect of changes in μ and π^e. This can be accomplished by rewriting the *AD* equation with π^e from (3.11) substituted into (3.5) to obtain

$$(3.5') \quad \pi = [1/(1 - a_3)][\mu + (m - p)_{-1}] - (a_2 + a_3/a_1)y - [a_3(a_1a_2 + a_3)/(a_1\{1 - a_3\})]y_e + [a_3/a_1(1 - a_3)]a_0 + x_m + (a_3/a_1)x_g$$

Thus the *AD* curve shifts upward to *AD''* by $1/(1 - a_3)$ times the change in μ which is, of course, larger than the change in μ by itself. The *AS*

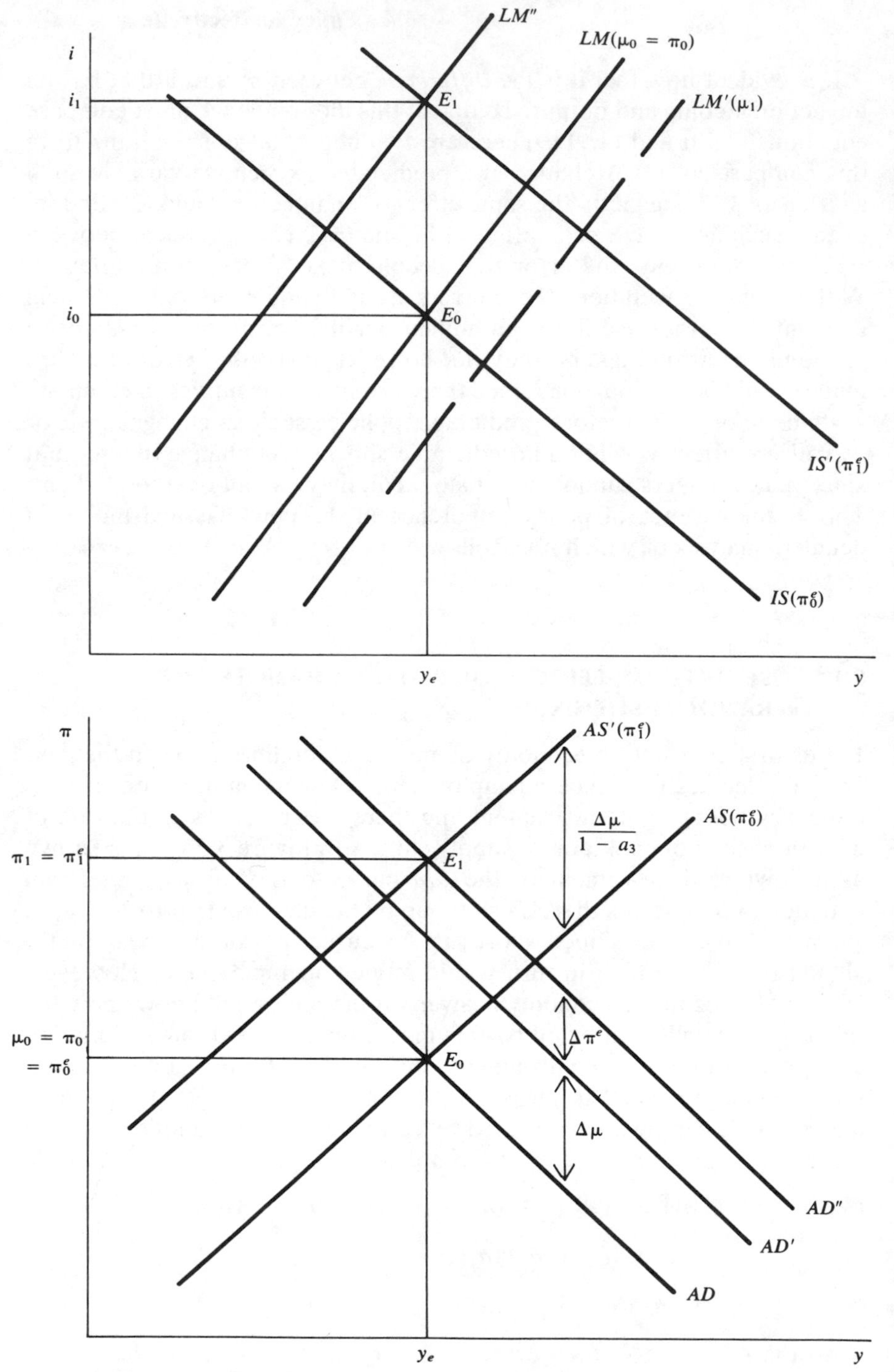

Figure 3-5 The effects of expansionary monetary policy.

curve is also influenced by the increase in μ through π^e. Substituting for π^e from (3.11) into (3.3) produces

$$(3.3') \quad \pi = [1/(1 - a_3)][\mu + (m - p)_{-1}] - (1/a_4)y$$
$$- [1/a_4 + (a_1a_2 + a_3)/(a_1\{1 - a_3\})]y_e$$
$$+ [a_3/a_1(1 - a_3)]a_0 - [(1 + a_4)/a_4]x_s$$

It is now easily seen that the AS curve shifts upward to the same extent as the AD curve, so that the new intersection of AS' and AD'' is at the same y_e as before. The other important variables can be determined sequentially. The real interest rate is impervious to this policy. From the IS curve of equation (3.1) the real interest rate can be written as

$$(3.13) \quad i - \pi^e = (a_0 - y)/a_1 + x_g$$

Since monetary policy was not able to change y, it could not alter the real interest rate. However, the IS curve does shift up by the increase in π^e. It is now located at IS'. To maintain y_e, the nominal interest rate must rise by the increase in π^e or π. This is also necessary to keep the real interest rate constant. Finally, the same y and a higher i generate a reduced demand for real money balances. To make $(m - p)$ smaller, the LM curve must backtrack all the way to LM'' where it intersects IS'. This is accomplished by $\pi > \mu$ for at least part of the adjustment period. Indeed, from equation (3.10) we can see that π exceeds μ by $a_3/(1 - a_3)$. At this point, since μ does not equal π we cannot be in full equilibrium and the continuing dynamics will be taken up shortly.

For purposes of comparison, predictable fiscal policy in the form of a_0 *can* change the real interest rate, but that still does not make it a potent macroeconomic policy instrument since equations (3.5′) and (3.3′) inform us that both AD and AS curves shift equally for a change in a_0 and therefore y remains constant. Expansionary fiscal policy would lead to reduced investment expenditures to make room for the higher government demand. This is referred to as the "crowding-out" effect of fiscal policy.

From these results one is tempted to ask why private individuals in the economy would want to frustrate the efforts of the authorities to bring down the unemployment rate? The answer is essentially simple: y_e is an equilibrium to which everyone wants to move and from which no one wants to depart. To obtain a higher y requires that π^e fall below π. This also means that the real wage is falling: Firms expand their demand for labor, but workers are now "forced" to work more than they wish. Such a situation is not an improvement in economic welfare and maximizing output is not, by itself, a goal for which governments should strive. To prevent this result, workers will try to incorporate the likely effect of such policy changes on the real wage and attempt to keep π^e from deviating systematically from π. In other words, expansionary policy relies on workers being "tricked" into increasing their work effort; if they were aware of the trap, they could and would avoid it.

It is still possible for workers to make errors in their calculations of π^e because they cannot anticipate the x's that also affect π. In these circumstances, can the government through its policy instruments help to reestablish equilibrium? To answer this question we assume that, from a position of equilibrium, a random shock occurs. More specifically, assume that x_m becomes positive because of an unanticipated change in the relationship between bank reserves and the money supply. It has the same effect on the *LM* curve as an increase in μ and shifts the *LM* curve downward. This is shown in Figure 3-6. Also, the *AD* curve shifts up by the value of x_m. Neither the *AS* curve nor the *IS* curve is disturbed by this change since π^e remains at its previous level. At the intersection of *AS* and *AD'*, y is now y_1 and the inflation rate rises to π_1. At the intersection of *LM'* and *IS*, i is now lower at i_1. The economy is in short-run equilibrium but in long-run disequilibrium since π and π^e do not coincide. Is there an opening here for the government to use its macroeconomic policies to avert this situation? In the new classical model the answer is no, since the authorities cannot anticipate x_m any better than private individuals, and therefore they can only react after x_m appears. At that point, if the government now lowers μ to counteract the increase in x_m it would not have any different real effect than if it did nothing and allowed the economy to return to long-run equilibrium when x_m becomes zero again. The decision about μ is only important for the inflation rate.

Perhaps it could be argued that the government has superior information and advance intelligence on random shocks. If that is true, and it remains an arguable point, it suggests that the government should announce the impending value of x_m and let individuals incorporate it into π^e rather than try to offset x_m by an adjustment in μ. By sharing its information the authorities enable all agents to treat x_m as if it were μ and equilibrium would be sustained. Therefore, if there is an asymmetry between public and private information, the role of government is to correct this "distortion," not to exploit it.

Stabilization policy would "work" if μ looks like x_m, but the economy is best served if x_m looks like μ. In a world where only random events can upset the equilibrium position of the economy, it would seen improbable that the central bank would follow an unpredictable pattern for μ just to prove that it can influence y. In fact, many central banks now follow a procedure of announcing target rates of growth for the money supply in advance to make monetary policy more predictable. This is particularly useful for antiinflationary policy, which is discussed in Section 3.6.

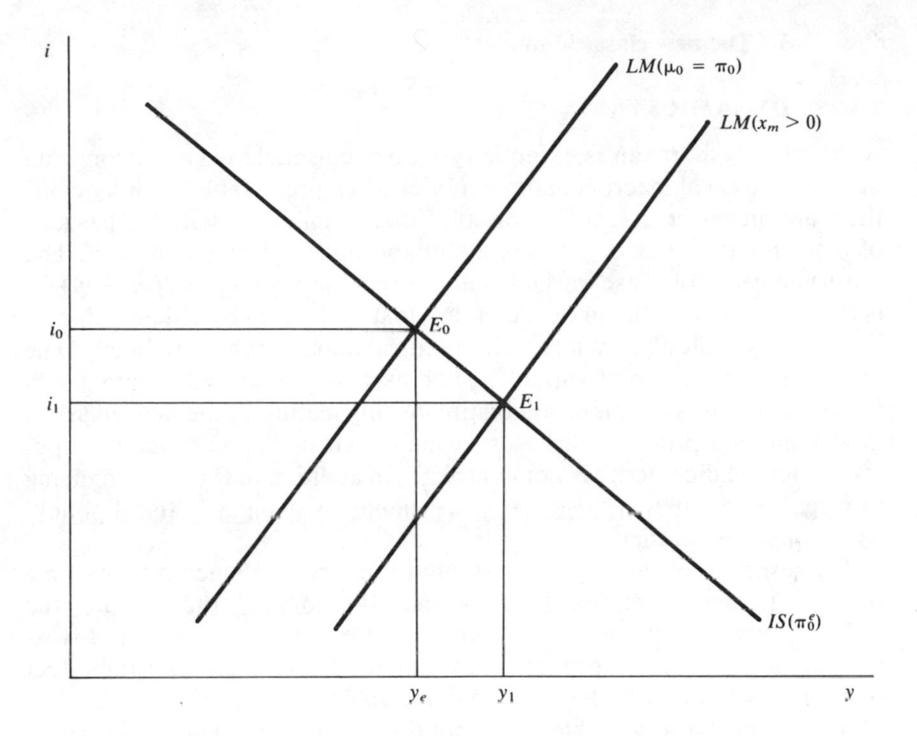

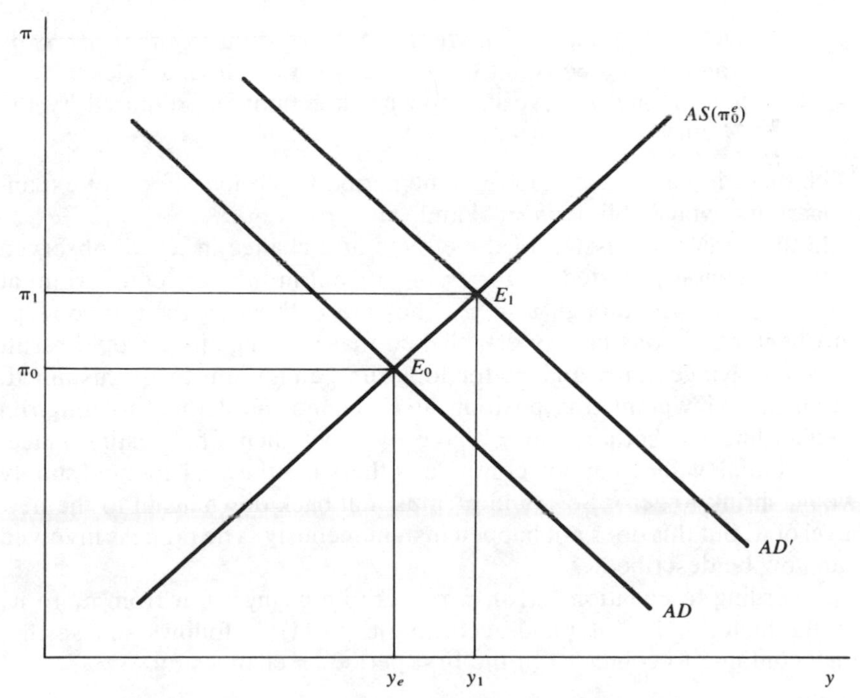

Figure 3-6 The effects of a monetary shock.

3.4.2 DYNAMICS

Although the short run is essentially indistinguishable from the long run in a new classical macroeconomic model when predictable events occur, there are, nevertheless, some variables that change only with the passage of time and until they come to rest equilibrium is not fully achieved. The most important of these variables is the real money supply, $(m - p)$. It is the only real variable in the economy that is affected by either a change in monetary policy or by a random nominal shock such as x_g or x_m. The dichotomy between real variables such as y or $i - \pi^e$ and nominal variables such as μ is an important distinguishing feature of the new classical model and is a prime contributor to the conclusions about policy impotence, but the dichotomy is not complete. In addition to $(m - p)$ changing in response to a new μ, also $i - \pi^e$ responds to changes in fiscal policy, as we observed earlier.

The response of $(m - p)$ is particularly interesting since it takes time to reach its new level and in the process the nominal interest rate, the inflation rate, and the expected inflation rate continue to adjust. Investigating this adjustment process allows us to understand better the effect of monetary policy on these nominal variables.

In tracking these variables over time there are two general forces at work:

1. i and π move together, since the *IS* curve stipulates that i exceeds π^e and π by a constant $(a_0 - y_e)/a_1$ if $x_g = 0$; and
2. $(m - p)$ and i move in opposite directions, as required by the *LM* curve.

With these in mind we can look at the period-by-period effects of expansionary monetary policy on π, i, and $(m - p)$.

In the earlier discussion of the effects of a change in μ, we observed that the economy started at $\mu = \pi = \pi^e$, but in the new equilibrium at E_1 in Figure 3-4, although $\pi = \pi^e$, they are both larger than the new μ. In Chapter 2, it was clearly established that a change in μ would result in *equal* changes in π and π^e for long-run equilibrium to be sustained. From that viewpoint, the position at E_1 cannot be defined as long-run equilibrium and both π and π^e have overshot their final resting place. Their initial values cannot continue, otherwise the real money supply would shrink to zero. So π and π^e must fall back down again to the new level of μ, but this does not happen instantaneously. The process involved can now be described.

According to equation (3.10), π reacts to a change in μ from μ_0 to μ_1 by the factor $1/(1 - a_3)$ and according to (3.11) π^e follows suit so that they continue to coincide. In the first period, π changes by

$$(3.14) \quad \pi_1 - \pi_0 = [1/(1 - a_3)][\mu_1 - \mu_0]$$

EXAMPLE

> Assume $\mu = \pi = \pi^e = .10$ or 10%, initially; then μ rises to .12; since everyone "knows" this information and the fact that $a_3 = .25$, both π and π^e rise to $.10 + (1/.75)(.02) = .1267$ or 12.67%.

From Chapter 2, we can repeat equation (2.5):

$$(3.15) \quad (m - p) - (m - p)_{-1} = \mu - \pi$$

which indicates how $(m - p)$ changes over time based on what μ and π are at a point in time and assuming that $x_m = 0$ in this instance. Thus at the end of the first period

$$(3.15') \quad (m - p)_1 - (m - p)_0 = \mu_1 - \pi_1$$
$$= (\mu_1 - \mu_0) - (\pi_1 - \pi_0) + (\mu_0 - \pi_0)$$
$$= -[a_3/(1 - a_3)][\mu_1 - \mu_0]$$

from (3.14) and remembering that $\mu_0 = \pi_0$. In other words, $(m - p)$ falls by $a_3/(1 - a_3)$ times the increase in μ. The fall in $(m - p)$ creates excess demand in the money market forcing i to rise. From the *IS* curve of equation (3.13), $i = (a_0 - y_e)/a_1 + x_g + \pi$ and therefore

$$(3.16) \quad i_1 - i_0 = \pi_1 - \pi_0 = [1/(1 - a_3)][\mu_1 - \mu_0]$$

since $\pi^e = \pi$ at every point and $x_g = 0$. In summary, expansionary monetary policy forces both the interest rate and the inflation rate to rise initially by more than the increase in the growth rate of the money supply.

In the second period π is forced to react to the change in $(m - p)_1$. Again using (3.10), we note that π changes by the factor $1/(1 - a_3)$ to the change in $(m - p)$ in the previous period. During the second period the inflation rate begins to fall according to

$$(3.14') \quad \pi_2 - \pi_1 = -[1/(1 - a_3)][a_3/(1 - a_3)][\mu_1 - \mu_0]$$
$$= -[a_3/(1 - a_3)^2][\mu_1 - \mu_0]$$

Now, at the end of the second period, the real money supply has risen, as seen from

$$(3.15'') \quad (m - p)_2 - (m - p)_1 = \mu_2 - \pi_2$$
$$= [a_3^2/(1 - a_3)^2][\mu_1 - \mu_0]$$

since $\mu_2 = \mu_1$. In fact, because $\mu_1 > \pi_2$, π_2 is now below its new long-run value.

EXAMPLE CONTINUES

> $\pi_2 = .1276 - (.25/.75^2).02 = .1178.$

Continuing one more period, we see that

$$(3.14'') \quad \pi_3 - \pi_2 = [1/(1 - a_3)][(m - p)_2 - (m - p)_1]$$
$$= [a_3{}^2/(1 - a_3)^3][\mu_1 - \mu_0]$$

which is now once more positive.

EXAMPLE CONTINUES

> $\pi_3 = .1178 + (.25^2/.75^3).02 = .1208$. This value is getting close to its final destination of .12.

This pattern suggests that π, i, and $(m - p)$ will cycle around their new long-run values, with period-to-period changes becoming smaller and smaller until the final equilibrium is reached. At that point, $\pi = \mu_1$, $i = \mu_1 + (a_0 - y_e)/a_1$, and $(m - p)$ will be lower by a_3 times the change in i, which is equal to $a_3(\mu_1 - \mu_0)$. The paths of $(m - p)$, i, and π are drawn in Chart 3-1. Because π^e has been able to track π throughout this process, the equality of $y = y_e$ is maintained. Even though the economy has not been in full equilibrium, income and output have been insulated from these cycles.

In making these calculations it is obvious that the value of a_3 is important. The reason for this is that it is the only parameter that connects a real variable, $(m - p)$, to a nominal variable, i. If a_3 were zero, this link would be broken and π would move immediately to its long-run value.

By way of comparison, the initial increase in the interest rate and the inflation rate in response to expansionary monetary policy counters directly the predictions of the *IS–LM* model, taken by itself. In fact the dynamics in that model (see Section 2.2.3) dictate an initial *fall* in the interest rate that is larger than is consistent with long-run equilibrium. The difference arises from the role of expected inflation in the new classical model and the assumed knowledge of all agents about the effects of monetary policy on all the important macroeconomic variables.

There are also dynamics involved in reacting to a nominal shock such as $x_m > 0$. The main difference is that a change in μ is considered to be permanent, whereas x_m is supposed to last for only one period. If $x_m =$

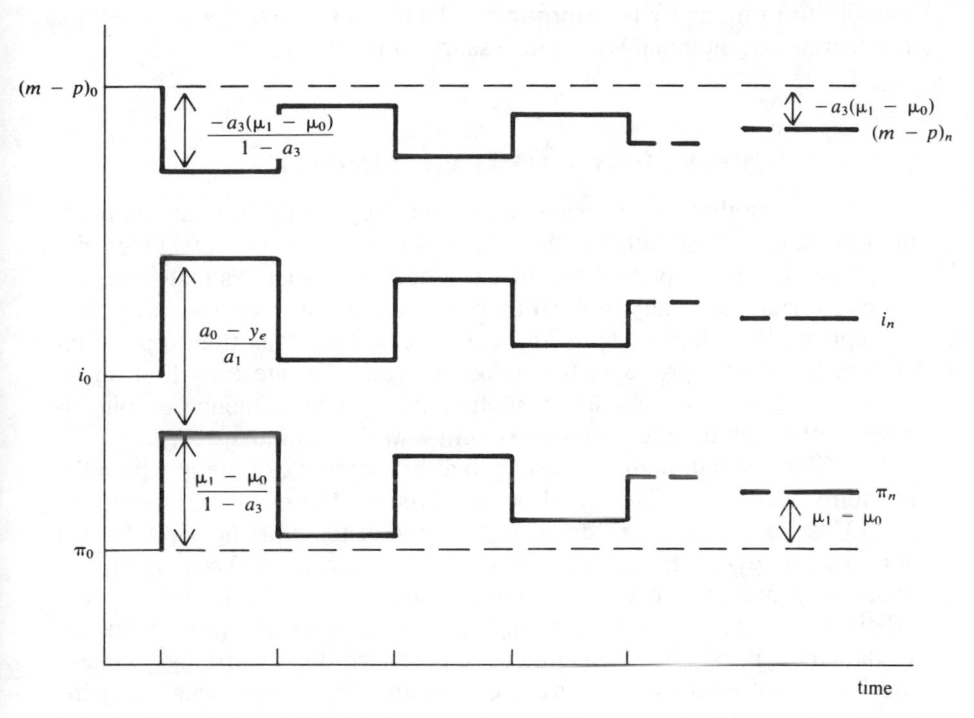

Chart 3.1 The path of $(m - p)$, i, and π after an increase in μ.

0 in the second period and thereafter, y will return to y_e and π, i, and $(m - p)$ will move back to their original levels. Since $\mu + x_m > \pi$ in the first period, $(m - p)$ will rise. This is the opposite movement to the one generated by an increase in μ, where $\mu < \pi$ initially. After that, the values of π, i, and $(m - p)$ will cycle until they come to rest at their *old* levels. The additional complication here is that y will also adjust after the first period, during which $\pi^e < \pi$. In the second period, $E[x_m] = 0$, and if that forecast is indeed fulfilled, π and π^e will once again coincide. However, if the rate of change of nominal wage is now set equal to π^e, there will be a lasting reduction in the real wage. If that is not corrected, the economy will remain at y_1. This is most easily seen by referring back to the original *AS* curve, equation (2.12) in Chapter 2. It is written as

$$(3.17) \quad y = y_{-1} - a_4(\omega - \pi)$$

where ω is the rate of change of nominal wages. If $\omega = \pi^e$, then $y = y_{-1}$. To restore equilibrium in the labor market, second-period wage negotiations must include a "catch-up" element that makes up for the previous difference between π and π^e, allowing the real wage to rise to its equilibrium rate and y to return to y_e. That is, $\omega = \pi^e + \pi_{-1} - \pi^e_{-1}$ is the increase in nominal wages necessary to reach y_e.

3.5 A SUPPLY SHOCK TO THE ECONOMY

So far the new classical model has been used to examine a deliberate policy of stimulating aggregate demand and an unexpected demand shock. To complete the picture it is necessary to investigate a supply shock as well, especially to see if there is room for macroeconomic policy to improve the situation after an adverse event such as the oil-price increase. It will also prove useful to take up again the question, first raised in Section 2.5, as to whether monetary policy can influence output indirectly through its effect on investment and the capital stock.

Consider a situation in which $x_s < 0$ after a period of time in which the economy was at y_e. This could be triggered by the oil-price increase of the 1970s that essentially "destroyed" some of the existing capital stock such as energy-inefficient machinery. The capacity of the economy to produce goods and services is reduced temporarily until new, energy-efficient capital is put in place through increased investment expenditures. In the labor market, the demand curve is shifted downward and employment and real wages are lowered. Our main interest is in what happens to output and the inflation rate. When $x_s < 0$, the *AS* curve shifts to the *left* by x_s times $(1 + a_4)$, as indicated in Figure 3-7. Since π^e cannot incorporate this event, the *AS* curve does not respond through this channel. This time there is nothing that happens to the *AD* curve and a new short-run equilibrium is found at E_1, where inflation is higher and output is lower. These results can be verified by inspection of equations (3.10) and (3.12). For instance, the effect of x_s on π is given by $-(a_1a_2 + a_3)(1 + a_4)/(a_1 + a_3a_4 + a_1a_2a_4)$ in equation (3.10). Furthermore, this combination of an increase in π and a fall in y allows us to identify it as a supply shock; with a demand shock, π and y move together.

Rising inflation and falling output are particularly painful and such a situation is described as "stagflation." From a political perspective, there is great incentive to do something about it. However, it is not clear what policy should be implemented and how it could improve on current conditions. Even if the government had advance warning of the shock, it could not take preventive action. In fact, advising the public of the impending event would exacerbate the decline in output. With full information, $\pi = \pi^e$, and from the *AS* equation $y = y_e - (1 + a_4)x_s$, which is lower than y_1. Only because $\pi > \pi^e$ does y fall by a smaller amount to y_1.

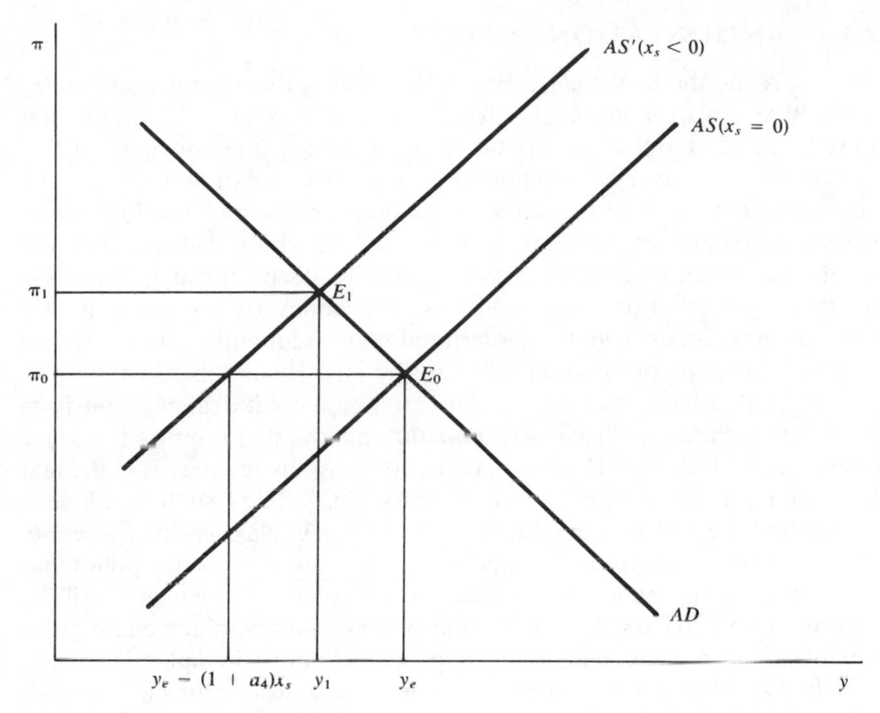

Figure 3-7 A supply shock.

If x_s is a temporary event, the economy will return to y_e of its own accord, just as it does when disturbed by a demand shock such as x_m. However, if x_s turns out to be permanent, then macroeconomic policy will not be able to restore y_e. Instead, the new equilibrium is $y_e - (1 + a_4)x_s$. All that the government can do is to regulate the inflation rate, but since it can do that under all circumstances, adjusting monetary policy when a supply shock appears has no special appeal to a new classical macroeconomist.

In Section 2.4, it was noted that monetary policy might be able to influence output by stimulating investment in the short run, which is subsequently translated into a permanent addition to the capital stock. However, this requires a temporary reduction in the real interest rate. According to equation (3.13), monetary policy cannot change the real interest rate since i and π^e move together in response to a change in μ. Therefore, in a new classical model monetary policy is also impotent as a "supply-side" instrument.

3.6 ANTIINFLATION POLICY

While the new classical model renders active stabilization policy ineffective, it also enhances the effectiveness of monetary policy that aims to reduce and stabilize the inflation rate. Although it is now evident that an economy can be in full equilibrium at *any* rate of inflation, it is generally conceded that any positive rate of inflation causes some misallocation of resources. There are some "unproductive" activities that are triggered by the existence of inflation: People have to keep informed about the prospects for inflation; they hold less real money than is optimal, and catalogs and menus have to be reprinted more frequently. These are just some of the costs of inflation, even in the long run when it is fully perceived. In that light, it is not surprising to find a great deal of enthusiasm for policy measures, particularly monetary policy, that promise to reduce a high rate of inflation. However, that enthusiasm is tempered by the fear that such a policy might have temporary side effects such as reduced output and increased unemployment. To the new classical macroeconomist such fears are groundless as long as the antiinflationary policy has *credibility*. If the policy is believed, it will succeed because it will be incorporated into expectations and allow the economy to move to a lower rate of inflation while maintaining constant output and employment. The credibility of the government's intentions is therefore crucial. To verify this, let us follow the effects of an antiinflationary policy, comparing a situation of a credible policy with one that is not believed until after it has achieved its goal.

To reduce the rate of inflation permanently, the central bank must reduce the rate of growth of the money supply. Assume that such a policy is announced and implemented. If the policy is believed, it will reduce π and π^e by $1/(1 - a_3)$ times the change in μ according to equations (3.10) and (3.11). Therefore, in Figure 3-8, the economy will stay on the vertical line at y_e. Reducing the growth rate of the money supply from μ_0 to μ_1 lowers the position of the *AD* curve by $1/(1 - a_3)$ times the change in μ to *AD'*. As was the case before, the inflation rate overshoots its final target, and ultimately the *AD* curve will have to shift upward again to *AD''*, where the vertical distance E_2E_0 is equal to $\mu_1 - \mu_0$. Not only is credibility important for this result, but so is the requirement that all market participants be aware of the overshooting phenomenon. If, for instance, π^e is adjusted by only $(\mu_1 - \mu_0)$, then a short-run *AS* curve would be relevant. From its initial position of *AS*, it would fall to *AS'* by the vertical distance $(\mu_1 - \mu_0)$. Since π^e is now exogenously determined, we can go back to the *AD* curve of equation (3.5) to find its adjustment. The change in μ will lower the vertical intercept by $(\mu_1 - \mu_0)$ plus a_3 times the change in π^e for a total of $(1 + a_3)(\mu_1 - \mu_0)$, which

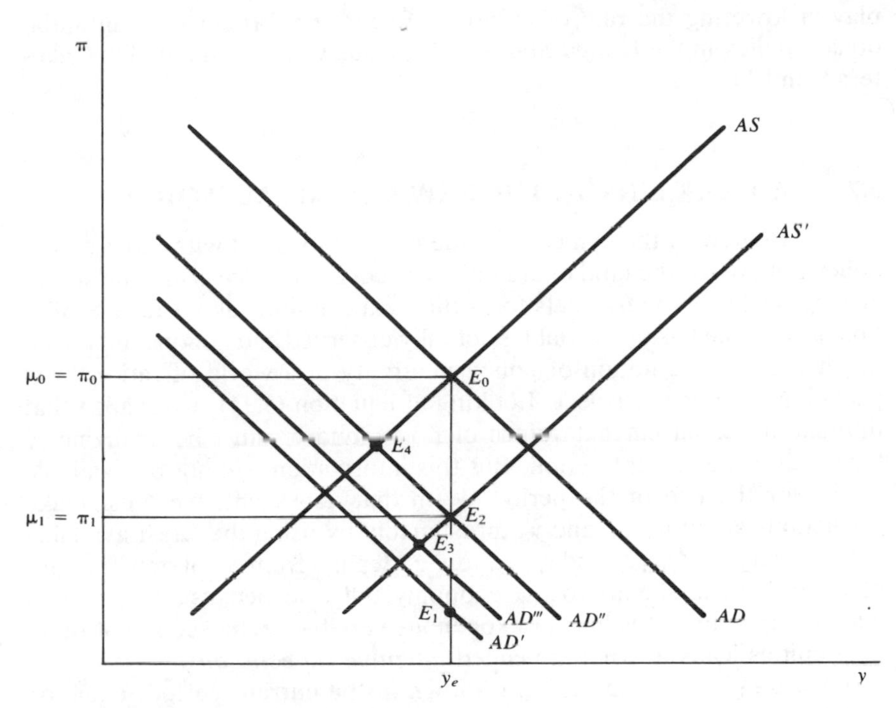

Figure 3-8 Antiinflation policy.

represents a downward shift greater than that for the *AS* curve. Assume that *AD*‴ is now relevant. Its intersection with *AS*′ at E_3 must lead to lower output and increased unemployment.

Even worse would be a situation in which π^e did not adjust at all to the announcement of a lower μ. If workers took the view that antiinflation policy was merely propaganda to encourage them to accept lower *real* wages, they might continue to bargain for nominal wages based on current π. In that case the *AS* curve would not shift at all, while the *AD* curve would shift down by $(\mu_1 - \mu_0)$, which is again *AD*″, and equilibrium would be at E_4. In general, the smaller is the change in π^e relative to the shift of the *AD* curve in the wake of a policy change, the greater is the departure of income from its equilibrium level. Credibility of policy intentions has much to do with this, and not surprisingly central banks have gotten into the habit of announcing in advance their target rates of growth for the money supply and the public has also acquired the habit of checking on the performance of the central bank with respect to its announced goal. In other words, monetary policy not only influences π but also π^e, and the more predictable the central bank is, the more active a role it can play in lowering the rate of inflation. Recent performance of antiinflationary policy in the United States and Canada will be examined in Chapters 8 and 11.

3.7 A WEAK LINK IN THE NEW CLASSICAL MODEL

In view of the cynical attitude often associated with government policy initiatives, the kind of credibility needed for success may be sorely lacking. In fact, if individuals form their expectations about future inflation only on the basis of variables actually observed and not on announced targets, the whole notion of policy neutrality in a world of rational expectations becomes suspect. Looking at equation (3.11), we realize that information about current values of μ, a_0, and y_e must be available to form π^e for the current period. But this information will not be available until after the end of the period. With that constraint, we must make predictions about μ, a_0, and y_e, presumably by using the latest available data, namely μ_{-1}, $a_{0_{-1}}$, and $y_{e_{-1}}$. Now π^e departs from π not only because of unpredictable shocks to the economy but also because of errors in guessing the current values of exogenous variables. The second of these possibilities leads to what are called *adaptive expectations*.

Since μ_{-1}, $a_{0_{-1}}$, and $y_{e_{-1}}$ are known in the current period, equation (3.10) allows us to calculate π_{-1}, assuming all the previous x's were zero. This one variable summarizes all the known information about the economy and is the best available predictor of π in the current period. Thus, $\pi^e = \pi_{-1}$, or if the x's were nonzero in the last period, the following expectations process is applicable:

$$(3.18)\quad \pi^e = \pi_{-1} - [1/(a_1 + a_3 + a_1a_2a_4)] \times [a_3x_{g_{-1}} + a_1x_{m_{-1}} + (a_1a_2 + a_3)(1 + a_4)x_{s_{-1}}]$$

For example, if $x_{m_{-1}} > 0$, π^e should be lower than π_{-1} because the inflationary shock is not expected to last. Equation (3.18) is a specific version of the general case of adaptive expectations, written as

$$(3.19)\quad \pi^e - \pi^e_{-1} = j(\pi_{-1} - \pi^e_{-1})$$

Equation (3.19) stipulates that individuals change their expected inflation in direct proportion to their previous error; that is, they adapt their current thinking about inflation on the basis of past experience. In general, j lies between zero and one, but equation (3.18) is derived from (3.19) if $j = 1$. Adaptive expectations lead to systematic errors in π^e because π^e will always be below π when inflation is rising and it will be above π when prices are decelerating; only when π is steady will π^e "home in" on π.

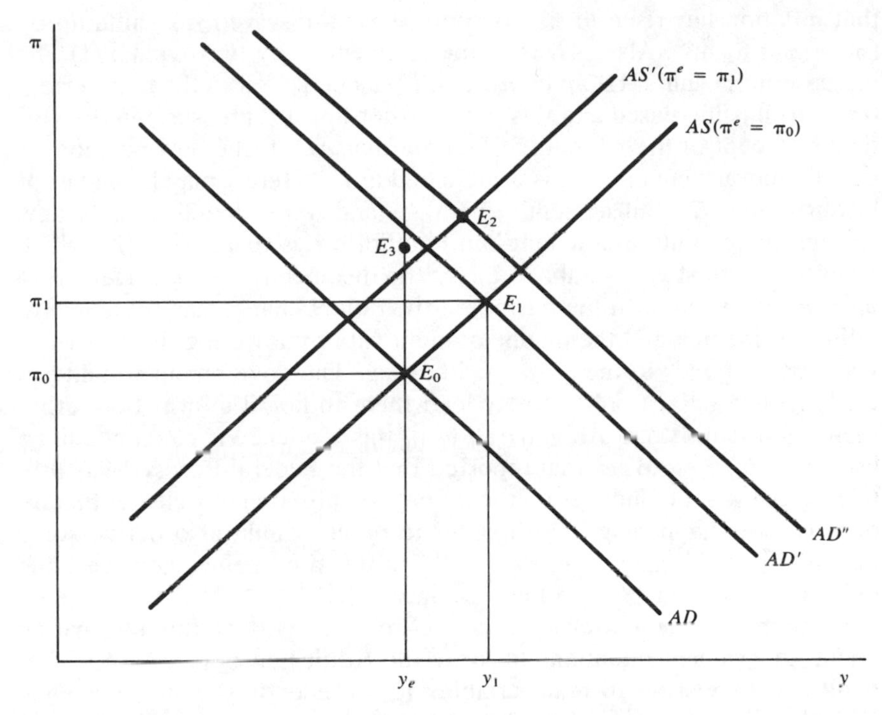

Figure 3-9 Expansionary monetary policy with adaptive expectations.

Although individuals try to eliminate such errors, they cannot improve their performance without knowing what has yet to be measured. This puts extra pressure on the government to announce its goals for μ and a_0 and abide by them. But since the authorities are unlikely to accept the limited role of "automatic pilot" and because they cannot guarantee the quality of the information they provide if they do make announcements about economic policy, they are likely to hedge with target *ranges* and multiple provisos for all sorts of emergencies. Moreover, the public's inability to know the current value of μ opens the door to an activist policy regime, and the government may not shy away from the opportunity to reap some political rewards from short-term economic gains.

An economy operating with adaptive expectations as expressed by equation (3.18) can move away, although only temporarily, from its equilibrium level of output through deliberate but unknown policy changes. Starting from y_e, assume an increase in μ. Since π^e is still geared to π_0, the economy must move along the short-run *AS* curve in Figure 3-9. The *AD* curve shifts up by the increase in μ, and therefore the new equilibrium is established at E_1. But this is not a final position for the economy. Now that inflation has risen to π_1, as soon as it is observed AS shifts up by $(\pi_1 - \pi_0)$ to AS'. Also, AD is further influenced by two events: (1) The increase in π^e shifts AD up by a_3; and (2) since $\mu > \pi$ in the first period, $(m - p)$ has increased and this puts further upward pressure on the vertical intercept of the AD curve. Assume that AD'' is the new position. A new temporary equilibrium is established at E_2. Here y may be higher or lower than at E_1. Subsequently, both AS and AD keep adjusting to new circumstances until a new long-run equilibrium is reached at E_3, which is on the vertical y_e line, above E_0 by the distance $(\mu_1 - \mu_0)$. Here $\pi = \mu = \pi^e$ once again. In the meantime the policy change has been able to influence income and the unemployment rate by lowering the real wage when π^e responds to the change with a lag. The government's ability to exploit such activist policies may lead them to hoard information rather than to disseminate it. An illustration of this tendency is contained in an article in *Business Week* that reported that the Federal Reserve was producing a new set of indexes on the money supply "to get a clearer picture of what was happening." Although the public would also derive some benefit from this new information, "for the time being, however, the indexes will be available to Fed officials only."[3]

In summary, the new classical model relies heavily on full information about government intentions to draw the result that policies are in fact neutral with respect to real variables in the economy, without dealing with the pressing issue of the incentives and constraints involved in the provision of complete information.

3.8 SUMMARY

The new classical model of the macroeconomy is based on the *IS–LM–AS* model of Chapter 2 with the addition of stochastic variables to distinguish between predictable and unexpected events and an expectations process for inflation that incorporates the former but not the latter. Robert Gordon, a critic of some of the excesses of this school of thought, summarizes this model as one "in which universal auction markets allow prices to adjust instantly to perceived nominal changes, and in which agents fail to select the quantity that would maintain an aggregate equilibrium only when imperfect information prevents them from discerning the true value of nominal aggregate demand."[4]

[3] "Economic Diary," *Business Week,* September 22, 1980, p. 25.

[4] R. J. Gordon, "Output Fluctuations and Gradual Price Adjustment," *Journal of Economic Literature,* 19, June 1981, p. 494.

The main features of the new classical model are as follows:

1. It is an equilibrium model, not only because $AD = AS$ at all times, but also because it has a built-in tendency to move quickly and painlessly to long-run equilibrium where $\pi = \pi^e$.
2. It incorporates "rational expectations" that use all the information that is available for forming π^e.
3. Although computationally more difficult than "adaptive expectations," rational expectations eliminate systematic errors but not random errors.

Its chief results are the following:

1. Predictable monetary policy does not affect real variables in the economy, except the real money supply.
2. The economy can be displaced from equilibrium by random shocks, but monetary policy cannot prevent or alleviate the consequences of such events.
3. Monetary policy is the most important variable for determining the rate of inflation, especially if the actions of the central bank are predictable and therefore credible.

Its weakness is its rather cavalier attitude toward the availability of full information because it does not pay much attention to a number of important factors:

1. the problem of distinguishing between information and misinformation;
2. the possibility that the government and the private sector have different interests in the provision of information; and
3. the question of when information becomes available.

Nevertheless, this model has caused macroeconomists of all persuasions to rethink the entire perception of macroeconomic policy. It is no longer taken for granted that stabilization policy can always improve the performance of the economy. Rational expectations and the self-equilibrating forces in the economy make it at best arguable that the government can do things that the private sector cannot. But new classical macroeconomists have not won the argument outright. The next chapter will evaluate the counteroffensive taken by those economists who remain convinced that a useful role remains for monetary and fiscal policy, without going back to the simple *IS–LM* model. Their analysis of the economy is just as sophisticated and convincing as that of the new classical economists, and their argument is just as persuasive.

EXERCISES

1. Toss two dice 25 times. Keep track of the outcomes. Calculate the mean and standard deviation. Does the distribution look like Figure 3-3?
2. Develop an equation for π^e that is based on rational expectations and given the "information" in exercise 4 in Chapter 2.
3. Check to see that the changes in μ, π, i, and $(m - p)$ from equations (3.14), (3.15), and (3.16) are consistent with the *LM* curve of equation (3.2) after the first period and in the final equilibrium when μ is increased.
4. Assume that x_m suddenly takes on a value of $-.03$.
   (a) Calculate the first-round effects on y, π, i, and $(m - p)$ using the model in exercise 4, Chapter 2.
   (b) What are the long-run effects?

FURTHER READING

Barro, R. J., "Rational Expectations and the Role of Monetary Policy," *Journal of Monetary Economics,* 2, January 1976, pp. 1–32. Develops the argument against activist policies.

Fellner, W., "The Credibility Effect and Rational Expectations," *Brookings Papers in Economic Activity,* 1, 1979, pp. 176–78. Deals with the issue of policy credibility.

Sargent, T. J., *Macroeconomic Theory,* New York, Academic Press, 1979. Later chapters present the new classical macroeconomic model.

CHAPTER 4

The institutionalist model

THE CASE FOR STABILIZATION POLICY

4.1 INTRODUCTION

To a new classical macroeconomist the principal guiding light is *equilibrium*. Equilibrium is in everyone's best interest and therefore each of us will try to achieve it. To Robert Barro the identification of equilibrium with optimality is derived from his belief that the equality of supply and demand "implies that . . . the private market manages to exhaust trades that are to the perceived mutual advantage of the exchanging parties."[1]

Underlying this belief is the perception that all markets are organized as auction markets, clearing at almost every instant in time, and that prices determined in these markets provide the participants with the signals that allow them to respond to changing conditions in ways that maximize their individual benefits as well as those of society as a whole. In such a world, other institutional arrangements do not make sense since they cannot improve on the results available from a complete set of auction markets. There is no room in the analysis for the influence of such institutions as labor unions and union contracts. If unions do not disrupt equilibrium, they are tolerated but irrelevant; if they do cause disequilibrium in the labor market, they will be eliminated by a new institutional arrangement for setting wages that does not produce this undesirable result. Nevertheless, we observe markets that are emphatically not auction markets. In particular, the labor market is characterized by contracts, not auctions. Because there are considerable adjustment costs to both workers and employers of moving from one job to another, both sides restrict competitive behavior in response to short-run changes in labor-market con-

[1] R. J. Barro, "Second Thoughts on Keynesian Economics," *American Economic Review,* 69, May 1979, p. 56.

ditions and agree to formal or informal contracts that are binding through either legal sanctions or tradition. Both workers and firms find these arrangements advantageous or they would have gotten rid of such contracts long ago.

A union contract is only one of many ways in which a long-term relationship is established between a worker and a firm. More loosely structured arrangements also exist: An employer offers a job to a prospective employee, outlining wages and working conditions, often for an indefinite period into the future; by accepting the job, the employee "promises" to abide by these conditions. In a very few cases, there is recontracting during the period for which the previous contract was presumed to be binding, but this is limited to occasions when there are large-scale departures from previous expectations. The renegotiation of contracts between the United Auto Workers and the Big Three automobile manufacturers in the United States in 1982 is a rare example of such recontracting, but was probably inevitable given the large drop in demand for North American automobiles in the wake of the oil-price increase and the 1981–3 recession. Nevertheless, the rule is still long-term contracts that specify not only wage increases for the first year but also for subsequent years. This is not consistent with an auction market, and the existence of such long-term contracts must be acknowledged in our macroeconomic model.

One would not want to suggest that the length of a union contract is an institutional constant. In fact, contracts have tended to become shorter as unpredictability about inflation and other matters tended to increase in the 1970s.[2] Nevertheless, even though contracts introduce rigidity into the labor market and may prevent equilibrium from being established at all times, they still serve a useful purpose to all concerned and are not likely to be completely eliminated. In other words, institutions such as labor contracts will adjust to new circumstances, but they will adjust slowly since there is always the possibility that the new circumstances may give way to the old once more and the costs of institutional change are high. In the absence of a more descriptive term, the macroeconomic model that takes labor contracts into account will be labeled the *institutionalist* model.

There are other features of the new classical model that have been questioned by those economists who believe that institutions other than

[2] According to the *Current Industrial Relations Scene in Canada, 1981* (Kingston, Queen's University Industrial Relations Centre), in 1973, only 5% of Canadian employees were covered by contracts lasting for 18 months or less; by 1980, contracts of this duration covered 22% of the employees. Long-term contracts of 30 months or more fell from 41% in 1973 to 34% in 1980. However, for the United States, John B. Taylor has shown that three-year contracts still dominate collective bargaining agreements: in 1975, they covered 65% of workers in major union settlements; by 1980, coverage had increased to 78%. See his table 1 in "Union Wage Settlements during a Disinflation," *American Economic Review,* 73, December 1983, p. 984.

auction markets are important to the working of the economy. For example, Robert Gordon has suggested reasons why some product markets are not organized as auction markets and therefore have preset prices that prevail for some period even if they are patently disequilibrium prices. He argues, "There is nothing arbitrary about pre-set prices; they simply substitute for pre-set locations and times of hypothetical auction markets by allowing transactions locations and times to be freely chosen."[3] The late Arthur Okun also made a distinction between auction markets and customer markets, justifying this distinction on the basis that they served different purposes.[4]

Whatever the approach to recent criticism of the new classical model, the aim of these economists is to show that the economy is not as self-regulating as is depicted in Chapter 3 and that there is room for stabilization policy to improve the performance of the economy. This view of the structure of the economy is not as monolithic as that of the classical model, and there is as yet no agreement on the distinguishing feature or features of the institutionalist model, with the result that it is more difficult to represent this school of thought in one specific version of the *IS–LM–AS* model, but it is possible to do this by incorporating certain institutional characteristics of the labor market.

In this chapter the feature of long-term labor contracts will be substituted for the wage-determination process of the new classical model. This, together with pervasiveness of random shocks, is enough to make the case for stabilization policy. In this regard, it is important to show not only that government activity *can* influence output and employment but that it *should* do so from a perspective of improving economic welfare. Then, when dealing with antiinflationary policy, it will become evident that credibility of the policy is not the only problem; predictions of a temporary loss of output and jobs are likely to be another. After that, other features of the labor market such as cost-of-living-adjustment clauses will be discussed. Finally, an argument that the natural rate of unemployment is really endogenous and capable of policy-induced improvement will be considered.

4.2 LONG-TERM WAGE CONTRACTING

The essential ingredient of long-term wage contracts is that the wage is changed less frequently than every unit of analytical time. While it is impossible to specify the length of a "period," this requirement is

[3] R. J. Gordon, "Output Fluctuations and Gradual Price Adjustment," *Journal of Economic Literature,* 19, June 1981, p. 519.

[4] A. M. Okun, *Prices and Quantities: A Macroeconomic Analysis,* Washington, D.C., Brookings Institution, 1981.

likely to be met in most circumstances. Wages are fixed for periods of as long as a year and predetermined for periods of up to three years. Even though new information becomes available frequently, transactions costs of negotiations create incentives to make contracts that last for some time.

To incorporate long-term wage bargains into the model, it is convenient to assume that there are *overlapping contracts,* a concept introduced by Stanley Fischer.[5] This means that contracts last for several periods but are not all signed at the same time. To put matters more concretely, suppose that unions and firms bargain over wages every two years, stipulating a wage not only for the first year of the contract but also for the second year. Half of all agreements are signed at the beginning of odd years (1979, 1981, 1983, etc.), and the other half are signed at the beginning of even years (1980, 1982, 1984, etc.).[6] In each case, the rate of growth of nominal wages is set equal to the inflation rate expected to prevail for the period during which the wage is binding. This will keep the expected real wage constant and the labor market in equilibrium if supply and demand curves in that market are presumed to stay in place. Therefore, in every contract

$$\omega = \pi^e \tag{4.1a}$$

$$\omega_{+1} = \pi^e_{+1} \tag{4.1b}$$

where ω and ω_{+1} are the rates of growth of nominal wages for the two years in the contract and π^e and π^e_{+1} are the expected rates of inflation for the first and second years of the contract, both expectations being formed just before the contract is signed.

At any one time there are two types of contracts in existence, old and new. The average wage paid during any period is a weighted average of old and new contracts and is represented by

$$\omega = .5\omega_o + .5\omega_n \tag{4.2}$$

where the subscripts o and n refer to old and new contracts. In this example, the weights are equal for both kinds of contracts, but if more workers are covered by one than by the other, the weights would reflect that fact. Now ω_o and ω_n, although they cover the same period, need not be the same, since ω_n is based on newer information than ω_o.

[5] See S. Fischer, "Long-term Contracts, Rational Expectations, and the Optimal Money Supply Rule," *Journal of Political Economy,* 85, February 1977, pp. 191–206.

[6] Such overlapping contracts are a distinguishing feature of North American industrial relations, but in Europe wage bargaining is much more coordinated and centralized. See C. L. Barber and J. C. P. McCallum, *Controlling Inflation* (Ottawa, Institute for Economic Policy, 1982), for a summary of the bargaining process in Austria, Belgium, Germany, and the Netherlands.

EXAMPLE

> Assume that in 1980 a contract covering half the workers in the economy was signed allowing for $\omega = .15$ and $\omega_{+1} = .13$ for 1980 and 1981; then in 1981, another contract covering the other half of all workers was signed stipulating $\omega = .14$ and $\omega_{+1} = .13$ for 1981 and 1982. Thus for 1981, $\omega = .5(.13) + .5(.14) = .135$ or 13.5%.

This suggests that for any one year there will exist two separate expectations about inflation, one old and one new, which will be designated by π_o^e and π_n^e. Even if these expectations are "rational," they will typically differ because new expectations can incorporate new information, whereas π_o^e, having been made a year ago, remains constant in the face of new developments.

In an abstract sense, labor contracts that specify a wage rate for a year or two in advance but make no provision for employment levels are not really written in the best way possible. A contract with a fixed wage is bound to lead to excess supply or demand in the labor market when either the demand curve or the supply curve shift after the contract has been signed. Since the preservation of equilibrium in the labor market is the ultimate goal, it would be better to specify employment levels for various contingencies and let the wage adjust in an equilibrating fashion. If such contracts are superior to the ones in force today, why is there so little incentive to use them? The answer lies in the existence of enforcement costs. It is very difficult for unions and management to agree on the current state of the economy and the cause of disturbances to the labor market and that could make enforcement of the contract a litigious affair. In fact, a firm that attempts to maximize profits would have every incentive to minimize prosperous conditions and emphasize a gloomy picture. From that perspective, we can see that current contracts that stipulate wages but allow employment decisions to be made unilaterally by management are an effective compromise between transactions costs and enforcement costs of contracts.

4.3 PERVASIVE SHOCKS

Before addressing the issue of policy intervention in a world of long-term contracts, random shocks have to be reintroduced into the analysis and expectations formation has to be discussed. As in Chapter 3, random events that cannot be predicted beforehand are presumed to play a leading role in the performance of the economy. Such events affect the goods market, the money market, and the labor market.

The *IS–LM–AS* equations of the model are written as follows:

$$y = a_0 - a_1(i - \pi^e) + x_g \tag{4.3}$$

$$\mu - \pi + x_m = a_2 y - a_3 i - (m - p)_{-1} \tag{4.4}$$

$$y = y_e - a_4(\pi^e - \pi - x_s) + x_s \tag{4.5}$$

As in previous chapters, y is the natural log of income, i is the nominal interest rate, μ is the growth rate of the money supply, π is the inflation rate, $(m - p)_{-1}$ is the natural log of the real money supply at the end of the previous period, and y_e is the natural log of the equilibrium level of income. Turning to the x's, x_g is a goods-market shock, x_m is a monetary shock, and x_s is a supply shock.

Unlike the treatment in Chapter 3 where the expected value of each x in each period was zero, here it will be assumed that shocks are to some extent pervasive. This means that this period's shock is related to the one that occurred in the previous period, or more accurately that the shock lingers for more than one period. Of course, x and x_{-1} cannot be equal or they would become entirely predictable. To preserve the unpredictable nature of shocks and to incorporate pervasiveness, the x's are now expressed as

$$x_g = b_g x_{g-1} + z_g \tag{4.6a}$$

$$x_m = b_m x_{m-1} + z_m \tag{4.6b}$$

$$x_s = b_s x_{s-1} + z_s \tag{4.6c}$$

where the z's represent new developments during the current period. They have an expected value of zero and a known standard deviation. Thus the z's in this chapter are treated as the x's were in Chapter 3. The b's represent the relationship between current and past shocks and measure the lingering effects of these shocks. Each b will lie between zero and one. The closer b is to one, the more pervasive a shock is; if $b = 0$, then shocks have no lasting effect and the z's become the x's once more. In this way, the structure of random shocks is more versatile than in Chapter 3.

The pervasiveness of a shock is contained in the dynamics of equation (4.6). Starting from $x = 0$, z now becomes positive and in the first period $x_1 = z_1$. In the second period, if $z_2 = 0$, then $x_2 = bx_1 = bz_1$. In the third period, $x_3 = bx_2 = b^2 z_1$; and so on.

EXAMPLE

Let $z_1 = 1$ and $b = .7$. The sequence for the shock would be 1, .7, .49, .34, .24, .17, etc. If $b = .4$, the shock decays faster as indicated by the sequence 1, .4, .16, .06, .03, .01, etc.

4.4 FORMATION OF INFLATIONARY EXPECTATIONS

Individuals are still assumed to use all the information available to them and to process this information rationally when they form their expectations about inflation. In this regard there is no distinction between the new classical model and the institutionalist model. However, the existence of two-period wage contracts does lead to a problem of timing in forming expectations. For any one period there are now two values for π^e, one formed a year ago and the other brand-new. To derive π^e_o and π^e_n we need to go through the same procedure as in Section 3.3. First we "invent" an equation for π that captures all of the influences on the rate of inflation without attempting to assign an order of importance and without allowing the expected rate of inflation any independent influence.

$$\begin{aligned}(4.7)\qquad \pi = {} & c_0\mu + c_1(m - p)_{-1} + c_2 b_m x_{m-1} + c_3 a_0 + c_4 b_g x_{g-1} \\ & + c_5 y_e + c_6 b_s x_{s-1} + c_7 z_m + c_8 z_g + c_9 z_s\end{aligned}$$

which is the same as equation (3.7) in Chapter 3 except that the x's have been separated into their pervasive and new components. The c's are again the undetermined coefficients of equation (4.7). Rational expectations involves using this structure for predicting the inflation rate to the extent that the information is available at the time that the prediction is made. Thus for old contracts, starting from a position where all x's were zero, the relevant expectation of π is

$$(4.8)\qquad \pi^e_o = c_0\mu + c_1(m - p)_{-1} + c_3 a_0 + c_5 y_e$$

whereas new contracts allow for the occurrence of shocks during the previous period and their degree of pervasiveness. The expected rate of inflation now becomes

$$\begin{aligned}(4.9)\qquad \pi^e_n = {} & c_0\mu + c_1(m - p)_{-1} + c_3 a_0 + c_5 y_e \\ & + c_2 b_m x_{m-1} + c_4 b_g x_{g-1} + c_6 b_s x_{s-1}\end{aligned}$$

Because π_o^e and π_n^e coexist, π^e is an average of the two as indicated by

$$(4.10)\quad \pi^e = .5\pi_o^e + .5\pi_n^e$$

$$= c_0\mu + c_1(m - p)_{-1} + c_3a_0 + c_5y_e$$

$$+ .5(c_2b_mx_{m_{-1}} + c_4b_gx_{g_{-1}} + c_6b_sx_{s_{-1}})$$

assuming that μ, $(m - p)_{-1}$, a_0, and y_e have not changed in the meantime. The next step in the process is to eliminate the c's by substituting equations (4.8) and (4.9) into a structural equation for π which is the same as equation (3.6) in Chapter 3 and then solving for the c's in terms of the structural parameters, the a's of the *IS–LM–AS* model.

Although some of the c's are exactly the same as for the new classical model of Chapter 3, others are quite different. Specifically, c_0, c_1, c_3, and c_5 are equal to the same values as in Chapter 3; c_7 is the same as c_2 was previously, $c_8 = c_4$ before and $c_9 = c_6$ in Chapter 3. The following parameters are new:

$$c_2 = a_1/[a_1(1 - .5a_3) + .5a_3a_4 + .5a_1a_2a_4] > 0$$

$$c_4 = a_3/[a_1(1 - .5a_3) + .5a_3a_4 + .5a_1a_2a_4] > 0$$

$$c_6 = -\frac{(a_1a_2 + a_3)(1 + a_4)}{a_1(1 - .5a_3) + .5a_3a_4 + .5a_1a_2a_4} < 0$$

Even though the *IS–LM–AS* structure has been preserved, the pervasiveness of the shocks and the more complicated structure of π^e do make a difference: Predictable policies and new shocks still have the same effect on inflation as before, but continuing shocks now have effects that are somewhere between them. Compare c_0, c_2, and c_7, the coefficients attached to the completely predictable, the previously unpredictable, and the currently unpredictable changes in the growth rate of the money supply, μ, $x_{m_{-1}}$, and z_m, respectively. Now $c_0 > 1$, so that μ has a magnified effect on π, as discussed in Chapter 3. On the other hand, $0 < c_7 < 1$, so that a monetary shock has a dampened effect on π. Here c_2 has the same numerator as c_7 but a smaller denominator; therefore, $c_2 > c_7$. Since they are now quite complicated expressions, it is less space-consuming to continue to use the c's to measure the effect of various exogenous variables on π; it is, of course, possible to recapture the a's from the derivations above.

Before going on with the final version of the *AS* curve, it should be noted that expected inflation also plays a role in investment decisions and that in the new classical version of the model the real interest rate prevailed for one period at a time since π^e was formulated at the beginning of each period. Are there reasons to believe that investors are similarly "locked in" by previous π^e's? The answer is probably yes, since binding investment decisions are often made in advance of being carried out. To avoid complicating the model further, it is simplest to force both workers and investors to have the same overlapping contracts and therefore the same π^e as formed by equation (4.10); otherwise, we would need separate expectations processes for the two groups.

Now if μ, $(m - p)_{-1}$, a_0, and y_e are constant or change only in predictable ways, the *AS* curve is derived by substituting equations (4.8) and (4.9) into (4.10) and in turn into (4.5) to arrive at

$$(4.11) \quad y = y_e - a_4[-.5(c_2 b_m x_{m-1} + c_4 b_g x_{g-1} + c_6 b_s x_{s-1}) - c_7 z_m - c_8 z_g - c_9 z_s - x_{s-1} - z_s] + x_{s-1} + z_s$$

This version of the *AS* curve is much different from the new classical one. We can see that not only current shocks (i.e., the z's) but also previous shocks that are likely to prevail (i.e., the x_{-1}'s) will cause a divergence between y and y_e. If policy actions can allow y to stay closer to y_e, then they have an important role to play.

4.5 A ROLE FOR STABILIZATION POLICY

To analyze the role of macroeconomic policy in an economy with overlapping contracts and pervasive shocks it is best to work through a specific example of a shock to the economy and its subsequent performance. Starting from a position of full equilibrium, consider a negative monetary shock to the economy (i.e., $z_m < 0$). Just before this event, one half of all wage contracts were signed; the other half were signed a year before. Since no information became available in the interval, both π^e_o and π^e_n are the same. The *AS* curve is equation (4.5) with $x_s = 0$ and is drawn in Figure 4-1. The *AD* curve, again derived from the *IS–LM* curves of equations (4.3) and (4.4), is written as

$$(4.12) \quad \pi = \mu + (m - p)_{-1} - (a_2 + a_3/a_1)y + a_3 a_0/a_1 + a_3\pi^e + b_m x_{m-1} + z_m + (a_3/a_1)(b_g x_{g-1} + z_g)$$

but $x_{m-1} = x_{g-1} = z_g = 0$. A negative z_m will cause the *AD* curve to shift down by the size of z_m without affecting the location of the *AS* curve. Short-run equilibrium for the economy at the end of the first period is at E_1.

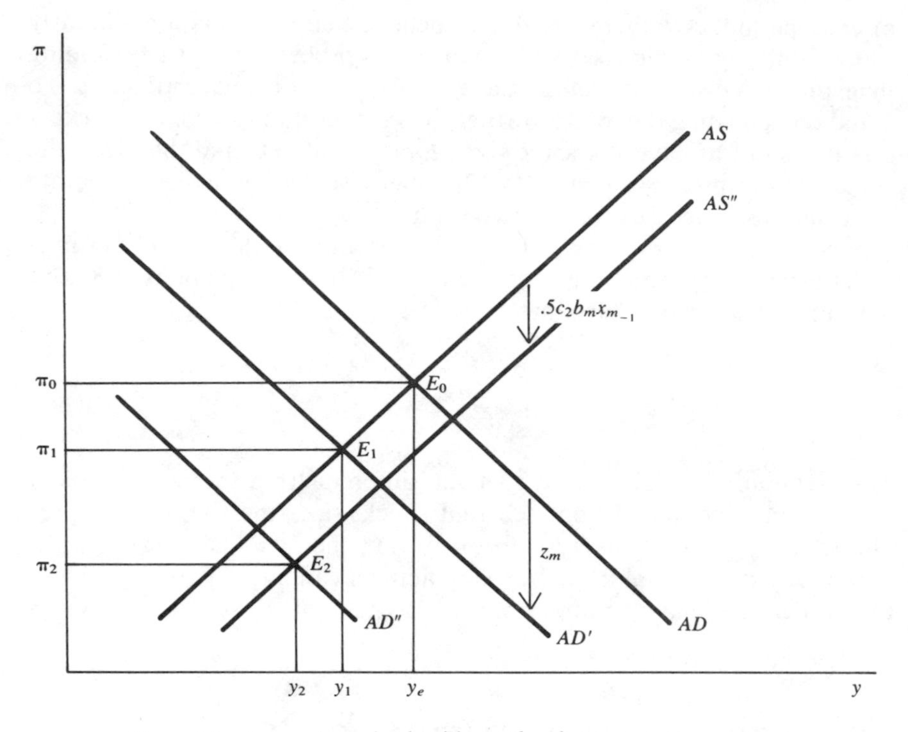

Figure 4-1 A monetary shock with overlapping contracts.

EXAMPLE

> Assume that the economy had an initial inflation rate and growth rate of the money supply equal to 12%. Now $z_m = -2\%$, so that $\mu + z_m = 10\%$ and the distance between AD' and AD in Figure 4-1 is 2%. As a result, let us say that π fell by 1% to 11%, which means that the real wage rises by 1%. If $a_4 = 3$, then y_1 will be below y_e by 3%.

Stabilization policy cannot overcome the decline in output from y_e to y_1 since the government was not able to anticipate the shock any better than private individuals. So far the situation is exactly the same as in the new classical model and no case can yet be made for activist policies, but in the second period a possible role for compensatory monetary policy does exist.

After the end of the first period z_m is translated into $b_m x_{m-1}$ for the second period. This is the value of the shock for that period, assuming that z_m is now zero. New wage contracts covering half of the workers will take into account the prediction for a lower inflation rate and the rate of change of wages will be correspondingly lower, but the second-year wage increases of the old contracts cannot be adjusted for this development and the average wage will not fall enough to get the economy back to equilibrium. The *AS* curve will be lower by $.5c_2b_mx_{m-1}$ to AS'' because of the partial reduction in π^e. The *AD* curve will shift as well. Since $\pi > z_m + \mu$ in the previous period, $(m - p)_{-1}$ will now be smaller and cause the *AD* curve to shift down. Also π^e is now lower and causes a further downward shift of *AD*. In addition, b_mx_{m-1}, being smaller than z_m in the previous period, forces the *AD* curve to move upward. All of these factors lead to an uncertain outcome for the location of the *AD* curve and the new short-run equilibrium. However, by looking directly at the *AS* curve of equation (4.11) we can measure the effect on output. In the second period $y = y_{-1} + .5a_4c_2b_mx_{m-1}$. Since $x_{m-1} < 0$, y falls again. Therefore AD'' must be the location of the *AD* curve that intersects AS'' at E_2 to produce y_2 and π_2.

EXAMPLE CONTINUES

Let it be assumed that *new* contracts correctly anticipate the inflation rate in the second period at 10.5% since the persistence of z_m from the previous period (b_mx_{m-1}) is now known. For these workers, the real wage is constant; for old contracts, the real wage rises by 12% − 10.5% = 1.5%. The average nominal wage rises by .5(12) + .5(10.5) = 11.25%, while the average real wage rises by 11.25 − 10.5 = .75%. Therefore, y falls by a further 2.25% if $a_4 = 3$.

The important feature of this result is that it is known beforehand and therefore avoidable, at least in principle. At the beginning of the period everyone was aware that the adverse shock would prevail to some extent. Half of the workers adjusted to this information, but the other half were "stuck" with their previous contracts and hence could not adjust. The average wage is therefore too high to allow full employment to return. In this setting the central bank can act to improve the situation. It can increase the predictable portion of the growth rate of the money supply to cancel the effect of the decline in the previously unpredictable portion. That is, the central bank should use its control over μ to offset its lack of control over z_m when it becomes obvious that the shock is pervasive. In the first period it could not increase μ equal to the negative z_m because it could not act in time. In the second period, however, it knows that the growth rate of the money supply will again be too low by the amount $b_m x_{m-1}$, but there is a catch-up factor as well. The problem is that during the two periods inflation was too low to bring about the correct real wage for y_e. In the first period the real wage rose by the difference between π^e and π, namely $c_7 z_m$, as can be seen by comparing equations (4.8) and (4.7). In the second period, the real wage rises again by $.5c_2 b_m x_{m-1}$. The problem facing the government is to reduce the real wage by a total of $[c_7 + .5c_2 b_m] z_m$, since $z_m = x_{m-1}$, by definition.

EXAMPLE CONTINUES

In the first period the real wage rose by 1% and in the second period it rose again by .75% for a total of 1.75%.

How does the government reduce the real wage? It does this by increasing the rate of inflation. From equation (4.7) we know that increasing μ will also increase π by c_0. Although equations (4.7) to (4.9) contain the undetermined coefficients, c_0 to c_9, the government will have made the calculations necessary to translate the c's into the a's of the structural model. It should be noted at this point that monetary policy is the appropriate instrument to use in this case since the original shock was of a monetary nature. If, instead, there had been a goods-market shock with z_g being negative, then the appropriate response would have been to use expansionary fiscal policy. The essential difference between the two instruments is their effect on the inflation rate and the real interest rate. From Chapter 2 it will be remembered that increasing the growth rate of the money supply will have a permanent effect on the inflation rate but no effect on the real interest rate, while increasing government expenditures has only a temporary effect on the inflation rate but raises the real interest rate in the long run. The same distinction applies to z_m and z_g. Since the aim of the government is to return the economy to its previous equilibrium, it wants to cancel the effects of shocks with an instrument that has essentially the same features as the shock: monetary policy for dealing with monetary shocks and fiscal policy for coping with goods-market shocks.

Once the economy is back in equilibrium the central bank will have to announce its plans for μ in the future so that negotiations for new labor contracts can take its actions into account. Although the shock will continue into the third period with a value of $b_m^2 z_m$, which of course is equal to $b_m x_{m-1}$, it is no longer necessary for the central bank to change the value of μ, since both old and new labor contracts can now incorporate the initial z_m into their expected inflation. If, on the other hand, the central bank continues to adjust μ, without an announcement to that effect, it will become the source of a new shock and therefore contribute to instability in the economy.

While dealing with the issue of information we can ask the question whether a government announcement of the continuation of the shock in the second period would have been sufficient to bring the economy back to equilibrium. The answer is clearly no, since everyone already had that information but because of overlapping contracts could not act on it. Accommodating policy was the only resource available to the government to achieve full employment. It may next be asked whether the government should discourage such overlapping contracts if they are known to lead to disequilibrium in the labor market from time to time. The answer depends largely on a comparison of the costs of contracting and the costs of disequilibrium in the labor market. If the economy is subjected to a large shock, it will become evident to all parties that recontracting is in their best interests. If, on the other hand, shocks are small relative to the costs of negotiating and the threat of strikes, then both workers and firms will accept the inevitable disequilibrium and continue to make long-term contracts.

So it would appear that active policy intervention is the only way in which the government can forestall a recession in the economy. However, before we conclude that stabilization policy will always improve the performance of the economy, it is important to consider what damage the central bank might cause if it does not take the correct action for a particular set of circumstances. Errors in policy may be caused by a lack of complete information. Although it was earlier posited that everyone knew the size of the first-period shock, one can never be certain about its pervasiveness. In other words, the parameter b_m may itself be a stochastic variable. If it is overestimated, then the central bank will provide too much stimulus to the economy. In an attempt to bring the growth rate of the money supply back on course it will in fact cause it to overshoot its target, raise the rate of inflation too high for it to be consistent with equilibrium, and create a new round of disequilibrium. Thus the issue is not whether the government has better information than the public, but how accurate the information is in an absolute sense. When the information is reliable, a strong case can be made for active policy intervention in an economy characterized by contracts, rather than auctions, and by pervasive shocks, rather than by completely random ones.

Next, we should consider the temptation for the government to use contractual obligations for its own purposes. Stanley Fischer, himself a critic of the new classical model, sounded a note of warning about the possibilities for activist policies: ''An attempt by the monetary authority to *exploit* the existing structure of contracts to produce behavior far different from that envisaged when contracts were signed would likely lead to the reopening of the contracts and, if the new behavior of the monetary authority were persisted in, a new structure of contracts."[7]

One final question needs to be answered: Which of the two features is more important in describing the institutionalist macro model, overlapping contracts or pervasive shocks? The answer is that they are both equally important. If contracts lasted only one period but shocks were pervasive, then in each period all the available information would be included in π^e and only random events would cause a divergence between y and y_e. Government intervention would not be needed in the second period of a continuing shock since all contracts are "new" every period and the real wage would come back into line. If there are long-term contracts but shocks last only one period, then they are again completely unpredictable and cannot be overcome by policy intervention.

4.6 ANTIINFLATION POLICY

At the same time as stabilization policy looks more attractive in an institutionalist model, antiinflation policy looks less attractive because it has undesirable real effects on the economy's output and employment. By way of comparison, the new classical model allows an economy to lower its rate of inflation without any side effects merely by lowering the growth rate of the money supply in a credible way. In the previous chapter it was established that announcing a lower μ and sticking to it would allow π and π^e to move down simultaneously and leave y undisturbed. However, in an economy with overlapping contracts this is not possible.[8] To consider this problem, we again postulate an economy starting from equilibrium with the central bank announcing and implementing a lower growth rate of the money supply at the beginning of a period. New labor contracts will be able to incorporate this information and one-half of all wages will increase at a lower rate. Starting from an initial position of $\pi_o^e = \pi_n^e = \mu_0$, π_n^e will now equal $\pi_o^e + c_0(\mu_1 - \mu_0)$, where μ_1 is the newly announced monetary growth rate. Now c_0 will *not* equal $1/(1 - a_3)$ as before because the expectations structure has been changed once more, and thus all the c's would have to be recalculated. No wonder the mechanics of rational expectations are so complicated! Since π_o^e has not changed, we have

$$\pi^e = \pi_o^e + .5c_0(\mu_1 - \mu_0) \tag{4.13}$$

[7] S. Fischer, "Long-term Contracts," p. 204; emphasis added.

[8] Since all events are predictable in this analysis, the pervasiveness of shocks is not at issue.

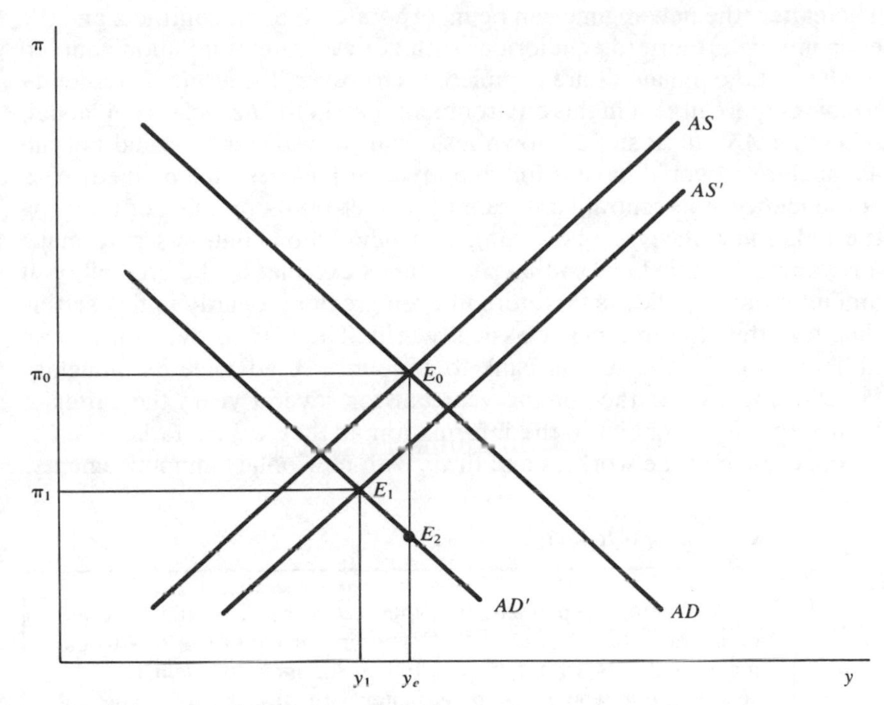

Figure 4-2 Antiinflation policy with overlapping contracts.

Whatever the value of c_0, we know that π will fall by that amount times the change in μ. However, π^e falls by only half that amount. Diagrammatically, this asymmetry can be shown in Figure 4-2. Starting from E_0, the AD curve shifts down by $\mu_1 - \mu_0$ plus a_3 times the change in π^e for a total of $(1 + .5a_3c_0)(\mu_1 - \mu_0)$. On the other hand, the AS curve shifts down by less than this amount, namely by $.5c_0(\mu_1 - \mu_0)$. The new equilibrium at E_1 must be to the left of y_e because the average real wage is too high to maintain full employment in the first period.

EXAMPLE

> Initially $\pi = \pi^e = \mu = 12\%$. Then the central bank announces and implements a lower growth rate of the money supply at 10%. Let us assume that both π and π^e for new contracts fall to 11%. But $\pi^e = .5(12) + .5(11) = 11.5\%$ and the average real wage rises by .5%. If $a_4 = 3$, y will fall by 1.5%.

Thereafter, the new regime can be incorporated into all contracts and the economy will return to equilibrium with a lower rate of inflation equal to μ when all the dynamics are completed. However, the issue of credibility becomes more urgent in this environment than in the new classical model. Since the *AS* curve shifted down less than the *AD* curve, π did not fall as much as it would have if full employment had been maintained. As a consequence, the central bank cannot deliver on its promise of reducing the inflation rate by $c_0(\mu_1 - \mu_0)$, and new labor contracts may make allowances for this fact, so that π_n^e declines even less. The credibility of antiinflationary policy is therefore in even greater jeopardy in this setting than was the case in a new classical world. The way to overcome these difficulties is for the central bank to announce in advance its monetary targets, not just for the coming year but for several years thereafter to allow contracts to build in the information as they expire rather than to surprise some of the workers and firms with new policy announcements.

EXAMPLE CONTINUES

A year before implementation the central bank should have announced its target of $\mu = 10\%$. The first group of workers would make contracts with 12% and 10% wage increases, whereas the second group would start a year later with 10% and 10%. The real wage would remain constant as $\mu = \pi = 12\%$ in the first year and $\mu = \pi = 10\%$ in the second.

In the new classical model, antiinflation policy reduces the nominal interest rate but maintains the long-run real interest rate, since expected inflation and the nominal rate fall together. The real interest rate must remain constant to prevent a change in aggregate demand and thus output. In the institutionalist model, however, since π^e is sluggish, the real interest rate will rise, as is consistent with lower output. The nominal interest rate may rise or fall. Rewriting the *IS* curve of equation (4.3), we get

$$(4.3') \quad i = (a_0 - y)/a_1 + x_g + \pi^e$$

With $x_g = 0$ and y and π^e both lower, the net effect on i cannot be determined a priori.

4.6.1 CANADIAN AND U.S. EXPERIENCE WITH ANTIINFLATION POLICY

Since 1975, both the Canadian and U.S. monetary authorities have instituted well-publicized antiinflation policies. They hoped to bring down

Table 4-1. *Growth rates of the money supply, inflation, unemployment, and interest rates in Canada and the United States, 1975–82*

	Growth rate of money supply		Inflation rate		Unemployment rate for prime-aged males		Short-term interest rate	
Year	Canada	U.S.	Canada	U.S.	Canada	U.S.	Canada	U.S.
1975	14.0	4.9	10.8	9.3	4.3	6.8	7.4	5.8
1976	8.0	6.7	9.5	5.2	4.2	5.9	8.9	5.0
1977	8.5	8.1	7.1	5.8	4.9	5.2	7.4	5.3
1978	10.1	8.3	6.5	7.4	5.2	4.3	8.6	7.2
1979	6.9	7.1	10.3	8.6	4.5	4.2	11.6	10.0
1980	6.4	6.6	11.0	9.3	4.8	5.9	12.8	11.5
1981	4.0	6.4	10.1	9.4	4.9	6.3	17.8	14.1
1982	1.2	8.5	10.7	6.0	8.1	8.8	13.8	10.7

Note: The money supply is defined as M1, inflation is measured by the GNE deflator, and interest rates are 90-day Treasury bill rates, in both countries. Unemployment is for males 25 years and over in Canada, 20 years and over in the United States.
Sources: Canada, *Bank of Canada Review*, tables 1, 57; U.S., *Economic Report of the President for 1983*, tables B61, B3, B31, B67.

the inflation rate by reducing the growth rate of the money supply, announcing in advance their targets for these growth rates. According to the new classical model, the inflation rate should fall, perhaps even faster initially than the reduction in money growth rates, nominal interest rates should also decline, but output and employment should be unaffected since predicted and actual inflation will continue to coincide. The institutionalist model, on the other hand, recognizes that expected inflation cannot fall quickly enough; therefore, inflation will be reduced by a smaller amount, and in the process, output will decline and the real interest rate will rise, while the nominal interest rate may rise or fall.

The evidence on this issue for the period 1975 to 1982 is presented in Table 4-1. In both countries the aim was to reduce the growth rate of M1 gradually from year to year. Except for 1978, the Canadian experience seems to conform to that goal, but in the United States the downward trend is not very evident. This may be explained by the fact that the Federal Reserve Board had targets for M2 and M3 as well and had to make compromises when not all targets could be reached simultaneously. This matter will receive further attention in Chapters 7 and 8. In both countries the inflation rate has not decreased to the same extent as the growth rate of M1. Especially in the period 1979–82, the inflation rate exceeded the growth rate of money by a substantial margin. This suggests that both economies were behaving more in line with the institutionalist model than with the new classical model. Moreover, by 1982 it was clear that output and employment were taking the brunt of the fight against inflation. The unemployment rate for prime-aged males, presumably the best available indicator of cyclical unemployment, reached levels that were unprecedented since the 1930s in both countries. The case for the institutionalist model is made even stronger when we look at nominal interest rates. Instead of falling, as they are required to do in a new classical model, they rise fairly consistently in both countries. Real interest rates must also have risen since π^e should have fallen. But even here there is a caveat. While antiinflation policy was a dominant theme in economic policy in the 1970s, government budget deficits increased as well. These can be predicted to increase both nominal and real interest rates and may have had a stronger influence than monetary policy. All in all, it is difficult to choose a clear winner from these two models on the basis of the evidence at hand, but the institutionalist model does have an advantage in explaining the deep recession of 1982.

4.7 WAGE INDEXATION

Another institutional feature of the labor market that has become prominent in the last decade is the reliance on cost-of-living adjustment (COLA) clauses in union contracts. One of the legacies of the inflationary experience of the 1970s is the great difficulty of predicting with any accuracy the rate of inflation for even a short time horizon. It did not take long for workers and firms to realize that instead of trying to achieve a certain real wage ex ante, it would be better to do it ex post. As a result, COLA clauses have appeared in more and more labor contracts. This institutional adaptation in the labor market has an important effect on the macroeconomy when it is subjected to different kinds of shocks, a matter that has been studied by Joanna Gray and Stanley Fischer, who concluded that full wage indexation helps to preserve the economy's equilibrium when it is faced with a money-market or goods-market shock, but that supply-side shocks are made worse by COLA clauses that prevent any adjustment of the real wage. In other words, indexation is a mixed blessing: It is desirable under some sets of circumstances, but not under others. With the aid of our *IS–LM–AS* model we can determine the basis for these conclusions.

Up to now the wage determination process has been forward-looking in the sense that ω was geared to π^e; with COLA clauses, wage determination becomes backward-looking because ω is set to whatever π happens to be. A contract with a COLA clause will not specify a timetable for specific nominal wages, but instead will contain a formula providing for wage adjustments at specific times in relation to changes in a price index, usually the Consumer Price Index (CPI). There are various formulae that are used: Some have a maximum amount to be paid in COLA, others provide a threshold value for inflation before COLA clauses come into effect; some are stated as "cents per point of the CPI," others are written in proportional terms. For our purposes, to pinpoint the effects of wage indexation, COLA clauses with proportional features will be used. The rate of change of nominal wages now becomes

$$\omega = f\pi + (1 - f)\pi^e \tag{4.14}$$

where f is the indexation factor, which can take any value between zero and one. Equation (4.14) stipulates that ω is a weighted average of π and π^e. If $f = 1$, there is full indexation, while $f = 0$ means that indexation is absent and $0 < f < 1$ involves partial indexation.

Since it is the labor market that is affected by the choice of indexation, it is the slope of the AS curve that will be influenced by indexation. If labor agreements are negotiated before shocks make themselves evident, unions and firms will have to make a choice about COLA clauses. If they choose not to use a COLA clause, then ω is predetermined by all the factors that are known at the time, but it cannot be changed afterward if shocks intervene; then the AS curve is as it was before. But if any degree of indexation is incorporated into labor contracts, then equation (4.14) is substituted into the AS curve, which is now

$$y = y_e - a_4(1 - f)(\pi^e - \pi) \tag{4.15}$$

The slope is now $1/[a_4(1 - f)]$. If $f = 1$, the AS curve becomes vertical and the distinction between π and π^e is unimportant. With $0 < f < 1$, the AS curve has a slope between $1/a_4$ and infinity.

We can now subject the economy to various shocks to see how it reacts with and without indexation. Let us consider demand shocks as contained in the AD curve, such as x_m or x_g. Suppose that z_m becomes either positive or negative after a period in which all x's were zero. From an inspection of equation (4.12), a positive z_m causes the AD curve to shift upward, while a negative z_m moves AD in the opposite direction. Both are shown in Figure 4-3. We also have two AS curves, $AS(f = 0)$ for zero indexation and $AS(f = 1)$ for full indexation, both of which intersect at E_0, the initial equilibrium before the shock appears.

With a positive shock and no indexation, the economy will move to E_1 with both higher inflation and higher output (π_1, y_1). With full indexation, the inflation rate rises more, to π_2, but output remains insulated at y_e. If y_e is an optimal point for the economy, then full indexation is the preferred way of setting wages. The same result applies if there is a negative shock, since E_3 is inferior to E_4.

Why does indexation have an advantage in this context? In a world buffeted by shocks it is impossible to maintain equilibrium because of the

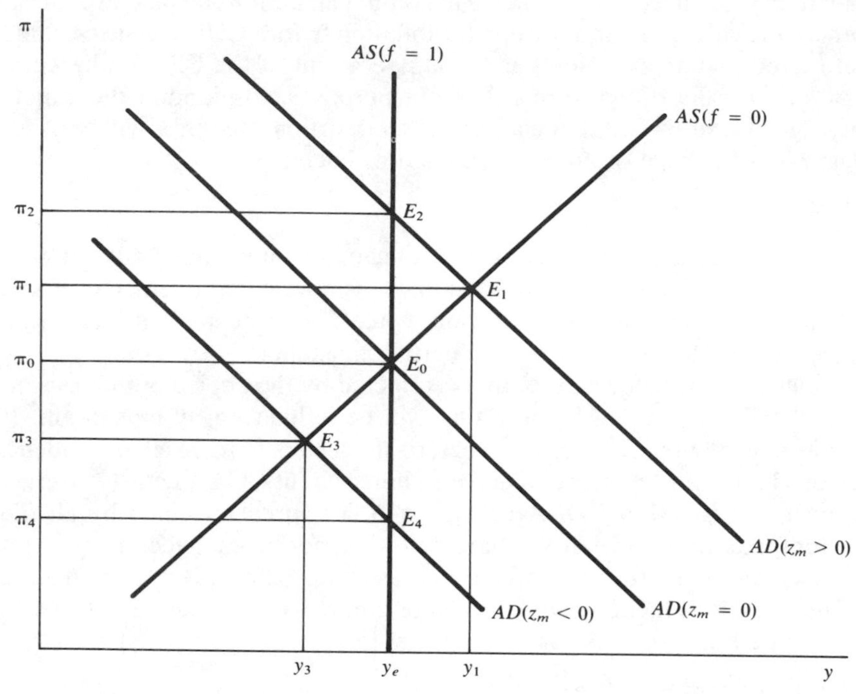

Figure 4-3 A monetary shock, with and without indexation.

difficulty in changing the nominal wage continuously. But contracts, rather than auctions, can provide the necessary flexibility of the nominal wage if these contracts incorporate COLA clauses. By making the nominal wage more flexible, it gives the real wage greater stability. Therefore, in a stochastic environment what is needed are *contingent contracts* that stipulate certain outcomes depending on a list of events that may transpire. COLA clauses are an example of such contingent contracts. They are easily defined and enforced: All that is needed is a price index that is acceptable to both sides. Since individual unions and firms cannot influence the CPI to any extent, it is the one used most often in COLA clauses.[9]

In summary, we can have both long-term contracts and equilibrium if full indexation is included in such contracts when the economy faces unknown influences on the location of the *AD* curve. This advantage of COLA clauses is, unfortunately, not universal. When the economy is subjected to supply shocks from the labor market, the optimum is only partial indexation.

[9] Why would unions oppose the use of a price index heavily weighted by the firm's own product?

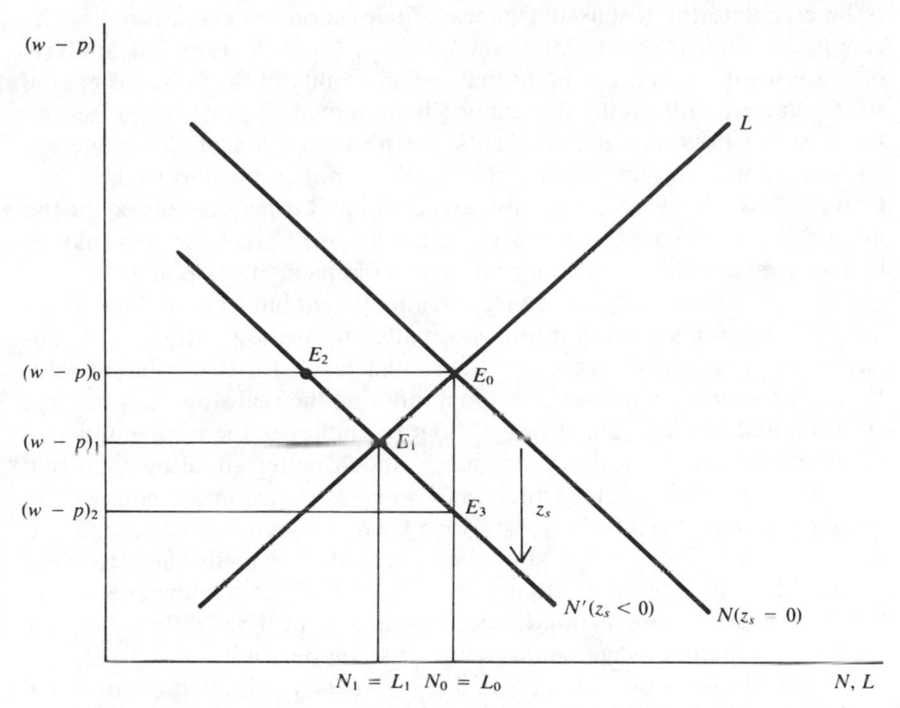

Figure 4-4 A supply shock, with and without indexation.

Let us therefore explore the effects of a supply shock. In this instance, it is no longer possible to identify the preshock y with equilibrium in the labor market, and for that reason it is necessary to see how shocks affect that market directly. In Figure 4-4, the supply and demand curves for labor are drawn. Initially $z_s = 0$. Allow z_s to take a negative value. This shifts the N curve down by the value of z_s because it represents an unexpected deterioration in the marginal product of labor. To move to a new short-run equilibrium at E_1, the real wage should fall to $(w - p)_1$, but unless there is just the right degree of indexation this will not happen. With full indexation, $(w - p)_0$ remains, leading to unemployment equal to E_0E_2. Without any indexation, π will rise by $[(a_1a_2 + a_3 + a_3a_4 + a_1a_2a_4)/(a_1 + a_3a_4 + a_1a_2a_4)]z_s$ as shown by equation (3.10) in Chapter 3, where all the determinants of π are indicated in a rational expectations framework. If $a_2 = 1$ and $a_3 = 0$, as both Gray and Fischer assume, then $(w - p)$ will fall by the value of z_s, leading to $(w - p)_2$, which is now too low for the new equilibrium at E_1, and the labor market moves to E_3 on the demand curve. Thus $(w - p)_1$, the optimal real wage, requires partial indexation with the optimal size of f depending on the slopes of the N and L curves.

To complete the discussion of wage indexation we should look at its role in the context of antiinflationary policy. From the previous analysis of this issue it was quite evident that the credibility of the policy was vital to its success. But credibility cannot be assumed; it must be earned on the basis of previous achievements. If the reputation of the monetary authority for living up to its stated goals is not particularly high, then COLA clauses may be especially attractive, and it may be easier for the authorities to convince the private sector to use COLA clauses than to believe in the ability of the central bank to implement its policy.

The lack of credibility can cause unemployment but COLA clauses can keep the economy at equilibrium no matter what the relationship is between the announced target and the actual result for the inflation rate. By setting wages according to ex post inflation the real wage can be kept constant and the only uncertainty about the policy is the timing and size of the reduction in the inflation rate, a much better situation than one with rising unemployment, which makes perseverance in the policy even more suspect. With COLA clauses, long-term contracts can be maintained and the complications of credibility are avoided. Of course, the other side of the coin is the possibility that supply shocks will also intervene just as full indexation is implemented, making adjustment more difficult than it would be if the real wage could maintain some flexibility.

In view of these conclusions it is not surprising to find that in countries such as Brazil, Israel, and Italy, where high and variable inflation is the primary concern, almost all contracts are fully indexed, whereas in Canada and the United States partial indexation is more prevalent, presumably because of the realization that real shocks such as the energy crisis are also sources of uncertainty.

4.8 CAN MACROECONOMIC POLICY CHANGE THE NATURAL RATE OF UNEMPLOYMENT?

In a new classical model of the economy, predictable macroeconomic policy is unable to move the economy away from the natural rate of unemployment, nor is it able to change this rate, because the natural rate is an equilibrium concept in the labor market. In an institutionalist model, however, we know that even announced changes in monetary policy can increase output and reduce unemployment in the short run because of the existence of long-term contracts. Given the ability to do this, is it worth the effort? To a new classical economist the answer is no because he would point not only to the temporary effects of the policy but also to the undesirability of "disequilibrium" that it creates. To an institutionalist, however, the possibility of a permanent improvement in the labor market makes this a useful experiment. But how can macroeconomic policy affect the long-run equilibrium in the labor market when we had previously concluded that only microeconomic policies that increase labor mobility could be counted on for such results? To answer this question James Tobin has suggested that

> it is hard to resist or refute the suspicion that the operational [natural rate of unemployment] gravitates toward the average rate of unemployment actually experienced. Among the mechanisms which produce that result are improvements in unemployment compensation and other benefits enacted in response to higher unemployment, loss of on-the-job training and employability by the unemployed, defections to the informal and illegal economy, and a slowdown in capital formation as business firms lower their estimates of needed capacity.[10]

Remember that a positive natural rate of unemployment arises from the general fact that there are some square pegs (the unemployed) that do not fit into an equal number of round holes (vacancies). If the economy experiences excess demand in the labor market, this would be analagous to forcing some of the square pegs into some of the round holes by force. The longer that pressure is applied, the rounder the pegs and the squarer the holes become, with the end result that the number of mismatches has been permanently reduced. For instance, on-the-job training for low-skilled youth, in an economy that has no room for them in their original state, may give them the skills they need to increase their employability thereafter. The same argument can probably be made about improving geographic mobility.

The main force of this proposition is that pushing the economy past the natural rate of unemployment will reduce that rate permanently; conversely, trying merely to stay at the natural rate will increase it over time as market rigidities set in. In this setting monetary policy can take an activist role. With overlapping contracts, expanding the growth rate of the money supply can lower the real interest rate as the nominal rate falls faster than expected inflation. Aggregate demand will expand as the *AD* curve shifts up to *AD'* in Figure 4-5. The *AS* curve will also shift up, but by less than the *AD* curve. The new short-run equilibrium is at E_1, where the increased output is produced by some of the square pegs that are precariously sitting in round holes. This part of the sequence of events is no different from what we had looked at before, but an additional feature in this context is the possibility that y_e will also increase, and even if E_1 cannot be sustained in the long run, the economy will not move back to E_0. In this light, many economists who do not share the fatalist view of the new classical school that the natural rate of unemployment is a fixed quantity are afraid that the lack of activist policies will in fact lead to a

[10] J. Tobin, "Stabilization Policy Ten Years After," *Brookings Papers on Economic Activity*, 1:1980, p. 61.

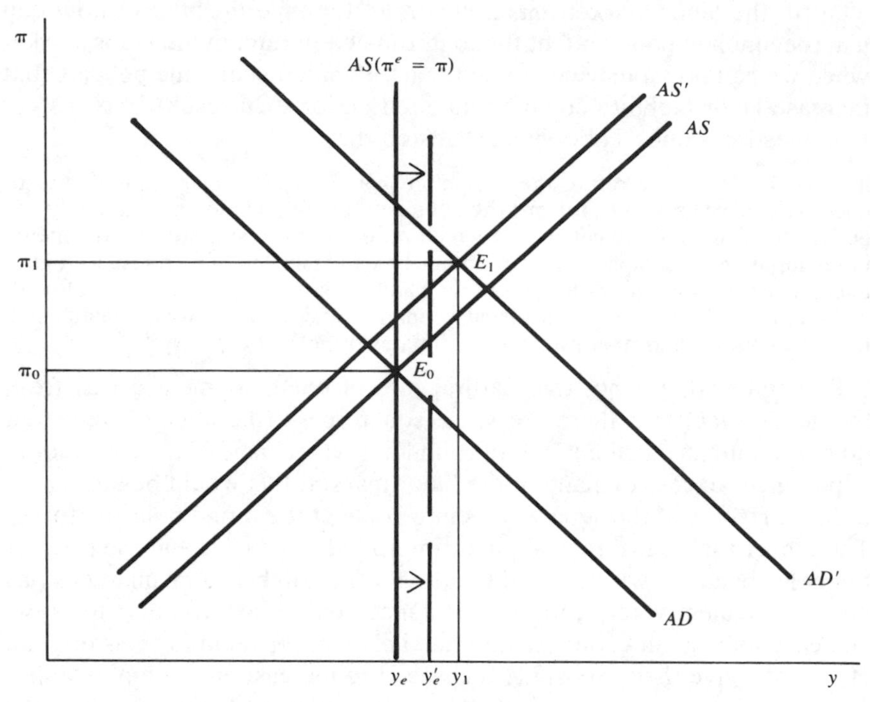

Figure 4-5 Expansionary monetary policy and equilibrium output.

continuing erosion of our goal of full employment. However, they would also have to concede that forcing y above y_e for a period of time may not be the most efficient way of reducing the natural rate of unemployment; it may be better to concentrate on "micro" policies that improve job matching.

4.9 SUMMARY

In this chapter the case for stabilization policy has been presented. It has been based on the same *IS–LM–AS* model developed in Chapter 2. It also shared some similarities with the new classical model outlined in Chapter 3, such as the insistence that expectations about future inflation be "rational." However, it does differ in a number of important respects:

1. The operation of the labor market is based on contracts, not auctions, making disequilibrium in that market possible.
2. These contracts are often in the best interests of all concerned, because equilibrium in the labor market is not the only goal; minimizing transactions costs is another.

3. Although it is difficult to define a "period" in terms of calendar time, it is possible that shocks last for more than one period.
4. The pervasiveness of shocks makes long-term contracts less desirable, but still does not provide an overwhelming argument in favor of auctions in labor markets.
5. Instead of wages always being determined by expected inflation, some contracts provide for COLA clauses that essentially determine the real wage ex ante and the nominal wage ex post.

From these differences in the structure of the model arise differences about the role of stabilization policy. In the institutionalist model, the chief results are as follows:

1. Predictable monetary policy does affect real variables such as output and employment in the short run because of the long-term contracts.
2. Monetary policy can help to bring the economy back to equilibrium faster after a random monetary shock to the economy that becomes pervasive than if it were left to its own resources.
3. Monetary policy has a less easily predictable effect on inflation, making it a less reliable instrument for reducing inflation.
4. Full wage indexation is optimal when monetary uncertainty is the primary problem facing an economy, but only partial indexation is best when supply shocks intervene.
5. Activist monetary policy may be able to reduce the natural rate of unemployment and increase output permanently by improving the workings of the labor market, but it may not be the best policy to achieve this result.

Which is the better model for contemporary macroeconomic analysis? Which will give the better answer to certain pressing questions about our current state of affairs? What should and should not be done about the rate of inflation and the rate of unemployment? We still do not have a satisfactory answer to these questions and we may never have one. In some circumstances one model dominates the other, but "truth" in economics is neither universal nor eternal. As a student of macroeconomics and monetary policy you should be less persuaded by dogma and more by common sense.

EXERCISES

1. Compare and contrast, μ, x_{m-1}, and z_m.
2. Assume that predictions about the inflation rate were made two years in advance according to the following pattern: 1978 – 14%, 13%;

1979 – 10%, 11%; 1980 – 11%, 11%; 1981 – 12%, 11%; and 1982 – 10%, 8% (e.g., at the beginning of 1978, π^e for 1978 was 14% and π^e for 1979 was 13%).

(a) Calculate ω for 1979 to 1982 using the overlapping contract model of this chapter.

(b) Given the answer in (a), if the central bank happened to stabilize the inflation rate at 11% for the entire period, predict movements in y using the AS curve in exercise 4, Chapter 2.

(c) What could the central bank do to keep y closer to y_e?

3. Assume that all labor contracts are signed at the same time and last for two years. Also shocks last for two years and then disappear entirely. Substitute these features in the macro model and indicate whether they change the conclusion about policy effects in the institutional model.

4. Assume that workers form inflationary expectations according to the equation $\pi^e = .67\pi_{-1} + .33\pi_{-2}$. Actual inflation in 1977 was 7.1%, in 1978 6.5%, in 1979 10.3%, in 1980 11.0%, in 1981 10.1%, and in 1982 10.7%.

(a) What happens to the real wage between 1979 and 1982 if $f = 0$ and if $f = .5$?

(b) On a cumulative basis, does the real wage rise more with $f = 0$ or $f = 1$?

FURTHER READING

Fischer, S., "Long-term Contracts, Rational Expectations, and the Optimal Money Supply," *Journal of Political Economy,* 85, February 1977, pp. 191–206. This article points out the macroeconomic effects of overlapping contracts in the labor market.

Gordon, R. J., "Output Fluctuations and Gradual Price Adjustment," *Journal of Economic Literature,* 19, June 1981, pp. 493–530. Makes a counterattack on the new classical model.

Gray, J. A., "Wage Indexation: A Macroeconomic Approach," *Journal of Monetary Economics,* 2, April 1976, pp. 221–35. The first published work on the macroeconomic effects of different degrees of wage indexation.

Okun, A. M., *Prices and Quantities: A Macroeconomic Analysis,* Washington, D.C., Brookings Institution, 1981. Also seeks to explain why labor and goods markets may not clear at all times.

CHAPTER 5

The demand for money

5.1 INTRODUCTION

Given its prominence in the previous three chapters it would appear that behavior in the labor market is the crucial element in the performance of the economy, but the money market is equally important for a full understanding of the *IS–LM–AS* model, especially on the issue of what monetary policy can and cannot do. In this chapter the demand for money will be investigated more closely than was done in Chapter 2, and then in Chapter 6 we will look at the process by which monetary policy influences the supply of money, that is, the links between the central bank on the one hand and commercial banks and the public on the other. Whereas the last two chapters have been concerned with the debate about the position and slope of the aggregate-supply curve, the next two chapters will introduce the reader to the disagreements among economists about the nature and the role of the *LM* curve in determining macroeconomic variables such as the inflation rate, the interest rate, and output.

From Chapter 2 we can write the *LM* curve, the equilibrium condition in the money market, as

$$(5.1) \quad m - p = a_2 y - a_3 i$$

where m is the natural log of the nominal money supply, p is the natural log of the price level so that $(m - p)$ is the natural log of real money balances, y is the natural log of income, and i is the interest rate. The two parameters, a_2 and a_3, are both positive elasticities. Since the money market is presumed to be in equilibrium at all times, given that the interest rate can respond almost instantaneously to disequilibrium, m measures not only the supply of money but also the amount of money demanded. From that perspective, equation (5.1) stipulates that the demand for real money balances is determined by income and the interest rate. This is a strong statement about behavior in the money market, because it isolates only a few, readily measurable variables to pinpoint the location of the *LM* curve and leaves out of the demand function all other possible influences. It also makes the *LM* curve a useful analytical device since we can identify the mechanism by which monetary policy is transmitted to macroeconomic activity.

In an inflationary environment, we can write the *LM* curve as

$$(5.2) \qquad \mu - \pi = a_2 y - a_3 i - (m - p)_{-1}$$

where μ is the growth rate of nominal money balances and π is the rate of inflation since $(m - p) - (m - p)_{-1} = \mu - \pi$. From this specification, it is clear that μ, under the control of the central bank, influences π, y, and i, the three important macroeconomic variables. If the demand for money were more complicated than equations (5.1) or (5.2), in the sense of having more explanatory variables or having a large random component, then "manipulating" the *LM* curve through monetary policy and thereby influencing the other variables in the economy becomes a much more tenuous proposition. Furthermore, in order to *use* the *LM* curve in practice, we must be able to agree on how to measure μ, y, π, i, and $(m - p)_{-1}$ and we need "robust" estimates of a_2 and a_3. If this cannot be done, the monetary authorities would be unable to decide on the current position of the *LM* curve nor on the appropriate value of μ to reach the targets for y, π, and i that they want to achieve.

Despite earlier disputes about the slope of the *LM* curve between Keynesians and monetarists, there is now fairly universal agreement that income and the interest rate are indeed both important determinants of the demand for real money balances. Although there may be many motives for holding money and many theories to explain these motives, the end result is almost always that y and i are identified as *the* important determinants. Nevertheless, disagreements continue, both at the theoretical level and at the empirical level. In the former category such questions as (1) what should we expect the size of a_2 to be? (2) what is the role of total wealth? and (3) what is the importance of other rates of return? remain contentious. In the latter category, (1) the appropriate measure of y and i and (2) the relevant definition of money to estimate the demand function have not been settled with finality. We now turn to these two sets of issues and then look at some of the empirical evidence for money-demand functions in Canada and the United States.

5.2 THEORETICAL FOUNDATIONS FOR THE DEMAND FOR MONEY

Why do people hold money? This question has exercised economists for many generations and we still have no satisfactory answer. Unlike goods and services, money does not provide utility directly. Instead, the existence of money must be able to increase utility indirectly by improving the transactions technology whereby we exchange goods that we have for those that we want. An improvement in this technology allows us to consume more goods with the same endowment of resources and thereby increases welfare. Money is therefore useful because it represents an improvement in transactions technology over barter trade. In this chapter, it will be taken for granted that people want money, and we ask the following question: What determines the amount of money demanded in the macroeconomy?

John Maynard Keynes provided us with three motives for holding money balances: (1) the *transactions* motive, (2) the *precautionary* motive, and (3) the *speculative* or idle-balance motive. Of these, the second motive is becoming of less and less importance. With the increasing availability of all-purpose credit cards, such as Mastercard and Visa, and of standby credits from banks, very few individuals or firms keep sizable money balances specifically as a precaution against unexpected expenditures. In any case, the precautionary motive would add little to our understanding of the total demand for money balances; income and interest rates have been found to be important here as well. We can now look more closely at the transactions motive and the speculative motive.

5.2.1 THE TRANSACTIONS MOTIVE

One of the reasons that people hold money is that their income stream does not coincide exactly with their expenditure stream. In general, households spend more frequently than they receive income, while businesses spend less frequently than they receive income. A typical profile of money balances for households and firms is shown in Figure 5-1. Notice that the "sawtooth" effect differs for the two groups: For the former, money balances decline from the beginning to the end of the period; for the latter, they increase. Since income is a *flow* per period of time whereas money holdings refer to a *stock* at a point in time, the relationship between them is one of *velocity,* the speed at which money moves through the economy or the number of times a dollar turns over per unit of time. As an example, in Canada, GNP in current prices for 1981 was $328,501

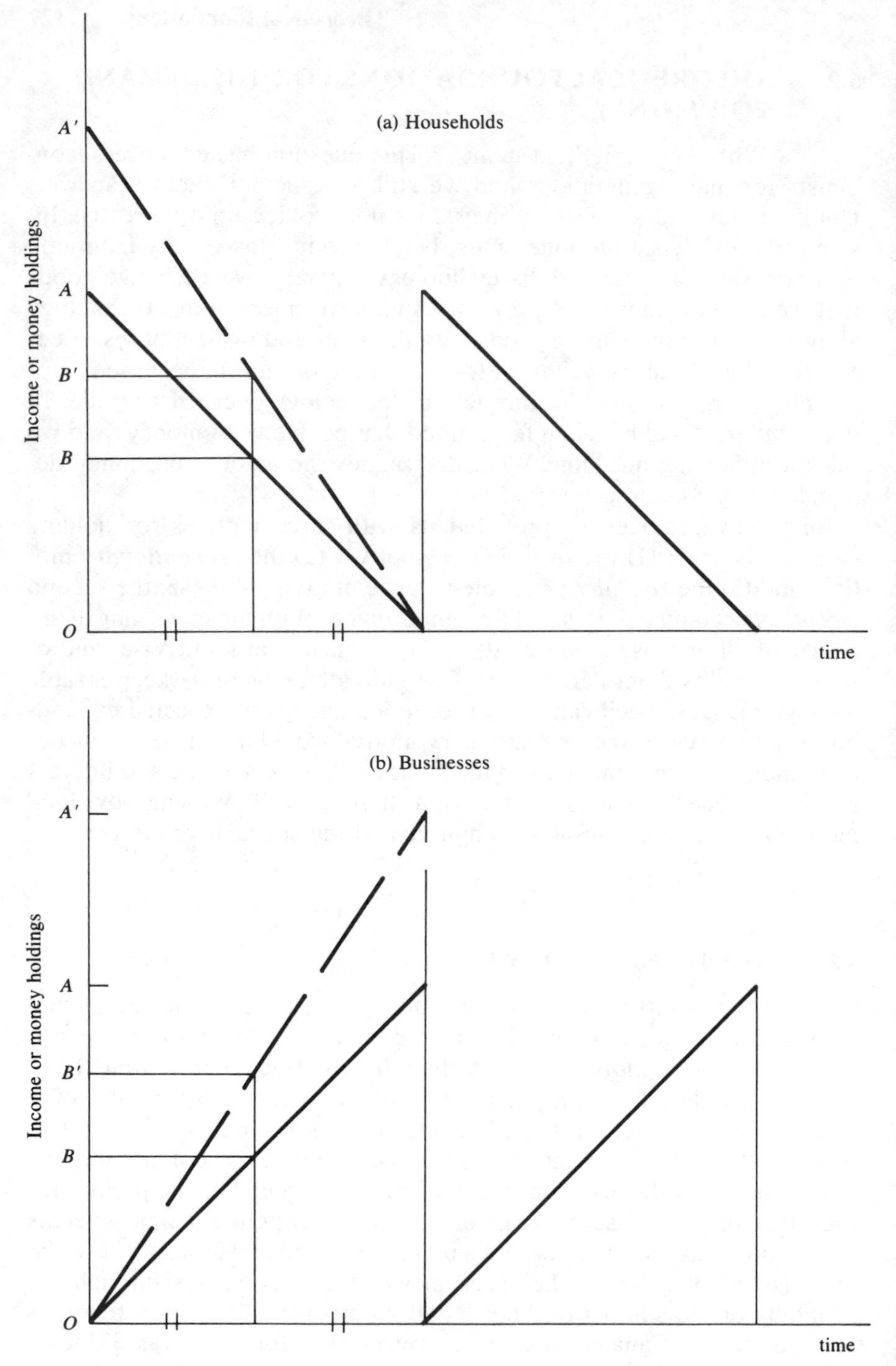

Figure 5-1 Income and expenditure patterns of households and businesses.

million, whereas the amount of money (measured by M1) at the end of 1981 was $26,592 million. This allows us to calculate the velocity (measured at the end of 1981) as 12.4. This means that each dollar was used about 12 times in generating income in 1981. In the United States, GNP in current prices was $2,937.7 billion in 1981, whereas M1 was $440.9 billion at the end of the year, giving rise to a velocity of 6.7. At present we are not concerned with the fact that velocity in Canada is twice as large as in the United States; interest centers instead on the evidence that the United States, with a much higher income than Canada, also has much larger money holdings. If velocity is treated as constant over time, the relationship between income and money is as follows: A given proportionate increase in real income will lead to the same proportionate increase in real money balances. Therefore, as a first approximation a_2 should be equal to one, remembering that a_2 is an elasticity represented by the ratio of percentage changes in real money to percentage changes in real income. This can be seen in Figure 5-1. Household income is initially *OA* per period of time. *Average* cash holdings, assuming a straight-line expenditure pattern, are equal to one-half of income or the amount of money held halfway during the period. This is equal to *OB* or *BA*.

EXAMPLE

> If income is $1,000 per month, average cash holdings will be equal to .5(1000) + .5(0) = $500, if we use the beginning and end of period holdings to calculate the average. This number does not change if we measure cash holdings more frequently. In the middle of the first week the household has $875, in the second week it has $625, and so on; the average is still $500.

For businesses, average cash holdings can be measured in a similar manner. Their initial money holdings are zero, but end-of-period cash is *OA*, for an average of *OB*. Halfway through the period, households and firms each hold *OB* of money to support a total income of *OA*. Now assume that income for the economy rises to *OA'*. For both groups, average cash holdings rise to *OB'*. Since the distance *BB'* is a constant proportion of *AA'*, the stipulated increase in income leads to the same proportional increase in money holdings, and for that reason $a_2 = 1$.

Velocity, in natural logs, can be written as

$$v = p + y - m \tag{5.3}$$

remembering that p, y, and m are also expressed in natural logs. The antilog of v is the ratio of nominal income to nominal money balances. Is v a constant? On a trivial level, we can change velocity merely by redefining income for a shorter or longer period. For example, Canadian GNP in the fourth quarter of 1981 was $85,196 million; with M1 still $26,592 million at the end of 1981, velocity is now 3.2, about one-fourth of its previous level. Thus velocity can change with alterations in the accounting period, but this is of no great consequence in a macromodel and will henceforth be disregarded.

More important, velocity reacts to changes in interest rates. The reason for this is that holding money balances causes individuals to incur an opportunity cost that can be measured by the interest income forgone from holding other assets such as bonds. The higher is this opportunity cost, the smaller are desired money balances for any given level of income and the larger is velocity. In other words, an increase in the interest rate causes people to "economize" on money balances. But there are limits to this process. It is unlikely that anyone would run to the bank or a broker to sell a bond for just the right amount to make each purchase of goods and services because there are transactions costs incurred, even if they only involve wearing out shoe leather. In general, there will be an optimal amount of money to hold that just equates the marginal cost of holding money (i.e., interest forgone) with the marginal benefit of money (i.e., the transactions costs forgone).

EXAMPLE

> An individual is paid $52,000 once a year; the current interest rate is 12%; a trip to the bank costs $2.30. This person chooses to place the $52,000 in an interest-earning asset and withdraw $1,000 a week for spending. This is the optimal decision since the forgone interest on $1,000 is $1{,}000 \times .12/52 = \$2.3077$ per week. If transactions costs now rise, it will pay to go to the bank less frequently and make larger withdrawals; if the interest rate rises, the individual will go to the bank more frequently and make smaller withdrawals.

This type of behavior gives rise to the so-called square-root inventory rule, because optimal inventories of money are related to the square root of income, interest rates, and transactions costs. On this basis the demand for money is determined by

$$(5.4) \qquad m = .5(y + p + \ln J - \ln 2 - \ln i)$$

where J is the cost of a trip to the bank or other transactions cost.

PROOF

> Transactions costs are nJ, where n stands for the number of trips to the bank; the opportunity cost of holding money is $iY/2n$ since $Y/2n$ represents the amount of money held between trips to the bank, defining Y as nominal income. Adjusting n to minimize the sum of these two costs involves differentiating the total cost function with respect to n and setting the result equal to zero. Thus $J - 2iY/4n^2 = 0$. Solving for n produces the optimal number of trips to the bank, $n = (iY/2J)^{.5}$. Thus average cash holdings should be $Y/2n = Y/2(iY/2J)^{.5}$. Squaring this result produces $Y^2/4(iY/2J) = JY/2i$. Taking the square root again finally gives the optimal level of money holdings as $(JY/2i)^{.5}$. This is the same as equation (5.4) above, once we take logs of all variables.

This forces a_2 and a_3 to be equal to .5 and also places a parameter of .5 next to p, instead of the previous coefficient of one. Incidentally, the requirement that $a_3 < 1$ was an important assumption in the dynamics of Chapter 3; we now have a theoretical argument for it.

Nevertheless, there are two factors that may make it impossible to follow the square-root rule with any precision. First there is the *integer constraint*. For example, if interest is paid only on the minimum monthly balance in a savings account, it makes no sense to optimize over a shorter period than one month. In general, people hold larger balances when integer constraints apply than when they do not. Thus a_2 becomes larger as more money is held at each level of income and a_3 becomes smaller as people react less to interest-rate changes. Therefore, $.5 < a_2 < 1$ and $0 < a_3 < .5$ are what we expect to find in the empirical evidence.

Second, there is the issue of money balances following a *random walk*. Instead of the highly predictable pattern of money balances as shown in Figure 5-1, income and/or expenditures could have a large stochastic element, which implies that money balances "wander" up and down, almost aimlessly. Retail stores may be especially affected by such a pattern. However, they should still optimize their money holdings in such a way that when they hit a lower bound (perhaps zero), they cash some bonds to replenish their cash balances, or when they hit some upper bound, they buy bonds to reduce cash to some predetermined amount. Average money holdings in this environment, according to a paper by Merton Miller and Daniel Orr, turn out to be $(4/3)(3J \text{ var } Y/4i)^{1/3}$.[1] From this formula it can

[1] M. Miller and D. Orr, "A Model of the Demand for Money by Firms," *Quarterly Journal of Economics*, 80, August 1966, pp. 413–35.

be seen that the variance of income is the scale variable instead of income itself; therefore, the greater the random element in income or expenditure patterns, the larger should money holdings be. Also, the income and interest-rate elasticities, a_2 and a_3, are now reduced to $\frac{1}{3}$; however, since a_2 is now attached to var Y, no direct comparison can be made to the square-root rule.

One other aspect of the inventory rule for money holdings requires elaboration. Unlike the *LM* curve of earlier chapters, where the natural log of money holdings was related to the interest rate, equation (5.4) suggests that the relationship is really between money and the interest rate, *both* expressed as natural logs. This presents a problem for the *IS–LM* model. Remember from the discussion in Chapter 2 that the cost of transferring goods from one period to the next was $(1 + i)$, the natural log of which is approximated by i. This is the appropriate relative price of goods between two periods and is relevant for the investment decision in the *IS* curve. But the opportunity cost of holding money from one period to the next is given by i, not $(1 + i)$.

EXAMPLE

Goods carried in inventories rise in value from $1,000 to $1,100 in one year if the interest rate is 10%. The relative price from one year to the next is $1 + i$ or 1.1. The return on $1,000 held as money for one year is zero, whereas the return on a $1,000 bond is $100 if the interest rate is 10%; the opportunity cost of holding money is $100 or 10 cents on the dollar.

Therefore, the *LM* curve should have $\ln i$ as the interest rate variable to make a_3 the appropriate elasticity. But we cannot have both i and $\ln i$ in the same model without hopeless confusion; therefore, we will retain i as *the* interest rate variable in the theoretical model, since both i and $\ln i$ move in the same direction. However, because the value of a_3 plays an important part in the dynamics, discussion of empirical results for the money market will focus on $\ln i$.[2]

Substituting equation (5.3) into the *LM* equation of (5.1) leads to

$$v = (1 - a_2)y + a_3 i \tag{5.5}$$

Velocity rises with increases in the interest rate because people will absorb the higher transactions costs of going to the bank or to the broker

[2] Technically speaking, a_3 is a semielasticity when i is used, but a full-fledged elasticity when $\ln i$ is used.

when the opportunity cost of holding money rises. Furthermore, since $0 < a_2 < 1$, velocity also increases with income. If equation (5.4) is the appropriate relationship, then

$$(5.5') \quad v = .5(y + p) + .5(\ln i + \ln 2 - \ln J)$$

Aside from being more specific about the value of a_2 and a_3, equation (5.5′) also stipulates that velocity depends on the price level and transactions costs as people economize on money holdings.

It is sometimes argued that the expected rate of inflation has an effect on velocity and therefore should be included in the demand-for-money function. For example, with inflation expected to be 10%, the demand for real balances is lower than when expected inflation is only 5%. But this link must be carefully explored. When assets consist only of money and bonds, both denominated in nominal terms, neither asset has an advantage over the other when inflation rises; in both cases their purchasing power is reduced by the rate of inflation. However, higher inflation leads to higher nominal interest rates, which we know will reduce the demand for real money balances. Therefore, it is not necessary to include expected inflation as an additional variable in the demand-for-money function. The nominal interest rate captures both the real opportunity cost of holding money and the inflationary effects on the purchasing power of money balances.

In summary, the transactions motive for holding money provides a theoretical underpinning for the *LM* curve. Not only does it make for an easier understanding for the reasons behind the positive relationship to income and the negative relationship to interest rates, but we also can get some idea of the factors that influence the absolute size of the parameters, a_2 and a_3. Finally, the relationship between the demand for money and velocity is established by the existing transactions technology.

5.2.2 THE SPECULATIVE MOTIVE

Having dismissed earlier the importance of the precautionary motive for holding money, we are left with the speculative motive. In his book *General Theory,* Keynes broke with the past by asserting that individuals may hold money balances in addition to those required for transactions purposes. Previously, classical economists argued that it made no sense to have *idle* money balances in a portfolio, when bonds pay interest but money does not. However, since most bonds are *marketable* (with the exception of savings bonds), they can fluctuate in value as interest rates change. In fact, the price of a bond moves inversely with the interest rate.

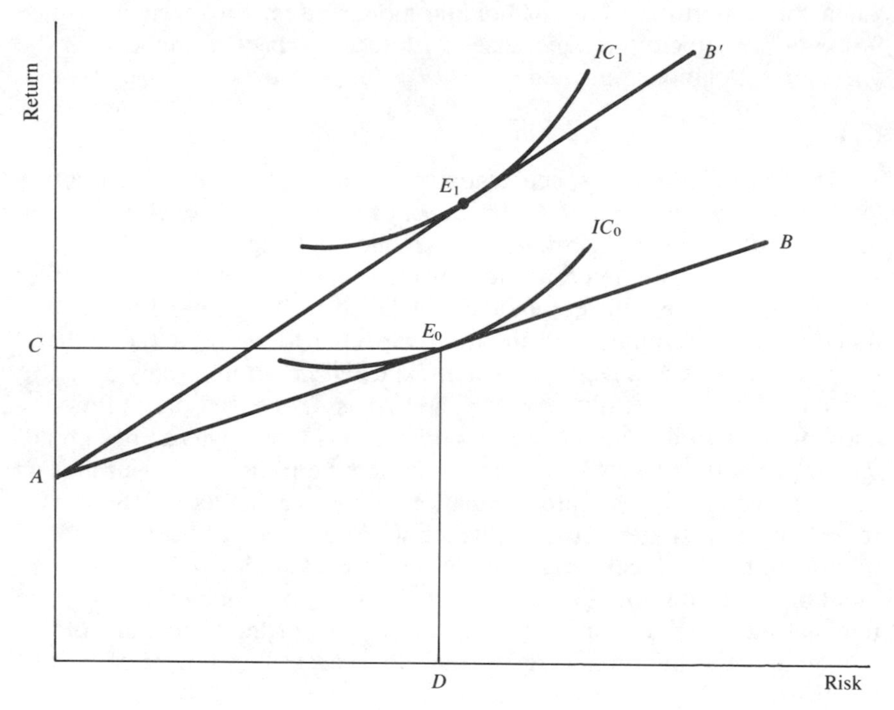

Figure 5-2 An equilibrium portfolio.

EXAMPLE

> A long-term bond with a 10% coupon rate and a face value of $100 will fall to a market value of $80 when interest rates rise to 12.5%, since the $10 interest payment represents a 12.5% return on $80.

This variability in the market value of bonds forces us to think of two characteristics associated with assets: *return* and *risk*. Money has zero return but it also has zero risk, whereas bonds have both a positive return and positive risk. Since return is desirable but risk is not – leaving out those individuals who love risk for its sense of adventure – the typical portfolio will contain some of both assets.

In Figure 5-2 an equilibrium portfolio is depicted with return and risk measured on the two axes. Since the investor is trying to minimize risk, an indifference curve between return and risk will have a positive slope. The market constraint, drawn as the line *AB*, also has a positive slope. The slope of this line indicates the extent to which the market for bonds allows the individual investor to combine risk and return; an investor who wants a higher return is forced to accept higher risk as well. Thus *OA* is the measure for the return on an absolutely riskless bond (e.g., a Treasury bill). The optimal position for the investor is the highest attainable indifference curve, moving northwest, subject to the market constraint. This is the position E_0 on IC_0. Given the attributes of money and bonds, we can translate *OC* of return and *OD* of risk into a unique portfolio of these two assets.

From the point of view of consistency with the *LM* curve we can conduct the mental experiment of an increase in the interest rate to determine its effect on money holdings. A higher interest rate causes the market constraint *AB* to rotate upward to *AB'* as more return is available with the same level of risk. The investor can now reach a higher indifference curve and finds a new equilibrium at E_1, which is drawn to the right of E_0. Here more risk is accepted, and this can only be done by holding more bonds and less money, verifying the inverse relationship between interest rates and money holdings. But we cannot be sure that this will always be the outcome. If the new equilibrium is to the left of the old one, less risk is accepted and money balances will increase. From price theory we are familiar with this ambiguous outcome. The substitution effect dictates that an increase in return should lead to larger holdings of the asset that provides that return, but the greater income allows one to get rid of some of the risk and still reach a higher indifference curve. Thus we cannot be sure that higher interest rates lead to lower money balances unless we make additional assumptions about the degree of risk aversion. Furthermore, the level of income seems to be totally unrelated to the portfolio decision, unless income determines the amount of wealth that is allocated to the portfolio; therefore, the *LM* curve does not appear to be derivable from the speculative motive for holding money.

But there may be an even more important argument against the speculative motive as the basis for holding money. In the discussion so far, money has been assumed to have extreme characteristics: no risk and no return. But there are assets that have "moneyness" to them and yield a return as well. Savings accounts are an example of a riskless asset that pays interest and can be used, perhaps indirectly, as money. If we are now faced with three assets, namely "narrow" money (defined to *exclude* savings accounts) with zero risk and zero return, "broad" money (defined to *include* savings accounts) with positive return and zero risk, and bonds with positive return and positive risk, investors would not hold any narrow money since it would be dominated by broad money no matter what the interest rate happened to be. For that reason, a portfolio model as described here is not very useful for predicting the demand for narrowly defined money.

5.3 THE DEMAND FOR MONEY AND OTHER ASSETS

If an argument can be made that money should be more broadly defined to include some riskless interest-earning asset, it can also be argued that the alternative asset, bonds, is probably too all-encompassing. If we distinguish between bonds and equities, the market value of the capital stock in the economy, on the basis of differences in risk and return, we then have three assets competing for a place in a portfolio, each with its own characteristics. In the 1960s, James Tobin made the telling point that a three-asset model made the traditional *LM* curve a much more tenuous analytical device than it is in the two-asset situation. A three-asset model poses two complications for the standard macro model:

1. Investment decisions will depend not only on the real interest rate, but also on the real return to equities, which Tobin called the *supply price of capital*.
2. The equilibrium condition in the money market requires an additional argument and is by itself no longer sufficient for asset-market equilibrium in general.

Although the first point is not directly relevant to the discussion of the *LM* curve, it is worth some elaboration. Consider how firms make investment decisions. A piece of capital earns a stream of income for the firm over its lifetime. This is called the marginal efficiency of capital (MEC), a concept similar to the marginal productivity of labor. If the rate of return on equities or the supply price of capital (SPC) is lower than MEC, firms will issue more shares in order to buy more capital. In the process MEC is driven down and SPC rises as share prices fall with the new supply, until they are equal, at which point firms have no further incentive to make investment expenditures. A similar reaction takes place if the interest rate on bonds is lower than MEC, except that firms will sell bonds to finance their investment. In equilibrium, there is a tendency for MEC, SPC, and the interest rate to be equal, but during the period in which investment is taking place this is not necessarily true, and it is for this reason that Tobin objected to the notion that the interest rate was the appropriate indicator of the stance of monetary policy. A falling interest rate may be associated with a rising supply price of capital under some circumstances, making it difficult to establish whether monetary policy is "tight" or "easy." For that reason we may want to allow for the SPC in the *IS* curve in addition to the interest rate.[3]

[3] Actually Tobin argued that only SPC mattered for investment decisions on the basis that firms maximized the market value of their shares. But with differences in tax treatment and bankruptcy risk between bonds and equities, both the interest

Let us now turn to the second issue raised by the three-asset model. With two assets, equilibrium in the money market *or* equilibrium in the bond market suffices to derive the *LM* curve. Because of Walras's law, there is only one relative price for the two assets to be determined; therefore, *the* interest rate is relevant for both money demand and bond demand. When we expand to three assets, there are now two relative prices, and we need to ensure that equilibrium exists in two markets before we invoke Walras's law to allow us to disregard the third market. Let i_B and i_K be the rates of return to bonds and equities relative to the return on money, respectively. The demand for money is positively related to income and negatively related to both rates of return. On the other hand, the demand for real bond holdings is negatively related to income, since higher transactions money balances means cashing in some bonds. It is also negatively related to i_K, but positively related to i_B, since an increase in its own rate of return, ceteris paribus, will increase the demand for that asset. The equilibrium equation for the equities market is not needed separately.

If bonds and equities are perfect substitutes in portfolios, then $i_B = i_K$ under all circumstances and we can aggregate bonds and equities. If bonds and equities are not perfect substitutes, we need equilibrium conditions for both money and bonds. Differences in tax treatment, bankruptcy risk, and other factors suggest that they cannot be perfect substitutes. How close is close enough? We really do not know, but for some purposes it may not really matter. One important role of the *LM* curve is the transmission of monetary policy changes to the rest of the macroeconomy, and much of that mechanism is preserved in the three-asset case.

Expansionary monetary policy is depicted by increases in public money holdings offset by decreases in bond holdings through open-market operations, a concept to be explored in greater detail in the next chapter. The excess supply of money and the excess demand for bonds will force the price of bonds to rise and i_B to fall. But there will be a spillover into the equities market, with excess demand developing for equities unless bonds and equities are not at all substitutable for each other. Thus i_K will fall as well. Now i_B and i_K may not change to the same extent, but they will move in the same direction. While this point is obviously important for empirical work on the effects of monetary policy, it does not change the theoretical conclusion that expansionary monetary policy stimulates investment if, of course, inflationary expectations do not adjust immediately.

rate and SPC will be important. Tobin's seminal article is "A General Equilibrium Approach to Monetary Theory," *Journal of Money, Credit, and Banking,* 1, February 1969, pp. 16–29.

Fiscal policy operations, on the other hand, may have ambiguous effects now that we have three assets to consider. Previously expansionary fiscal policy raised the real interest rate and reduced investment expenditures. Now an increase in public bond holdings, from financing a budget deficit, creates excess supply in the bond market and forces i_B to rise. There will again be spillover effects in the equities market, but depending on the strength of wealth and substitution effects, i_K may rise or fall. If i_K falls enough, investment may in fact be stimulated. However, since we are mostly concerned with monetary policy in this book, the three-asset representation does not create any additional complications for the macro model and equation (5.1) can continue to serve as the appropriate *LM* curve.

Nevertheless, there is one last aspect of this model that requires our attention. It was argued earlier that the demand for real money balances was related to the nominal interest rate. In the long-run version of the *IS–LM–AS* model this is the only link between real and nominal variables. Therefore, any rate of inflation is consistent with a unique set of real variables, such as output, the real wage, and so forth except for real money balances, which will respond to the rate of inflation. Both money and bonds are nominal assets, and inflation reduces their value equally, so that the nominal interest rate is the only opportunity cost of holding money. Does this situation change when the alternative asset is not a bond but an equity that should maintain its real value in an inflationary period, since it is a claim to ownership of real goods such as machines or office buildings? The answer is essentially no, since the opportunity cost of holding money is the real return to equities plus the inflation rate, or again the nominal return to equities, which may or may not be equal to the nominal interest rate depending on the degree of substitutability between bonds and equities. But if banks pay a return to money holders equal to the inflation rate, either directly through interest payments or indirectly through the elimination of service charges, then the real value of money is also constant and the opportunity cost is the real return on bonds or equities, depending on which is the alternative asset.[4] In essence therefore, the characteristics of money are more important than the distinguishing features of the alternative asset in deciding whether to use the nominal or real return to measure the opportunity cost of holding money balances.

[4] In the United States demand deposits cannot earn interest and Regulation Q limits payments on time deposits, but the process of deregulating the banking industry will eventually eliminate these constraints.

5.4 MONETARY AGGREGATES

Up to this point we have avoided the question of "demand for what?" The previous discussion makes it evident that it is time to deal with this thorny issue. How should we define money? Sophists may suggest that money is anything that is accepted as money, but this circular reasoning does not take us very far. Instead we will go directly to the definitions that are currently in use in Canada and in the United States and then cope with the problem of deciding whether some monetary aggregates are "better" than others.

5.4.1 MONETARY AGGREGATES IN CANADA

At the present time, the following monetary aggregates are defined by the Bank of Canada, with values in December 1982 indicated in millions of dollars, in the *Bank of Canada Review,* March 1984, table 9 (seasonally unadjusted figures):

M1 = currency and demand deposits = $27,983
M1A = M1 plus daily interest checkable and nonpersonal notice deposits = $34,457
M2 = M1A plus other notice deposits and personal term deposits = $132,057
M3 = M2 plus other nonpersonal fixed-term deposits plus foreign-currency deposits of residents booked in Canada = $186,612

As can be verified from these definitions, we move from narrow monetary aggregates with M1 to broad aggregates with M3, since any aggregate includes all the assets of the lower-order aggregate. For instance, M1A includes all of M1 plus other deposits on which checks can be written and nonpersonal notice deposits.

5.4.2 MONETARY AGGREGATES IN THE UNITED STATES

For December 1982, monetary aggregates in the United States were defined in the *Federal Reserve Bulletin,* March 1984, table 1.21, to be as follows:

M1 = (1) currency outside the Treasury, Federal Reserve Banks, and the vaults of commercial banks; (2) traveler's checks of nonbank issuers; (3) demand deposits at all commercial banks other than those due to domestic banks, the U.S. government and foreign banks and official institutions less cash items in the process of collection and Federal Reserve float; and (4) negotiable order of withdrawal (NOW) and automatic transfer service (ATS) accounts at banks and thrift institutions, credit union share draft (CUSD) accounts and demand deposits at mutual savings banks = $478.2 billion

M2 = M1 plus money-market deposit accounts, savings and small-denomination time deposits at all depository institutions, overnight repurchase agreements at commercial banks, overnight Eurodollars held by U.S. residents other than banks at Caribbean branches of member banks, and balances of money-market mutual funds = $1,959.5 billion

M3 = M2 plus large-denomination time deposits at all depository institutions, term RPs [repurchase agreements] at commercial banks and savings and loan associations, and balances of institution-only money-market mutual funds = $2,377.6 billion

By way of comparison, the first thing one notices is the greater detail in the definitions used by the Federal Reserve. But more important for analytical purposes is the fact that M1 in Canada includes only non-interest-earning assets, whereas M1 in the United States includes some deposits, such as NOW and ATS accounts, that do pay interest. The fact that M1 is broader in the United States than in Canada may explain why velocity is lower in the former country. A final characteristic to note is that the Federal Reserve is much less reluctant to change the definition of its monetary aggregates than the Bank of Canada. Until 1982 the Fed had two versions of M1: M1A, which excluded NOW and ATS accounts, and M1B, which included them. Prior to 1982, these innovations in transactions technology were considered to be imperfect substitutes for demand deposits; after that they were considered to be perfect substitutes.[5] The Bank of Canada, on the other hand, does not include daily-interest savings accounts, which have many of the same features as NOW accounts, in M1; they remain in M1A or M2. However, as of March 1983, M1A replaces an older definition, M1B, which included currency plus all checkable deposits.

5.5 EMPIRICAL EVIDENCE ON THE DEMAND FOR MONEY

For both Canada and the United States equation (5.1) has served as the basis for empirical estimates of the demand-for-money function. It is important for us to review this evidence to see if we have "robust" estimates of a_2 and a_3. Standard demand-for-money functions differ in one significant respect from equation (5.1). Since y and i are assumed to determine *desired* real money balances and since there can be a short-run gap between desired (i.e., unobserved) and actual (i.e., observed) money balances, we first have to consider how people close that gap. The

[5] Compare table 1.21 in the December 1981 issue of the *Federal Reserve Bulletin* with that in the March 1984 issue.

assumption in this regard is specified as a partial adjustment mechanism, written as

$$(5.6) \quad (m - p) - (m - p)_{-1} = g[(m - p)^d - (m - p)_{-1}]$$

where $(m - p)^d$ represents desired real money balances. Since $0 < g < 1$, in each period we partially close the gap between desired and actual real money balances; adjustment ceases when the gap is closed. Rewriting equation (5.1) as

$$(5.1') \quad (m - p)^d = a_2 y - a_3 i$$

and substituting (5.6) into (5.1′) produces

$$(5.7) \quad m - p = ga_2 y - ga_3 i + (1 - g)(m - p)_{-1}$$

We now have a distinction between short-run and long-run responses to changes in y and i. For instance, an increase in y raises $(m - p)$ initially by ga_2. In the second period, $(m - p)_{-1}$ also contributes to $(m - p)$ by the factor $(1 - g)ga_2$ and so on until finally actual money balances catch up with desired money balances, which is indicated by $(m - p)$ being constant. Therefore, a_2 is the long-run income elasticity, whereas ga_2 is the short-run response; similarly, a_3 is the long-run interest elasticity, and ga_3 measures the initial response. Equation (5.7) is the equation that has become the standard for empirical work on the *LM* curve.

Before we turn to estimates of this equation for Canada and the United States, we need to question the use of a partial adjustment mechanism in the money market. Earlier, in Chapter 2, it was argued that money-market adjustment was rapid, in fact fast enough that we would not observe excess demand or supply for very long. Although equation (5.6) does not imply disequilibrium, it does suggest that a given change in y or i would initially open a gap between desired and actual money balances. Why cannot individuals close that gap immediately, since it is possible to buy and sell bonds or other assets in any amount at almost any time? We have no clear answer to that question. All we can do is point to the fact that equation (5.7) with parameters a_2, a_3, and g to be estimated does a better job of explaining $(m - p)$ than does equation (5.1), which assumes implicitly that the adjustment is completed within one period.

There are two complementary explanations for this finding. They both involve a different interpretation of equation (5.7) than that given above. One has to do with the possibility that it is *permanent income,* not measured income, that is the true determinant of money demand. It is normal to approximate permanent income as a weighted average of past income. For example, the value of permanent income this period may be equal to $.5y + .33y_{-1} + .17y_{-2}$. An increase in y raises $(m - p)$ by a_2 times .5

times the change in y during the first period. Subsequently, if y remains higher, $(m - p)$ in the second period adjusts by a_2 times .33 times the original change in y, and so on. In this way, a one-time change in income has a continuing effect on the demand for money, but the interpretation is different. With a partial adjustment mechanism, desired and actual money balances need not coincide; with the permanent-income hypothesis, desired and actual balances are always the same, but permanent income and actual income need not coincide.

Next, there may be sluggish adjustment to changes in the interest rate. If the expected holding period for bonds is less than their maturity, then the interest rate is *not* the only return to bonds. In addition to coupon payments, investors will receive capital gains or losses when they sell bonds in the market. If interest rates have dropped since they purchased these bonds, their price will have risen and there are capital gains; if interest rates have risen, there are capital losses. Thus individuals need to know not only the current interest rate, but they also try to guess the interest rate at the time they expect to dispose of their bonds. If they use the past trend in interest rates to forecast the future interest rate, the total return on holding bonds will depend on current and past interest rates. For example, in addition to the interest payment, i per unit of time, asset holders may anticipate capital gains on the basis of past movements in interest rates according to a formula such as $.5(i_{-1} - i) + .2(i_{-2} - i_{-1})$, where $(i_{-1} - i)$, if positive, measures the capital gains in the previous period. Thus the total return is $i + .5(i_{-1} - i) + .2(i_{-2} - i_{-1})$ or $.5i + .3i_{-1} + .2i_{-2}$. Now an increase in the interest rate in one period causes people to want to hold less real money balances, but they adjust their expected total return on holding bonds by less than the increase in observed interest rates. Thus their reduction in $(m - p)$ will be equal to $.5a_3$ times the change in interest rates. Only if i remains at the higher value for three periods will the total adjustment in $(m - p)$ be measured by a_3. Here again the interpretation differs from the partial adjustment mechanism: Desired and actual money balances are always the same, but the interest rate does not always indicate the total expected return on a bond. For both of these reasons, $(1 - g)(m - p)_{-1}$ in equation (5.7) may be capturing, not slow adjustment of money balances, but instead slow adjustment of permanent income and expected rates of return on bonds, which are the true determinants of real money balances.

5.5.1 CANADIAN DEMAND-FOR-MONEY FUNCTIONS

A recent estimate of equation (5.7) for Canada was provided by Gregory and MacKinnon. Although their primary interest was in measuring the effect of postal strikes on the demand for money, in the process they provided estimates for a_2, a_3, and g. Using quarterly data for the period 1956I to 1978IV and using M1 as the monetary aggregate, they found that $a_2 = .763$, $a_3 = .229$, and $g = .248$. They also obtained a constant of 1.992 for equation (5.7). These parameters allow us to calculate the short-run elasticities: $ga_2 = .763 \times .248 = .189$ and $ga_3 = .229 \times .248 = .057$.[6]

One of the primary purposes of an equation such as (5.7) is that it can predict $(m - p)$ if we know y, i, and $(m - p)_{-1}$, plus any postal-strike variables that may be appropriate. If it cannot do this job, the *LM* curve is not a very useful concept. Let us now try our hand at prediction. For 1980, real GNP increased by 0.5%. Also, the 90-day commercial-paper rate, the interest rate used for this purpose, increased from 14.20% in December 1979 to 17.75% in December 1980, for a proportionate increase of 25%. Over a four-quarter period, real money balances should increase by $ga_2 + (1 - g)ga_2 + (1 - g)^2 ga_2 + (1 - g)^3 ga_2$ times the change in income minus $ga_3 + (1 - g)ga_3 + (1 - g)^2 ga_3 + (1 - g)^3 ga_3$ times the change in the interest rate. This works out to $.189 \times 2.743 \times .5\% - .057 \times 2.743 \times 25\% = -3.65\%$. During the year, nominal M1 increased by 6.4% while the GNE deflator rose by 10.3%, so that real M1 fell by 3.9%. Are these numbers consistent with each other? They are fairly close: only a .35% error in predicting the change in $(m - p)$ for 1980. (There were no postal strikes that year.) If the error were "large" (e.g., 10%), then it would have meant that other (unknown) variables were contributing to the determination of the demand for money and the *LM* curve could not have been accurately located.

So far, so good, but the predictive ability of any equation for M1 begins to fall apart in 1981 because of major innovations in financial markets that made holdings of M1 less attractive relative to broader definitions of money. (There was also a postal strike in 1981, but this should have *raised* the demand for M1 when it actually fell.) Let us first make the same calculations for 1981 and then see why we get such a large error in the prediction. For 1981, y increased by 3.1%, and the interest rate fell from 17.75% in December 1980 to 15.65% in December 1981, which represents a fall of 11.8%.[7] The predicted change is therefore $.189 \times 2.743 \times 3.1 - .057 \times 2.743 \times -11.8\% = 3.45\%$. The actual change in nominal M1 was 3.9%. With a rate of inflation equal to 10.1%, real M1 fell by 6.2%. We now have an error of 10%, which represents a substantial overpre-

[6] A. R. Gregory and J. G. MacKinnon, "Where's My Cheque? A Note on Postal Strikes and the Demand for Money in Canada," *Canadian Journal of Economics*, 13, November 1980, pp. 683–87, table 1, col. 2.

[7] During that year, interest rates were on a roller coaster; they hit a high of 22.4% in August 1981.

Table 5-1. *Composition of personal and nonpersonal deposits at Canadian chartered banks, 1979–82 (%)*

	Nonpersonal accounts		Personal accounts	
End of period	Checking	Notice	Checking	Savings
1979	29	71	5	95
1980	30	70	5	95
1981	25	75	4	96
1982	22	78	4	96

Source: *Bank of Canada Review*, table 8.

diction of actual cash holdings. What happened? Throughout the period of rising interest rates, there is pressure to hold less M1 since it contains only non-interest-earning assets and to shift to other banks accounts that pay some interest. This process is captured in the existing demand-for-money function and should not be the source of difficulty. In fact, for 1980, interest rates rose, and demand for money was predicted to fall, and indeed it fell. In 1981, interest rates finally turned down again, but real M1 continued to fall. During the entire period, new assets were being created by banks or old ones made more attractive by a substantial advertising campaign. For large corporate accounts, Canadian chartered banks introduced centralized concentration accounts, which essentially allow firms to operate with a zero balance in their demand accounts at the end of each day. This is attractive to both parties: Firms earn interest on transactions balances and banks need fewer reserves for these accounts.[8] For households, banks had always offered checkable savings accounts, but recent advances in computer technology made it possible for them to offer daily-interest accounts, which made movements of funds between checking and savings accounts easier and resulted in lower balances in the former. Both of these developments were stimulated by higher interest rates, but once the adjustment was made and the fixed costs incurred, there was no reversal, as would be predicted by our previous estimates. Firms and households continued to manage their cash balances more tightly, even though the opportunity cost of doing so had fallen in late 1981.

The data in Table 5-1 seem to verify this irreversible process. During the period of rising interest rates, nonpersonal deposits, mostly held by

[8] Reserve requirements for Canadian chartered banks will be discussed in Chapter 6.

firms, shifted to interest-earning categories (i.e., notice deposits), and their share continued to increase in 1981 and 1982 even though interest rates started to fall. For households, the picture is a little less clear, since demand deposits have always been a very small proportion of total personal deposits, but even here the proportion held as savings accounts did not fall in 1982.

Does this suggest that M1 should be redefined to include these new accounts? As we saw earlier, M1 in Canada does not include any bank liabilities except demand deposits, with concentration accounts and daily-interest accounts included only in broader definitions. By comparison, the Federal Reserve has made adjustments to the definition of M1 whenever financial innovations occur. In either case, the past history of asset choices is no longer relevant, and our estimates of a_2, a_3, and g are not as robust as they once were. This has very important implications for monetary policy, because the location of the *LM* curve is no longer as predictable as it was. We shall return to this topic in Section 5.9.

5.5.2 U.S. DEMAND-FOR-MONEY FUNCTIONS

The "conventional" demand-for-money function for the United States has been estimated by Stephen Goldfeld, most recently in 1976, for the period 1952II to 1973IV, using quarterly data. The basis of his estimates is also equation (5.7), except that he uses two interest rates to measure the opportunity cost of holding M1 balances. An increase in the short-term commercial paper interest rate will cause firms to move from M1 to other assets, whereas an increase in the rate on time deposits will have the same effect on households. Since these rates do not always move together, they have to be included separately. Thus we have a_{31} to measure the effect of the former and a_{32} to capture the effect of the latter. Goldfeld's estimates are given as: $ga_2 = .179$, $ga_{31} = .018$, $ga_{32} = .042$, and $(1 - g) = .676$.[9] We can also calculate the long-run elasticities as $a_2 = .552$, $a_{31} = .056$, and $a_{32} = .130$. Compared to the Canadian estimates, we see that the income elasticity is much lower. Adding a_{31} and a_{32} to get the effect of an equal increase in all interest rates shows a much lower interest elasticity as well. Finally, since g is larger, adjustment to equilibrium is faster than in Canada.

Unfortunately, we cannot perform the same experiment of predicting the change in the real money supply for 1980 and 1981 as we did for Canada, since the data for the time deposit rates are no longer collected

[9] S. F. Goldfeld, "The Case of the Missing Money," *Brookings Papers on Economic Activity,* 3:1976, pp. 683–730, table 1, line 1.

by the Federal Reserve Board. Instead we can look at Goldfeld's own forecasts for the immediate postsample period. By the end of 1974, the cumulative error in his forecast is −9.5%, and by the end of the second year it is −19.4%. This means that a two-year forecast for real money balances would be 20% higher than what actually occurred. For that reason, we must conclude that much the same innovation process in financial markets must have occurred in the United States, except that it probably started much earlier than in Canada. John Judd and John Scadding have investigated this situation and they conclude that:

> the most likely cause of the observed instability in the demand for money after 1973 is innovation in financial arrangements. These innovations, which allowed the public to economize on its holdings of transactions balances, appear to have been induced by the combination of high inflation rates (and therefore interest rates) and legal impediments to the payment of a market rate of return on transactions balances.[10]

5.6 FINANCIAL INNOVATION AND THE DEMAND FOR MONEY

Since this issue of a predictable demand for money is so important for the conduct of monetary policy, we need to look further at the role of financial innovation as the source of instability in the demand for money. Donald Hester has put forward the following argument.[11] Imagine a situation in which inflation is absent and the rate of return on money is zero. Now inflation becomes positive after a positive growth rate for money becomes established. Since nominal interest rates also rise, we know that the real money supply will decline. Banks that lend at the nominal interest rate but borrow at zero cost find an increased profit margin and competition will cause them to offer assets that pay some interest, as long as at the margin it is less than what they receive from borrowers. If they are prevented from doing this with existing assets (i.e., checkable deposits), they will find a new name for a similar asset. But this new asset will not be included in the definition of the money supply previously in existence, and holdings of this aggregate will be overestimated for known values of y and i. Moreover, Hester argues that this process is irreversible. When interest and inflation rates fall later on, people will continue to hold these new assets instead of going back to the old ones. The demand-for-money equation has thus become unstable, and unless the central bank can stay on top of these developments it will not

[10] J. P. Judd and J. L. Scadding, "The Search for a Stable Money Demand Function: A Survey of the Post-1973 Literature," *Journal of Economic Literature,* 20, September 1982, p. 1014.

[11] D. D. Hester, "Innovations and Monetary Control," *Brookings Papers on Economic Activity,* 1:1981, pp. 141–89.

be able to make adjustments to its monetary policy. For instance, a declining value of real M1 may appear to show that monetary policy is tight, but if broader aggregates show higher growth rates, can we really be sure that inflation will be reduced? We will not try to answer this question now, but it is already apparent that financial innovation in response to monetary policy changes can reduce the control the central bank has over the performance of the economy.

An example of such irreversible financial innovation is the NOW account. "Negotiable orders of withdrawal" are checkable demand deposits in everything but name and therefore escape the restriction on interest payments that exists for ordinary checkable deposits. These accounts made their first appearance in the late 1970s when interest rates were generally rising. In December 1978, these and similar accounts (i.e., ATS) amounted to $8.4 billion. By December 1981, they totaled $78.4 billion. Although interest rates peaked in 1981 and fell dramatically through 1982, these accounts continued to grow, standing at $87.9 billion in July 1982. Until NOW accounts were included in the latest definition of M1, a given y and i overpredicted the demand for M1 and became a misleading indicator of the stance of monetary policy. Realization that NOW accounts are a permanent feature of the transactions technology seemed to take at least a year, and one has to be worried about the ability of the Federal Reserve to predict accurately the location of the *LM* curve for the U.S. economy.[12]

These doubts exist for the Bank of Canada as well. As recently as February 1980, the governor of the Bank of Canada appeared unconcerned about the effects of financial innovation. He stated, "Provided M1 movements are interpreted with care in the context of banking practices, it seems likely that they will continue to be useful as a guide for monetary policy."[13] But, by early 1982 the governor is forced to report, "The movement of M1 over the past few months is well outside of the range of what can be explained by changes in total spending and interest rates even after allowance is made for the shift of funds into daily interest saving accounts."[14]

5.7 STRUCTURAL CHANGES IN THE DEMAND FOR MONEY AND VELOCITY

For both Canada and the United States the evidence points to the conclusion that previously estimated demand-for-money equations

[12] For a more sanguine view, see L. E. Gramley, "Financial Innovation and Monetary Policy," *Federal Reserve Bulletin*, 68, July 1982, pp. 393–400.
[13] *Annual Report of the Governor of the Bank of Canada*, Ottawa, 1979, p. 25.
[14] *Annual Report of the Governor of the Bank of Canada*, Ottawa, 1981, p. 31.

now overpredict the amount of money demanded for a given y and i. A financial innovation such as the introduction of daily-interest or NOW accounts increases the velocity of the existing monetary aggregate, M1, holding y and i constant. From the definition in equation (5.3)

$$(5.8) \quad v - v_{-1} = p + y - m - (p + y - m)_{-1}$$
$$= \pi - \mu + (y - y_{-1})$$

But if $\mu = \pi$ and y remains at y_e as we move through time, then velocity must remain constant. The only way in which v can change independently of these variables is to allow for structural change to take place in the demand-for-money function. Substituting equation (5.7) into (5.3) produces

$$(5.9) \quad v = (1 - ga_2)y + ga_3 i - (1 - g)(m - p)_{-1}$$

which is similar to (5.5). For given values of y, i, and $(m - p)_{-1}$, v will rise after financial innovations if ga_2 decreases in size, ga_3 increases and/or $(1 - g)$ decreases. What is the recent evidence for these predictions? Christopher Holling has added four years' worth of observations to the Gregory–MacKinnon estimate of the Canadian demand-for-money function, which had ended with 1978IV. Holling's new estimates are $a_2 = .940$, $a_3 = .479$, and $g = .136$, and the constant is .691. Therefore, $ga_2 = .128$, $ga_3 = .065$, and $(1 - g) = .864$, compared to .189, .057, and .752 previously. Only $(1 - g)$ does not conform to the predictions.

We can now compare velocity estimates for a particular period, say 1982IV, using the two sets of parameters and see which is larger. For 1982IV, $y = 10.372$ (ln of seasonally unadjusted real income at a quarterly rate), $i = 2.414$ (ln of 90-day commercial paper rate), and $(m - p)_{-1} = 9.134$. Using the Gregory–MacKinnon parameters, $(m - p) = 9.189$; therefore, estimated $v = 10.372 - 9.189 = 1.183$, the antilog of which is 3.26. With the Holling parameters, $(m - p) = 9.182$ and estimated $v = 1.190$, the antilog being 3.29, which is approximately 1% higher than the Gregory–MacKinnon estimate. Actual velocity for that quarter, measured as quarterly GNP divided by the nominal money supply, is 89,539/26,477 = 3.38, suggesting that the Holling estimates are more accurate because they incorporate the financial innovations that took place between 1980 and 1982.[15]

At the time that the financial innovation takes place the central bank is probably not aware of the structural nature of the event and is likely to interpret the higher velocity as a temporary phenomenon caused by a

[15] A similar reestimation of the Goldfeld equation for the United States is not possible since data on time-deposit rates are not available after 1979.

negative monetary shock. Since $m - m_{-1} = \mu + x_m$, equation (5.8) can be rewritten as

$$(5.8') \quad v - v_{-1} = \pi - \mu + (y - y_{-1}) - x_m$$

showing how an increase in velocity can be blamed on a negative x_m. Only later, when v remains higher, does it become obvious that the parameters of the *LM* curve are no longer the same.

In summary, one very important source of monetary uncertainty in the Canadian and U.S. economies during the 1970s and early 1980s was the series of financial innovations that drastically changed the concept of transactions balances. Before, these balances were restricted to currency and demand deposits, neither of which earned interest; afterward, they included a whole host of interest-earning assets that can be used directly or indirectly in making everyday transactions. In the process the *LM* curve, based on a narrow monetary aggregate, became unstable.

5.8 REDEFINING THE MONEY SUPPLY

Since money is anything that is acceptable as money, it would appear sensible to redefine monetary aggregates whenever it is clear that new assets have become part of the transactions technology. This is what the Fed has done from time to time, but the Bank of Canada has not. What happens to the *LM* curve when a monetary aggregate such as M1 is redefined to include some new asset? Let us call this new aggregate M1′. Before the innovation, the *LM* curve was described by equation (5.1), with M1 as the choice for M. After the change, equilibrium in the money market, with money defined as M1′, is depicted as

$$(5.10) \quad (m' - p) = a_2'y - a_3'i$$

with new parameters a_2' and a_3'. What can we say about the relative sizes of a_2 and a_2' and a_3 and a_3'? First, let us look at the interest elasticity of the demand for money. Since M1′ contains interest-earning assets but M1 does not, we should expect that $a_3 > a_3'$. Consider an increase in the interest rate. Before the financial innovation, investors would shift out of money and into other assets, probably bonds, the extent of which was measured by a_3. Now they will shift less into bonds, having acquired some of the new asset that also bears some interest. Thus a_3' is smaller than a_3, and the demand for money becomes less interest sensitive after the innovation. Second, we can look at the income elasticity of the demand for money. Optimal transactions balances will still be given by the

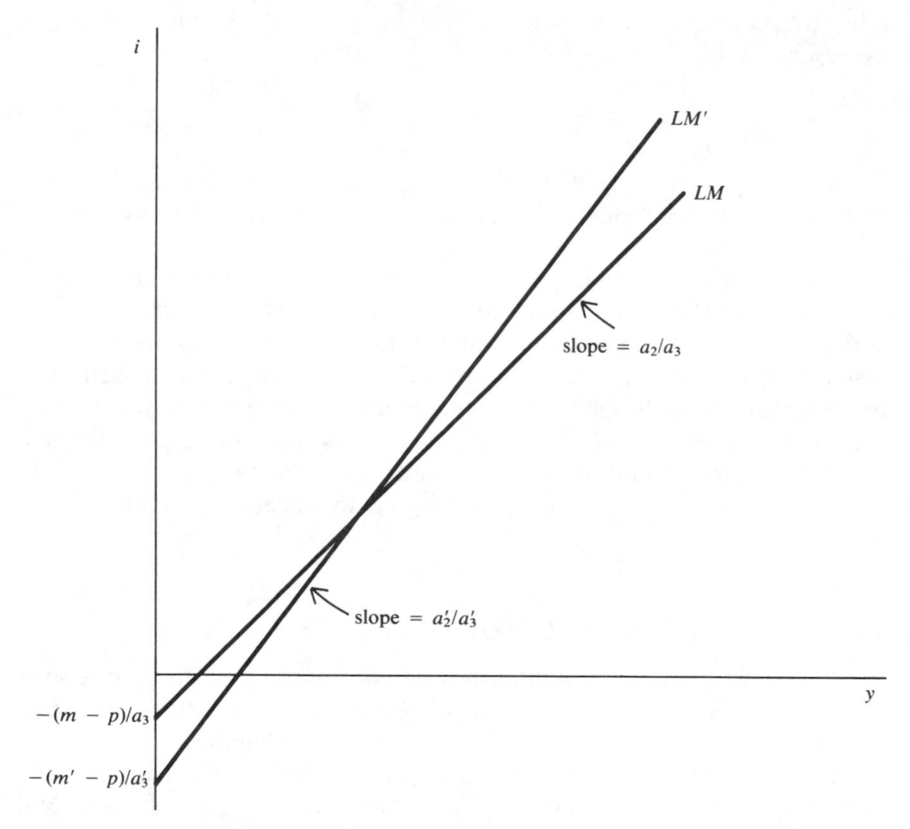

Figure 5-3 Shift of the *LM* curve after a redefinition of the money supply from M1 to M1′.

"square-root rule" or its modified version that takes integer constraints and random walks into account. Thus a_2' should not differ from a_2, which lies between zero and one. But M1′ may include not only transactions balances but also idle balances, since this aggregate includes interest-earning assets. Now it is possible for $a_2' > a_2$ to allow for both kinds of balances at every level of income.

The important point is that both a_2 and a_3 may have been altered and the slope and position of the *LM* curve is no longer the same. The slope of the *LM* curve is a_2/a_3, which increases in size after M1′ becomes relevant because the numerator either stays the same or increases while the denominator becomes smaller. The vertical intercept of the *LM* curve is $-(m - p)/a_3$, the numerator of which increases while the denominator becomes smaller. Both the old *LM* curve and the new one are drawn in Figure 5-3.

Table 5-2. *Growth rates of monetary aggregates and inflation rates, Canada and the United States, 1978–82 (%)*

	Canada				United States			
Year	M1	M2	M3	Inflation	M1	M2	M3	Inflation
1978	10.1	11.1	14.5	6.7	8.3	8.2	11.2	7.4
1979	6.9	15.7	20.2	10.3	7.1	8.2	9.2	8.6
1980	6.4	18.9	16.9	11.1	6.6	9.0	10.3	9.3
1981	3.8	15.2	13.1	10.6	6.4	10.1	11.5	9.4
1982	0.6	9.3	5.0	10.1	8.5	9.7	9.9	6.0

Note: The inflation rate is measured by the GNE deflator.
Source: Canada, *Bank of Canada Review*, March 1984, table 1, col. 1, 3, 4, 14; United States, *Economic Report of the President for 1983*, tables D61, D3.

5.9 MONETARY POLICY IN A PERIOD OF FINANCIAL INNOVATION

One of the important features of financial innovation is that its occurrence has not been predicted ex ante. This poses serious problems for the conduct of monetary policy, especially antiinflationary policy, where credibility is such an important ingredient. Consider an initial high-inflation equilibrium. During the previous period in which inflation developed, the standard *IS–LM* model would predict a reduction in $(m - p)$ as nominal interest rates rose. However, the very existence of this inflationary period creates incentives for financial innovation that are not observed until after the fact. Now the central bank announces and implements an antiinflationary policy by reducing μ, the growth rate of a narrowly defined monetary aggregate such as M1. However, the *actual* reduction in the growth rate of M1 is larger since x_m also appears to be negative during the period of financial innovation. Thus M1 will grow more slowly than the announced target range. In the meantime, π, y, and i are being determined by broader aggregates, which are growing faster now as the transactions technology is changing. It will therefore appear that the central bank "overachieved" its target for the money supply but "underachieved" its goal for the inflation rate, suggesting that M1 is an irrelevant variable in controlling the rate of inflation. Only later does it become obvious that NOW accounts and daily-interest accounts are virtually perfect substitutes for demand deposits and that they are a permanent part of the transactions technology, but in the meantime the financial innovation has made monetary policy unpredictable.

This sequence of events is close to the experience of the Canadian and American economies during the period 1978–82. Table 5-2 indicates what happened to monetary aggregates, not only M1, but also M2 and M3 in both countries, when both central banks followed a contractionary policy. Although growth rates for M1 did fall during the period, in fact more than was targeted for by the Bank of Canada, broader aggregates had an upward trend.[16] Perhaps even more important for the monetarist position behind these policies is the fact that the inflation rate seems much more closely related to M2 or M3 than to M1, making it difficult for the central bank to argue that its downward pressure on M1 will reduce the inflation rate eventually.

5.10 SUMMARY

The demand for money is largely determined by income and interest rates. There is both theoretical and empirical support for this proposition. At the theoretical level, the transactions demand for money is the most reliable basis for narrowly defined money, with the speculative demand playing a role only in more broadly defined monetary aggregates. The theory suggests that the income elasticity should lie between .5 and 1 and the interest elasticity between 0 and .5. The empirical evidence for Canada and the United States verifies this requirement. Most of the empirical work has dealt with M1, the narrowly defined money supply, although both countries have data series for more broadly defined aggregates.

Standard demand functions based on equation (5.7) begin to overpredict actual demand for M1 on a consistent basis, starting in the late 1970s in the United States and in 1981 in Canada. These shifts in the demand functions can be explained by financial innovations that make interest-earning moneylike assets more attractive during a period of high inflation and high interest rates, a process that is not reversed when inflation subsides and interest rates fall. Although the existence of these new assets is now acknowledged and their effect on M1 can now be calculated, they were largely unpredicted by the Bank of Canada and the Fed before the event. These financial innovations therefore will initially appear as negative monetary shocks, but subsequently can be interpreted as permanent changes in the parameters of the demand function. Also, the *LM* curve becomes steeper as broader definitions of money are used.

If financial innovations occur at the same time as the monetary authorities are attempting to pursue an antiinflationary policy, the combined

[16] In the United States, the Fed had targets for M1, M2, and M3 with target ranges being generally higher for broader aggregates. More on this in Chapters 7 and 8.

effect will be that the growth rate of narrowly defined money will fall more than was announced and the inflation rate will drop less than predicted. Also, broader aggregates will have higher growth rates. One is forced to conclude that during such periods the *LM* curve becomes difficult to locate and the conduct of monetary policy becomes a precarious endeavor.

EXERCISES

1. Assume that a person has a choice between two assets: demand deposits and bonds. Every check written on the demand deposit costs 10¢; a conversion from bonds to money costs $2.50. Money income is $1,000 per month, all of which is spent at a constant rate during the month, and the interest rate is 10% per annum.
   (a) Calculate the optimal number of conversions and the optimal average balance in the demand deposit.
   (b) How are these changed if there are integer constraints?
   (c) If there are no bonds but instead a noncheckable savings account that pays 10% interest on the minimum monthly balance, what is the optimal strategy?
   (d) If there are no bonds but instead a checkable daily-interest account which pays 6% interest with a 10¢ charge per check, what is the best strategy?
2. If $(m - p) = a_2 y_p - a_3 i_t$, where $y_p = gy + (1 - g)gy_{-1} + (1 - g)^2 gy_{-2} + \cdots + (1 - g)^n gy_{-n}$ represents permanent income and $i_t = gi + (1 - g)gi_{-1} + (1 - g)^2 gi_{-2} + \cdots + (1 - g)^n gi_{-n}$ represents the total opportunity cost of holding money, with $0 < g < 1$, show that you will obtain equation (5.7).
3. Landy estimated $ga_2 = .184$, $ga_3 = .046$ and $g = .208$ for Canada.
   (a) Calculate the predicted change in $(m - p)$ for 1980.
   (b) Do her estimates predict $(m - p)$ better than those of Gregory and MacKinnon?
4. In the United States in 1977I, real GNP was $1,306.7 billion, the price index was 138.27, the commercial paper rate was 4.81%, and the time deposit rate was 4.92%. Also, in the previous quarter, M1 was $311.1 billion and the price index was 136.35.
   (a) Using Goldfeld's estimates and assuming that his regression constant was −.880, predict $(m - p)$ for 1977I.
   (b) Actual $(m - p)$ was .827. Calculate the error in the predicted nominal money balances.
   (c) Calculate velocity for 1977I.

FURTHER READING

Hester, D. D., "Innovations and Monetary Control," *Brookings Papers on Economic Activity,* 1:1981, pp. 141–89. Argues that the effect of financial innovations is not reversible.

Judd, J. P., and J. L. Scadding, "The Search for a Stable Money Demand Function: A Survey of the Post-1973 Literature," *Journal of Economic Literature,* 20, September 1982, pp. 993–1023. Reviews some of the reasons for the recent instability of money demand functions in the United States.

Laidler, D. E. W., *The Demand for Money,* third edition, New York, Harper & Row, 1985. A thorough treatment of the subject.

Landy, L. "Financial Innovation in Canada," *Federal Reserve Bank of New York Quarterly Review,* Autumn 1980, pp. 1–8. Compares recent financial developments in Canada and the United States and their effect on money demand functions.

CHAPTER 6

The supply of money

6.1 INTRODUCTION

It has been a useful fiction in the previous chapters to treat the money supply as being entirely determined by the central bank as if the bank notes that it issues were the only medium of exchange. But since much of what we treat as money is a liability of various private banking institutions, it is now time to explore the actual process by which the money supply is made to grow over time and to evaluate the central bank's control over that process. At the same time, the other forces that play a role in the money supply will come to the fore. In particular, it is vital to distinguish between predictable and unpredictable changes in the money supply. From the discussion in Chapters 3 and 4, we know that they have different effects on the macroeconomy. So far, the unpredictability in the money market has been identified in only a very general way; it is now time to be more specific on this issue: Randomness exists both on the demand side and on the supply side.

Control of the money supply by the central bank relies on a fundamental relationship between the liabilities of the central bank, which are called *high-powered money,* and the liabilities of the commercial banks, which are referred to as *private money*. This fundamental relationship is established by the power of the state to grant to the central bank a monopoly for the production of high-powered money and to insist that private money be linked to high-powered money by *minimum reserve* requirements. Nevertheless, despite the unquestioned ability of the state to regulate the private banks in minute detail, this link has some flexibility and randomness. From that perspective, if the central bank is going to follow a monetarist strategy of announcing and following a target growth rate of the money supply, it must be able to ensure that it can enforce its view on the banking system. If it cannot deliver on that promise because the banking system is able to circumvent the requirements of monetary control techniques, then much of the credibility of the policy is lost. For example, we saw in Chapter 5 that financial innovations involving the creation of checkable interest-earning accounts in both Canada and the United States made the then-existing narrowly defined monetary aggregate, M1, almost meaningless and caused concern that the monetary authorities had picked an irrelevant monetary target. For that reason alone, the process by which money is created and the role of the monetary authority in that process are important elements of a macro model.

This chapter will review some of the material usually covered in an intermediate macroeconomics textbook and thus should be familiar to the student, but since we are going to compare Canadian and American institutions and experience, it will be useful for the reader who has not studied the banking system in both countries to work through this chapter. Also, the emphasis on distinguishing between predictable and unexpected money supply changes may be a novel feature and therefore requires special attention.

6.2 THE BALANCE SHEETS OF THE BANKING SYSTEM

To establish the link between the central bank and deposit-taking institutions, we need to look at the balance sheets of the banking system and to find the connection between central-bank and commercial-bank liabilities through the legal requirement of reserves. Against their deposit liabilities, commercial banks must hold certain liabilities of the central bank in prescribed proportions. These minimum reserve requirements vary by type of liability and differ, of course, between the Canadian and American banking laws. With that in mind, we can look at typical balance sheets of the two banking systems and see the connection between the central banks and the commercial banks.[1] It should be noted that in both countries, commercial banks are not the only deposit-taking institutions and that components of monetary aggregates are liabilities of other financial intermediaries such as credit unions, trust companies, savings and loan associations, which are generally referred to as "thrifts." It used to be a distinguishing feature of commercial banks that they alone maintained reserve deposits with the central bank, but now even thrifts in the United States are forced to maintain legally required reserves. Under the provisions of the Monetary Control Act of 1980, depository institutions sub-

[1] In Canada, banks are referred to as *chartered banks,* but we will use the more generic term, *commercial banks,* where appropriate in this chapter.

Table 6-1. *Balance sheets of the Canadian banking system, December 1982*

Bank of Canada (millions of dollars)			
Assets		*Liabilities*	
Government of Canada securities	$15,371	Notes in circulation	$12,719
		Chartered bank deposits	4,838
Foreign-currency deposits	264	Other deposits	244
		Other liabilities	1,642
Advances	143		
Other	3,645		
	$19,423		$19,443

Chartered banks (millions of dollars)			
Assets		*Liabilities*	
Bank of Canada deposits and notes	$ 7,067	Demand deposits	$ 19,114
Earning assets	361,995	Personal savings deposits	100,037
		Nonpersonal term and notice deposits	48,541
		Advances from Bank of Canada	143
		Other liabilities and equity	201,227
	$369,062		$369,062

Reserve requirements	
Demand deposits	10%
Notice deposits	
Less than $500 million	2%
Over $500 million	3%
Foreign currency deposits of Canadian residents	3%

Sources: Bank of Canada Review, March 1983, tables 3, 7, 8, and H. H. Binhammer, *Money, Banking, and the Canadian Financial System*, fourth edition, Toronto, Methuen, 1982, p. 245.

ject to reserve requirements include commercial banks, mutual savings banks, savings and loan associations, credit unions, agencies and branches of foreign banks, and Edge Act corporations.

6.2.1 THE CANADIAN BANKING SYSTEM

The assets and liabilities of the Bank of Canada and the chartered banks as of December 1982 are recorded in Table 6-1. These entries are considerably simplified compared to what an accountant would like to see, and even then our interest is mainly in the size of the liabilities of these institutions. The main components of chartered-bank liabilities are the various kinds of deposits from the public, which in turn are the major portion of the conventional monetary aggregates. From Chapter 5, it will be remembered that demand deposits are contained in M1, while personal savings accounts and nonpersonal term and notice deposits are in M1A or in M2. Except for currency held by the public and deposits at thrift institutions, these liabilities represent the total money supply according to these definitions. The link connecting this private money to the high-powered money of the central bank is provided by the reserve requirements stipulated in the Bank Act. These are also listed in Table 6-1. Because of their relatively high liquidity and turnover, demand deposits have the highest reserve requirement. The acceptable reserves are (1) coins held by the chartered banks, (2) Bank of Canada notes in their vaults, and (3) deposits at the Bank of Canada.

EXAMPLE

At the end of 1982, required reserves were roughly equal to $.10 \times \$19{,}114 + .03 \times \$100{,}037 + .03 \times \$48{,}541 = \$6{,}368.7$ million. Actual reserve requirements were somewhat different because the calculations are not quite that simple; statutory requirements were $6,430 million.

Except for coins,which are only of minor importance, reserves of the commercial banks are liabilities of the central bank.

Chartered bank deposits at the Bank of Canada were $4,838 million, and their total reserves were $7,067 million, which implies that of the total notes in circulation amounting to $12,719 million, banks had in their vaults $2,228 million, the rest, $10,491 million, being held by the public. We can also calculate some of the monetary aggregates from these balance sheets. For example, M1, which is equal to currency held by the public plus demand deposits, amounted to $\$10{,}491 + \$19{,}114 = \$29{,}605$ million.

As we shall see in Section 6.4, the central bank can change the size of the deposit liabilities of the banks and therefore the money supply by changing its own liabilities through open-market operations or other transactions that have a direct bearing on its balance sheet.

6.2.2 THE U.S. BANKING SYSTEM

Table 6-2 presents the balance sheets of the American banking system. Although some of the names are different, the basic components have approximately the same function as in the Canadian system. Commercial banks in the United States have various types of deposit liabilities against which they must hold reserves of prescribed proportions, as shown at the

Table 6-2. *Balance sheets of the U.S. banking system, December 1982*

Federal Reserve banks (billions of dollars)			
Assets		*Liabilities*	
U.S. Government securities	$139.3	Federal Reserve notes	$142.0
Loans to depository institutions	.7	Deposits of depository institutions	26.5
Gold, SDRs, and foreign currency	21.5	Other deposits	6.4
Other	25.3	Other liabilities	12.0
	$187.0		$187.0
All commercial banks (billions of dollars)			
Assets		*Liabilities*	
Deposits with FRBs, currency and coin	$ 49.8	Demand deposits	$ 376.2
Earning assets	1,922.4	Savings deposits	296.7
		Time deposits	736.7
		Borrowings	278.3
		Other liabilities and equity	284.3
	$1,972.2		$1,972.2
Reserve requirements			
Net transactions accounts	3–12% – rising with size of deposit liabilities		
Nonpersonal time deposits of less than 3½ years maturity	3%		
Eurocurrency deposits	3%		

Source: Federal Reserve Bulletin, March 1983, tables 1.15, 1.18, 1.25

bottom of Table 6-2. These reserve requirements are somewhat more complicated than those in Canada, not only because they vary by type of deposit but also because they are graduated by volume of these deposits. They involve some new terminology. "Net transactions accounts" are essentially all checkable accounts. Also, the range varies from 3% to 12%, compared to 2% to 10% in Canada. Some deposits, such as nonpersonal time deposits with an original maturity of more than 3½ years, escape reserve requirements altogether. Because of this more complex structure it is not possible simply to multiply the reserve requirements times the deposit liability to arrive at required reserves. Instead, Table 1.12 of the *Federal Reserve Bulletin* shows that required reserves for December 1982 were $41.9 billion. These reserves must be in the form of deposits with the Federal Reserve banks, which were equal to $24.8 billion at the end of 1982, and vault cash, which was estimated at $20.4 billion. This adds up to $45.2 billion in total reserves, somewhat less than the $49.8 billion listed in the first item of the asset side of the commercial-bank balance sheet, suggesting that they held something like $4.6 billion in excess reserves. In turn, the deposits at the Federal Reserve banks are somewhat smaller than the $26.5 billion listed under "Deposits of depository institutions" because this item includes reserves of thrifts. Much more important in the U.S. banking system than in Canada is the amount of borrowing that commercial banks do. Of the total of $278.3 billion, only a small proportion represents borrowed reserves of $.7 billion from the Federal Reserve banks. A much larger proportion involves individual banks borrowing reserves from each other. This is referred to as the Federal funds market, where banks with excess reserves lend funds to those who do not have enough to meet their requirements temporarily, sometimes just overnight. For the system as a whole however, net borrowings must be zero, and therefore the largest part of the borrowing category represents Eurodollar loans from overseas.

6.3 A SIMPLIFIED BANKING SYSTEM

For analytical purposes we want to simplify these balance sheets even further, allowing only enough detail to show the workings of the system. After eliminating the complications of the real world, Table 6-3 presents this simplified banking system. There are now two important links between the central bank and the commercial banks:

1. The central bank liabilities include reserves that are assets of the commercial banks.
2. The central bank can make loans to commercial banks that are carried as assets of the former and liabilities of the latter.

With the fictitious numbers in Table 6-3, we can make a number of useful calculations and in the process introduce a number of important concepts.

First, we see that in the initial position commercial banks hold $300 in reserves, composed of currency in their vaults valued at $50 and deposits at the central bank for the remainder. Next, given the assumed reserve requirements at the bottom of Table 6-3, we can calculate required reserves as .10 × $1,000 + .04 × $5,000 = $300. Therefore, banks hold no excess reserves at this point. Also, since they have not borrowed from the central bank, *free reserves*, which are defined as excess reserves minus borrowed reserves, are also zero.

Now, if we define M1 as currency held by the public plus demand deposits, we have $500 + $1,000 = $1,500. Then, M2 = M1 + time deposits or $1,500 + $5,000 = $6,500. Although the greater part of both M1 and M2 is private money provided by commercial-bank liabilities, the central bank does make available the currency held by the public. There-

Table 6-3. *Simplified banking structure*

		Central bank		
Assets		*Liabilities*		
Government securities	$700	Currency in circulation		$550
Foreign-currency assets	100	At commercial banks	50	
Advances to commercial banks	0	Held by the public	500	
		Deposits of commercial banks		250
	$800			$800
		Commercial banks		
Assets		*Liabilities*		
Currency	$ 50	Demand deposits		$1,000
Deposits at central bank	250	Time deposits		5,000
Earning assets	5,700	Borrowings from central bank		0
	$6,000			$6,000
Reserve requirements				
Demand deposits	10%			
Time deposits	4%			

fore, high-powered money, consisting of currency plus deposits of the commercial banks, which is $800 in this case, can also be defined as reserves of the commercial banks plus currency held by the public. Because the central bank liabilities represent a base for any of the monetary aggregates, this $800 is also referred to as the *monetary base*.

At the starting point of the analysis, currency is 33.3% of M1 and demand deposits are 66.7%. In M2, currency held by the public represents 7.7%, demand deposits are 15.4%, and time deposits are 76.9%. These proportions will be taken as given for now, but we shall see later that changes in interest rates will cause these proportions to be adjusted. Also, for later use, it is more useful to think of currency and time deposits as multiples of demand deposits. Thus the currency ratio is 500/1,000 = .5 and the time deposit ratio is 5,000/1,000 = 5.

Finally, the link between M1 or M2 and the monetary base is provided by the *money multiplier*. For M1 the value of the money multiplier is 1,500/800 = 1.875, while for M2 it is 6,500/800 = 8.125.

In more general terms, *the money supply equals the money multiplier times the monetary base*. In our macro model, since we use natural logs, this can be expressed as

$$m = k + m_b \quad (6.1)$$

where m is the natural log of the money supply (M1 or M2), k is the natural log of the money multiplier, and m_b is the natural log of the monetary base. Since both M1 and M2 are related to the same monetary base, the two multipliers must differ in size.

EXAMPLE

$k1 = .629$, while $m_b = 6.685$, so that $m1 = 7.314$, of which we can take the antilog to arrive at 1,500. Also, $k2$ is equal to 2.095 in this example and when added to $m_b = 6.685$, then $m2 = 8.780$, which leads to 6,500 when the antilog is taken.

Equation (6.1) makes the important point that by controlling the monetary base and knowing the money multiplier, the central bank can dictate the money supply. Furthermore, remembering that $m - m_{-1} = \mu$, and $m_b - m_{b-1} = \mu_b$, where μ is the growth rate of the money supply and μ_b is the growth rate of the monetary base, we can convert (6.1) into

$$(6.2) \quad \mu = k - k_{-1} + \mu_b$$

Now if k can be presumed to be constant over time, the central bank can control the growth rate of the private money supply merely be setting the growth rate of high-powered money equal to its target.

6.4 OPEN-MARKET OPERATIONS AND THE MONEY SUPPLY

But what is the technique used by the central bank to achieve the monetary base that it wants and the money supply target that it announced to the public? In general, the central bank has the ability to change its assets and liabilities in equal proportions. In the process, the rising or falling liabilities change the monetary base in the same proportion and, if the money multiplier remains constant, the same proportional change applies to any of the monetary aggregates. The most common method of changing the size of its assets and liabilities is through *open-market operations*. This involves the central bank buying or selling government securities in the bond market. If it buys securities, it increases the monetary base, and such an operation is considered expansionary; if it sells securities, the monetary base declines and the operation is thought to be contractionary. Buying securities is also considered expansionary from another viewpoint; since it creates excess demand in the bond market, interest rates, which move in the opposite direction to bond prices, will fall and stimulate investment. Consider an open-market purchase of $40 of securities. This shows up as an increase in holdings of government securities from $700 to $740. The central bank pays for these bonds with a check written on itself, which is likely to find its way into the deposit account of the commercial banks at the central bank raising this amount from $250 to $290. Thus both assets and liabilities of the central bank have risen equally by $40 or 5%. An open-market sale of $40 worth of securities would have had symmetrical effects; the monetary base would have declined by $40 or 5%.

Although the central bank is now in a new equilibrium, the commercial banks and the public in general are likely to want to restructure their assets and liabilities after the commercial bank reserves have risen by $40. First, the banks will have $40 more in assets but it is unlikely that they would want to hold this $40 as a nonearning asset since deposits at the central bank are not paid any interest. Commercial banks are, after all, profit-maximizing institutions, and they are likely to hold only those reserves that they need for the extra deposits that they create when they make new loans. Also, the public will want to hold currency and demand and time deposits in certain proportions, presumably the same with which they started. This suggests that the structure of the banking system has not changed, merely its scale. Therefore, the money multipliers for M1 and M2 remain the same as before. With this information, we can calculate the new M1 and M2, as well as its components, and show the final outcome for the balance sheets.

First, since the monetary base has risen by 5%, M1 increases by 5% from $1,500 to $1,575, as can be seen from solving $m1 = .629 + 6.733 = 7.362$ and taking antilogs. If currency held by the public remains 33.3% of M1, then it rises from $500 to $525. Also, demand deposits rise by 5% to $1,050 and remain 66.7% of M1. Next, time deposits rise by 5% from $5,000 to $5,250; they also remain at 76.9% of M2, which is now $6,825.

Are these numbers consistent with the balance-sheet requirements? First let us check required reserves. They are now equal to $.10 \times \$1,050 + .04 \times \$5,250 = \$315$. Since banks are assumed to hold no excess reserves, actual reserves must also equal $315. They are composed of deposits at the central bank equal to $290 plus $25 held as currency. In this case, the composition of reserves has changed, since individuals wanting to hold more currency to go along with their extra deposits got $25 more from the commercial banks. Finally, banks have increased their earning assets from $5,700 to $5,985. The final outcome is shown in the balance sheets in Table 6-4.

This way of changing the monetary base is not the only one available to the central bank. As an alternative, the monetary authorities could have purchased some foreign-currency assets worth $40 and could have produced the same result. This is not an unusual maneuver in an open economy where the central bank is attempting to influence the supply of and demand for foreign exchange, but for now we will not be concerned with this technique.

The important point to note from this exercise is that it verifies equation

Table 6-4. *Balance sheets of the banking system after an open-market operation*

	Central bank			
Assets		*Liabilities*		
Government securities	$740	Currency in circulation		$550
Foreign-currency assets	100	At commercial banks	25	
Advances to commercial banks	0	Held by the public	525	
		Deposits of commercial banks		290
	$840			$840
	Commercial banks			
Assets		*Liabilities*		
Currency	$ 25	Demand deposits		$1,050
Deposits at central bank	290	Time deposits		5,250
Earning assets	5,985	Borrowings from central bank		0
	$6,300			$6,300

(6.2) when k is constant. It shows that target growth rates for monetary aggregates can be achieved by applying those same target growth rates to the monetary base, which in turn requires that the central bank engage in open-market operations so that it increases its holdings of government securities from year to year at the same rate which it has chosen for the money supply. It should be noted that the central bank controls the entire monetary base but not the reserves of the commercial banks. Because the central bank is unable to influence the public's choice of currency holdings, it cannot specify the amount of currency in the banks' vaults, but only the total amount of currency outstanding.

Up to this point, it appears relatively easy for the central bank to follow a monetarist prescription of dictating the pace at which any of the conventional monetary aggregates is allowed to grow, but it must be reiterated that this mechanism relies on the assumptions that the central bank never relinquishes its control over the monetary base and that the money multiplier remains constant. Both of these assumptions, while useful as first approximations, are not as robust as one would wish. We can look at each of them in turn.

6.5 COMMERCIAL BANK BORROWING

In almost all countries the central bank acts as the lender of last resort to the government and to the commercial banks. If the commercial banks use this borrowing facility, the central bank is no longer able to determine the size of its own asset and liabilities. In Table 6-3, banks are

Table 6-5. *Balance sheets of the banking system after commercial-bank borrowing*

		Central bank		
Assets		*Liabilities*		
Government securities	$700	Currency in circulation		$550
Foreign-currency assets	100	At commercial banks	25	
Advances to commercial banks	40	Held by the public	525	
		Deposits of commercial banks		290
	$840			$840
		Commercial banks		
Assets		*Liabilities*		
Currency	$ 25	Demand deposits		$1,050
Deposits at central bank	290	Time deposits		5,250
Earning assets	6,025	Borrowings from central bank		40
	$6,340			$6,340

assumed to have no borrowings from the monetary authority, but we can perform an experiment that has the same result as the open-market operation shown in Table 6-4, without the central bank taking the initiative; instead, the commercial banks are assumed to want to increase their loan portfolio because of perceived profit opportunities. If they borrow $40 from the central bank, this shows up as an increase in their liabilities as well as an asset of the central bank. However, since these loans count as reserves, the commercial banks are again in a position of having $315 in reserves, which leads to the same expansion of the money supply (both M1 and M2), as was the case with the $40 open-market operation, except that commercial bank liabilities will be $6,340. The details are shown in Table 6-5.

In this situation, the central bank has been *forced* into expanding the monetary base, and together with a constant money multiplier, M1 or M2 will rise, not because the monetary authorities saw this as desirable, but because the commercial banks and the public did. Of course, it would be wrong to think of the central bank as being completely helpless in these circumstances. For example, it could offset the borrowing by open-market sales of securities, which would leave the monetary base at its original position, but since banks could then borrow even more reserves, we have to look at the ultimate constraint on this activity. Borrowing reserves involves a cost to the banks, and they will borrow only if the extra revenue from the loans to the public increase more than the cost of borrowing from the central bank. At the margin, the extra revenue should equal the additional cost so as to maximize profits. Because the central bank dictates the rate of interest at which commercial banks borrow reserves, it essentially controls the profit margin of these reserves.[2] By moving the discount rate relative to the rate of interest at which commercial banks lend their assets, the central bank can manipulate the borrowing of the commercial banks. For instance, raising the discount rate above the highest rate of interest charged by the commercial banks should almost entirely eliminate borrowing by the commercial banks. On the other hand, lowering the discount rate below the prime rate will encourage the banks to borrow reserves. In general, the central bank can gauge the borrowing level of the commercial banks for all feasible differentials between general interest rates and the discount rate; however, there may be circumstances where the predictions of the central bank are wrong and borrowings will be more or less than anticipated, leading to a money supply that is larger or smaller than expected. In this sense, there is randomness in the money market on the supply side as well as on the demand side. More specifically the monetary base has a predictable element, m_b and an unpredictable portion, x_b. Thus, equation (6.1) is expanded to

$$(6.3) \qquad m = k + m_b + x_b$$

In its dimensions x_b represents the proportionate change in the monetary base from its expected level. If x_b takes on a value of zero, as it is expected to do, then the money supply is entirely predictable; if $x_b > 0$, the monetary base rises by the value of x_b and so does the money supply.

EXAMPLE

Using the data in Table 6-5, if the $40 borrowed by the banks is unexpected, then $x_b = .05$ (i.e., 40/800) while m_b remains at 6.685 and $k1$ at .629, so that $m1$ becomes 7.362 as opposed to 7.314 previously, for a 5% increase.

The banking systems in Canada and the United States seem to differ with respect to the extent to which commercial banks borrow from the central bank. Whereas it is quite normal for commercial banks in the United States to borrow from each other and from the Federal Reserve, chartered banks in Canada are considered to be more reluctant to do so. However, there is another practice that essentially duplicates the effect of borrowing without it appearing in the balance sheets of the banks. This involves traditional relationships between the chartered banks and investment dealers on the one hand and between these investment dealers

[2] In Canada, this rate is called the *bank rate*, while in the United States, it is referred to as the *discount rate*.

and the central bank on the other. Investment dealers who hold government securities as their assets obtain day-to-day loans from the banks to finance these portfolios. However, if the banks call some of these short-term loans, the investment dealers can get an indirect loan from the Bank of Canada by agreeing to sell and then repurchase securities at a later date at stipulated prices. The investment dealers are middlemen in this operation but it has the same effect as direct borrowing by the chartered banks from the Bank of Canada.[3]

6.6 THE MONEY MULTIPLIERS

As the next step, we want to find the factors that determine the money multipliers and how they change over time. This information will establish the link between the monetary base and the money supply. Again, the main emphasis is on distinguishing between predictable and unpredictable changes in the money multipliers. Only the latter are cause for concern. If the monetary authorities know that certain events will force the money multiplier to rise, they merely need to lower the monetary base by the appropriate amount to achieve the targeted money supply; but if the money multiplier rises and the central bank is not yet aware of this, it will not be able to prevent the money supply from departing from its target path.

Two money multipliers need to be defined, one for M1 and the other for M2. We will use the example of the banking system in Table 6-3 to show how these multipliers are calculated. First, let us define in natural units and *not* in natural logs:

C_p = currency held by the public

C_b = currency in the vaults of the commercial banks

D_d = demand deposits held by the public

D_t = time deposits held by the public

D_b = deposits of the commercial banks at the central bank

q_c = currency ratio = C_p/D_d

q_t = time deposit ratio = D_t/D_d

e_d = reserve ratio for demand deposits

e_t = reserve ratio for time deposits

[3] Data on investment dealer activity is contained in the *Bank of Canada Review*, table 36 for inventories of securities, table 19 for purchase and resale agreements between the dealers and the Bank of Canada, and table 10 for chartered-bank loans to investment dealers.

Using the definitions of q_c and q_t, it can be verified that currency and demand deposits are in the proportions $q_c/(1 + q_c)$ and $1/(1 + q_c)$ in M1, while currency, demand and time deposits are in proportions $q_c/(1 + q_c + q_t)$, $1/(1 + q_c + q_t)$, and $q_t/(1 + q_c + q_t)$ in M2.

First, the multiplier for M1 is defined as

$$\text{(6.4)} \qquad \text{M1 multiplier} = (C_p + D_d)/(C_p + C_b + D_b)$$

Remember that the monetary base which forms the denominator of the multiplier includes all currency outstanding, which is the sum $C_p + C_b$. Also, reserves of the commercial banks can be defined as $C_b + D_b$. If commercial banks carry no excess reserves, then all reserves are required to back the two types of deposits of the public and therefore

$$\text{(6.5)} \qquad C_b + D_b = e_d D_d + e_t D_t$$

Required reserves are a weighted average of D_d and D_t. Since it is typically true that $e_d > e_t$, an increase in D_t at the expense of D_d will lower the amount of reserves that the banks have to carry. Substituting equation (6.5) and the definitions for q_c and q_t into (6.4) produces

$$\text{(6.6)} \qquad \text{M1 multiplier} = (1 + q_c)/(e_d + e_t q_t + q_c)$$

It is important to note that (6.3) is an identity because it involves a definition, but (6.6) contains assumed behavioral information about excess reserves and desired proportions of currency and demand and time deposits. From the data in Table 6-3, we know that $q_c = .5$, $q_t = 5$, $e_d = .10$, and $e_t = .04$. Therefore, the M1 multiplier is $(1 + .5)/(.10 + .04 \times 5 + .5) = 1.875$ and when we take natural logs we obtain $k1 = .629$.

Next we want to investigate how the M1 multiplier may change. First, an increase in q_c raises both the numerator and the denominator to the same extent, but since the numerator is always larger than the denominator, the proportionate increase for the former is smaller than for the latter, and hence the multiplier falls. An increase in the currency ratio reduces both the reserves that the banks have and those that they need. If the public chooses to hold more currency relative to demand deposits, they obtain it from the commercial banks, who find that the reserve drain of each dollar is greater than the reduction in required reserves from the lower demand deposits. The value of q_c is essentially established by technological factors and does not change much over time, except that it has seasonal features. However, such innovations as the introduction of universal credit cards reduce the need for currency and lower q_c once and for all. Second, an increase in either e_d or e_t will reduce the size of the multiplier. In the past, both the Bank of Canada and the Fed were able to make alterations in minimum reserve requirements, but now the Bank Act of 1981 in Canada and the Monetary Control Act of 1980 in the United

States have fixed the reserve requirements, as shown in Tables 6-1 and 6-2. Therefore, these parameters should be thought of as institutionally given constants.[4] Finally, an increase in q_t will also lower the M1 multiplier. When the public decides to have more time deposits for every dollar of demand deposits, more reserves are required to hold against the new time deposits but no more are available. Thus the existing monetary base supports a smaller amount of M1 and the multiplier must fall. However, the M2 multiplier will be affected in a different way, as we shall see shortly.

PROOFS

From calculus, $\partial(\text{M1 multiplier})/\partial q_c = (e_d + e_t q_t - 1)/(e_d + e_t q_t + q_c)^2 < 0$ since e_d, e_t, and q_t are all much smaller than one. Next, $\partial(\text{M1 multiplier})/\partial q_t = -e_t(1 + q_c)/(e_d + e_t q_t + q_c)^2 < 0$.

Not directly observable in equation (6.6) is the effect of introducing excess reserves into bank behavior, but we can calculate their influence on the multiplier. If total reserves exceed required reserves, the value of the multiplier falls because the existing level of reserves will be able to support a smaller money supply. Assume that banks hold excess reserves in the ratio q_e to demand deposits. Then

$$\text{(6.7)} \quad \text{M1 multiplier} = (1 + q_c)/(e_d + e_t q_t + q_c + q_e)$$

which is smaller than the multiplier in (6.6). Since it was asserted earlier that banks are profit-maximizing institutions, we need to explore the reasons for their holding non-interest-earning excess reserves. In general, banks are unable to calculate precisely what reserves they will need in each accounting period, and since e_d and e_t are defined as legal minima, they must always allow for a positive margin of error. Of course, banks can borrow reserves from each other or from the Fed, but it may be cheaper to hold some excess reserves. The cost of borrowing reserves is the discount rate, whereas the opportunity cost of excess reserves is the market interest rate. If the discount rate is a "penalty rate" in the sense that it is above the market rate, then holding excess reserves seems to be the better strategy. From that viewpoint, the larger is the difference between the discount rate and the market rate, the larger are systemwide excess reserves. Thus the multiplier is sensitive to the interest rate; with

[4] In Canada, there is a secondary reserve requirement that can vary between 0 and 12%. Secondary reserves are defined as Treasury bills, day-to-day loans to investment dealers, and excess primary reserves.

a given monetary base and discount rate, both under the control of the central bank, a rise in the market interest rate will reduce excess reserves and increase the money multiplier and M1.

In summary, the value of the M1 multiplier depends on decisions of the central bank (i.e., the discount rate and perhaps e_d and e_t), the commercial banks (i.e., q_e), and the public (i.e., q_c and q_t).

Turning now to M2, the multiplier is defined as

$$\text{(6.8)} \quad \text{M2 multiplier} = (C_p + D_d + D_t)/(C_p + C_b + D_b)$$

which becomes

$$\text{(6.9)} \quad \text{M2 multiplier} = (1 + q_c + q_t)/(e_d + e_t q_t + q_c)$$

when the previously discussed behavioral relationships are substituted. In equation (6.9) excess reserves are again assumed to be zero, but their existence can be reintroduced by adding q_e to the denominator of the equation. The M2 multiplier is exactly the same as the M1 multiplier except that it has q_t in the numerator which makes it larger. Thus from Table 6-3 the M2 multiplier is equal to $(1 + .5 + 5)/(.10 + .04 \times 5 + .5) = 8.125$, and when we take natural logs, $k2 = 2.095$. Changes in q_c, e_d, and e_t have the same effect on the M2 multiplier as on the M1 multiplier, but an increase in q_t now seems to have an ambiguous effect on the multiplier for M2 because it appears in both the numerator and the denominator of (6.9). However, this multiplier will always increase if q_t rises, since this parameter appears by itself in the numerator but is multiplied by e_t, which is much less than one, in the denominator, forcing the numerator to rise in greater proportion than the denominator.

PROOF

$$\partial(\text{M2 multiplier})/\partial q_t = [(e_d - e_t) + q_c(1 - e_t)]/[e_d + e_t q_t + q_c]^2 > 0 \text{ since } e_t < e_d < 1.$$

Earlier, in Chapter 5, we saw that rising nominal interest rates in a period of accelerating prices increased the opportunity cost of M1 more than of M2. This was especially true in the period 1975–81 when the public shifted out of demand deposits and into time deposits and the newly created checkable interest-earning accounts such as NOW and ATS. This is essentially captured by an increase in q_t. Therefore, interest rates once more have an effect on the value of the multipliers, but in different directions for M1 and M2. A higher interest rate increases q_t, which lowers the M1 multiplier but raises the M2 multiplier. For this reason, the central bank is unable to force both M1 and M2 to grow at the same rate at a time when inflation is rising, as is evident from Table 5-2.

Much of the adjustment in these two multipliers is predictable, but some of it clearly is not. It was found in Chapter 5, for instance, that the shift of money demand from demand deposits to interest-earning checkable accounts seemed to catch the central banks in both Canada and the United States by surprise, especially by the size of the adjustment and its permanence. Thus, changes in the multipliers are partly determined by interest rates and other predictable factors and partly by random events that cannot be evaluated until after the fact. This leads to one final change in equation (6.1) to

(6.10) $m = k + x_k + m_b + x_b$

where a positive x_k represents an unpredictable increase in the money multiplier over what is given by k.

EXAMPLE CONTINUES

> If, in addition to the $40 borrowed reserves, q_t rises unexpectedly from 5 to 6, then $k1 = .579$ and $k2 = 2.189$, so that $m1 = 7.312$, which is lower, and $m2 = 8.922$, which is higher.

We now have a host of x's that in Chapter 3 were all identified with x_m, a shock to the money market in general. Although it may appear easy now to pinpoint the supply-side and demand-side shocks, this is not really the case. Consider, for example, an increase in q_t. This involves a change in the public's habits with respect to the form in which they hold money balances and appears to be a demand-side event, but it has its impact on the supply of money by changing the money multipliers. Nevertheless, as we shall see later, it is important to try to identify the source of any monetary shock.

6.7 MONEY MULTIPLIERS IN CANADA AND THE UNITED STATES, 1975–82

In order to make target growth rates for one or more of the monetary aggregates useful macroeconomic policy instruments, the central bank must be able to determine the size of the money multipliers and be able to predict the effect of its own policy changes and other exogenous events on the value that these multipliers take at a point in time. It is, of course, not possible to know how much information the Canadian and

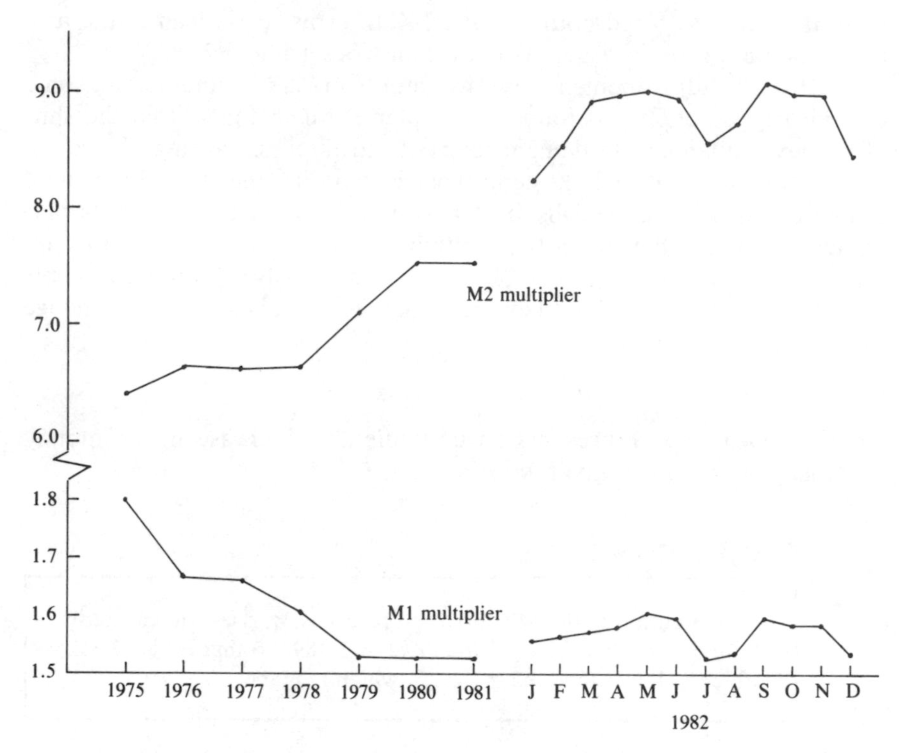

Chart 6-1 Money multipliers in Canada, 1975–82. *Source: Bank of Canada Review,* table 9 for M1 and M2 and table 3 for the monetary base, end of period, not seasonally adjusted.

American central banks have on the money multipliers with which they work, but their variability over the past few years must give cause for concern.

Let us first look at the M1 and M2 multipliers for Canada for the period 1975–82. Chart 6-1 shows the December figures for each year from 1975 to 1981 to indicate the trend of these multipliers and monthly figures for 1982 to exhibit the short-run properties of the multipliers. The most obvious feature of the trend for the M1 and M2 multipliers is that the former fell rather steadily while the latter rose.[5] This pattern is entirely consistent with the rise in q_t, the time deposit ratio, throughout this period. This in turn was caused by the rising nominal interest rates during the period as actual and expected inflation grew. Over the short run, the picture is somewhat different. There seems to be a lot of "noise" in the monthly

[5] The scale is not the same for the two lines, so that the rise in the M2 multiplier is actually more dramatic than would appear.

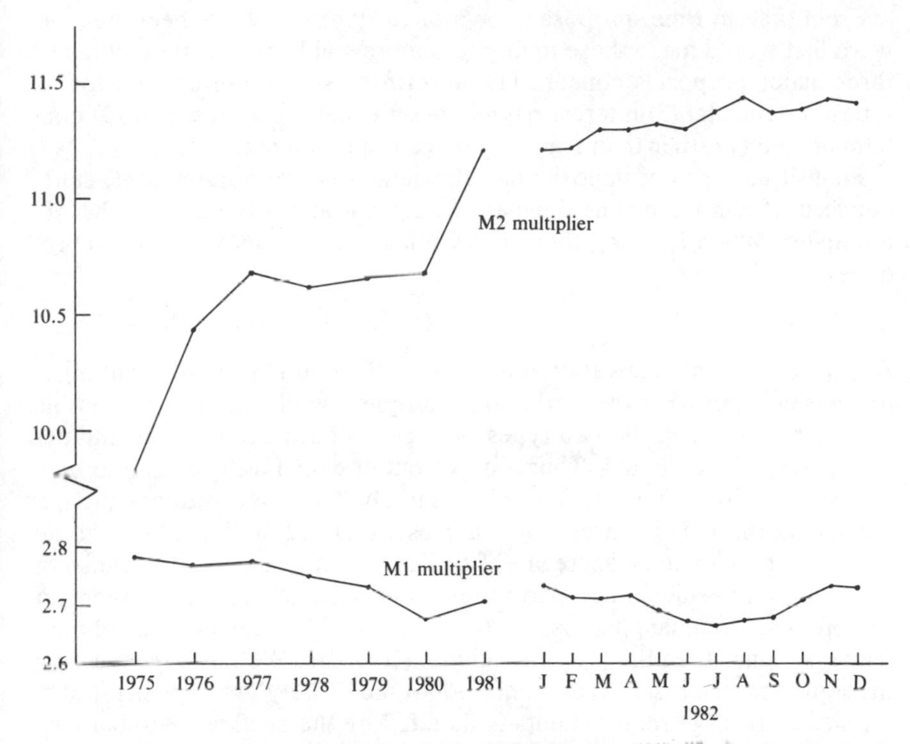

Chart 6-2 Money multipliers in the United States, 1975–82. *Source: Economic Report of the President,* Washington, D.C., 1983, table B61 for M1 and M2 and table B66 for the monetary base, end of period, seasonally adjusted.

values for the multipliers, some of which may be seasonal, since the data for the monetary base are published only in seasonally unadjusted values. One thing to note is that in 1982, both multipliers seemed to move up and down together rather than in opposite directions. It is not clear how much of this variability the Bank of Canada can predict, but there must be changes in q_c, q_t, and q_e that come as surprises to the monetary authorities.

For the United States the two multipliers are consistently larger than in Canada, but that fact is of no great importance. Chart 6-2 shows the same general pattern of a falling M1 multiplier and a rising M2 multiplier. The same general reason of rising opportunity cost of holding M1 balances is at work here, although, as will be recalled, American M1 includes interest-earning checkable accounts. The month-to-month changes in these multipliers are noticeably smaller than in Canada, mainly because they are seasonally adjusted, but there are still variations, some of which are surely unpredictable.

From time to time, proposals for monetary reform have been put forward that would make these multipliers more stable and predictable. The three major proposals concern (1) uniform reserve requirements for all types of deposits, (2) interest payments on excess reserves, and (3) contemporaneous rather than lagged reserve requirements.

First, if all types of deposits had the same reserve requirement, shifts between demand and time deposits would not affect the size of the M2 multiplier. When $e_d = e_t$, then substituting equation (6.5) into (6.8) produces

(6.11) M2 multiplier $= [C_p + D_d + D_t]/[C_p + e_d(D_d + D_t)]$

As long as the only substitution is between D_d and D_t, the M2 multiplier remains constant. However, the M1 multiplier would still be susceptible to switches between the two types of deposits because only demand deposits are included in M1. Thus a move out of demand deposits into time deposits will lower the M1 multiplier, merely because it reduces the numerator of (6.4). This observation suggests that M2, and not M1, should be the target monetary aggregate if this proposal is accepted because of its improved predictability. However, it may be difficult to implement any proposal for changing reserve requirements if the new universal minimum is higher than the present weighted average. We no longer rely on the argument that reserves are required for the "safety" of deposits; today the size of reserve requirements is dictated by the need to keep banking profits in line with those in related industries.

The second proposed measure dealing with interest payments on excess reserves would also affect profits, but favorably, making a combination of the reforms more palatable to the banking system. More important, interest payments on excess reserves at the same rate as the discount rate would make the money multipliers more stable. At the present time, excess reserves tend to expand as market interest rates fall in relation to the discount rate because the opportunity cost of holding excess reserves is currently measured by the rate at which banks make loans. With interest receipts on excess reserves at the same rate as interest payments on borrowed reserves, banks would be indifferent between the two for meeting temporary reserve needs. Thus q_e in equation (6.7) would become more predictable as would the money multipliers.

The third proposal is concerned with the timing of reserve requirements. Under a *lagged* reserve requirement, as exists in both countries at the present time, banks must post their required reserves in any given period based on deposits for an earlier period, whereas *contemporaneous* reserve requirements are calculated on the basis of current deposit liabilities. It is claimed that the former lead to more volatile multipliers. The M1 multiplier of equation (6.6) was based on the assumption of contemporaneous reserves as dictated by (6.5). Alternatively, lagged reserves would involve

(6.12) $C_b + D_b = e_d D_{d-1} + e_t D_{t-1}$

and the M1 multiplier would become

(6.13) M1 multiplier $= [1 + q_c]/[e_d(D_{d-1}/D_d) + e_t q_t(D_{t-1}/D_t) + q_c]$

Comparing (6.13) and (6.6) reveals that lagged reserves introduce two new sources of variability in the multipliers, D_{d-1}/D_d and D_{t-1}/D_t. If demand or time deposits increase from one period to the next, these ratios become smaller than one and the M1 multiplier becomes larger. From that point of view, contemporaneous reserve calculations are to be preferred, but they in turn can introduce greater volatility in short-term interest rates as banks make last-minute adjustments in their reserve positions to meet requirements at the end of the period. This is particularly problematic in the United States, where banks are often forced to borrow reserves in the Federal funds market even with lagged reserves, which eliminate uncertainty about the base on which reserves must be calculated. In 1981, the Federal Reserve Board requested public comment on a proposal to implement contemporaneous reserve requirements, but no action has yet been taken.[6]

6.8 EQUILIBRIUM IN THE MONEY MARKET

So far, the discussion has concerned itself with the supply of money, but by bringing forward the major conclusions about the demand for money from Chapter 5, we are now in a position to examine the equilibrium properties of the money market when supply and demand interact. In Chapter 2, it was asserted that the interest rate was the equilibrating variable in the money market. In fact, because transactions in asset markets can be virtually instantaneous, the interest rate can adjust immediately to any disturbance in the money market. Therefore, we can take income and prices as given for the time it takes the interest rate to clear the market.

In looking at the money market, only one monetary aggregate will be considered. At this stage, the distinction between M1 and M2 is not as important as before. On the demand side, given income and the price level, the demand for money is inversely related to the nominal interest

[6] See *Federal Reserve Bulletin*, 67, November 1981, pp. 856–7; for details of the calculation of the Canadian "statutory cash reserve ratio" see H. H. Binhammer, *Money, Banking, and the Canadian Financial System*, fourth edition, Toronto, Methuen, 1982, p. 243.

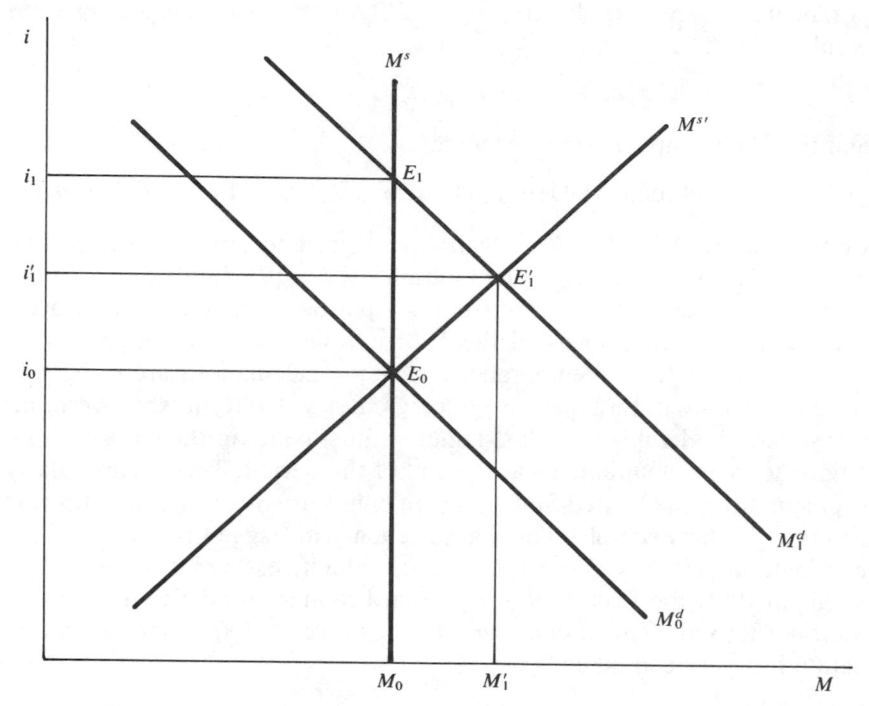

Figure 6-1 Equilibrium in the money market after a shift of the M^d curve.

rate. Thus, M^d is drawn with a negative slope in Figure 6-1. An increase in either income or the price level will shift the M^d curve upward, since at the existing interest rate excess demand for money would appear because of the need for larger transactions balances. Until we reached this chapter, the supply of money was considered to be completely exogenously determined by the central bank. This presumption is captured by the vertical M^s curve in Figure 6-1. However, for two reasons the supply of money may now be positively related to the interest rate. First, the monetary base will expand if commercial banks borrow from the central bank, and the higher is the market rate of interest relative to the discount rate, the larger will be borrowed reserves. Second, the money multiplier rises with the interest rate, since excess reserves will be reduced. In other words, in equation (6.1) both m_b and k increase with the interest rate; therefore, so does the money supply. For that reason, $M^{s\prime}$ is drawn with a positive slope as an alternative supply curve. They all intersect at E_0, with i_0 as the equilibrium interest rate and M_0 as the amount of money in the economy for both supply curves.

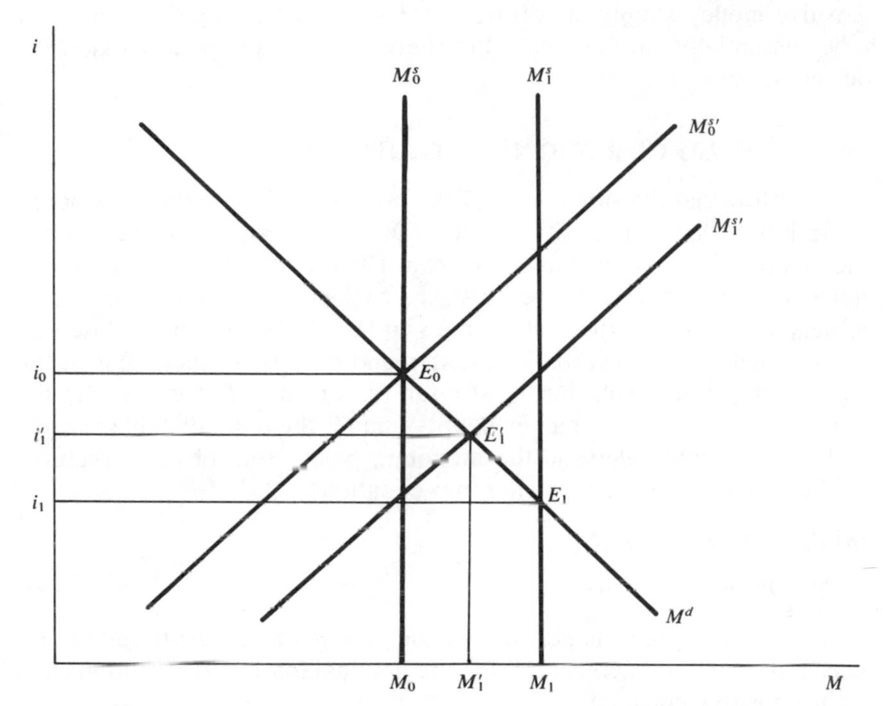

Figure 6-2 Equilibrium in the money market after a shift of the M^s curve.

What difference does the alternative supply function make to money-market equilibrium? To answer this question we conduct a number of experiments and predict their effect on the interest rate and the quantity of money. First, consider an upward shift of the M^d curve to M_1^d caused by one of the reasons enumerated above. As a result, if M^s is relevant, the interest rate jumps to i_1, but the amount of money in the economy remains unchanged. Here, the entire shock is taken up by price adjustment and none by quantity adjustment. With $M^{s\prime}$ as the supply curve, the interest rate rises only to i_1', but the amount of money rises to M_1', allowing for both price and quantity changes. Next consider an exogenous change on the supply side. In Figure 6-2, the two supply curves are shifted to the right by equal amounts because of an increase in the monetary base or a larger multiplier. With M_1^s, the new equilibrium is at E_1, with i lower and M higher, but if $M_1^{s\prime}$ is the relevant curve, the equilibrium is established at E_1', with smaller adjustments in both i and M.

On the basis of these comparisons it is not clear which supply function is to be preferred. There is nothing inherently wrong with an interest-sensitive money supply, and it does not make the conduct of monetary policy essentially more difficult, but there are differences in reactions to various shocks.

6.9 THE *LM* CURVE ONCE AGAIN

Now that the supply side of the money market has been explored in depth, the slope and position of the *LM* curve needs to be reexamined once more. It will be remembered from Chapter 5 that the demand for money can be conveniently summarized by income and the interest-rate influences, but that structural changes in the 1970s caused existing empirical equations to overpredict the demand for M1 balances. From the supply side, two conclusions will alter the existing *LM* curve: (1) the interest sensitivity of the money supply and (2) the unpredictable aspects of the money multiplier and the monetary base. Both of these features can be captured by the following two equations:

(6.14) $k = k_0 + b_{13}i$

(6.15) $m_b = m_{b0} + b_{14}i$

where k_0 and m_{b0} are the portions of the multiplier and the base that are independent of the interest rate, i is the nominal interest rate, and b_{13} and b_{14} are positive constants.

Substituting (6.14) and (6.15) and (6.10) produces

(6.16) $m^s = k_0 + b_{13}i + x_k + m_{b0} + b_{14}i + x_b$

where m^s is used to signify the natural log of the money supply. On the demand side of the money market we have

(6.17) $m^d - p = a_2y - a_3i + x_d$

where p and y are the natural logs of the price level and income, respectively, a_2 and a_3 are positive constants, and x_d is a random element in the demand for money. If the money market is always in equilibrium, $m^s = m^d = m$ and (6.14) and (6.15) can be equated to produce

(6.18) $k_0 + b_{13}i + x_k + m_{b0} + b_{14}i + x_b - p = a_2y - a_3i + x_d$

which is rewritten as

(6.18′) $k_0 + m_{b0} + x_k + x_b - p = a_2y - a_3''i + x_d$

where $a_3'' = a_3 + b_{13} + b_{14}$. In other words, the interest elasticity of the *LM* curve, now measured by a_3'', is larger.[7] This makes the *LM* curve as

[7] a_3' was used in Chapter 5 to measure the interest elasticity of a broader aggregate than M1; $a_3' < a_3$.

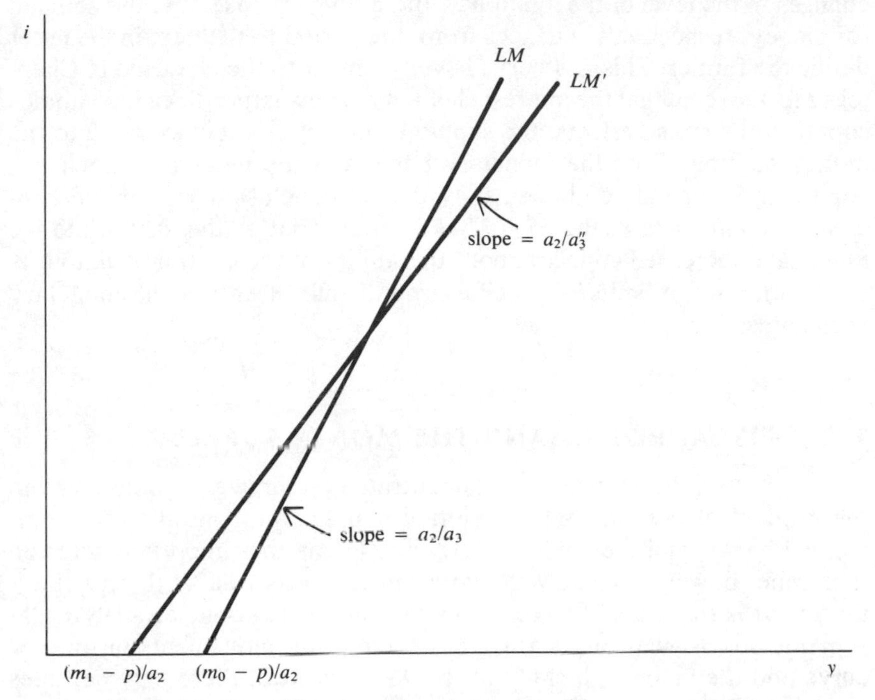

Figure 6-3 The *LM* curve with an interest-sensitive money supply.

shown in Figure 6-3 flatter than previously. It also has a smaller horizontal intercept, since at very low levels of the interest rate the money supply becomes smaller than its exogenous counterpart. In (6.18′), $k_0 + m_{b0}$ comprise the controllable portion of the amount of money in the economy and $x_k + x_b - x_d$ represents the sum of the unpredictable elements.

In an inflationary environment, the focus is on the growth rate of both money and prices. The nominal amount of money in the economy grows according to

$$(6.19) \quad m - m_{-1} = (k_0 - k_{0_{-1}}) + (x_k - x_{k_{-1}}) + \mu_b + (x_b - x_{b_{-1}}) - (x_d - x_{d_{-1}})$$

while the inflation rate is given by $\pi = p - p_{-1}$. Equation (6.18′) is now written as

$$(6.20) \quad k_0 - k_{0_{-1}} + \mu_b + x_m - \pi = a_2 y - a_3'' i - (m - p)_{-1}$$

where x_m, previously referred to as a general monetary shock, is equal to $(x_k - x_{k_{-1}}) + (x_b - x_{b_{-1}}) - (x_d - x_{d_{-1}})$. Since x_m represents a shock to the growth rate of money while x_k, x_b, and x_d refer to unexpected changes in the level of the multiplier, the monetary base, and the demand for money, respectively, changes from one period to the next in the latter define the former. This *LM* curve is very similar to the one used in Chapters 2 to 4, except that the interest elasticity is now larger since it combines supply and demand effects, the supply of money is decomposed into the money multiplier and the monetary base, and the monetary shock has supply and demand components. With that conclusion we can have increased confidence in the *IS–LM–AS* model, but at the same time we must have increased concern about the ability of the central bank to dictate, within close limits, a specific growth rate of any of the monetary aggregates.

6.10 FISCAL POLICY AND THE MONEY SUPPLY

So far, the analysis has concentrated on three groups involved in the process of determining the money supply: the central bank, commercial banks, and the public. There may be another important actor on the scene, however, namely the government in its role as the fiscal authority. It is traditional to keep monetary and fiscal policies analytically separate so that we can identify the former with movements in the *LM* curve and the latter with shifts of the *IS* curve. But there may be times and circumstances when monetary policy is not independent of fiscal policy and the money supply may be determined in part by the interactions of the Treasury and the central bank. For instance, in the early post–World War II period, governments had large debts created by war finance. These debts required refinancing from time to time, and to keep interest costs as low as possible central banks were "encouraged" to buy some of these bonds to raise their price or lower the interest rate beyond what would otherwise prevail.

With the aid of the simplified banking system, first presented in Table 6-3, we can investigate how fiscal policy influences the monetary base and the money supply. In Table 6-4, an open-market purchase of $40 of government bonds was assumed to take place at the initiative of the central bank; however, the same transaction and the same outcome would occur if the government had a budgetary deficit of $40, which is financed by issuing bonds in this amount, and if the government can convince the central bank to buy all of these bonds. The extent to which this can happen depends very much on the historical independence of the central bank from the government. Although central banks are owned by governments, central bankers usually have some independence from the Treasury or Finance Department in making decisions about open-market operations. For the immediate postwar period that independence was not great, but

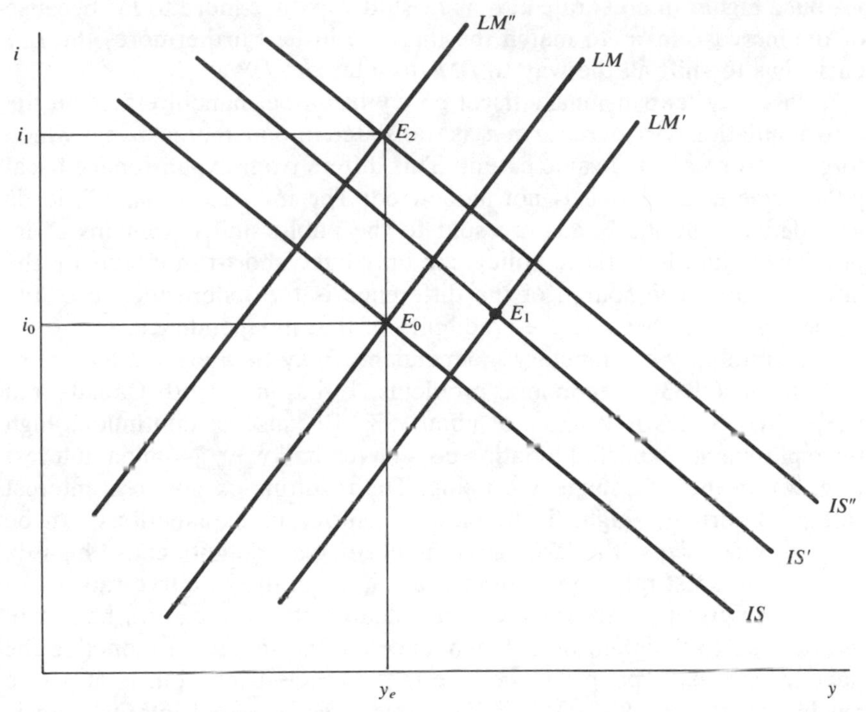

Figure 6-4 Fiscal policy effects on the money supply.

in more recent times central bankers have tried to establish the position that they are not required to finance the government's need without reference to the macroeconomy's needs.

The possibility of fiscal-policy effects on the money supply is examined in the *IS–LM* diagram of Figure 6-4. From a position of long-run equilibrium, assume that the government increases its expenditures relative to tax revenue once and for all, leading to a permanent budget deficit. This is captured by an increase in a_0 in the *IS* curve, which now shifts upward by $1/a_1$ times the increase in a_0. If the central bank is forced to finance this deficit by buying the bonds, there will be a permanent increase in the growth rate of the money supply as the central bank increases its holdings of government securities by the size of the deficit in each and every subsequent time period. Therefore, μ rises relative to π and the *LM* curve shifts down by $1/a_3$ times the increase in μ or a_0. At the new short-run equilibrium, E_1, there will be an increase in y, but the effect on the interest rate is ambiguous without information about the relative size of a_1 and a_3. This, of course, is not the long-run outcome of such an experiment. In the final equilibrium, there will be the same level of output,

y_e, but a higher interest rate at i_1 as *IS* shifts up once more to *IS*″ because of the increase in π^e to match the increase in μ. Furthermore, the *LM* curve has to shift all the way to *LM*″ to intersect *IS*″ at E_2.

In this way, expansionary fiscal policy has a permanent effect on the rate of inflation: An increase in a_0 is translated into an increase in μ which forces π to rise to the same extent. This differs from expansionary fiscal policy where the deficit is not monetized: The increase in a_0 still leads to a deficit, but the bonds are sold to the public and μ remains at its previous value; here fiscal policy can only have short-run effects on the inflation rate. The source of the difference is the independence of the monetary authorities and the credibility of that independence.

The credibility of monetary independence may be a critical feature of the current (1983–4) economic problems. Inflation in both Canada and the United States is running at about 5%. Because of continuous high unemployment, expected inflation could even be lower. Nominal interest rates are in the 10% range and rising. The resulting ex post real interest rate is abnormally high. Two somewhat different explanations can be offered. One is that the large government budget deficits cause high ex ante real interest rates since an increase in a_0 in the *IS* curve raises $i - \pi^e$ for any given y. Alternatively, it is feared that the central bank will not be able to maintain its independence and be forced to monetize the debt, which leads people to believe that expected inflation is at a rate much higher than 5%, say 7–8%. In that case, the real interest rate is much lower, at about 3%. Which of these explanations is closer to the truth makes a large difference in terms of predicting aggregate demand and wage behavior, but since we cannot observe π^e directly, it is not possible to decide in favor of one over the other.

6.11 SUMMARY

The central bank does not control the money supply directly. Instead, the money supply has two components:

1. the money multiplier, which depends for its value on decisions of the central bank, the commercial banks, and the public; and
2. the monetary base, which is largely determined by the central bank through open-market operations and the setting of the discount rate at which the commercial banks borrow.

Both the money multiplier and the monetary base are also subject to random shocks, which in turn create some unpredictability of the money supply. Despite these additional features, the *LM* curve is not altered very much; it becomes more interest-elastic since the money supply is positively related to the interest rate and the money-market shock can be decomposed into supply and demand shocks. Fiscal policy can influence the money supply if the central bank is forced to "monetize" budget deficits.

EXERCISES

The following monthly data for 1982 for Canada and the United States refer to *measured* $k1$, $k2$, and m_b, including unobservable x_k and x_b (m_b is measured in natural logs of millions of dollars for Canada and billions for the United States).

Canada

	Jan.	Feb.	Mar.	Apr.	May	June	July	Aug.	Sep.	Oct.	Nov.	Dec.
$k1$	.437	.447	.471	.482	.509	.476	.417	.425	.473	.459	.463	.424
$k2$	1.999	2.029	2.065	2.074	2.088	2.078	2.028	2.051	2.097	2.087	2.087	2.012
m_b	9.719	9.700	9.675	9.674	9.669	9.686	9.737	9.714	9.674	9.688	9.686	9.773

United States

	Jan.	Feb.	Mar.	Apr.	May	June	July	Aug.	Sep.	Oct.	Nov.	Dec.
$k1$	1.004	.999	.998	1.000	.990	.984	.981	.984	.985	.997	1.006	1.005
$k2$	2.416	2.418	2.424	2.425	2.426	2.425	2.431	2.438	2.431	2.433	2.437	2.435
m_b	5.102	5.104	5.107	5.115	5.122	5.129	5.131	5.136	5.147	5.152	5.157	5.165

1. Calculate the mean and the standard deviation of $k1$ and $k2$ for each country.
   (a) Are the M1 multipliers more stable than the M2 multipliers?
   (b) Are Canadian multipliers more stable than U.S. multipliers?
2. (a) Calculate the average monthly growth rate of the monetary base for the period January to December 1982 in each country.
   (b) Calculate x_b for each month on the basis that the predictable portion of m_b grows at that rate calculated in exercise 2(a) from a December 1981 base of 9.668 in Canada and 5.093 in the United States. Show that the sum of the x_b's is zero.
   (c) In which country is the growth rate of the monetary base more stable?
3. (a) Calculate monthly $m1$ under two assumptions: (i) $m1 = k1 +$

$m_b + x_b$ (use the average multiplier) and (ii) $m1 = k1 + x_k + m_b$ (use the predictable portion of m_b). Also calculate actual $m1$ from the data in the above tables.

(b) Which of x_k or x_b creates greater problems for stable $m1$ growth?

FURTHER READING

Binhammer, H. H., *Money, Banking, and the Canadian Financial System,* fourth edition, Toronto, Methuen, 1982. Chapters 14–18 deal with the control of the money supply in Canada.

Cathcart, C. D., *Money, Credit, and Economic Activity,* Homewood, Ill., Irwin, 1982. Chapters 13–14 offer a more detailed discussion of the money-supply process in the United States.

CHAPTER 7

The monetary mechanism

7.1 INTRODUCTION

From the previous chapters we have learned what monetary policy can and cannot do to stabilize income and employment. In this chapter we can start to look at how the monetary authorities should approach their task in the light of their limited capabilities. In other words, we are now more concerned with techniques than with ultimate goals. In this chapter, then, the emphasis is not on *monetary policy* but on the *monetary mechanism* while we look into the "control room" of the central bank. We know that the macroeconomy is subjected from time to time to random shocks from all directions, causing output, employment, inflation, and the interest rate to deviate from long-run equilibrium values. The aim of stabilization policy is to find a monetary mechanism that mitigates the effect of these shocks, especially on income and employment. This involves finding a *policy instrument* over which the monetary authority has complete control, which has a predictable effect on the important macroeconomic variables, and which creates countercyclical forces automatically. Therefore, there are three important features to look for in an optimal monetary mechanism: *controllability, effectiveness,* and *automaticity*. There is no sense in choosing a policy instrument that is only very imprecisely regulated by the central bank. An example would be the amount of currency held by the public, since the central bank cannot "force" individuals to hold a certain fraction of the total currency outstanding. Also, it would not be wise to choose a policy instrument that has unpredictable effects on output or inflation. An example here is the amount of total currency outstanding; although the central bank can dictate this amount to the last dollar, the availability of virtually perfect substitutes in the form of bank deposits makes this a highly unreliable policy instrument. Finally, it would be wrong to rely on a policy instrument that cannot be adjusted until after the shock has had its effect when it might be the cause of further instability rather than an instrument of stabilization. An example of a *discretionary* policy in the present institutional relationship between the central bank and commercial banks is a change in the discount rate. Instead, what is needed is a policy instrument that counters the shock as it occurs. This does not mean that monetary policy should always be on "automatic pilot." Such servomechanisms have their benefits in an environment of the existing *IS–LM–AS* model subjected to random disturbances from known sources, but if the structure of the economy changes, then we need to change the policy regime as well. Therefore, there is no universal optimal monetary mechanism; the best choice depends on the circumstances. The focus of this chapter is on how that choice should be made.

7.2 WHAT SHOULD THE CENTRAL BANK CONTROL?

The central bank basically has a choice of controlling one of two financial variables: the monetary base or the interest rate. In Chapter 6, we saw how the central bank can literally dictate the size of the monetary base through its open-market operations or through setting of the rate at which it lends to commercial banks. Alternatively, because of its importance in asset market transactions it can also have a large influence on the interest rate. For instance, in the weekly auction of Treasury bills, both the Canadian and U.S. central banks make bids for substantial portions of each offering. The price of their bids acts as a pace setter for the other participants in the market. In this way and through daily open-market operations they can virtually peg the interest rate at whatever rate they wish. However, the central bank cannot establish separate goals for the monetary base and for the interest rate, because there is only one equilibrium interest rate and one equilibrium monetary base or money supply. Therefore, in the long run controlling the money supply is equivalent to choosing the equilibrium interest rate, whereas pegging the interest rate is tantamount to determining the growth rate of the money supply and the inflation rate. In this setting, there is no conflict in the control mechanism, and this is the first proposition that we want to establish in Section 7.3. However, when the economy is subjected to shocks, the choice between controlling interest rates or the monetary base is very much dependent on the source of the shocks. This proposition is taken up in Section 7.4.

7.3 THE CHOICE OF INSTRUMENTS IN EQUILIBRIUM

To analyze these issues we will concentrate on the *IS–LM* part of the macro model. The *AS* curve will be assumed to be quite flat so that changes in output dominate changes in the inflation rate. The *IS–LM* curves, which together form the *AD* curve, allow us to determine the demand for output in the economy. A shift of the *AD* curve creates a discrepancy between supply and demand in the goods market; a policy mechanism that minimizes this discrepancy is considered optimum. The *IS* and *LM* curves can be written as

$$y = a_0 - a_1(i - \pi^e) + x_g \tag{7.1}$$

$$\mu - \pi + x_m = a_2 y - a_3 i - (m - p)_{-1} \tag{7.2}$$

where y represents the natural log of income, i is the nominal interest rate, π and π^e are the actual and expected rates of inflation, $(m - p)_{-1}$ is the natural log of the real money supply prevailing at the end of the previous period, and μ is the growth rate of the money supply. Now x_g and x_m are potential random shocks to the economy, the former in the goods market and the latter in the money market; they have expected values of zero, but from past observation they have known variances. In equilibrium, $x_g = x_m = 0$, $y = y_e$, $\pi = \pi^e = \mu$. In this environment, it does not matter whether the central bank chooses to set μ or i, as long as they are consistent with equilibrium as described above. If it chooses μ, then π and π^e must match this choice and equations (7.1) and (7.2) can be used to solve for y and i. If i is chosen as the controlled variable, then the same equations solve for μ and y. The only difference between them is that the first choice dictates the supply of money directly whereas the latter makes the supply of money demand-determined, since choosing i and knowing $y = y_e$ allows the central bank to calculate $(m - p)$ that is consistent with equilibrium. As a consequence, there is nothing that differentiates between these two methods of monetary control in a fully predictable long-run economy. To make a purposeful choice we need to introduce the possibility of random shocks to the economy.

7.4 THE CHOICE OF INSTRUMENTS FOR STABILIZATION POLICY

Stabilization policy only has a role to play when the economy is exposed to unexpected events that can cause y to diverge from y_e. Unlike in previous chapters, we are not now concerned with discretionary changes in policy in response to shocks, but instead in picking a policy instrument that will be held constant in the face of these shocks. There

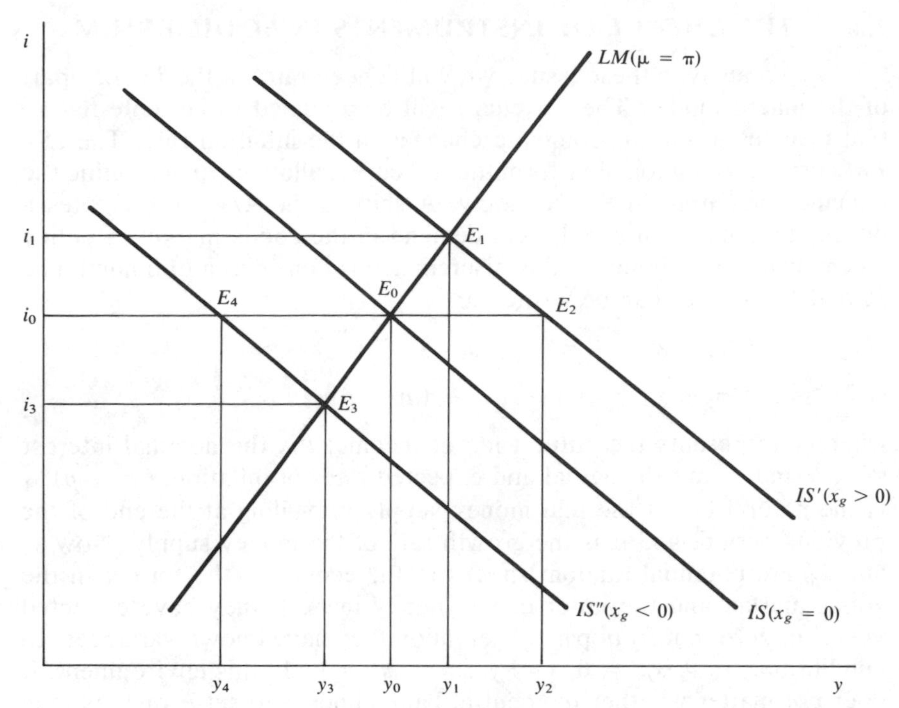

Figure 7-1 Controlling the money supply or the interest rate when the *IS* curve is unstable.

are goods-markets shocks, represented by positive or negative values for x_g, or money-market shocks, indicated by nonzero values for x_m, or both. Here x_m is a combination of x_b (shocks to the monetary base), x_k (unpredictable elements in the multiplier), and x_d (random changes in the demand for money) from Chapter 6. If x_b is nonzero, the central bank cannot control precisely the monetary base as argued above.

First, let us look at an economy experiencing shocks in the goods market but having a very stable *LM* curve. In Figure 7-1, we start at E_0, which represents the intersection of *IS* and *LM* consistent with long-run equilibrium. Thus y_0 is equal to y_e as given by the unseen *AS* curve. Also, i_0 is the interest rate necessary for long-run equilibrium. Now assume that x_g takes on a positive value. This shifts the *IS* curve to *IS*′. How the economy adjusts to this unexpected event depends very much on the control mechanism of the central bank. If the monetary authorities have chosen to fix μ, then the *LM* curve remains in its original location and the economy moves to E_1 with y rising to y_1 and the interest rate rising to i_1. Alternatively, if the central bank has chosen to defend the existing interest rate, then short-run equilibrium is established at E_2. In this case the *LM* curve has to shift to the right as the central bank is forced to increase μ, which allows the real money supply to expand as is necessary for a higher y and constant i. This indicates that the central bank cannot simultaneously keep μ and i at their previous levels. More important, holding i constant forces income to rise to y_2, which is higher than y_1. Which of these two mechanisms is better? Clearly, controlling μ reduces the variability of y in this case. Could it not be argued, however, that a higher y is always desirable? The answer is definitely no, since y_e is the optimum; only at y_e are both workers and firms satisfied in the labor market. Both y_1 and y_2 represent excess demand in the labor market, with workers being forced to work more than they wish, but y_1 has less excess demand than y_2 and is therefore preferable. How has this been made possible? Remember that when x_g appears, the central bank is unable to respond to it directly, but has a rule that it follows, regardless of events. If it holds μ constant, the nominal interest rate rises automatically and with π^e constant, since x_g is unexpected, the real interest rate also rises, thus choking off some investment expenditures, which now offsets, in part, the increase in aggregate demand created by $x_g > 0$ such as a surge in consumer demand.[1]

A negative value for x_g shifts the *IS* curve to *IS*″. With control over μ the *LM* curve remains in place and equilibrium is established at E_3, whereas holding the interest rate at i_0 means that the economy moves to E_4. Again, the latter mechanism creates a greater divergence of y from y_e or larger unemployment in the labor market, and therefore the previous conclusion that control over μ is preferable to control over i continues to hold. In summary, in an economy subjected to goods-market shocks the optimal control mechanism for the central bank involves a choice for μ and sticking to it, regardless of what happens to the nominal interest rate when these shocks appear.

Now let us consider an economy subjected to monetary shocks, but in which the *IS* curve is stable. In Figure 7-2, we again start with equilibrium at E_0. Then $x_m > 0$ appears, which shifts the *LM* curve down and to the right to *LM*′ as the nominal money supply has increased more than the price level and the real money supply is now higher. If the central bank maintains μ in this situation, then a new short-run equilibrium is reached at E_1, with y rising and i falling. On the other hand, if the central bank maintains the existing interest rate, the economy miraculously stays at the original equilibrium. In this case, controlling the interest rate is preferable to holding the growth rate of the money supply constant. In fact, fixing the interest rate allows the central bank to stabilize the economy

[1] By assuming the *AS* curve to be flat, one complication has been avoided: the shift of the *LM* curve through higher inflation in response to the rise in output; y_2 would still be the same, but y_1 would be lower.

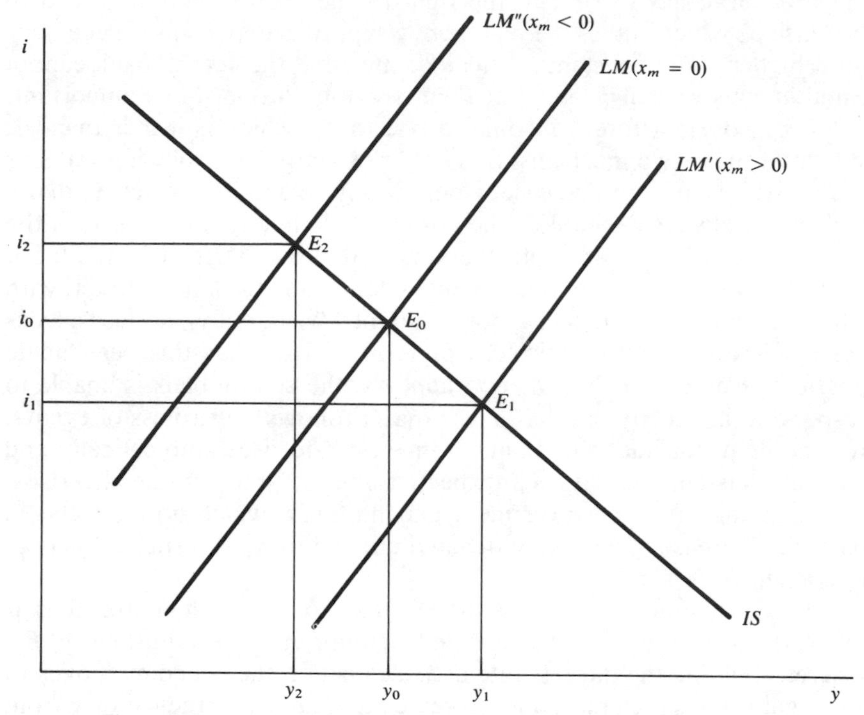

Figure 7-2 Controlling the money supply or the interest rate when the *LM* curve is unstable.

completely. By determining the demand for money, it allows the supply of money to adjust automatically. Here x_m represents an increase in the growth rate of the money supply with the same features as μ, except for the fact that the central bank is unaware of its existence. If the central bank maintains μ at a certain level, then $\mu + x_m$ leads to a volatile growth rate of the money supply, but if it holds i constant, then it is forced to compensate for whatever value x_m takes by adjusting μ so that $\mu + x_m$ remains constant throughout.

In summary, the central bank should control the money supply if there is believed to be a lot of "noise" in the demand for goods and services, but it should hold the interest rate constant if the money market is thought to be unpredictable. If there are shocks to both markets, the optimal mechanism is a weighted average of a money-supply target and an interest-rate target, with the weights dictated by the relative size of the shocks. For instance, if x_g and x_m are both positive, then the central bank might decide to reduce μ somewhat and let the interest rate rise to some extent.[2]

[2] Supply shocks require the *AD–AS* framework and will be dealt with in Chapter 8 as a case study of U.S. monetary policy during the oil-price shocks.

These theoretical propositions about the optimal control mechanism for the monetary authorities were made popular in the literature by William Poole. His analysis has also had an important impact on the actual conduct of monetary policy in recent years. In the halcyon days of Keynesian economics in the 1950s and 1960s, there was a strong belief in the predictability of the *IS* curve but considerable debate about the slope and position of the *LM* curve. In that environment, it is not too surprising to find that central banks tried to peg interest rates to what they thought would be the appropriate level for stabilizing the economy at full employment. Then in the 1970s Friedman's monetarist position gained considerable ground and the economics profession began to believe that the *LM* curve was more stable than the *IS* curve. In response, central banks switched to controlling growth rates of the money supply. Now in the 1980s, this position is again being reassessed, and proposals for controlling interest rates are being put forward. Some of the reasons for the presumed instability of the *LM* curve derive from financial innovations that were discussed in Chapter 5 and from the unpredictability of the money multiplier and the monetary base that was explored in Chapter 6. But now the question is whether it is nominal or real interest rates that should concern the central bank. To make this a meaningful issue we need to bring actual and predicted inflation back into the analysis.

7.5 CONTROLLING INTEREST RATES IN AN INFLATIONARY ENVIRONMENT

There are two avenues by which the government influences the demand for goods and services: a_0 and $(i - \pi^e)$ in the *IS* curve respond to fiscal and monetary policy. Both are real variables, whereas the monetary mechanism discussed so far offers us a choice between two nominal variables, μ or i. In an inflationary environment, controlling the nominal interest rate can mean losing sight of the real interest rate. Consider again an initial equilibrium depicted in Figure 7-3. Now let there be a goods-market shock such that $x_g > 0$, which would shift the *IS* curve to *IS'*. If the central bank controls μ and does not alter it, then the economy moves to E_1 with increased output and a higher nominal interest rate. However, if the central bank holds the interest rate at i_0, short-run equilibrium is established at E_2. In the process the central bank must allow μ to rise so that the *LM* curve can shift down to intersect at E_2. If the increase in μ calls fourth a higher π^e, as is evident from the discussion of expected inflation in Chapter 3, then the *IS* curve will shift up again by the extent of the increase in π^e and another short-run equilibrium is established at E_3, which further increases the gap between y and y_e and necessitates

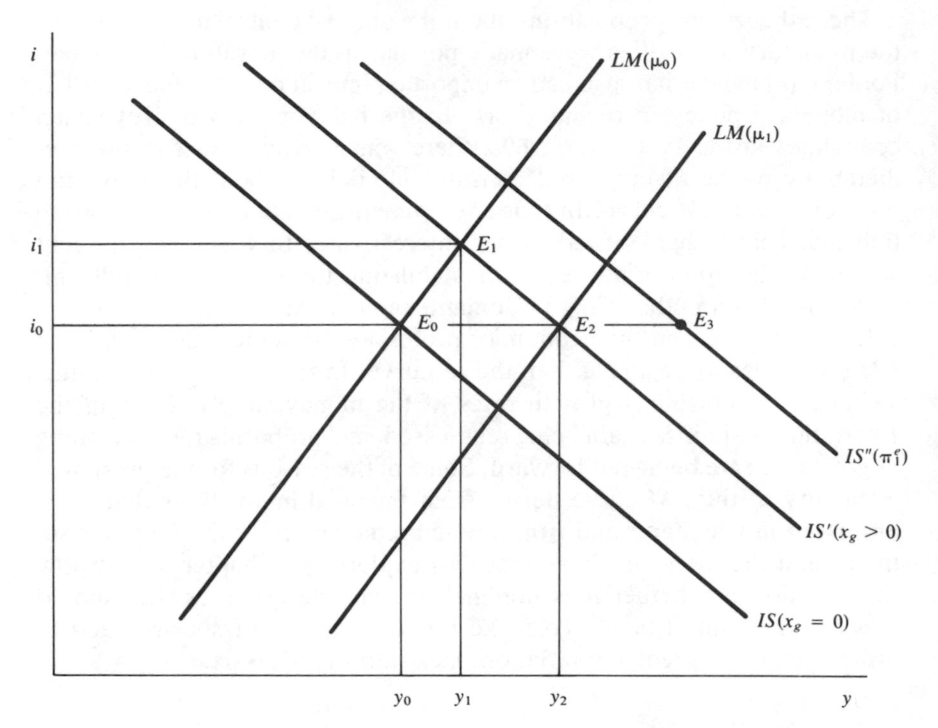

Figure 7-3 Controlling the nominal interest rate in an inflationary environment.

another increase in μ. Clearly such a mechanism is unstable as the central bank tries to hold down the nominal interest rate in the face of rising inflation, forcing the real interest rate to become smaller and smaller and perhaps even negative. On the other hand, holding μ constant in the face of this shock provides a built-in stabilizing effect, since π^e will remain constant and inflation cannot become a self-fulfilling prophecy.

The central banks of the Western world learned this lesson the hard way in the late 1960s and early 1970s when inflation took root precisely because they attempted to keep nominal interest rates constant at the wrong time when the Vietnam War pushed up the aggregate-demand curve and the oil crisis reduced aggregate supply. Throughout the period 1970 to 1975, the Bank of Canada and the Fed watched the nominal interest rate closely and were able to keep it fairly constant during this period, as Table 7-1 documents. But in the process they had to let the growth rate of the money supply rise, which in turn fueled inflation. Consequently, the real interest rate dropped and stimulated investment expenditures in an already overheated economy. To calculate the real interest rate we cannot merely subtract π from i; instead we need π^e. Since

Table 7-1. *Interest rates, growth rates of the money supply, and inflation rates, Canada and the United States, 1970–75 (%)*

	Canada				United States			
Year	i	μ	π	π^e	i	μ	π	π^e
1970	6.1	2.3	4.7	4.0	6.4	5.9	5.4	4.5
1971	3.6	12.7	3.1	4.3	4.3	6.3	5.2	5.0
1972	3.6	14.3	5.0	3.8	4.1	8.7	4.8	5.1
1973	5.4	14.4	9.1	4.4	7.0	5.8	5.0	4.7
1974	7.8	9.5	15.3	6.8	7.8	4.7	5.8	5.1
1975	7.4	13.8	10.7	11.3	5.8	4.2	6.3	6.9

Note: i is defined as the 3-month Treasury bill rate, μ is the growth rate of M1, and π is the rate of change of the GNE deflator, in both countries; π^e is calculated from a weighted average of the past four π values with weights .5, .3, .15, and .05 – see the text for details.
Sources: Canada, *Bank of Canada Review*, January 1979, table 1, cols. 1, 14, 32; United States, *Federal Reserve Bulletin*, table 1.36 for i, and Federal Reserve Bank of St Louis, *International Economic Conditions: Annual Data, 1962–1981*, pp. 67, 68 for μ and π.

we cannot measure π^e directly, Dornbusch and Fischer suggest that an equation like $\pi^e = .5\pi_{-1} + .3\pi_{-2} + .15\pi_{-3} + .05\pi_{-4}$ may capture all the information that is available in order to form expectations about inflation for the next period.[3] Although it is recognized that the weights and the lags are arbitrary choices, it is important to note that information about μ, a critical variable for forming π^e, as Chapter 3 showed, is not available at the time that we really need it. The last column for each country in Table 7-1 uses this formula for calculating π^e. We can see expected inflation rising for most of the period, leading to reductions in the real rate of interest until in 1975 it actually becomes negative. This outcome is especially noteworthy in the United States since the Fed began to look at monetary aggregates as early as 1970 and by 1974 the Federal Open Market Committee (FOMC) had explicit μ and i targets simultaneously. For instance, the FOMC announced that

> for the April–May [1974] period the Committee adopted ranges of tolerance of 3 to 7 per cent and $5\frac{1}{2}$ to $8\frac{1}{2}$ per cent for the annual rates of growth in M_1 and M_2, respectively . . . and they decided that . . . the weekly average Federal funds rate might be permitted to vary in an orderly fashion from as low as $9\frac{3}{4}$ per cent to as high as $10\frac{3}{4}$ per cent.[4]

The lesson that was learned was that the nominal interest rate is not a very good signal for macroeconomic developments in an inflationary en-

[3] R. Dornbusch and S. Fischer, *Macroeconomics*, second edition, New York, McGraw-Hill, 1981, p. 432, chart 13-5. This chart does not appear in the third edition.

[4] *Federal Reserve Bulletin*, 60, July 1974, p. 498.

vironment and that movements in the real interest rate are better predictors of what is likely to happen to aggregate demand. But by 1975, central banks in Canada, the United States, and elsewhere had converted to monetarism and their goals and announcements were made in terms of growth rates for the money supply. The modus operandi of monetarism in Canada and the United States will be examined in the next two sections.

7.6 MONETARY CONTROL TECHNIQUES IN CANADA, 1975–82

From 1975 to 1982 the Bank of Canada established targets for the growth of M1. From time to time, these targets were reduced in an effort to bring down the rate of inflation. This policy was enunciated by Governor Bouey in what is called the "Saskatoon Manifesto" in September 1975. He stated, "Whatever else may need to be done to bring inflation under control, it is absolutely essential to keep the rate of monetary expansion within reasonable limits."[5] Although this episode of macroeconomic policy will be analyzed in much detail in Chapter 11, at this point we can discuss the monetary mechanism that was used by the Bank to make this policy work. The Bank had target ranges for the growth of M1 (e.g., in 1976 the range was 8–12%), but this policy was enforced by the use of the Bank's control over interest rates. Does this present an inconsistency, especially since it was observed earlier that a central bank cannot simultaneously control the money supply and the interest rate? Also, why would the Bank choose such a complicated procedure when it could have allowed the money supply to increase at whatever rate it had set in its announcement? The answer to both questions lies in the distinction between the short run and the long run. Even though the Bank of Canada had taken a monetarist position after 1975, it was still convinced that on a day-to-day basis the *LM* curve was quite unpredictable; only on a year-to-year basis did the Bank feel that it could reduce the rate of inflation by its control over the money supply. In other words, the *LM* curve is "blurred" if it is observed frequently, but it comes into sharp focus if one looks at it infrequently. From our previous analysis, this suggests that keeping the growth rate of the money supply constant day by day or even month by month may not be the optimal strategy. For instance, if $\mu = 12\%$ a year, this also means $\mu = 1\%$ per month. But if x_m is very large relative to μ for such a time period (say $+1\%$ or -1% per month), then the total $\mu + x_m$ will exhibit considerable variability

[5] *Bank of Canada Review*, October 1975, p. 24.

(either 0% or 2% per month). Over the year, positive x_m values and negative x_m values will tend to cancel each other so that μ will dominate x_m. Therefore, the Bank of Canada was convinced that it should set a steady course for the money supply in the long run, but that it should not worry about being blown off course in the short run. Also, since the *LM* curve was thought to be unpredictable in the short run, it chose to use the interest rate as the monetary mechanism for its day-to-day operations to keep the Canadian economy on the *IS* curve.

To ensure consistency between its long-term targets for M1 and its short-term operating procedures, it did have to use the *LM* curve, rewritten as

$$i = [1/a_3][a_2 y - (m - p)_{-1} - \mu - x_m + \pi] \tag{7.3}$$

From this equation we can see that i and μ are negatively related and that the Bank can ensure a consistent result if it knows the value of a_3. In other words, if the money supply is growing too fast the Bank will realize this by the fact that the interest rate is falling and it can correct this by putting upward pressure on the interest rate during the next few days. What is involved here is the control over the money supply through the demand for it. The advantage of this mechanism is that the Bank does not have to distinguish between μ and x_m; it need only be concerned about their sum. If x_m takes on a positive value, then μ is cut back *automatically* to the same extent so that $\mu + x_m$ remains constant.

Let us take the year 1978 as a specific example to investigate. At the beginning of the year the target range for the growth rate of M1 was 7–11%. Presumably the target for the inflation rate was also in that range; let us assume $\pi = 9\%$, which represents the midpoint of that range. If μ was at the top of the range at 11%, then $(m - p)$ would rise by 2%, but if it were at the bottom of the range at 7%, then $(m - p)$ would fall by 2%. At the end of 1977 $(m - p)$ was 9.374 (i.e., the money supply was $19,919 million and the price index was 1.734). Therefore, the Bank expected $(m - p)$ to be in the range 9.354–9.394 at the end of 1978. This in turn allows us to calculate the range for the interest rate that would be consistent with this real money supply and other information that the Bank needs about the *LM* curve. From the estimates of Gregory and MacKinnon presented in Chapter 5, we know that $a_2 = .763$ and $a_3 = .229$. Also, their equation contained a constant, for which they obtained a value of 1.992. Furthermore, assuming that the Bank can guess correctly the value of y at 10.359 for 1978, we can now estimate the upper and lower bounds for the interest rate. First, the upper bound is obtained from equation (7.3):

$$i = [1/.229][.763 \times 10.359 - 9.354 + 1.992] = 2.367 \tag{7.4}$$

If we take the antilog of 2.367, we obtain an interest rate of 10.665%.[6] Next, the lower bound is

(7.5) $i = [1/.229][.763 \times 10.359 - 9.394 + 1.992] = 2.192$

or an interest rate of 8.953%. The only difference between these two numbers is the value taken for $(m - p)$: In (7.4) we took the minimum value and in (7.5) we took the maximum value, both based on $(m - p) = (m - p)_{-1} + \mu + x_m - \pi$, with x_m presumed to be zero.

The operating mechanism worked as follows. If the interest rate remained within the range 8.953–10.665%, the Bank was assured that the growth rate of the money supply was within the bounds that it had set and it would not alter its current stance. But if the interest rate fell below 8.953%, then the Bank had reason to believe that the money supply was growing more quickly than it had wanted. Presumably this was caused by a positive value for x_m. In response, the Bank would buy fewer Treasury bills at the next auction or cut back its demand for government bonds in open-market operations, thus causing bond prices to fall and the interest rate to rise. With the higher interest rate, demand for M1 would fall off until it was within the targeted range once more. Alternatively, if the interest rate was higher than 10.665%, it would assume that x_m had been negative and that it should increase its demand for government securities, which would raise their price and lower the interest rate. In fact, it could calculate precisely the adjustment that was needed. Assume that the interest rate is 11%. This means that $(m - p)$ is equal to $1.992 + .763 \times 10.359 - .229 \times 2.398 = 9.347$, which is .007 below the bottom of the acceptable range. From that information it would increase open-market purchases to push the growth rate of M1 up by .7%. Following this procedure, the Bank of Canada did not have to worry about trying to anticipate x_m. It merely manipulated the demand for money in such a way so that the "right" supply was forthcoming; whether this was accomplished by μ or x_m did not matter.

It now becomes apparent why the Bank of Canada used targets for M1 and why it was reluctant to change definitions of monetary aggregates when financial innovations occurred. If the Bank were to use interest-rate control on a day-to-day basis, M1 would have a higher interest elasticity of demand, a_3, than would a larger monetary aggregate such as M2 or M3, because these latter contain interest-earning components.[7] From equation (7.3) we see that the larger is a_3, the smaller is the change in i when μ moves outside its bounds. In this way the Bank is able to work

[6] Remember that in the empirical estimates of the *LM* curve i is the ln of the interest rate.

[7] See Section 5.8 for a more detailed discussion of this point.

with a smaller range for the interest rate, reducing its variability. It must be remembered that although i is a nominal variable, large and unpredictable changes can have adverse effects on borrowers and lenders who have made contracts with each other in nominal terms and who would be reluctant to use such contracts in the future.

Even if M1 became less relevant after 1980, the Bank of Canada adhered to target ranges for its growth rate because it would have to acquire information about a_2 and a_3 for the new aggregate before it could resume using the interest-rate control mechanism. Although there are empirical estimates available for M2, the Bank did not seem to trust them; it remained convinced until 1982 that the demand for M1 was more predictable than that for broader monetary aggregates.

Even before 1981 the Bank's interest-rate servomechanism was not without difficulties. Equations (7.4) and (7.5) provide signals to the Bank and a technique for responding to them. But the signal may sometimes be misleading. One assumption that was made earlier was that the Bank could guess correctly the level of GNP in 1978 at the beginning of that year. Alternatively, y could be lower, say 10.250, rather than 10.359 because of some shock to the *IS* curve. This lowers the interest-rate range by $1/.229 \times .763 \times .109 = .363$ or 1.44%. Now assume that the Bank observes an interest rate of 8.5%, which is below its acceptable lower limit. Not aware of the development in the *IS* curve, it would follow a contractionary policy in the belief that the growth rate of the money supply is too large. This, of course, is the wrong response in these circumstances; the Bank should either have done nothing if it wanted to take a neutral stance to stabilization policy or followed an expansionary policy if it thought that active intervention was advisable. The difficulty arises from the fact that the Bank cannot distinguish among the many possible causes for the interest rate to be outside of its limits. The basis of its position must be that whereas the *LM* curve is noisy in the short run, the *IS* curve is not; yet it was precisely because of the assumed instability of the *IS* curve that the Bank of Canada converted to monetarism in 1975.

Consider another problem. Assume now that the inflation rate is running higher than the expected 9%, but the Bank does not yet know this since GNE deflators are published only once every three months. If inflation is in fact 12% and the nominal money stock is allowed to grow in the range of 7–11%, then the real stock of money will be 1–4% lower at the end of 1978 compared to 1977. This causes the interest rate to rise, and the Bank responds by easing its policy stance in the unwarranted belief that it was operating too stringently before. But this merely fuels the rate of inflation further, making it even more difficult to succeed with its antiinflationary policy.

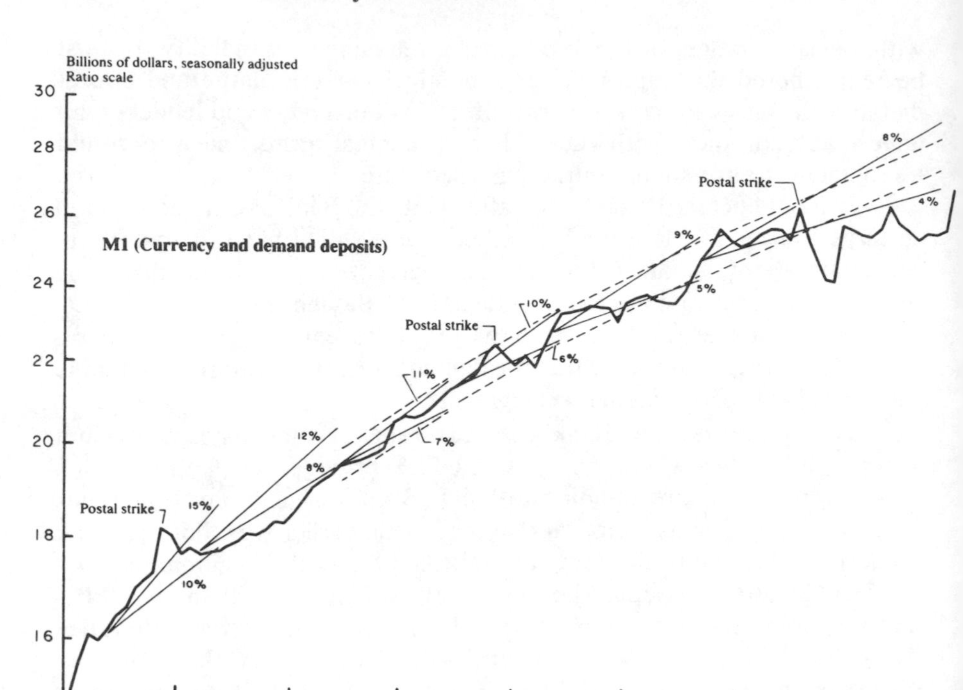

Chart 7-1 Target and actual growth of money in Canada, 1975–82. *Source: Annual Report of the Governor of the Bank of Canada,* 1982, p. 26.

In summary, the Bank of Canada set targets for growth rates of M1 during 1975 to 1982 in the conviction that this was the most effective way of gradually reducing the rate of inflation. Because it believed that the short-run *LM* curve was subject to a lot of uncertainty, it controlled the money supply by regulating its demand through the process of manipulating interest rates. On the whole it was successful in keeping the money supply within the bounds that it had announced until 1981 when financial innovations led to the collapse of reliable estimates of the demand for M1 and made targets for this monetary aggregate useless.

Chart 7-1 displays the performance of the Bank of Canada relative to its announced aims. Starting in 1975 we see the "cones" that represent the upper and lower limits for M1 given the target range and the starting point. The first range was 10–15% growth in M1 per annum, but later target ranges were lower in accordance with the monetarist position that antiinflation policy must rely on reductions in the growth rate of the transactions medium. The postal strikes in 1975 and again in 1978 forced the Bank of Canada to let M1 move above the upper bound of the cone, but in general the Bank was able to keep the money supply moving within the preannounced bounds. Then after the postal strike in 1981, M1 fell below the bottom of the 4–8% growth rate and stayed there. Interest rates had peaked but the demand for demand deposits did not pick up as expected because of the permanent shift into daily-interest accounts. At this stage, the Bank of Canada could have redefined M1 to include these interest-bearing accounts or it could have lowered the starting point of allowable growth rates for the existing monetary aggregate, if it was convinced that the process of financial innovation was now complete. Instead, the Bank hesitated. In early 1982, the governor wrote that "the Bank is, *for the time being,* not inclined to draw inferences about monetary conditions from the recent pattern of M1 growth beyond those that can be confirmed by other economic and financial indicators."[8] Then, in November 1982, the governor announced, "The recorded M1 series is not a useful guide to policy at the present time. In these circumstances I want to make it known that the Bank no longer has a target for it."[9]

As of 1983 the Bank of Canada did not have a publicly stated monetary mechanism or any announced monetary targets, although it was widely believed that the Bank was then attempting to influence the exchange rate, an issue that will be taken up after the open-economy framework is presented in Chapter 9. Several proposals have been made to fill this void, the most seriously considered being that the Bank of Canada should control the real interest rate. This is much different from controlling nominal interest rates, as the Bank tried to do before 1975. A target real interest rate is on a much better theoretical foundation as the *IS* curve reveals: It is the variable that helps to determine the demand for goods and services, and it can be moved to keep the economy in equilibrium. In terms of the monetary mechanism, the Bank of Canada would be expected to follow an expansionary policy if the real interest rate moved above its equilibrium level or to adopt a contractionary stance if the real rate was too low.

Despite its general appeal, such a strategy has a number of serious flaws, any one of which may be fatal. First, the real interest rate is not observable, since the expected rate of inflation is a subjective variable. This would make it extremely difficult to gauge the right policy stance if there is disagreement over what the real interest rate actually is. One way of remedying this problem is to introduce a new type of government bond for which principal and interest are indexed to the CPI or the GNE deflator. This would make the return on such a bond impervious to the rate

[8] *Annual Report of the Governor of the Bank of Canada,* Ottawa, 1981, p. 32; emphasis added.

[9] *Bank of Canada Review,* December 1982, p. 7.

of inflation, and its price would establish the current market evaluation of the real interest rate.

EXAMPLE

A \$100 bond would promise to pay \$3 interest plus \$1 for every 1% increase in the CPI. The real return would be 3%, no matter what happened to the inflation rate. Now consider an alternative bond that pays \$10 a year with no indexing provision. If the inflation rate is expected to be 7%, then both bonds have a real return of 3% and they should have the same value. If, however, the expected inflation rate is greater than 7%, the return on the unindexed bond falls below 3% and its price relative to the indexed bond should also fall and vice versa. By watching the relative price of the bonds we can "read" the expected rate of inflation and observe the real interest rate.

Second, the Bank of Canada is not the only government agency that influences the real interest rate; the fiscal authorities also play a role here with their budgetary decisions. Thus the Bank cannot set a target for the real interest rate independently of what the Department of Finance is doing. This lack of accountability may ultimately impinge on the Bank's credibility. Third, and even more fundamental than the second point, predictable policies by the Bank of Canada should not influence the real interest rate at all. Consider again the reaction of the monetary authorities to an increase in the real interest rate: They would allow the growth rate of the money supply to rise. But to the extent that this move is predictable, both the nominal interest rate and the expected rate of inflation would increase equally leaving the real rate unaffected. Only if the policy were not incorporated into expectations would the real interest rate fall. Therefore, for the policy to be successful it must be unpredictable – hardly a desirable property for a policy instrument in the long run. Fourth, for Canada with its capital markets closely integrated with those in the United States, it may be impossible to have a real interest rate different from what prevails in the rest of the world, making it irrelevant as a target variable for the Bank of Canada. Since this involves an open-economy issue, further discussion of this point will be postponed until Chapter 9. Finally, an attempt to control real interest rates is tantamount to manipulating aggregate demand, a technique central banks in most countries favored before the great inflationary period of the 1970s but have now abandoned as being too ambitious.

7.7 MONETARY CONTROL TECHNIQUES IN THE UNITED STATES, 1975–82

The Canadian experience can be described by fairly abrupt changes in the policy instrument that the Bank of Canada chose to control. In the United States, on the other hand, there was a more gradual shift of emphasis during the same period. As early as 1970, the Federal Reserve Board started to look informally at monetary aggregates even though interest rates were still their primary target. By 1974, we saw that the Fed had explicit target ranges for M1, M2, and the Federal funds rate. Then, in the Full Employment and Balanced Growth Act of 1978, Congress declared that "inflation is a major national problem requiring improved government policies." The act called on the Federal Reserve Board to transmit to Congress twice a year "the objectives and plans of the Board of Governors and the Federal Open Market Committee with respect to ranges of growth or diminution of the monetary and credit aggregates." But there was no penalty for not achieving these objectives, since it allowed the Fed to judge whether new developments made them impractical. These Monetary Policy Reports to Congress are reprinted in the *Federal Reserve Bulletin* and contain both an appraisal of past economic performance as well as the Fed's objectives with respect to targets for monetary aggregates and the projections on which they are based. For instance, in its Report of February 1983 (reprinted in the *Federal Reserve Bulletin* of March 1983), it predicts real GNP to grow at 3–5½%, inflation to be in the range 3½–5½%, and unemployment at 9½–10½%. In these circumstances, it set target growth rates of 4–8% for M1, 7–10% for M2, and 6½–9½% for M3.

Also, the control mechanism for keeping monetary aggregates on target was revised in October 1979. Up until that time, the Fed used interest-rate manipulation to keep the demand for money growing at a rate consistent with its targets, much the same as the Bank of Canada did in that period. However, while the Bank of Canada tended to concentrate on a general interest rate such as the yield on Treasury bills, the Fed watched the more specific Federal funds rate, the overnight rate banks charge each other for the use of reserves. In that earlier period, if monetary aggregates were climbing too quickly, the Fed would put upward pressure on interest rates, including the Federal funds rate, which would reduce borrowing of reserves by commercial banks and induce them to lower their own loans and deposit liabilities. Then in 1979, the Board of Governors shifted to controlling nonborrowed reserves of the commercial banks. According to Stephen Axilrod, the staff director for monetary and financial policy at the Fed,

The shift to the new procedure, which meant that day-to-day fluctuations in the funds rate would freely reflect variations in the market demand for reserves, was made in an effort to find a more reliable way to control the money supply over the longer run.[10]

Not surprisingly, the Report to Congress for 1983 does not mention a target range for the Federal funds rate as it did in 1974, although the Fed still stipulates an "intermeeting" funds-rate constraint, the range of which was 6%.

The new procedure involves watching nonborrowed reserves, that is, the monetary base minus borrowed reserves and currency held by the public. Now a target range for monetary aggregates implies a target range for nonborrowed reserves on the basis of past relationships between these two variables. Thus if nonborrowed reserves rise too quickly, this is a signal that the monetary aggregates are also above the acceptable target range and that the FOMC should instruct the trading desk to decrease open-market purchases of bonds or increase open-market sales so as to "pinch" the reserve position of the banks. There is, of course, some slippage in this mechanism, since banks can borrow reserves to make up any short fall that they experience, but the Federal funds rate will rise, perhaps sharply when the Fed takes a restrictive stance and this reduces the incentives to borrow reserves.

We can now analyze the control techniques of the Fed at two levels: The first concerns the *strategy* of having multiple targets for monetary aggregates, and the second deals with the *tactics* of controlling nonborrowed reserves to achieve these targets. In contrast to the Bank of Canada, which had a target only for M1, the Fed has separate targets for M1, M2, and M3 as well as for "credit" aggregates. In general, these multiple targets exist because the Fed does not like to rely on any one of them exclusively. For example, in the Report of February 1983, the Board of Governors indicated that for the time being the targets for M2 and M3 would be given greater weight than the target for M1 because of its recent erratic behavior. Also, because of its multiple targets, the Fed is less reluctant to alter definitions of monetary aggregates as it did when it included NOW and ATS accounts in M1 in 1982. Nevertheless, we can ask why the Fed has different targets for these monetary aggregates? The answer lies in its prediction of compositional changes in currency, demand, and time deposits.

From the M1 and M2 multipliers derived in Chapter 6, it is evident that the growth rate of the monetary base will lead to equal increases in all monetary aggregates if all the money multipliers remain constant. But if these multipliers vary over time, then it is possible for the growth rate of

[10] S. H. Axilrod, "Monetary Policy, Money Supply, and the Federal Reserve's Operating Procedures," *Federal Reserve Bulletin,* 68, January 1982, p. 19.

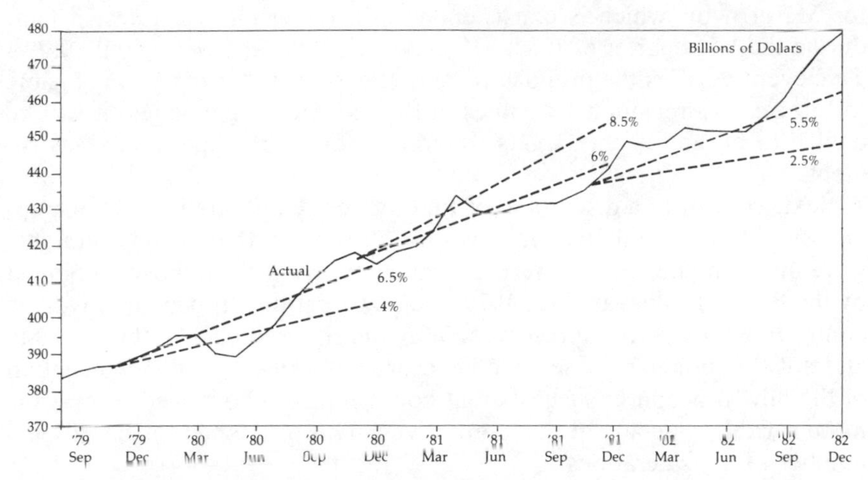

Chart 7-2 Target and actual growth of money in the United States, September 1979–December 1982. *Source: Brookings Review,* Spring 1983, p. 6. Copyright © by The Brookings Institution, Washington, D.C.

M1 to diverge from the growth rate of M2 and from the growth rate of the base. In turn these multipliers are strongly influenced by the public's desire to hold the various components of the monetary aggregates since they have different reserve requirements. If we take the ratio of the M1 and M2 multipliers from equations (6.6) and (6.9) in Chapter 6 we obtain $(1 + q_c)/(1 + q_c + q_t)$, where q_c is the currency-to-demand-deposit ratio and q_t is the time-deposit-to-demand-deposit ratio. Changes in either q_c or q_t can cause the two multipliers to diverge. In particular, an increase in q_t causes the M1 multiplier to fall while the M2 multiplier rises. Since q_t is positively related to the market interest rate, a Fed target of M2 growing faster than M1 suggests that they expect to see an increase in the interest rate. From that perspective, the job of the Fed is more complicated than that of the Bank of Canada, given that it must predict compositional changes in the monetary aggregates as well as control the monetary base or reserves. On the other hand, the Fed's credibility is not as much at stake if one of its several goals is not realized, whereas the Bank of Canada put all of its prestige on the line for M1.

Chart 7-2 displays the Fed's performance with respect to M1 for the period September 1979 to December 1982. Although the path of M1 moves outside the "cones" established by the target ranges, these errors are relatively small and self-correcting, except for the positive, cumulative error of substantial proportions in the last few months of 1982. This may have been caused by the precipitous drop in interest rates that reduced the opportunity cost of money, an event perhaps not fully anticipated by the Fed since it had a target range of 2.5–5.5% for M1 growth and 6–9%

for M2 growth, which is consistent with a rising interest rate. In fact, during the last quarter of 1982, M1 grew by 13.5% and M2 by only 9.2%. This event verifies the proposition stated earlier that if the Fed is unable to forecast compositional changes in the monetary aggregates, it will be unable to hit any of the targets squarely with its one operational instrument.

Next we turn to a discussion of Fed tactics. Until late in 1979, manipulation of the Federal funds rate was used to ensure that monetary targets were met. The mechanics were not much different from those employed by the Bank of Canada. Since 1979, the new operating procedure involves controlling nonborrowed reserves. Why did the Fed choose this variable and not the monetary base or total reserves? Axilrod, in his explanation of the new procedure, suggests that controlling nonborrowed reserves is more reliable than any of the alternatives. This assessment is based on a number of considerations.

First, nonborrowed reserves are more controllable by the Fed than the monetary base or total reserves. Despite the ability of the Fed to set the discount rate, it cannot predict exactly the amount of borrowing that will be done by commercial banks, but through open-market operations it can dictate the reserves that the banks own outright. However, by the same token, the possibility of borrowing reserves provides a useful buffer for total reserves in case of unexpected events.

This leads to the second consideration. Axilrod is convinced that in the short run there is a great deal of randomness both on the demand side and on the supply side of the money market, leading to a great deal of unpredictability in the variables that are determined in this market. Hence there are likely to be some operating procedures that better minimize these disturbances than others. Consider first a random shock to the demand side of the money market and observe the results. In Figure 7-4, there are two supply curves: M^s to depict a tightly controlled monetary base with a constant money multiplier and $M^{s\prime}$ to represent an interest-sensitive supply of money, as occurs if the Fed controls nonborrowed reserves and is not directly concerned with the size of borrowings that would rise with the market interest rate. The demand curve, M^d, is downward-sloping. If it shifts up to M_1^d because of a positive shock, equilibrium is then temporarily reestablished at E_1 if M^s is relevant, forcing the interest rate to absorb all of the adjustment. However, if $M^{s\prime}$ is the appropriate supply curve, equilibrium moves to E_2 with both price and quantity sharing in the adjustment. Axilrod notes that this "would tend to moderate short-term movements in interest rates. Such a procedure would be desirable in the degree that the monetary authority believed that some allowance should be made for transitory variations in money demand."[11]

[11] Ibid., p. 20.

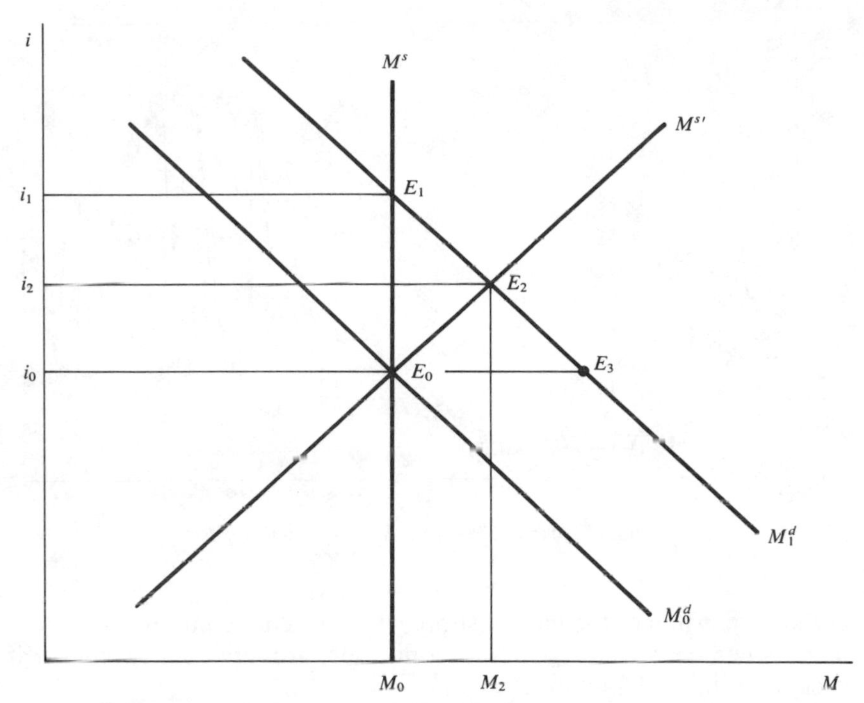

Figure 7-4 Adjustment to a demand shock with base control (M^s) and nonborrowed-reserves control ($M^{s'}$).

This concern with interest-rate variability should not be taken too literally. After all, the Fed abandoned the Federal funds rate to market determination in 1979 because it believed control over the money supply was more important than control over the interest rate. In fact, after November 1979 it allowed much greater variation in the Federal funds rate than before, as Chart 7-3 clearly shows. What can be said in favor of the new procedure is that it is a compromise between the two extremes of controlling interest rates that would move the money market to E_3 in Figure 7-4 and of controlling the actual money supply that leads to E_1.

Next, Axilrod suggests that we consider an unexpected fall in the money multiplier. If the Fed controls the monetary base, the money supply absorbs the entire shock. However, if only nonborrowed reserves remain constant, the excess demand in the money market, which raises interest rates, encourages banks to borrow reserves, allowing the base to expand and offset, to some extent, the drop in the multiplier. Now the decline in the money supply is smaller than it is with base control, and it allows the Fed to stay closer to its announced path for the money supply. Nevertheless, despite this advantage, the new procedure allows the banks to

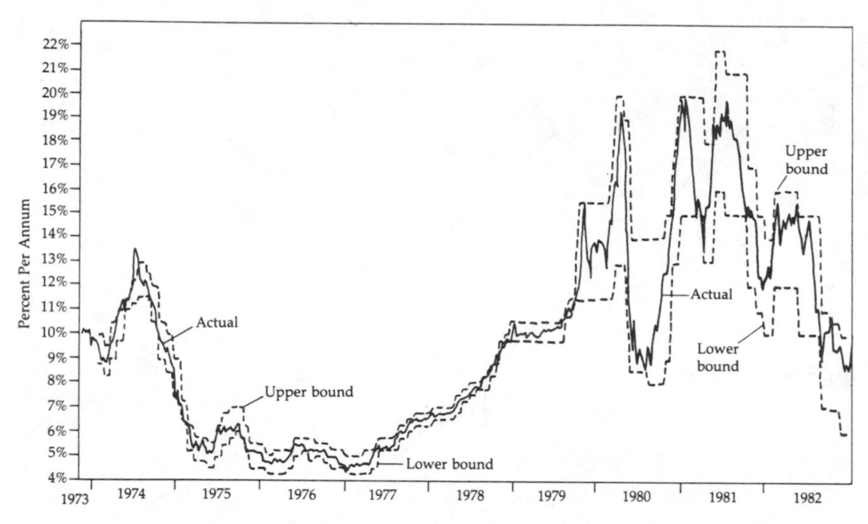

Chart 7-3. Federal funds rate, 1973–82. *Source: Brookings Review,* Spring 1983, p. 11.

force an expansion of the money supply even when the multiplier has not shifted, when borrowed reserves become more attractive for reasons that are beyond the Fed's control.

In general, Axilrod argues that the nonborrowed reserves target has just the right combination of control and flexibility. Control over the money supply is still indispensable for bringing down the rate of inflation, but flexibility in the monetary mechanism is necessary to minimize the effect of unexpected shocks on the macroeconomy.

Nevertheless, the Fed has been criticized for concentrating on control over *financial* variables and not over *economic* variables. As Robert Solow put it, "The true goal of monetary policy is not to achieve some financial or monetary result, but to achieve some national-economic objective."[12] Solow and some others have suggested nominal GNP as a better target for the Fed than money growth or interest rates. However, one must be careful in interpreting this criticism in terms of the choice of a monetary mechanism. The *target* that the Fed now has is stated in terms of monetary aggregates, whereas the *instrument* that it uses is nonborrowed reserves. It is possible to debate the choice of targets while agreeing on the choice of instruments or vice versa. Solow and the other critics differ from the Fed about targets but not necessarily about instruments. It is important to draw this distinction, to which we now turn.

[12] R. S. Solow, "Fiscal and Monetary Policy – Co-ordination or Conflict?" Frank E. Seidman Lecture, Memphis, September 1983, p. 17.

7.8 IS THERE A CONFLICT BETWEEN MONETARY MECHANISMS AND MONETARY POLICY?

The Bank of Canada or the Federal Reserve can control the interest rate or the monetary base to stabilize output automatically, but at the same time they are attempting to reduce the rate of growth of one or more monetary aggregates to push down the inflation rate. Is there a potential conflict between stabilizing output and reducing inflation? Put another way, is there an inconsistency between monetary mechanisms and monetary policy? The answer is essentially no, since these decisions are made in different contexts, one of which is stochastic in nature whereas the other is perfectly predictable. Stabilization of output is an automatic response to shocks of various kinds, whereas reducing the growth rate of money is a deliberate policy change. Also, it is possible to use the interest rate as the monetary mechanism and the money supply as the target of monetary policy without creating insuperable problems. In a world of diverse shocks it may not be possible to lower the growth rate of some monetary aggregate day in and day out along some fixed path, but it should be possible to do so on average. In other words, there may be periods in which the money supply is above trend, but there should be an equal number of periods in which it is below trend as long as the shocks have an expected value of zero and a symmetrical distribution as shown in Figure 3-3. It is for this reason that central banks tend to state their goals for monetary aggregates in terms of ranges rather than as fixed numbers. This allows them to preserve credibility of their commitment to the target even when events force the growth rate to deviate from the midpoint of that range. However, Charts 7-1 and 7-2 indicate prolonged departures of the money supply from the target "cone" in both countries, especially in 1982, suggesting either that the shocks are biased in one direction or a weakening of commitment to the target ranges. Even after a careful review of this period in the last few chapters it is difficult to sort out the exact source of the problem, but it does raise the question of whether in some circumstances the central bank may not be able to choose separately a monetary mechanism and a monetary policy.

7.9 SUMMARY

This chapter has focused on the choice of a monetary mechanism that provides the best response to random events that disturb the equilibrium of the economy. This mechanism is to be distinguished from discretionary policy changes that deliberately attempt to move the economy from one equilibrium to another.

In general, the central bank can control the monetary base or the interest rate. If the *IS* curve is subjected to large and frequent shocks but the *LM* curve is stable, control over the monetary base is the best mechanism. If, on the other hand, the *LM* curve is unstable and the *IS* curve is stable, then control over interest rates is the optimal approach.

Both the Bank of Canada and the Federal Reserve System have followed a monetarist strategy by announcing targets for monetary aggregates and attempting to stay within the bounds of these targets. However, both institutions feel that in the short run they cannot control these aggregates directly. Instead, the Bank of Canada manipulated interest rates to keep the demand for money moving along planned growth rates, whereas the Fed, since October 1979, chose to control nonborrowed reserves. In both countries, the monetary targets were generally achieved until 1982. In that year, the Bank of Canada discontinued its announcements of targets for M1 because of major changes in the transactions technology that made this aggregate less than useful. The Fed, at the same time, paid much more attention to M2 and M3 than to M1 for many of the same reasons. Recent suggestions have been made that the central bank should try to control the real interest rate, but there are many difficulties with that mechanism as well.

EXERCISES

1. Using the numerical version of the *IS–LM–AS* model in exercise 4 of Chapter 2, calculate the effect of the following shocks on y, π, i, and/or μ:
   (a) $x_m = -.05$ with money-supply control. [*Hint:* use equation (3.6) to determine π first.]
   (b) $x_g = -.08$ with interest-rate control.
   (c) The same shock with money-supply control. Can you confirm that money-supply control is better in this instance?
2. (a) Derive the *AD* curve for interest-rate control.
   (b) Why is it different from the *AD* curve for money-supply control?
3. (a) What instruments does the fiscal authority control?
   (b) Can you devise "fiscal mechanisms" analogous to the monetary mechanisms discussed in this chapter?

FURTHER READING

Axilrod, S. H., "Monetary Policy, Money Supply, and the Federal Reserve's Operating Procedures," *Federal Reserve Bulletin*, 68, January 1982, pp. 13–24. Argues the case for nonborrowed reserve targets for the Fed.

Courchene, T. J., *No Place to Stand? Abandoning Monetary Targets: An Evaluation,* Montreal, C. D. Howe Institute, 1983. A detailed discussion of recent Bank of Canada policy.

Leroy, S. F., and D. E. Lindsey, "Determining the Monetary Instrument: A Diagrammatic Exposition," *American Economic Review,* 68, December 1978, pp. 928–34. A diagrammatic treatment of the Poole analysis.

CHAPTER 8

U.S. monetary policy and the dilemma of stagflation

8.1 INTRODUCTION

During the past 10 years the U.S. inflation rate has been on a roller-coaster ride. Twice, during 1973–75 and again during 1979–81, the inflation rate rose dramatically, giving rise to fears of unstoppable hyperinflation, only to drop again almost as dramatically. In addition, during these episodes, output fell and unemployment rose. This unfortunate combination of inflation and recession has been dubbed "stagflation." Monetary policy played a prominent role in this stagflationary decade, and it is the purpose of this chapter to review and analyze the part played by the Federal Reserve's conduct of monetary policy in greater detail than was possible in previous chapters. It is not intended merely to record the events since 1972 but instead to fit them into the analytical framework formulated in Chapters 2–7. From the *IS–LM–AS* model it is possible to make a number of predictions about the macroeconomic consequences of policy changes or unpredictable shocks; these predictions will then be tested against the evidence of the time to see how.useful the *IS–LM–AS* model is in such a turbulent period.

In a sense, this is a case study; it is an attempt to use the macro model to analyze a specific real-world situation. At the same time, it should not be construed as the final word on the events that transpired during this period; there is not enough historical perspective for that. Nor should it be perceived as a newspaper account of current trends; the story ends in 1982 and subsequent developments are not treated, except incidentally.

It is possible to identify, without hesitation, the two supply shocks associated with the oil-price increases by OPEC in 1973 and again in 1979 as the major features of the U.S. macroeconomic environment in the 1970s. The earlier shock was compounded by the dismantling of the wage and price controls and by significant reductions in world food production in 1973–4. Hence the emphasis in this chapter will be on the predictions that such shocks would have on the inflation rate, output, employment, and the interest rate and on the analysis of actual and optimal responses to such shocks. In particular, the spotlight is on the Fed and more especially on the Federal Open Market Committee, the group responsible for day-to-day – or more accurately month-to-month – decisions about the conduct of monetary policy.

The analysis will proceed on the basis that the American economy is a closed one, without significant interactions with foreigners. This, of course, is not a true representation, but since open-economy macroeconomics will not be dealt with until the next chapter, it makes sense here to concentrate only on those issues where the distinction between closed and open economies is not important. Later, in Chapter 11, after the open-economy framework is laid out, Canada's experience, which was similar to that in the United States in many respects, will be examined in a worldwide environment.

8.2 HIGHLIGHTS OF THE PERIOD

As a preliminary step, the important macroeconomic trends need to be highlighted for the period 1972–82. Both the starting and ending dates are somewhat arbitrarily chosen but they encompass the period of greatest interest. Table 8-1 provides us with these data. All variables are defined in the same units as they were in the previous chapters.

1. For most of the 1950s and early 1960s, inflation was barely perceptible. The average annual inflation rate for 1950–65 was only 2.2%. Then, in the late 1960s the inflation rate began to move into and stay in the 4–5% range. In 1973–4 major increases in energy prices, which reached almost 30% in just one year, 1974, coupled with wage and price decontrols and food price increases caused the overall inflation rate to jump to the 10% range. Although the GNP and CPI versions of the inflation rate are not the same, since they measure somewhat different things, they tend to move up and down together and reinforce the view that inflation during 1974–5 was not just a large-scale measurement error. Thereafter, the inflation rate starts to subside, only to rise once again in the wake of the 1979 oil-price increase, which caused energy prices to rise by 25% in 1979 and 31% in 1980, with the overall inflation rate once again moving into the 10% range. Finally, in 1982 there was a major decline in the inflation rate. The novel feature of the inflationary experience in the 1970s was not so much the height of the inflation rate as its variability. From Chapters 3 and 4, it is readily appreciated that deviations of predicted inflation from actual inflation cause the economy to depart from equilibrium. If

Table 8-1. *Important macroeconomic variables in the U.S. economy, 1972–82*

	π											
Year	GNP	CPI	Energy	i	$\mu 1$	$\mu 2$	$\mu 3$	$(m1 - p)$	$(m2 - p)$	u	y	y_e
1972	4.2	3.3	2.8	4.1	9.2	13.0	14.1	5.53	6.69	4.0	7.08	7.07
1973	5.8	6.2	8.0	7.0	5.5	7.0	11.2	5.53	6.71	3.3	7.13	7.10
1974	8.8	11.0	29.3	7.9	4.4	5.6	8.4	5.48	6.67	3.8	7.13	7.14
1975	9.3	9.1	10.6	5.8	4.9	12.7	9.6	5.44	6.70	6.8	7.12	7.17
1976	5.2	5.8	7.2	5.0	6.7	14.1	11.9	5.46	6.79	5.9	7.17	7.20
1977	5.8	6.5	9.5	5.3	8.1	10.8	12.2	5.48	6.83	5.2	7.22	7.24
1978	7.4	7.7	6.3	7.2	8.3	8.2	11.2	5.49	6.84	4.3	7.27	7.27
1979	8.6	11.3	25.2	10.0	7.1	8.2	9.2	5.47	6.83	4.2	7.30	7.30
1980	9.3	13.5	30.9	11.5	6.6	9.0	10.3	5.45	6.83	5.9	7.30	7.33
1981	9.4	10.4	13.5	14.1	6.4	10.1	11.5	5.42	6.84	6.3	7.31	7.36
1982	6.0	6.1	1.5	10.7	8.5	9.7	9.9	5.44	6.87	8.8	7.30	7.39

Sources: π(GNP), growth of GNP deflator, *Economic Report of the President,* 1983, table B3; π(CPI), growth rate of consumer price index, year to year, ibid., table B55; π(Energy), growth rate of energy prices, year to year, ibid.; i, Treasury bill rate, 3 months, ibid., table B67; $\mu 1$, $\mu 2$, $\mu 3$, growth rate of M1, M2, and M3, respectively, ibid., table B61; $m1$, natural log of currency plus checkable deposits, ibid.; $m2$, natural log of M1 plus overnight repurchase agreements and Eurodollars, money-market mutual fund balances and savings and small time deposits, ibid.; p, GNE deflator, 1972 = 1, ibid., table B3; u, unemployment rate for males 20 years and over, ibid., table B31; y, natural log of real GNP, in billions of 1972 dollars, ibid., table B2; y_e, natural log of full-employment output, in billions of 1972 dollars, R. J. Gordon, *Macroeconomics*, third edition, Boston, Little, Brown, 1984, appendix B, table B1.

the inflation rate rises and falls in quick succession, it becomes difficult to predict, and errors are almost inevitable.

2. Both the unemployment rate for prime aged males and the ratio of actual to full-employment output indicate that the economy was out of equilibrium much of the time. The unemployment rate for adult males is considered to be more sensitive to demand conditions in the labor market than is the overall unemployment rate because of structural changes in the employment experience of young people and adult women. Both u and the differential between y_e and y show that the labor market moved toward excess demand in 1973–4, then to excess supply in 1975, with a slow recovery until 1978–9. Then another period of high unemployment ensued, culminating in the "Great Recession" of 1981–2.

3. Another novel development in the 1970s was the variability of interest rates, matching the fluctuations in the inflation rate. Moreover, when inflation rates rose, so did nominal interest rates and vice versa. This implies that nominal interest rates cannot be used to gauge the stance of monetary policy. In an earlier period, it was argued that higher interest rates implied tighter monetary policy, but now it is accepted that this would only happen if the change in monetary policy were unanticipated.

4. As a result, much greater attention is paid to growth rates of the money supply in assessing the position taken by the central bank. In Table 8-1, growth rates for three monetary aggregates are given, since these became the numbers that the Federal Open Market Committee (FOMC) set in its monthly meetings. It is evident that not only does each series display considerable volatility from year to year, but also that $\mu 1$, $\mu 2$, and $\mu 3$ do not move together very often. The former observation can be explained by the Fed's inability to hit its multiple targets with great precision; the latter fact is explained by the major shifts that occurred in the demand for various types of deposits as relative prices among them changed in the 1970s.

5. Since the growth rates of the money supply were set in some relation to inflationary pressures existing at that time or projected for the future, another way to judge the effects of monetary policy is to look at the real money supply existing at the end of each year. Only $(m1 - p)$ and $(m2 - p)$ are shown in Table 8-1. If the growth rate of a monetary aggregate is larger than the inflation rate, then $(m - p)$ will rise and vice versa. Thus if policy is intended to be "tight," the Fed would try to set μ less than π and the real money supply will fall. In general, both series show that the Fed did not intend to validate the inflation created by both supply shocks. In 1974 and again in 1980, $(m1 - p)$ fell; for $(m2 - p)$ the same is true in 1974 although in 1980 there was no change.

6. During the period, the Fed shifted gradually from controlling nominal interest rates to controlling the growth rate of several monetary aggregates as its monetary mechanism, that is, its automatic response to situations in which the economy was not reacting in predictable ways, presumably because of shocks that disturb the existing equilibrium. Additionally, from a longer-term perspective, the Fed attempted to lower the growth rates of money in order to bring inflation under control, but it did continue to respond to the temptation of fine-tuning, that is, gearing its policy stance to both unemployment and inflation. In other words, the Fed became more monetarist and less interventionist in its outlook as time went by, but it did not completely accept the new classical version of the macroeconomy.

8.3 SUPPLY SHOCKS AND THEIR MACROECONOMIC CONSEQUENCES

An oil-price increase is converted into a supply shock through its effect on the marginal product of labor. The unexpected increase in energy prices destroys some of the existing capital stock built on the basis of previously cheap oil. Although these capital goods will ultimately be replaced by energy-efficient versions, for some period of time each unit of labor will have less capital to work with and from the characteristics of the production function this reduces the marginal product of all workers. In the labor market the demand curve shifts down and to the left, leading to lower employment and a reduction in the real wage. In the output market this is captured as a negative value in the random variable x_s in the *AS* curve of

$$y = y_e - a_4(\pi^e - \pi - x_s) + x_s \tag{8.1}$$

where y and y_e are the natural logs of actual output and equilibrium output, π^e and π are expected and actual inflation, and a_4 is a positive constant. The variable x_s has an expected value of zero, but the economy can be thrown out of equilibrium by either a positive or negative value, which is then called a supply shock. It will be remembered from Chapter 3 that $x_s < 0$ has a double effect on y:

1. It reduces the marginal product of existing workers and has a direct effect on output, captured by the second appearance of x_s in equation (8.1).
2. Firms will reduce their labor force in an effort to raise the marginal product of the smaller labor input back to its previous level and in the process output falls again, by an amount equal to a_4x_s in equation (8.1).

Thus, the total effect is $(1 + a_4)x_s$, which is the horizontal shift of the *AS* curve in Figure 8-1.

To complete the picture we need an *AD* curve which is made up of the combination of the *IS* and *LM* curves given by

$$y = a_0 - a_1(i - \pi^e) + x_g \tag{8.2}$$

$$\mu - \pi + x_m = a_2y - a_3i - (m - p)_{-1} \tag{8.3}$$

where additional variables are defined as follows: i is the nominal interest rate, μ is the growth rate of the money supply, $(m - p)_{-1}$ is the natural log of the real money supply at the end of the previous period, a_0, a_1, a_2, and a_3 are all positive constants, and x_g and x_m are also random variables, the former representing an unexpected change in the demand for goods and services and the latter depicting an unanticipated change in the growth rate of the money supply. The *AD* curve is obtained by substituting the *IS* curve into the *LM* curve, eliminating i in the process:

$$\pi = \mu + (m - p)_{-1} + x_m - (a_2 + a_3/a_1)y + (a_3/a_1)(a_0 + x_g) + a_3\pi^e \tag{8.4}$$

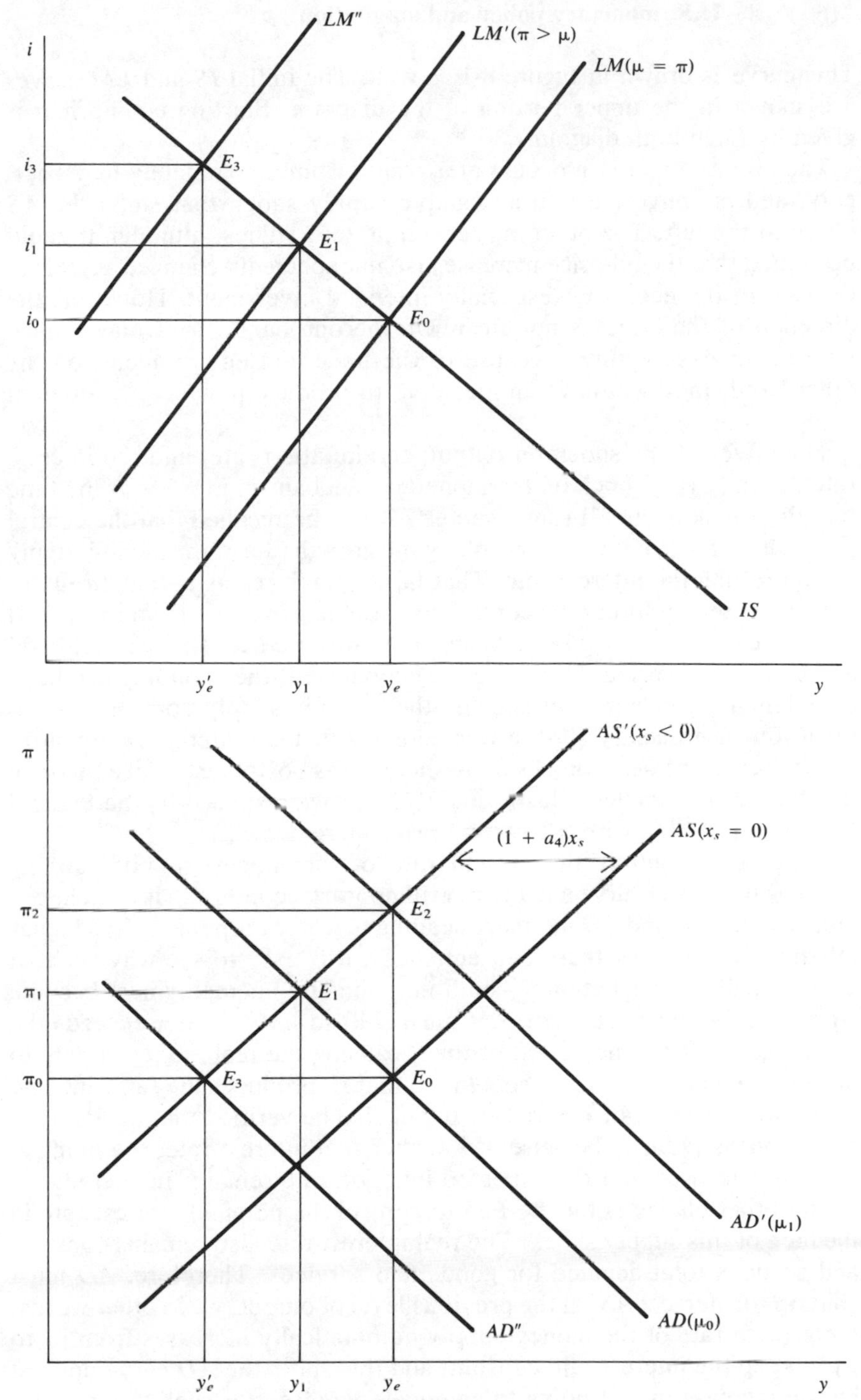

Figure 8-1 Supply shocks and possible responses.

This curve is drawn in Figure 8-1 as well. The initial *IS* and *LM* curves are shown in the upper portion of the diagram. Starting equilibrium is given by E_0 in both diagrams.

The oil-price increase occurs at a point in time, completely unexpectedly, and is converted into a negative supply shock that shifts the *AS* curve to the left. The other x's remain at zero values, although it could be argued that the oil-price increase also unexpectedly changed aggregate demand in the economy, especially intended investment. However, the direction of the effect is not clear. On the one hand, firms may reduce investment expenditures because of the uncertain environment; on the other hand, they will have an incentive to produce new energy-efficient equipment.

The effect of the shock on output, the inflation rate, and the interest rate depends very much on the monetary mechanism in place at the time that the shock occurs. From Chapter 7 it will be recalled that the central bank has a choice between controlling the growth rate of the money supply or controlling the interest rate. That is, the bank reacts automatically to any pressure that forces the controlled variable to deviate from its desired path. The choice between controlling μ or i was predicted on the likelihood and severity of various shocks to the economy. If the economy had been experiencing goods-market shocks, then money-supply control was optimal, but if monetary shocks were dominant, then interest-rate control was better. Consideration of supply shocks was postponed until now since it serves as an excellent illustration of the problems faced by the Federal Reserve in dealing with the two oil-price increases.

If the Fed controls the growth rate of the money supply, nothing changes in the *AD* curve and the new temporary equilibrium is established at E_1 where AS' and *AD* intersect, leading to lower output at y_1 and higher inflation at π_1. From these consequences, it is easy to see why such an event is called "stagflation" – both inflation and unemployment become worse. In the upper diagram, *LM* must shift to LM' since π exceeds the unchanged μ for some period of time, causing the real money supply to decline. The new LM' intersects *IS*, so that E_1 produces the same income as in the lower part of Figure 8-1. It can also be verified that the demand for output is reduced because of a higher real interest rate; the nominal interest rate rises, but the expected inflation rate remains unaltered.

The other choice is for the Fed to control the nominal interest rate in the face of this supply shock. The real interest rate also remains constant and so does total demand for goods and services. Therefore, *AD* must shift up to intersect AS' at the previous level of output, y_e. In other words, the growth rate of the money supply automatically increases from μ_0 to μ_1 to keep the interest rate constant and this shifts the *AD* curve upward by the increase in μ, leading to an equal increase in π such that the real money supply remains constant and the *LM* curve remains in place. Thus output and the interest rate remain the same as in the previous equilibrium, but the inflation rate rises to π_2 in response to the higher μ_1.

In comparing these results it is obvious that the interest-rate control mechanism is superior to the money-supply control mechanism in minimizing the effect of the shock on output and employment. In fact, if the Fed can keep the nominal interest rate constant, it allows the economy to be completely insulated from the shock. The only adverse effect is a higher rate of inflation. Nevertheless, it would be incorrect to argue that interest-rate control is the optimal monetary mechanism in the face of *all* supply shocks. The decision about optimality of automatic stabilizers depends not only on the source of the shock, but also on its longevity. If the shock is temporary (i.e., it lasts for one period and then disappears), then indeed interest-rate control is the best mechanism, but if the shock is converted into a permanent event, then money-supply control turns out to be a better choice.

To analyze the importance of permanence of the shock we need to look at the second and subsequent periods after the initial event. If the shock is of one-period duration, the *AS* curve will move back from *AS'* to *AS* in the second period and then stay there. All the original values of the important variables will be reestablished. In that case, interest-rate control can keep the economy at y_e for the one period in which it would depart from full equilibrium. In other words, the central bank merely validates the inflation attributed to the shock. To prevent subsequent side effects, the central bank would have to announce that the one-time increase in μ from μ_0 to μ_1 is not to be interpreted as a deliberate expansionary stance, but merely the result of the control mechanism. With such an announcement, inflationary expectations should not respond to the temporary increase in μ.

Now consider the shock being permanent. Regardless of what the central bank does, the economy will have to adjust to a new level of equilibrium output at y_e', which is $(1 + a_4)x_s$ lower than y_e. Neither monetary mechanism can keep the economy at y_e, but the interest-rate control mechanism is now undesirable, since it has a built-in tendency for the inflation rate to accelerate. If the Fed maintains i_0 by letting μ increase to whatever is necessary in a continued attempt to keep the economy at y_e through its influence on the *AD* curve, there must be excess demand in the labor market, for which equilibrium is now established at y_e'; hence the real wage will have a tendency to rise. How does this occur? Nominal wages must rise faster than prices. An increase in the growth rate of wages will shift the *AS* curve upward in the second period. This is not shown in Figure 8-1, but it becomes obvious that both the *AS* curve and the *AD* curve would have to keep shifting upward, leading to higher and higher inflation. On the other hand, if the Fed maintains μ at its original level throughout, the economy will move to E_3 in both parts of the diagram. Output falls to y_e', inflation is back to its original level, π_0, and the nominal interest rate rises to i_3. In this case, the short-run *AS* curve remains at *AS'*; the *AD* curve moves down to *AD''* even though μ remains constant, but $(m - p)$ falls from period to period and according to equation (8.4) this causes a downward shift of the *AD* curve. From a different perspective, it is known that $\pi = \mu$ in the long run; therefore, the *AD* curve must shift to *AD''*. The *LM* curve, however, shifts up to *LM''* because during the adjustment π exceeded μ for some time, which forces the real money supply to fall. The real interest rate rises to the same extent as the nominal rate since expected inflation is unchanged, and this chokes off some investment expenditures, as is needed to reduce total demand for goods and services.

Comparing these results indicates that interest-rate control can be a hindrance to making the necessary adjustment to a lower level of equilibrium output and leaves an inflationary legacy if the event is permanent. For that reason, the optimal control mechanism depends not only on the central bank's ability to identify the sources of shocks that are going to hit the economy, but also to guess correctly their permanence. This is a tall order for any central bank, especially in the case of the OPEC-induced oil-price increases, which were a new experience for all concerned. At the time that they occurred, there was considerable debate as to how long an oil cartel would survive the competitive pressures triggered by the oil-price increase, and therefore the permanence of these events could not be accurately predicted. In these circumstances, it would make sense to treat these oil-price increases as temporary until the evidence showed otherwise. In that case the Fed should have stabilized the interest rate for a while; then when it became obvious that the oil-price increases were here to stay, it should have shifted to controlling the money supply.

8.4 RECONCILING THE EVIDENCE WITH THE PREDICTIONS

In confronting the data, the first task is to establish that supply shocks rather than demand shocks were indeed the dominant feature of the macroeconomy of the 1970s. The distinguishing feature of negative supply shocks is that both inflation and unemployment rise, whereas demand shocks cause inflation and unemployment to move in opposite directions. Chart 8-1 shows graphically how the inflation rate and the GNP gap, measured as $y_e - y$, were related to each other in this period. A chart with inflation and unemployment on the axes would produce much the same result. Following the path in the chart clearly shows that in

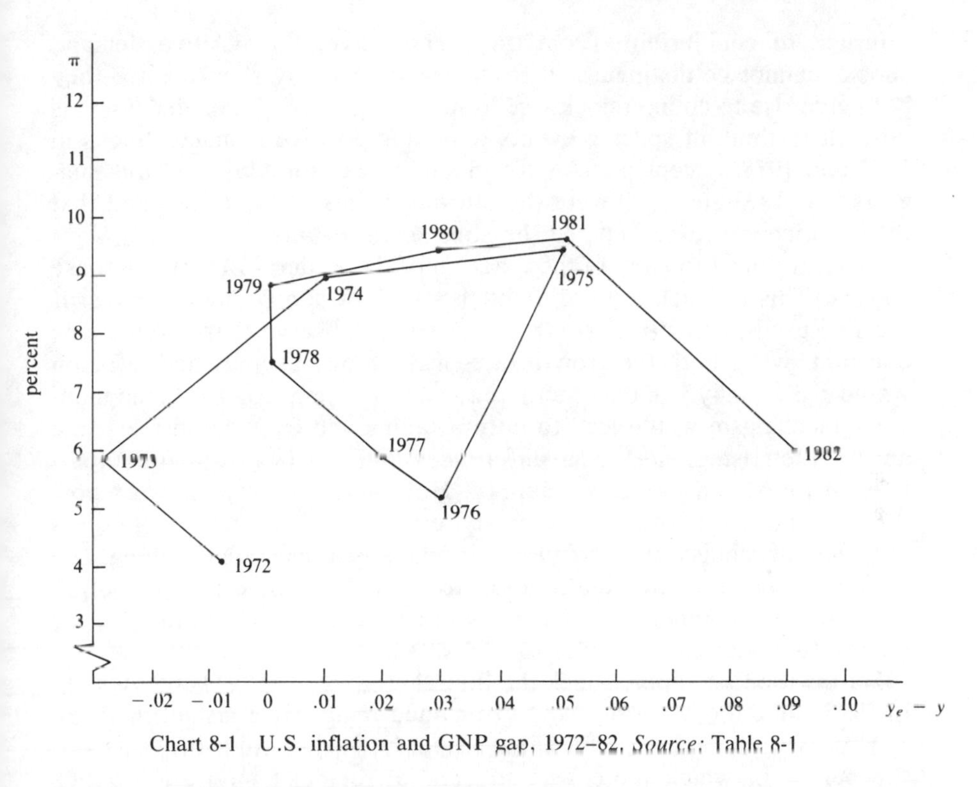

Chart 8-1 U.S. inflation and GNP gap, 1972–82. *Source:* Table 8-1

1973–5 the inflation rate and the GNP gap rose simultaneously. Since the first oil-price increase started in late 1973, these events are almost certain to be causally related. Then, after 1975, the effects of the shock begin to wear off until in 1978 the inflation rate and GNP gap are not much different from what they were in 1973. In 1979, following the second oil-price increase, inflation and unemployment rose once more. Using the CPI measure of inflation would show a much more pronounced positive slope in the chart for the period 1979–82. Since imported-oil prices rose faster than domestic-oil prices and since the latter are excluded from the GNP deflator but included in the CPI, the inflation rate based on the CPI rose more sharply – from 7.7% in 1978 to 11.3% in 1979 to 13.5% in 1980 – than the inflation rate based on the GNP deflator, for which yearly increases were from 7.4% to 8.6% to 9.3%.

Choosing 1973 and 1979 as the beginning years of these two cycles is important for identifying their origins as supply shocks instead of demand shocks. As an alternative hypothesis, it is possible to think of positive demand shocks occurring in 1972 and then again in 1978. The initial response would be higher inflation and lower unemployment or a smaller value of $y_e - y$. The subsequent events in 1973–5 and again in 1979–82 would then be interpreted as necessary adjustments before the economy returned to equilibrium. From this perspective, the positive demand shocks cannot be distinguished from negative supply shocks since they both give rise to counterclockwise loops in Chart 8-1. Nevertheless, it is difficult to think of specific events depicting positive demand shocks in 1972 and 1978, except perhaps for election-year stimulus, and this suggests that 1973 and 1979 were the starting points of the cycles and that the oil-price increases initiated the subsequent events.

Next, we need to explore the reaction of the Federal Reserve to these shocks. This is much more difficult because of conflicting evidence. If the Fed used interest-rate control, one would observe output remaining constant, while both the growth rate of the money supply and inflation would rise equally. On the other hand, money-supply control as the monetary mechanism would lead to output falling and both the interest rate and inflation rising. The crucial differences appear to be in terms of output, interest rates, and the money supply. However, since we know ex post that the shock was of a permanent nature, output had to fall regardless of which mechanism the Fed adopted; it is only a question of timing, and we do not have enough information to predict the time path of output under the two regimes. That leaves interest rates and growth rates of the money supply as the variables to be explained.

During the first supply shock the interest rate rose in 1974 and then fell in 1975 while the M1 growth rate remained relatively constant in 1973–5. However, the evidence for M1 may not be very useful, since this was the period in which there was substantial financial innovation which caused people to move from demand deposits to NOW and ATS accounts. Nevertheless, the large increase in $\mu 2$ between 1974 and 1975 is an indication that perhaps interest-rate control was in effect at this time.

Subsequent to the second oil-price increase in 1979, the control mechanism of the Fed is somewhat easier to identify. It is clear from Table 8-1 that the interest rate increased dramatically while all three growth rates of monetary aggregates remained relatively constant. There is also other evidence available to indicate that by 1979 the Fed had chosen to control monetary aggregates and to let interest rates respond entirely to market pressures. This evidence will be reviewed in greater detail in the next section.

8.5 THE SHIFTING EMPHASIS OF THE FEDERAL RESERVE'S MONETARY MECHANISM

The Federal Open Market Committee (FOMC) of the Federal Reserve System is charged with the responsibility of making monetary policy decisions. It consists of the 7 members of the Board of Governors of the Federal Reserve in Washington plus 5 of the 12 presidents of the regional Federal Reserve banks on a rotating basis, except that the president of the New York bank is always on the committee. The FOMC meets monthly to discuss current economic developments, analyze projections for the future, and issue instructions to the manager of the System Open Market Account in New York for the day-to-day conduct of open-market operations, the single most important tool of monetary policy. During this period, the chairmanship of the Federal Reserve and of the FOMC was held by Arthur Burns, G. William Miller (no relation to Barry Goldwater's running mate in 1964), and Paul Volcker.

Although the meetings of the FOMC are not open to the public – to prevent anyone gaining an unfair advantage from advance information – a Record of Policy Actions of the Federal Open Market Committee is released at a later date and published in the *Federal Reserve Bulletin*. These Records present the views of the committee, together with dissenting opinions of individual members, if any, on the current state of economic affairs, on the present stance of monetary policy, and on any changes that are thought to be necessary. It therefore represents a concise statement of what the Fed intends to do for the next month. Each year since 1975, one of the monthly issues of the *Federal Reserve Bank of St. Louis Review* (usually April) has contained a useful analysis and interpretation of these Records for the previous year.

From these documents it is possible to conclude that the FOMC gradually changed its monetary mechanism from interest-rate control to money-supply control by shifting its emphasis on what were the important variables to watch. The theoretical foundations for this change were presumably that the members convinced themselves of the greater stability of the *LM* curve relative to the *IS* curve, even in the short run. On the other hand, the increasing instability of the *AS* curve should have made interest-rate control more attractive in the 1970s. Commenting on events in 1972, Alan Blinder believed that "vestiges of the old policy of stabilizing interest rates induced the Fed to supply enough money to keep interest rate increases in bounds despite soaring demand for money and credit."[1] In addition, William Poole speculated that Arthur Burns, who was also chairman of interest and dividends in the Nixon wage and price control program had a vested interest in keeping interest rates from rising.[2] By 1974, however, FOMC operating instructions were stated in terms of growth rates of various monetary aggregates, although there was also an intermeeting range established for the Federal funds rate, outside of which

[1] A. S. Blinder, *Economic Policy and the Great Stagflation,* New York, Academic Press, 1981, p. 184.

[2] W. Poole, "Burnsian Monetary Policy: Eight Years After," *Journal of Finance,* 34, May 1979, pp. 473–84.

this market-sensitive interest rate was not supposed to move. Over the next few years, the Federal funds rate became less important, while monetary aggregates became more important in the sense that if there were a conflict between the two it would more likely be resolved in favor of the former instead of the latter. But this shifting emphasis was not continuous. In 1975, Chairman Burns stated:

There is a school of thought that holds that the Federal Reserve need pay no attention to interest rates, that the only thing that matters is how this or that monetary aggregate is behaving. We at the Federal Reserve cannot afford the luxury of any such a mechanical rule . . . we pay close attention to interest rates because of their profound effects on the workings of the economy.[3]

Nevertheless, at about the same time, Chairman Burns announced 12-month target ranges for M1, M2, M3, and a credit proxy. Although these target ranges could be changed, a public commitment of this sort made achievement of these targets important for the sake of attaining credibility. It will be remembered from Chapter 3 that predictable and credible reductions in the growth rate of the money supply make an antiinflationary policy easier than if they were unannounced or not credible. By 1976, "almost every financial report and the bulk of Congressional testimony was devoted to movements in M_1 relative to the ranges announced by the FOMC."[4] In 1977, the Federal Reserve Reform Act required quarterly consultations with congressional committees with respect to growth rates of monetary aggregates for the next 12 months, but not with respect to interest-rate projections. Now, not only the Fed but Congress as well became convinced of the importance of publicly announced target ranges for money. Nevertheless, short-run factors might cause growth rates from month to month to fall outside the ranges contemplated for the year ahead. In other words, the FOMC, although convinced that reductions of the growth rate of the money supply offered the best hope for reducing the inflation rate, was still worried about the short-run instability of the *LM* curve and therefore may have been ambivalent about interest-rate control or money-supply control as its best monetary mechanism. Then in 1978, interest-rate control was abandoned in all but name. The situation was described as follows:

At each monthly meeting, the FOMC sets an inter-meeting range for the Federal funds rate along with the two-month ranges for M1 and M2 growth. Within that range, the Committee's objective for the Federal funds rate is stated in terms of a specific level that is thought to be consistent with the short-run ranges set for M1 and M2. If the two-month growth rates of M1 and M2 appear to be deviating in specified ways from their respective ranges, the domestic policy directive pro-

[3] A. F. Burns, "Statement to Congress," *Federal Reserve Bulletin,* 61, February 1975, p. 64.

[4] A. E. Burger and D. R. Mudd, "The FOMC in 1976: Progress against Inflation," *Federal Reserve Bank of St. Louis Review,* 59, March 1977, p. 2.

vides that the Federal funds rate objective can be changed within its range, or the range itself can be reconsidered by the Committee.[5]

The FOMC issued both "aggregates directives" and "money-market directives." The former stipulated the range in which M1 and M2 were to be held and the latter set a range for the Federal funds rate. From the above quotation, it seems that the aggregates directive was to take priority over the money-market directive during the intermeeting period if a conflict between the two developed.

The final step in this process was taken in October 1979, after a special meeting of the FOMC was convened by the newly appointed chairman, Paul Volcker. At this meeting it was decided to control nonborrowed bank reserves and to abandon the Federal funds rate to the market. The directive issued at this meeting stated in part: "The Committee will consider the need for supplementary instructions if it appears that operations to restrain expansion of reserve aggregates would maintain the federal funds rate near the upper limit of its range."[6] Coupled with the fact that the range for the Federal funds rate, which previously had been about $\frac{3}{4}\%$, was now established at 4% indicated that in the presence of a shock, the FOMC would try to preserve the existing growth rates of M1 and M2 and let the interest rate adjust to whatever was necessary to establish money-market equilibrium. This procedure was described in detail in Section 7.7.

Since then the monetary mechanism has not changed much. Statements from the Fed have generally been of a clarifying nature. In March 1981 it was reported that the FOMC "has continued to set broad ranges of tolerance for . . . the federal funds rate. . . . They have not, in practice, served as true constraints in the period since October 1979, as the FOMC typically has altered the ranges when they become binding."[7] Also, it has become clear that the mechanism involved control of nonborrowed reserves, but the FOMC directives were to continue to be stated in terms of monetary aggregates. Achieving consistency between reserve targets and committee objectives was left to the staff of the Fed.[8]

8.6 SOME THOUGHTFUL CRITICS OF THE FED

The decisions and actions taken by the Fed during this period of supply shocks were not necessarily met with warm approval either by

[5] R. W. Lang, "The FOMC in 1978: Clarifying the Role of the Aggregates," *Federal Reserve Bank of St. Louis Review*, 61, March 1979, p. 4.

[6] "Record of Policy Actions of the FOMC," *Federal Reserve Bulletin*, 65, December 1979, p. 977.

[7] "Monetary Policy Report to Congress," *Federal Reserve Bulletin*, 67, March 1981, p. 204.

[8] A detailed description of this process is given in the *Federal Reserve Bank of St. Louis Review*, 63, August/September 1981, pp. 13–14.

the public or by the economics profession. In fact, considerable debate has been generated by the Fed's policies and their impact on the macroeconomy, much of it unfortunately on ideological grounds. Right-wing conservatives applaud the Fed's shrinking responsibility for macroeconomic fine-tuning, while old-fashioned liberals are displeased with the Fed's abdication from one of its chief functions. Instead of belaboring these issues once again, it is better to consider more moderate and practical critics of the Fed. Two such positions will be considered. First, Alan Blinder's assessment that the 1974–5 recession could have been minimized by appropriate Fed action will be explored and second, Ralph Bryant's critique of the Fed's operating procedures, that is, its choice of monetary mechanisms and targets, will be discussed.

8.6.1 BLINDER'S RECOMMENDED POLICY IN RESPONSE TO SUPPLY SHOCKS

In his book *Economic Policy and the Great Stagflation,* Blinder concludes,

> There was . . . an economic catastrophe in progress in late 1974 and early 1975, and no reading of the data will lead to the conclusion that the Fed took a vigorous antirecessionary stand. Furthermore, there can be no doubt that a preoccupation with inflation was the reason for this.[9]

This statement suggests another possible way of interpreting Fed policy: Instead of stabilizing output when a supply shock appears, the goal becomes stability of the inflation rate. Going back to Figure 8-1, when the *AS* curve shifts up and to the left in the wake of a negative x_s, the Fed would not want the economy to move to E_2 with interest-rate control or to E_1 with money-supply control, but rather to E_3 with inflation control by deliberately reducing the growth rate of the money supply or raising the interest rate sufficiently to move the *AD* curve down to *AD″*. Output would fall to y_e' but the inflation rate would remain constant at π_0. Looking at the evidence in Table 8-1 once more, one becomes convinced that even if the Fed was preoccupied with inflation at this time, it certainly did not succeed in keeping it constant. What we do not know is whether the Fed tried and lost or did not try at all. Blinder seems to believe the former to be the case.

Blinder then goes on to ask: "What could the Fed have done differently?" His answer:

> Many economists have advanced the view that an appropriate policy response to the oil shock would have been a step increase in the *money stock* large enough

[9] Blinder, *Economic Policy,* p. 192.

to finance the higher oil prices. . . . Since the shock was roughly 3.5% on the overall price level, and since it happened in 1973:4 and 1974:1, such a policy would have increased the annual money *growth rate* by about 7 points in each of these quarters, that is, roughly 12% for 1973:4 and 14% for 1974:1 (the figures apply to M_1).[10]

From such a policy Blinder believed that "things [presumably output and employment] could have been quite a bit better in 1974–1975."[11] In terms of Figure 8-1, such policy advice can be interpreted as moving to E_2 temporarily until the inflationary effects of the shock wear off and then back to E_0.

Blinder, who was one of the first economists to suggest that oil-price increases be treated as supply shocks, in this case does not make clear his views about the permanence of the shock. Therefore, the unresolved issue is whether the supply shock reduces y below y_e or whether it reduces y_e itself and for how long. The optimal policy response depends very much on an answer to that question. Trying to keep the inflation rate constant is the best policy response if it is known in advance that the supply shock will be permanent. In these circumstances, it would be optimal to adjust to y_e' with as little variation in inflation as possible to minimize the disturbances that arise from differences between π^e and π. On the other hand, trying to keep output constant is better if it is known beforehand that the supply shock is temporary. Probably neither of these conditions was satisfied in 1973–4, and it is not surprising to find the Fed groping in the dark as it learned to cope with the novelty of supply shocks.

8.6.2 BRYANT'S CRITICISM OF FEDERAL RESERVE POLICY MAKING

Ralph Bryant's criticism of the Fed deals with more fundamental issues than those of the best response to a supply shock; he is concerned with the question of what the Fed should try to control and what its targets should be. In his book *Controlling Money: The Federal Reserve and Its Critics,*[12] Bryant makes two major points:

1. No monetary mechanism is likely to do an adequate job and therefore the Fed should not rely on any one of them.
2. A two-stage strategy of stabilization policy, involving monetary

[10] Ibid., p. 192; emphasis in the original. Explanation: A 3.5% increase in the price level for a year is the same as a 7% increase in each of two quarters and no increase in the other two. To keep real money balances constant rather than letting them fall, the growth rate of the money supply must be raised to match the inflation rate.

[11] Ibid., p. 194.

[12] Washington, D.C., Brookings Institution, 1983.

aggregates as intermediate targets to influence output as the ultimate target, is inferior to a single-stage strategy in which the Fed would respond directly to departures of output from its full-employment level.

Each of these points can now be discussed.

First, there is the issue of the best monetary mechanism. Instead of just two, Bryant has five to choose from: (1) total Fed portfolio, (2) the monetary base, (3) total reserves, (4) unborrowed reserves, and (5) the Federal funds rate. In each case a "regime" involves holding one of these five variables close to a chosen target. He then analyzes the effect of various shocks on the economy using each of these five regimes or monetary mechanisms. These shocks include unexpected changes in float, unpredictable borrowing at the discount window, shifts in currency and demand deposits, and changes in aggregate demand. After this analysis, he concludes, "Given the dilemma that no one operating regime dominates for all types of disturbance, the Federal Reserve must choose that regime thought likely to prove best on average."[13] But since "economists at present do not have sufficiently reliable empirical knowledge about the (average) behavior of the U. S. economy to be able, with confidence, to assign relative weights to the various types of disturbance,"[14] he is reluctant to recommend any one of these regimes, although he does admit that his "own tentative personal view"[15] is that the unborrowed reserves regime may be a reasonable compromise. Since this is the same as that adopted by the Fed in October 1979, there seems to be no disagreement about the choice actually made, only about the strength of commitment that should be attached to any one regime.

The second issue deals with the two-stage strategy adopted by the Fed. Bryant writes:

> Few if any policymakers and economists perceive the money stock as a variable to be pursued in its own right as a final goal of monetary policy. The *ultimate targets* of policy are such variables as the volume of output, the level of employment, and the average price level. If the Federal Reserve chooses to aim at the money stock as a target variable, therefore, the rationale for doing so presumably rests on money being a useful surrogate for the ultimate targets of policy. Under such circumstances, the money stock is an *intermediate-target* variable. . . .
>
> Few advocates of an intermediate-target strategy pivoting on the money stock have provided a rationale for its two-stage characteristics. But six types of justification are conceivable. They assert that a money strategy (1) uses the flow of new information about the economy more efficiently, (2) copes more successfully with policymakers' uncertainty about how the economy functions, (3) incurs smaller resource costs, (4) provides better insulation for monetary policy from

[13] Ibid., p. 27. [14] Ibid., p. 29. [15] Ibid., p. 33.

the vagaries of the political process, (5) affords better protection for the economy from errors due to incompetence or mistakes in judgment on the part of central bankers, and (6) takes better advantage of game-theoretic, expectational interactions between policymakers and the private sector.[16]

Bryant examines each of these justifications and convinces himself that they are either "analytically inadequate" or "flatly wrong."[17] Instead of dealing with every point, it is more useful to discuss the general issue of information availability and processing and its impact on forming expectations about future inflation. Bryant's argument is that a two-stage strategy does not use all of the available information in the economy. For instance, monetary aggregates may be right on target, but if the Fed *knows* that inflationary pressures are increasing, it should react to this information with a strategy of "discretionary instrument adaptation."[18] That is, the Fed should strive for a lower growth rate of nonborrowed reserves or it should raise the Federal funds rate, in this way using the instruments which the Fed has under its control to influence directly one of its ultimate targets, in this case the inflation rate. Even if the information about the inflation rate is less than perfectly reliable, Bryant argues that it is still better for the Fed to use it rather than discard it. But if the Fed is faced with misinformation – for example, the Fed receives "news" that inflationary pressures are decreasing when in fact the opposite is true – then it would be better to disregard such news, since it would lead the Fed to follow an entirely inappropriate policy. The problem faced by the Fed is that it receives both information and misinformation at about the same time and it has no easy way to discriminate between the two. Hence the decision made by the Fed to use a two-stage strategy implies that it believes that it receives a lot more information about the money supply than misinformation, but the opposite is true about other economic events. Bryant, perhaps thinking of the problems of random shocks to the money supply creating misleading information, takes a contrary view. It is essentially an empirical matter to resolve this conflict between the Fed and its critics.

But even more important than the issue of the quality of information from various sources is the question whether information processing is essentially a zero-sum game (i.e., what one party gains, the other loses, leaving no improvement for both sides taken together). It will be recalled from earlier discussion that information about the growth rate of the money supply is an important ingredient in the process of forming expectations about future inflation.[19] If the Fed uses discretionary action

[16] Ibid., pp. 7–8, 83–4; emphasis in the original.
[17] Ibid., p. 84.
[18] Ibid., p. 85.
[19] See equation (3.11) in Chapter 3.

to deal with its ultimate goals, there will be a lot more "noise" in the growth rate of the money supply than there would be if the Fed tried to maintain a target growth rate for this variable. As a consequence, the private sector will have less information available and is likely to make more and larger errors in predicting inflation. This in turn creates more frequent and sizable discrepancies between π^e and π and between y and y_e, necessitating greater efforts by the Fed to stabilize the economy. To avoid depriving the public of useful information, Bryant suggests that "credible announcements of planned instrument settings would . . . give private decision makers a firmer basis for formulating expectations and decisions."[20] In other words, FOMC targets would be specified in terms of permissible ranges for reserves, borrowings at the discount window, and whatever else the Fed has under its control and the public thinks is important. Such a system may have important advantages over the present procedures, but Bryant concedes that

> it could be argued that many economic units in the private sector can understand what "money" is and why it plays an important role in the economy and will therefore react favorably to a Federal Reserve announcement of a money rule whereas they are not familiar with instrument variables such as bank reserves or the federal funds rate and will not react as favorably to announcements of an instrument rule.[21]

In summary, the debate comes down to the following question: Who provides information best and who uses it best? Those who argue in favor of a monetary-target strategy believe that the Fed should provide information on monetary aggregates and then let the public use this information in its expectations formation. In this view, money becomes an important step in the two-stage strategy. On the other hand, Bryant and like-minded critics of the Fed argue that the economy itself provides much useful information and that the Fed should use all of it in making its policy decisions. To them, money is only one aspect of the economy that bears watching; there are many others, including primarily the ultimate targets of stabilization policy, output, employment, and inflation. In other words, the Fed can use information much more efficiently than it produces it and the opposite holds true for the rest of the economy.

Once again, this dispute cannot be resolved on the basis of theory alone; empirical evidence is necessary, and, sad to say, we probably do not know enough about the provision and use of information to make a final judgment on this critical issue. Instead of taking sides in this debate, it is more important at this stage to try to gather the necessary data to make the choice easier in the future. For instance, it is vital to know which of the two competing models best describes the behavior of the macroeconomy.

[20] Bryant, *Controlling Money*, p. 87. [21] Ibid., pp. 87–8 fn.

A discretionary response by the Fed does not make much sense in the context of the new classical model of Chapter 3, where shocks last for only one period and the central bank does not have enough time to react before equilibrium is reestablished, but if it is more relevant to consider the institutionalist model of Chapter 4, where shocks are pervasive and disequilibrium in the labor market lasts as long as contracts do, then policies that respond to current economic events would improve the macroeconomic performance of the country.

8.7 THE "GREAT RECESSION" OF 1981–2

The debate about the proper role for stabilization policy has not only concerned itself with the actions of the Federal Reserve and the FOMC but also with the decisions made by those in charge of fiscal policy, namely the president and Congress, with the help of the Office of Management and Budget and the Congressional Budget Office. To complete the story of the period 1972–82 we need to look more carefully at the "Great Recession" of 1981–2 because of the alleged role that deficit spending had in its creation.

Although the Great Recession probably had its origins in the 1979 oil-price increase, its severity and length must be attributed to other factors. The general view is that extremely high real interest rates during 1981 were the main contributing factor and that the enormous deficits of the federal government in turn were the cause of the high borrowing costs faced by business and households. But the deficit spending alone cannot be blamed for both higher interest rates and falling output. Expansionary fiscal policy will "crowd out" investment expenditures of equal or of lesser value, thus leaving output constant or higher, but it would take more than complete crowding out to achieve the observed result. For that reason, we must look to monetary policy decision at that time as a contributing factor to the recession. Therefore, we will return to our *IS–LM–AS* model to see what events would predict such an outcome and then check these predictions against the data of the period.

Let us begin by examining how an economy can have both higher interest rates and lower output. In Figure 8-2, only the *IS* and *LM* curves are drawn, since we are concerned with the effect of monetary and fiscal policy on i and y and not on the inflation rate. Since the real interest rate is at the center of attention here, an $IS(\pi^e = 0)$ line is also drawn in Figure 8-2 to allow the vertical axis to measure both i and $i - \pi^e$. The original equilibrium is shown as E_0, somewhere in 1979–80. The economy was probably below y_e at that time as it was still recovering from the supply shock and would have required further adjustment even without policy

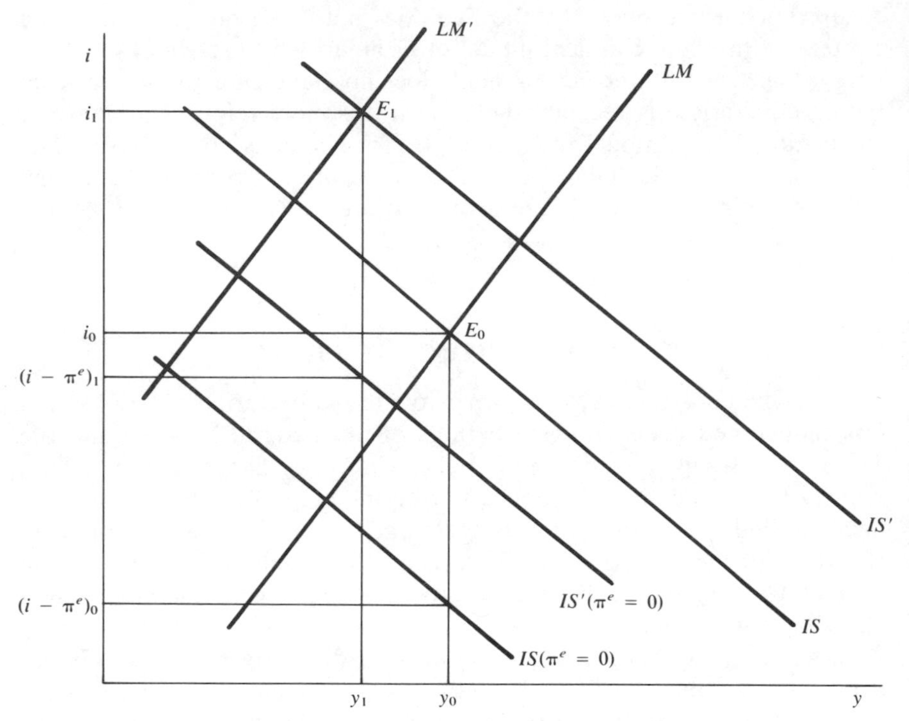

Figure 8-2 Fiscal and monetary policies in the Great Recession, 1981–2.

changes. In fact, Table 8-1 indicates that the GNP gap was 2% in 1980; therefore, original output, designated by y_0, is to the left of y_e, which is not shown. Falling output and rising interest rates could be observed by moving up and to the left along the original *IS* curve, but since it is taken for granted that fiscal policy was expansionary, the *IS* curve must move to *IS'*. Also, the $IS(\pi^e = 0)$ curve shifts by an equal amount to $IS'(\pi^e = 0)$. In this case, we would observe both $i - \pi^e$ and y increasing; for that reason, there must have been a major leftward shift of the *LM* curve to a position such as *LM'* to allow E_1 to be the new equilibrium in 1981–2. How should we characterize monetary events to get this result? We know that $(m - p)$ must fall to shift the *LM* curve to the left. This can be accomplished by μ falling or π rising, but since the inflation rate was falling in 1981–2, the latter can be ruled out. If contractionary monetary policy is predictable and credible, i will fall and $(m - p)$ will rise; but if it is unpredictable, i will rise, y will fall and $(m - p)$ will fall. Thus, it would appear that the continuing tight-money policy of the Fed, expressed as further reductions in the growth rates of the monetary aggregates, was not believed and was treated more like a negative monetary shock than

Table 8-2. *Some important data for explaining the Great Recession of 1981–2*

Year	Federal gov't. full-employment surplus (1972 $ bil.)	Gov't. purchases of goods and services (1972 $ bil.)	Gross private investment (1972 $ bil.)	i (%)	π^e (%)	$i - \pi^e$ (%)
1979	−32.9	278.3	229.1	12.7	6.7	6.0
1980	−76.3	284.6	213.3	15.3	7.7	7.6
1981	−26.5	287.1	216.9	18.9	8.6	10.3
1982	−97.8	291.2	205.4	14.9	9.2	5.7

Sources: Full-employment surplus, R. J. Gordon, *Macroeconomics*, third edition, Boston, Little, Brown, 1984, table B2, quarterly data; government purchases and gross private investment, *Economic Report of the President*, 1983, table B3; i, prime rate charged by banks, ibid., table B67; π^e, expected rate of inflation, based on the four previous years' actual inflation with weights of .5, .3, .15, and .05.

a predictable policy. In summary, a rightward shift of the *IS* curve through expansionary fiscal policy and an even larger leftward shift of the *LM* curve through contractionary, but not credible, monetary policy are predicted to lead to lower output and higher real interest rates.

The major evidence for testing this proposition is contained in Table 8-2. Although it is difficult to combine all the dimensions of fiscal policy in one variable, the federal government full-employment budget surplus comes close to measuring the stance taken by the fiscal authorities on stabilization policy. Since many components of both revenue and expenditures respond automatically to the current state of the economy, the actual surplus tends to rise with economic expansions and fall with recessions and is not a good indicator of policy changes. Hence, it is useful to pick an arbitrary point in the business cycle, that is, full-employment output, to measure the surplus or deficit for the given tax and expenditure decisions in force at that time. For the full-employment surplus, an increase would show a deliberately contractionary policy, whereas a decrease would indicate an intention toward expansion. The first column in Table 8-2 reveals that there was a full-employment deficit in all four years, with a dramatic rise from 1981 to 1982. From that viewpoint, 1981–2 represents an immense expansionary change in fiscal policy, not just the result of declining revenues engendered by the recession. Next, we can look at the crowding-out issue. The second and third columns of Table 8-2 are of interest here. Total expenditures for all levels of government rose thoughout the period in real terms, but of particular interest is the fact that the increase in 1982 was only 1.5%. At the same time, investment expenditures fell by 5%. It is seen that the fall in investment demand is much larger than the increase in government demand implying more-than-complete crowding out.[22] Finally, we can look at developments in the real interest rate during 1979–82. Because of the important relationship to investment, the prime rate charged by banks for loans is used here instead of short-term money-market rates. By 1981, the real interest rate reached a staggering 10%, which undoubtedly explains the major reductions in demand for capital goods in 1982, given the lags between the time that decisions are made and the time that they are carried out.

Because of the absurdity of more-than-complete crowding out, the high real interest rates are not just the result of fiscal policy, but also of continuing tight monetary policy which may not have been entirely credible. During 1981–2, the Fed continued to worry about inflation, and as a consequence it was prepared to keep downward pressure on the growth rate of the monetary aggregates. If such a policy were credible and capable of being incorporated into expectations and contracts, it should not have influenced the real interest rate; both the nominal interest rate and the expected rate of inflation should have fallen equally. If, on the other hand, the policy is not credible, inflationary expectations will not adjust; the nominal interest rate will rise, as does the real interest rate.

In setting the objective for the annual growth rates for 1981, the members of the FOMC "agreed that some further reduction in the ranges for monetary growth . . . was appropriate in line with the long-standing goal of contributing to a reduction in the rate of inflation and providing the basis for restoration of economic stability and sustainable growth in output of goods and services."[23] But those with an important stake in predicting future Fed action and its influence on the inflation rate may have questioned the Fed's resolve to maintain this stance in the face of rising unemployment, falling output, interest rates in the 20% range, and bankruptcy threatening even the most established corporations. They may have bet on a reversal of Fed policy and not adjusted inflationary expectations downward. Nevertheless, the Fed reaffirmed its 1981 goal for 1982. The "Record of Policy Actions of the FOMC" reveals that "the members were in agreement on the need to maintain the commitment to the long-standing goal of restraining growth of money and credit, thereby contributing to a further reduction in the rate of inflation and providing the basis for restoration of economic stability and sustainable growth in output."[24] In view of the fact that the 1982 statement is almost a word-for-word repetition of the 1981 statement, it is beyond doubt that the Fed was signaling its intention to stay the course despite many temptations

[22] Income-tax reductions, of some relevance at the time, can increase consumption expenditures, which could also crowd out some investment demand.

[23] "Record of Policy Actions of the FOMC," *Federal Reserve Bulletin*, 67, April 1981, p. 315.

[24] *Federal Reserve Bulletin*, 68, April 1982, p. 232.

to do otherwise, but the private sector was already convinced that the monetary authorities would succumb to these temptations. In that light, it would be fair to say that the fiscal authorities, the monetary authorities, and the private sector all contributed to the 10% real interest rate in 1981. Although in retrospect it is easy to see that tighter fiscal policy could have prevented such high interest rates, ironically we cannot say the same about easier monetary policy without knowing the expectational response of the public. Credibility of monetary policy makes all the difference to the result.

Whatever were the interpretations of Fed intentions, actual developments in the real money supply are hard to read. The Fed attempted to keep the growth rate of monetary aggregates below the rate of inflation, and this should have reduced the real money supply. In Table 8-1, $(m1 - p)$ falls fairly steadily from 1979 to 1981 but then rises by 2% in 1982. On the other hand, $(m2 - p)$ remains relatively steady until 1981 and then rises by 3% in 1982. Whether these results can explain the size of the leftward shift of the *LM* curve in Figure 8-2 is an open question. In other words, monetary policy appears to be tight from an interest-rate perspective but not necessarily from a real-money-supply perspective.

8.8 SUMMARY

The decade of the 1970s brought forth a new problem for stabilization policy, namely negative supply shocks, which caused output to fall and inflation to rise simultaneously. Such stagflationary phenomena were in contrast to the earlier experience of "trading off" inflation and unemployment in the short run along a "Phillips curve" when demand shocks hit the economy. In this new environment, monetary authorities must make some difficult decisions. Assuming that their aim is to stabilize output in the face of these supply shocks, they have to determine whether the shock is temporary or permanent. If it is the former, interest-rate control allows the economy to remain at full employment, but if it is the latter, any attempt to hold the interest rate constant imparts an inflationary bias to the economy. Money-supply control would be a better option in these circumstances.

During the first oil-price increase in 1973, the evidence favors an interest-rate control interpretation of Fed action, but during the subsequent period, the Federal Open Market Committee paid more attention to monetary aggregates and less to interest rates in setting its targets. When the 1979 oil-price increase occurred, money-supply control was dominant.

The policies adopted by the Fed were criticized from all sides. Only the more thoughtful critics were considered in this chapter. Alan Blinder believed that the Fed should have "financed" oil-price rises by a step increase in the money supply without, however, stating whether he thought the shocks were temporary or permanent in their effect on output. Also, Ralph Bryant attacked the Fed for its two-stage targeting procedure instead of aiming directly at the ultimate targets of full employment and price stability. But the difference between Bryant and the Federal Reserve lies in their respective views of optimal information processing, and in the absence of hard evidence one way or the other, one should not take sides easily.

The "Great Recession" of 1981–2 is often blamed on high interest rates, created in turn by monstrous budget deficits. However, such a view implies more-than-complete crowding out and therefore, tight but not credible monetary policy also shares some of the blame.

We have learned a lot about supply shocks in the 1970s, and if such events occur again, we may handle them better, but the danger exists that everything will now be interpreted as a supply shock and responses will be applied in these terms. One can only hope that the saying "generals always fight the last war" will not be applied to central bankers.

FURTHER READING

Blinder, A. S., *Economic Policy and the Great Stagflation,* New York, Academic Press, 1981. A thorough and critical review of macroeconomic policies in the 1970s.

Bryant, R. C., *Controlling Money: The Federal Reserve and Its Critics,* Washington, D.C., Brookings Institution, 1983. A very detailed and knowledgeable analysis of monetary shocks, monetary mechanisms and monetary targets with recommendations for improving Federal Reserve operating procedures.

CHAPTER 9

A model of an open economy

9.1 INTRODUCTION

The *IS–LM–AS* model has served us well so far in analyzing the recent macroeconomic experience in the United States. However, it is inappropriate to apply it in its current state to open economies such as Canada. We therefore need to make some adjustments to take into account the existence of international transactions, both in goods and in assets. Our main task in this chapter is to adapt the *IS–LM–AS* equations to an open economy. Once we have done that we can repeat some of our earlier experiments to compare how open economies react differently from closed economies when they are subjected to exogenous shocks and to compare the policy options that are available to the governments in these countries. First, we need to indicate the importance for Canada of international transactions compared to purely domestic trade.

There is no clear-cut method of classifying countries as closed economies or as open economies; there is really only a continuum of openness. Nevertheless, it is not unreasonable to think of the U.S. economy as being essentially closed with only 8.8% of its domestic output sold abroad in the form of exports of goods and services in the period 1976–80 and only 6.9% of its total expenditures going to foreign goods and services as imports. On the other hand, Canada exported 23.8% of its production during that same period and imported 27.5% of its needs. For that reason, international economic conditions play a much more important role in a country like Canada than in the United States and to explain Canadian macroeconomic events we therefore need an open-economy macro model.

Open-economy macroeconomics is always a little more complicated than closed-economy macroeconomics because there is at least one additional market to consider: the market for foreign exchange through which all international transactions must pass. This adds the exchange rate or the balance of payments to the list of important macroeconomic variables that must be determined by the model. Which of these variables is the equilibrating factor in the foreign exchange market depends on the exchange-rate regime adopted by the government. If a purely flexible exchange rate prevails, the government takes a hands-off attitude to the exchange rate and it is determined by the interaction of private demand and supply. On the other hand, if the government pegs its exchange rate to gold or to some numeraire currency, it must intervene in the market to make this rate prevail; this intervention is measured by balance-of-payments surpluses or deficits. In between, there is a managed exchange rate where the government has a target exchange rate but its value and the extent of its commitment to it are not known to the public. In essence, we not only have an extra market but also different ways of specifying the equilibrium condition for that market.

9.2 INTERNATIONAL TRANSACTIONS

An open economy consumes not only its own products but also those produced in the rest of the world, paying for these imports with exports, namely those items which the country sells in foreign markets. Thus, foreign demand adds to aggregate demand for the home country but imports subtract from it. This feature has to be incorporated into the *IS* curve and from there into the *AD* curve. Also, we must now draw a distinction between the price of goods produced in the country and the price of the bundle of goods consumed in the country. Although relative prices among individual goods produced either at home or abroad will be taken as fixed, there is still a relative price between domestic goods and foreign goods that can be changed by differences in inflation rates and by changes in the exchange rate. Therefore, prices faced by consumers may diverge from the price obtained by domestic producers. Let p remain the natural log of the price of domestically produced goods and define p_c as the natural log of the price of the consumption bundle. These are linked by the following relationship:

$$p_c = hp + (1 - h)(p^* + r) \tag{9.1}$$

where p^* is the equivalent to p in the foreign country and r is the natural log of the exchange rate, defined as the price of the foreign currency in terms of the domestic currency.

EXAMPLE

> If the price of £1 (the foreign currency in this example) is \$2, r would be .69.

The parameter h measures the importance of home goods in the consumption bundle; therefore, p_c is a weighted average of p and $p^* + r$ with the sum of the weights equal to one. Now $p^* + r$ is the price of foreign goods converted to the domestic currency, remembering that the product of the foreign price in the foreign currency times the price of the foreign currency is represented by the sum of their natural logs. One can think of p as the GNP deflator, measuring the price of goods and services produced in the home country, and of p_c as the Consumer Price Index (CPI), which measures price movements of a representative consumption bundle with fixed weights.

We need to make an additional assumption about the substitutability of domestic and foreign goods in the consumption bundle. If they are perfect substitutes, their prices must be equal and therefore $p = p^* + r$, which according to equation (9.1) stipulates that p_c and p would always move together. However, this is an unrealistic assumption. Because most countries are much more specialized in their production than in their consumption, foreign goods are likely to be imperfect substitutes for domestic goods, and therefore it will be possible for p_c and p to diverge when their relative price changes.

Since we are interested in rates of change of prices rather than their levels, we can define (9.1) for the previous period and together with property 4 of natural logs in the Appendix to Chapter 2, which dictates that $\pi = p - p_{-1}$, $\pi_c = p_c - p_{c_{-1}}$, $\pi^* = p^* - p^*_{-1}$, and $\rho = r - r_{-1}$, and we obtain

$$\pi_c = h\pi + (1 - h)(\pi^* + \rho) \tag{9.2}$$

Both π_c and π play a role in the macro model. For instance, in the labor market the real wage from the worker's perspective is the nominal wage deflated by consumer prices, whereas the real wage to the firm involves deflating the nominal wage by producer prices. Thus, we will have to be careful in choosing π_c or π as the measure of the inflation rate in the *IS–LM–AS* model.

If we let π measure the rate of growth of the GNE deflator and π_c the rate of increase of the CPI, we can see in Chart 9-1 that for Canada in the period 1971 to 1982 the two rates of inflation did not coincide very

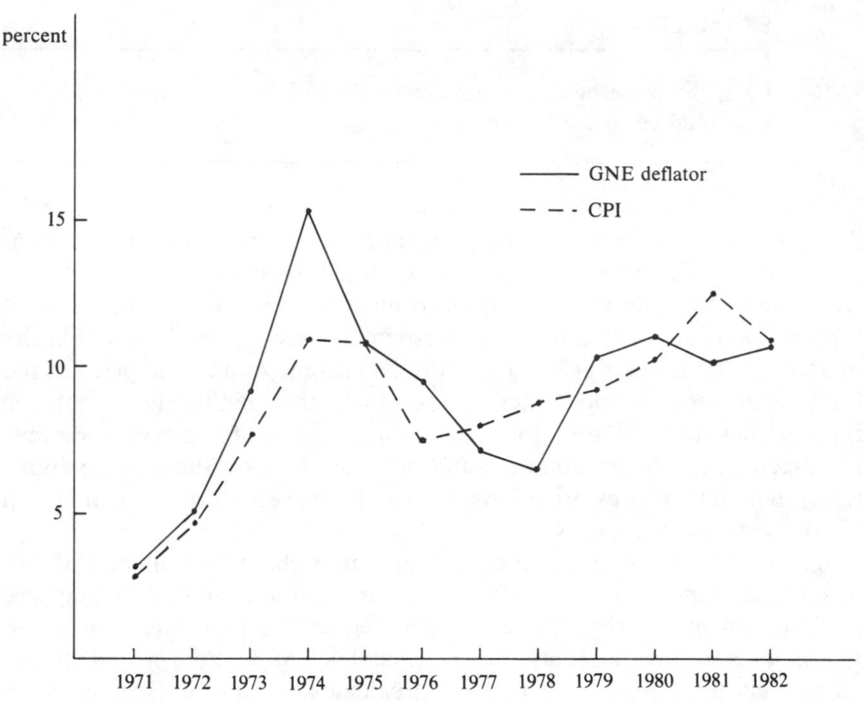

Chart 9-1 Inflation rates based on GNE deflator and Consumer Price Index, 1971–82. *Source: Bank of Canada Review,* table 1, cols. 14 and 36.

often. When π_c tends to be higher than π, it suggests that import prices are growing more quickly than domestic prices, which in turn implies that Canada's terms of trade are falling; when $\pi > \pi_c$, the terms of trade are rising.

There are also international transactions in assets. Money is mainly a transactions medium and therefore useful only in the domestic economy, as both domestic residents and foreigners use the home currency to buy goods and services. Bonds, however, which are held for their interest yield, can have an international clientele. In other words, both domestic and foreign bonds can be held in any one portfolio. What assumption about their substitutability is appropriate in this case? Unlike goods, it makes sense to think of government bonds from different countries as being alike in most respects: maturity, coupon rates, tax treatment, and other features of importance to the investor. However, they are distinguishable by the fact that they are denominated in different currencies. That means that domestic portfolios containing foreign-currency bonds are subject to capital gains or losses from changes in the exchange rate.

EXAMPLE

> If a Canadian investor purchased a £1,000 bond when the price of sterling was \$2.00, he would lose \$500 if the exchange rate dropped to \$1.50, but would gain \$200 if the exchange rate rose to \$2.20.

Despite this possibility, both bonds will yield an equal return if the interest rate on the domestic bond equals the interest rate on the foreign bond plus the rate of capital gain from exchange-rate changes. Equality of returns then would mean similarity in all respects, and there is no reason for not considering domestic and foreign bonds as being potentially perfect substitutes in investors' portfolios. Interest rates in the two countries are connected by

$$(9.3) \qquad i = i^* + \rho^e$$

where i and i^* are the interest rates on domestic and foreign bonds respectively and $\rho^e = r^e - r_{-1}$ is the expected change in the exchange rate for the next period.

EXAMPLE

> If the exchange rate at the beginning of the period is \$2.00 ($r_{-1} = .69$) but expected to rise to \$2.20 ($r^e = .79$) by the end of the period, then $\rho^e = .1$; if it is expected to fall to \$1.90 ($r^e = .64$), then $\rho^e = -.05$. In the former case the Canadian dollar is expected to depreciate vis-à-vis the pound or the pound is expected to appreciate vis-à-vis the Canadian dollar. The reverse is true in the latter case.

Equation (9.3) is an equilibrium condition because equality of yields on domestic and foreign bonds means that there is no pressure to exchange one kind of bond for the other as long as they are identical in every other respect. For that reason, equation (9.3) is called the *interest parity condition*. Let us explore its meaning. First, it suggests that if exchange rates are fixed and assumed to stay that way, interest rates will be equalized, since $\rho^e = 0$. If we observed $i > i^*$, everyone would want to buy domestic bonds and sell foreign bonds; the price of domestic bonds would rise and the price of foreign bonds would fall; interest rates would move in the opposite direction until $i = i^*$, at which point there is no further incentive to exchange one asset for the other.

Second, expected yields can still be equalized even if the exchange rate is expected to change as long as $\rho^e = i - i^*$. That is, the country with the higher interest rate must also have the currency that is expected to depreciate. But how can we check on such an assertion, especially when we are confronted again by an unobservable variable, ρ^e? Unlike the situation faced with measuring π^e, the expected rate of inflation, we believe that we have a very good proxy for ρ^e in the form of the *forward exchange rate*.

Currency markets not only have *spot* transactions where the exchange of currencies is effected immediately, but also future contracts where the price is agreed to at the time the contract is made but the transaction is not consummated until some specified date in the future, such as one or two months hence. The exchange rate for these different transactions will not, in general, be the same.

EXAMPLE

On January 5, 1983, the spot price of £1 was $1.9935 (Can.). One-month forward contracts were $1.9932, and the three-month forward rate was quoted at $1.9918, so that future pounds were cheaper than spot pounds.

The forward exchange rate represents the market's estimate of the spot rate that is expected to prevail at the time that the forward contract matures. The difference between the forward and spot rates, therefore, is our measure of ρ^e. It may not be everyone's estimate of ρ^e, but it summarizes the predictions of all those who enter the market, and since there is an incentive to speculate in currency markets if an individual believes that his or her prediction is better than that of the market, this *forward premium* is the "best" estimate of the expected change in the exchange rate.

EXAMPLE

Using the previous example for January 5, 1983, r(spot) = .6899, r(3 months) = .6890; therefore, the forward premium is −.09%, which is then converted to an annual rate by multipying by 4; therefore the annualized three-month forward premium is −.36%.

If the forward premium is positive, the exchange rate is expected to rise or the domestic currency is expected to depreciate; if the forward premium is negative, we have a forward discount, and the domestic currency is expected to appreciate or the foreign currency is expected to depreciate.

Equations (9.2) and (9.3) provide two important links between the home country and the rest of the world and they will be incorporated into the open-economy version of the *IS–LM–AS* model, but before embarking on that task we need to look at the direction in which causation takes place. Let us first explore this question for equation (9.3). Does i^* influence i, or vice versa, or both? The answer depends very much on the relative size of the home country and of the rest of the world. The smaller is the home country the less able it is to have any effect on the "world" interest rate through its own initiatives. Canada seems to fit that description of smallness rather well; it buys and sells in international asset markets at prices that it can take as given. Therefore, for countries like Canada, i^* is treated as exogenous and the Bank of Canada cannot influence this variable by its own actions. The answer for (9.2) is somewhat different since π and π^* refer to price changes of imperfectly substitutable goods. Thus equation (9.2) is not an equilibrium condition, but instead a definition of a price index, which indicates that a change in π^* will affect π_c, but says nothing about what happens to π. Since each country produces a unique bundle of goods, there is no sharp competition in international markets to make π and π^* exactly the same; therefore it is most appropriate to consider π as a domestically determined variable. By analogy, π_c^* is defined as $h^*\pi^* + (1 - h^*)(\pi - \rho)$, where h^* measures the importance of foreign-country goods in their own consumption bundle. Notice that home-country goods in the foreign-country currency are priced at $p - r$, with the rate of change denoted by $\pi - \rho$. The smallness of the home country makes h^* close to one so that π and ρ are of minor importance to the foreign country's π_c^*. Thus there is an assumed asymmetry: The "small" home country has an h significantly less than one; the "large" rest of the world has an h^* very close to one.

We can now summarize the international transactions of an open economy:

1. It produces one commodity but consumes both it and the foreign good, which are imperfect substitutes for each other.
2. It has a bond that is perfectly substitutable for the foreign bond when expected yields are equalized.
3. Domestic money is not accepted in any other country.

In these international transactions, the open economy takes the price of the import good as given but has some price-making power in the market for its export good; the open economy is also too small to affect the world interest rate.

9.3 THE STRUCTURE OF AN OPEN ECONOMY

The *IS–LM–AS* model remains as the framework for macroeconomic analysis, but the international transactions discussed above and the new relationships that they create must be incorporated into the *IS*, *LM*, and *AS* curves. In addition to the variables that were important in a closed economy, namely output, the interest rate, and the inflation rate, this framework tells us what is happening in the foreign exchange market, determining either the size of the balance-of-payments surplus or deficit if the exchange rate is fixed or the exchange rate if market forces are allowed to determine its level.

9.3.1 THE OPEN-ECONOMY *IS* CURVE

Previously, demand for goods and services was in equilibrium when unintended inventory adjustment was zero. This implied that saving plus taxes equaled investment plus government expenditures. Now, in an open economy, we add imports to the former and exports to the latter category. Therefore, let S represent the natural log of saving, taxes, and imports in real terms and I is now the natural log of investment, government expenditures, and exports, also in quantity (not in value) terms. In addition to income, the natural log of which is y, S is determined by the relative price of home and foreign goods. This relative price is defined as $t = p - p^* - r$ and is called the *terms of trade*. It is also in natural logs. Therefore

$$(9.4) \qquad S = b_0 + b_1 y + b_{15} t$$

where b_{15} is a positive parameter denoting the price elasticity of imports. An increase in p, for example, with p^* and r held constant will raise t and make domestic goods less attractive relative to imports; therefore, S rises. The parameter b_1 now contains the income elasticity of imports as well as the elasticities of savings and taxes.

The relative-price effect also operates on exports. For that reason we write

$$(9.5) \qquad I = b_2 + b_3 y - b_4(i - \pi^e) - b_{16} t$$

In this case an increase in t arising from a higher p causes a substitution away from domestic goods to foreign goods and reduces exports; for that reason b_{16} has a minus sign in front of it. From earlier discussion, we know that $(i - \pi^e)$ is the real interest rate that is inversely related to investment expenditures. In equation (9.5), π^e still refers to the expected rate of change of output prices since investment decisions focus on the price of goods produced by the firm.[1]

By setting equations (9.4) and (9.5) equal to each other we obtain the *IS* curve, which is again a relationship between y and i, written as

$$(9.6) \qquad y = a_0 - a_1(i - \pi^e) - a_5 t$$

where $a_0 = (b_2 - b_0)/(b_1 - b_3)$, $a_1 = b_4/(b_1 - b_3)$, and $a_5 = (b_{15} + b_{16})/(b_1 - b_3)$. In Chapter 2, we convinced ourselves that $b_1 > b_3$, a condition that is not changed by the addition of imports and exports to equations (9.4) and (9.5). Therefore the denominators of the a's are all positive. In addition we merely assume that $b_2 > b_0$ to ensure that $a_0 > 0$ and that the *IS* curve is drawn in the first quadrant.

Although we no longer keep track of imports and exports separately, we know that an increase in t will reduce exports and increase imports, thus reducing the trade balance, which is defined as the difference between exports and imports. At a particular level of t, the trade balance is zero. Let us call t_e the *equilibrium terms of trade* at which $a_5 t_e = 0$ since there is no net foreign demand for home goods at that particular constellation of domestic and foreign prices and the exchange rate.

To allow for continuing inflation in the home country and the rest of the world and its effect on the terms of trade we can write

$$(9.7) \qquad t - t_{-1} = \pi - \pi^* - \rho$$

Thus t increases over time if $\pi > \pi^* + \rho$. Substituting (9.7) into (9.6) produces

$$(9.8) \qquad y = a_0 - a_1(i - \pi^e) - a_5(\pi - \pi^* - \rho + t_{-1})$$

The new *IS* curve is drawn in Figure 9-1. Unlike the *IS* curve for the closed economy, it does not stay in place unless t is constant, which requires that $\pi = \pi^* + \rho$; that is, the terms of trade are constant. If that condition is not satisfied, the *IS* curve will keep shifting to the left or to the right. For instance, assume that $\pi > \pi^* + \rho$. That means that t is rising over time and demand for home goods will keep falling and the *IS* curve will keep moving to the left. On the other hand, if $\pi < \pi^* + \rho$, then *IS* continues to shift to the right. Therefore, in order to draw a particular *IS* curve we need to impose a constant t, but this can be achieved at any rate of domestic inflation as long as it is matched by the sum of foreign inflation and domestic-currency depreciation. This con-

[1] If saving were sensitive to the real interest rate, it would be defined as $(i - \pi_c^e)$, since savers are interested in the purchasing power of their accumulated wealth.

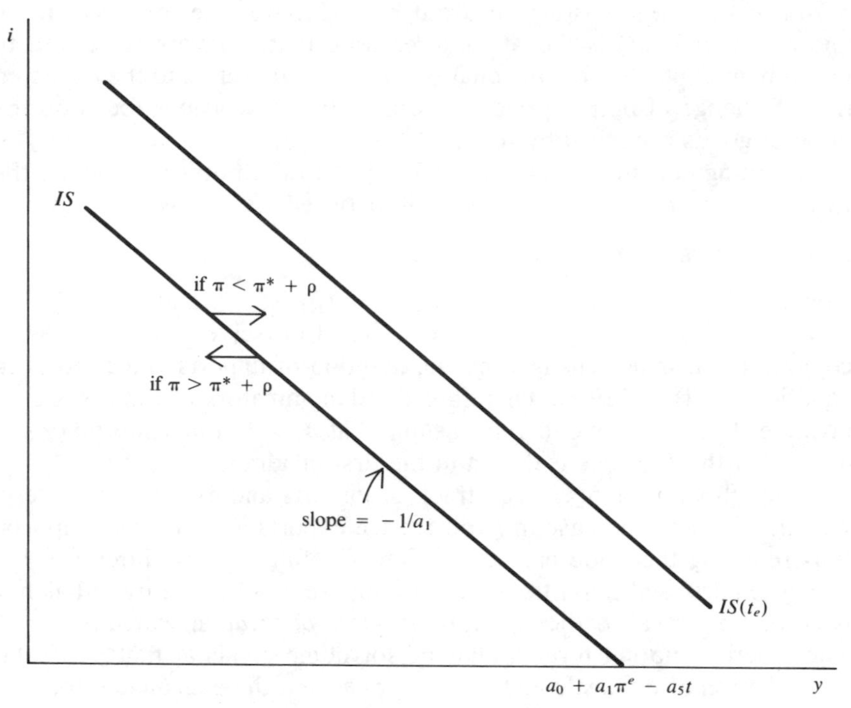

Figure 9-1 The open-economy *IS* curve.

dition is not the same as *purchasing power parity* (PPP) between any two countries which requires that $p_c = p_c^* + r$ according to the *absolute* version and $\pi_c = \pi_c^* + \rho$ according to the *relative* version. However, if $\pi = \pi^* + \rho$, then the relative version of PPP will hold.

By the same argument that the *IS* curve keeps shifting if t is rising or falling over time, so the trade balance must also be falling or rising. Therefore, if the *IS* curve keeps moving left because $\pi > \pi^* + \rho$, then the current account is moving to a smaller surplus or to a larger deficit, and if it is shifting to the right, the current account is experiencing a larger surplus or a smaller deficit. Only if t is constant is there an unchanging current account balance. Moreover, there is only one t, namely t_e, for which the current account is zero. Such an *IS* curve is drawn in Figure 9-1, as $IS(t_e)$. In this case, it is arbitrarily drawn to the right of *IS* to indicate a trade deficit at the existing t, which is greater than t_e. Now $IS(t_e)$ requires not only that demand for goods and services is in equilibrium, as it is on any *IS* curve, but also that there is no net foreign demand for these goods and services.

9.3.2 THE OPEN-ECONOMY *LM* CURVE

The openness of the economy does not change the demand side of the money market. The demand for real money balances is still determined by real income and by the domestic nominal interest rate, although the latter is now linked to i^* and ρ^e via equation (9.3). Also, nominal money balances will continue to be deflated by p and not by p_c, since transactions balances will be related to spending on home goods by domestic and foreign residents alike; therefore the "scale variable" continues to be domestic income or output, y, for which the deflator is still p.

But the process by which the money supply is created needs to be revamped to take into account international transactions that may involve the central bank. From Chapter 6, it will be remembered that the monetary base, equal to currency outstanding plus deposits of the commercial banks at the central bank, could be changed either by open-market operations in government securities or by purchases or sales of foreign-currency assets. Then through the money multiplier a rise or fall in the monetary base is translated into an equiproportionate change in the money supply, as defined by any of the conventional monetary aggregates. These techniques are interchangeable in their effect on the money supply, but there is one important distinction between them: open-market operations are the main policy instrument by which the central bank enforces its monetary policy, whereas transactions in foreign-currency assets are forced on the central bank if there exists a commitment to a fixed exchange rate and if excess demand or supply appears at that exchange rate. Thus, balance-of-payments surpluses show up as increases in central bank holdings of international reserves as they absorb the excess demand in the foreign exchange market. On the other hand, deficits involve reductions in international reserves. Because of this link, balance-of-payments surpluses increase the money supply and shift the *LM* curve down and to the right, whereas deficits shift the *LM* curve up and to the left.

Consider a balance-of-payments surplus equal to \$40 from the starting position of the banking system in Table 6-3 in Chapter 6. In other words, there is excess demand for the home currency equal to \$40 or excess supply of £20 if the exchange rate is \$2.00 for £1. In the absence of central bank intervention in the foreign exchange market, the exchange rate would fall to eliminate the excess supply of pounds. Instead, because the country is assumed to have a fixed exchange rate the central bank must buy the £20 and sell \$40. These dollars will wind up as commercial bank deposits at the central bank, and the various categories of assets and liabilities adjust as shown in Table 9-1. This end result is no different from that generated by open-market operations as reported in Table 6-4. The

Table 9-1. *Balance sheets of the banking system after a balance-of-payments surplus*

	Central bank			
Assets		*Liabilities*		
Government securities	$700	Currrency in circulation		$550
Foreign-currency assets	140	At commercial banks	25	
Advances to commercial banks	0	Held by the public	525	
		Deposits of the commercial banks		290
	$840			$840
	Commercial banks			
Assets		*Liabilities*		
Currency	$ 25	Demand deposits		$1,050
Deposits at central bank	290	Time deposits		5,250
Earning assets	5,785	Borrowings from central bank		0
	$6,300			$6,300

only difference is the composition of the monetary base between government securities and foreign-currency assets. In both cases, the size of the monetary base rose by 5% (i.e., 40/800). M1, defined as currency held by the public and demand deposits, also increased by 5%, as did M2, which is defined as M1 plus time deposits.

The growth rate of the monetary base and of the money supply now has two components: μ_s is the growth rate of central bank holdings of government securities, generated by open-market operations, and μ_r is the growth of international reserves, created by balance-of-payments surpluses. With a constant money multiplier,

$$\mu = s\mu_s + (1 - s)\mu_r \tag{9.9}$$

where μ is, as previously, the growth rate of nominal money balances and s is the proportion of government securities in the monetary base. In summary, unless the fixed exchange rate happens to be equal to the equilibrium exchange rate, the central bank will have to intervene in the foreign exchange market and in the process change both the monetary base and the money supply because μ_r will be other than zero. In that sense, a regime of fixed exchange rates reduces the ability of the central bank to follow an independent monetary policy.

The link between the foreign exchange market and the money supply is broken if we have a regime of flexible exchange rates. In that case the central bank does not intervene in the foreign exchange market because it has no commitment to a particular price for the foreign currency and therefore the exchange rate is the equilibrating factor in the market. Since international reserves at the central bank are now constant (i.e., $\mu_r = 0$), the monetary base changes only with open-market operations involving government securities, much the same as in a closed economy.

The *LM* curve in an open economy is written as

$$(9.10) \quad m - p = a_2 y - a_3 i$$

where m is the natural log of the nominal money supply and a_2 and a_3 are positive parameters interpreted as the income and interest elasticities of the demand for money. Since $(m - p) = (m - p)_{-1} + s\mu_s + (1 - s)\mu_r - \pi$, we can write

$$(9.11) \quad s\mu_s + (1 - s)\mu_r - \pi = a_2 y - a_3 i - (m - p)_{-1}$$

In summary, the *LM* curve looks very much like its closed-economy counterpart except for the important fact that the growth rate of the money supply is endogenously determined by balance-of-payments surpluses or deficits when the country operates with a fixed exchange rate. Only if $\mu_r = 0$ is the interpretation of equation (9.11) similar to that in Chapter 2.

9.3.3 THE OPEN-ECONOMY *AS* CURVE

The labor market, which provides us with the *AS* curve, remains a domestic market, but the open-economy version of the *AS* curve has to be adapted to the existence of two price indexes; p, which is relevant to producers, and p_c which is of interest to worker–consumers. Since it is assumed that the demand side of the labor market dictates actual employment when excess supply or demand appear, $(w - p)$ is the relevant wage for determining the actual level of employment, recalling that w is the natural log of the nominal wage. As $(w - p)$ rises employment and output fall; $(w - p)$ will rise if $\omega > \pi$, where ω is the growth rate of the nominal wage. Having given the right to determine employment to the firm, it is not inconsistent to give unions the right to determine ω. Since they try to keep the real wage $(w - p_c)$ constant over the life of a contract, they will set $\omega = \pi_c^e$.

Another feature of the open-economy labor market is that there does not exist a unique level of equilibrium employment and output, unlike the closed economy, where only supply-side policies or events could affect these variables. In the open economy, the terms of trade play a role in determining the work–leisure choice; although both supply and demand in the labor market respond only to *real* wages, the fact that there are two different real wages is important here.

The supply and demand curves in the labor market are shown in Figure 9-2. The demand curve, N, depends only on $(w - p)$, which is measured on the vertical axis, but the supply curve, L, is related to $(w - p_c)$. From

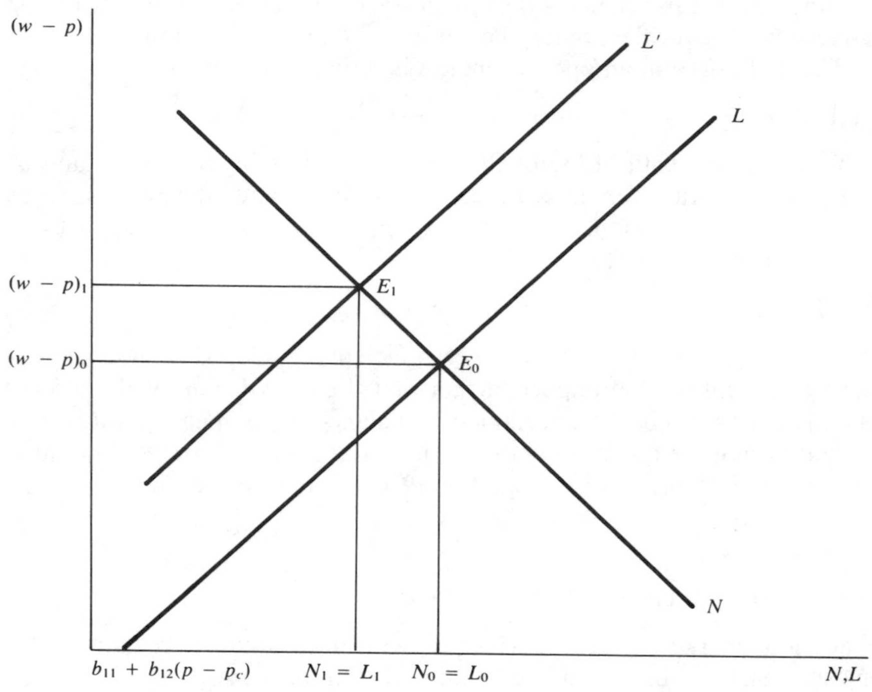

Figure 9-2 Adjustments in the labor market to a change in the terms of trade.

Chapter 2, the supply of labor is related to the real wage according to

$$(9.12)\quad L = b_{11} + b_{12}(w - p_c + p - p)$$
$$= b_{11} + b_{12}(p - p_c) + b_{12}(w - p)$$

Thus the horizontal intercept in Figure 9-2 depends not only on b_{11}, which incorporates all other factors determining the work–leisure choice, but also $b_{12}(p - p_c)$, which is determined by the terms of trade. In this setting, it is possible for an exogenous *nominal* change to affect the real equilibrium of the economy by changing full-employment output. Consider as an example an increase in import prices, p^*. This does not necessarily lead to an increase in domestic-goods prices, since they are only imperfect substitutes. Thus we can hold p constant and allow p_c to increase by $(1 - h)$ times the rise in $(p^* + r)$ according to equation (9.1). This can be referred to as a deterioration in the home country's terms of trade. The N curve remains in place, but the L curve will have to shift as if it were a supply-side event. Since $p - p_c$ is now smaller, the L curve shifts to the left, and a new equilibrium is established at E_1, with a higher real wage from the firm's perspective and lower employment. Through the production function, the reduced labor input also causes equilibrium output, defined as y_e, to fall.

Putting all this together we get the *AS* curve

$$(9.13) \quad y = y_{e-1} - a_4(\pi_c^e - \pi)$$

Since y_e is no longer unique, it has to be dated, and therefore equation (9.13) incorporates the assumption that the economy starts from a prior equilibrium position but it may not return there. In the closed economy, y changed only because of incorrectly anticipated inflation. Although errors in expectations are still important sources of income adjustments, they are not the only ones. Assume that $\pi_c^e = \pi_c$. Using equations (9.2) and (9.7) in the *AS* curve, allows us to rewrite it as

$$(9.14) \quad y_e = y_{e-1} + a_4(1 - h)(t - t_{-1})$$

The previously discussed increase in import prices causes t to fall and forces the *AS* curve to shift to the left. Unless there is a subsequent reversal in the terms of trade, the *AS* curve will stay in its new location and become the new y_e. This feature of the open-economy *AS* curve does not raise stabilization-policy issues that are any different from those in a closed economy. Although output is determined by the terms of trade now, equilibrium in the labor market is preserved at any terms of trade without policy intervention.

9.4 DIAGRAMMATIC REPRESENTATION OF THE OPEN ECONOMY

Although the open-economy macro model appears to be more complicated than the closed-economy version, it can still be represented diagrammatically in a rather straightforward manner. There are, however, two major differences from the diagrams that were used in earlier chapters. First, determination of equilibrium values of the endogenous variables differs between regimes of fixed and flexible exchange rates; second, because of the interest parity condition of equation (9.3), the *IS–LM* diagram is superfluous for the determination of the interest rate.

The macro model of the open economy should determine, in addition to the previously stated variables of output, the inflation rate, and the interest rate, either the exchange rate or the balance of payments. Thus from equation (9.3), the *IP* condition, equation (9.8), the *IS* curve, equation (9.11), the *LM* curve, and equation (9.13), the *AS* curve, solutions for y, π, i, and either ρ or μ_r can be obtained. Since the process by which these diagrams are put together differs for the two exchange-rate systems, it is necessary to deal with each of them in turn.

9.4.1 FIXED EXCHANGE RATES

In a country that is committed to a fixed exchange rate and is perceived to hold to that commitment, both ρ and ρ^e are equal to zero. Therefore, it is immediately obvious that $i = i^*$, which obviates the need for an *IS–LM* diagram. Previously, the *AD* curve was derived for a closed economy from a combination of the *IS* and *LM* curves. In an open economy only one of these is required: the *IS* curve for fixed exchange rates and the *LM* curve for flexible rates. The *LM* curve does not play a role in the determination of the interest rate; instead, in a country with fixed exchange rates its location is determined by the endogenously determined money supply which in turn depends on the state of the balance of payments. On the other hand, the *IS* curve now represents a relationship between y and π with the real interest rate held constant. The *AS* curve still plays a pivotal role in the determination of y and π.

The *AD* and *AS* curves are drawn in Figure 9-3. In both curves, expectational variables are treated as exogenous for the time being until the expectations process is reintroduced in the next chapter. Also, i^* and π^* are assumed to be determined in the rest of the world and impervious to home-country actions. Finally, past values of t and y_e are predetermined and a_0 is controlled by fiscal policy. The *AS* and *AD* (=*IS*) curves intersect to determine y and π, the only remaining variables. Once these variables are known and together with i from the *IP* condition, then the *LM* curve comes into play. It allows us to solve for μ_r, given μ_s by the monetary authorities and $(m - p)_{-1}$ from the previous period. If μ_r turns out to be positive, there is a balance-of-payments surplus, which forces the monetary base and the money supply to expand; if $\mu_r < 0$, then there is a deficit in the balance of payments and the money supply contracts. There are subsidiary variables that can also be determined. The current terms of trade, t, depend on t_{-1}, π, and π^*. Furthermore, whether $(m - p)$ is rising or falling depends only on the relative size of μ and π, with $\mu = (1 - s)\mu_r + s\mu_s$. Finally, π_c can be calculated from π^* and π and from knowledge of the value of the parameter h.

To sum up, the four variables of interest to us are determined in a sequential manner: (1) the interest rate is given by the *IP* condition, (2) the *IS* curve now becomes the *AD* curve and together with the *AS* curve they determine y and π, and (3) then the balance of payments is obtained from the *LM* curve. At this point we could perform any number of comparative-statics exercises to see how changes in any of the exogenous variables, as captured in the intercepts of the *AD* and *AS* curves, would cause these curves to shift and force y and π to adjust, but the results would be misleading if expectations were assumed to remain constant.

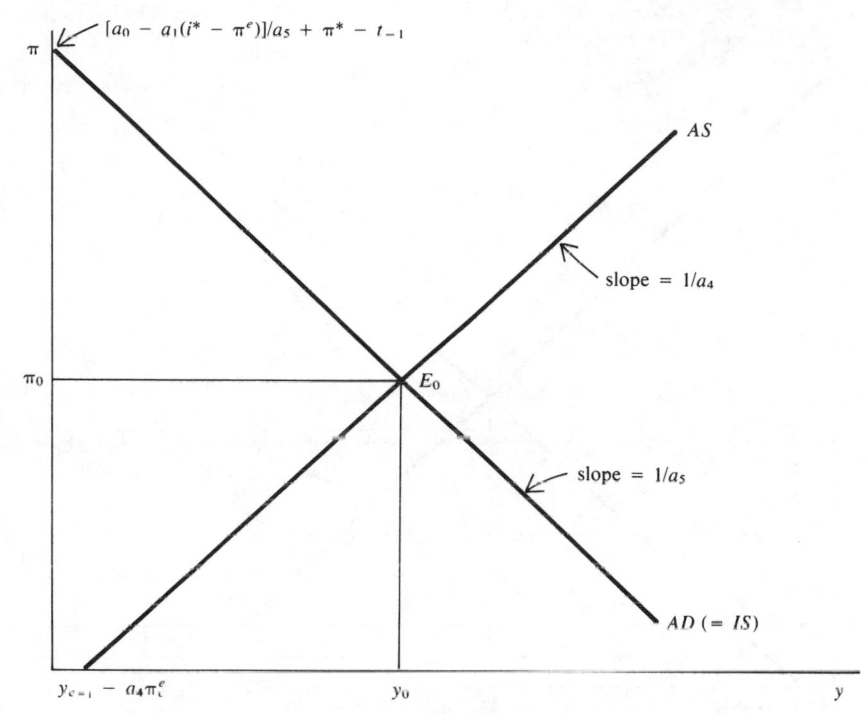

Figure 9-3 The *AD* and *AS* curves in an open economy with fixed exchange rates.

Instead, in Section 9.5, long-run characteristics are imposed on the model and exogenous changes are then interpreted in this environment.

9.4.2 FLEXIBLE EXCHANGE RATES

The sequence of solutions is different here. Now the *LM* curve becomes the *AD* curve, and the *IS* curve determines the rate of change of the exchange rate. The *IP* condition of $i = i^* + \rho^e$ is substituted into the *LM* equation, which then becomes the *AD* curve. The negative relationship between y and π now comes from the money market. Assume an increase in y; this creates excess demand for money, but since the interest rate cannot rise to equilibrate the money market when i^* and ρ^e are given, π is the only other variable that can adjust, and it falls to allow real money balances to rise. The *AD* (=*LM*) curve is drawn in Figure 9-4. The *AS* curve is also drawn. They again determine y and π simultaneously. Then the *IS* curve is rewritten as

$$(9.8') \quad \rho = [1/a_5][y - a_0 + a_1(i^* + \rho^e - \pi^e)] + \pi - \pi^* + t_{-1}$$

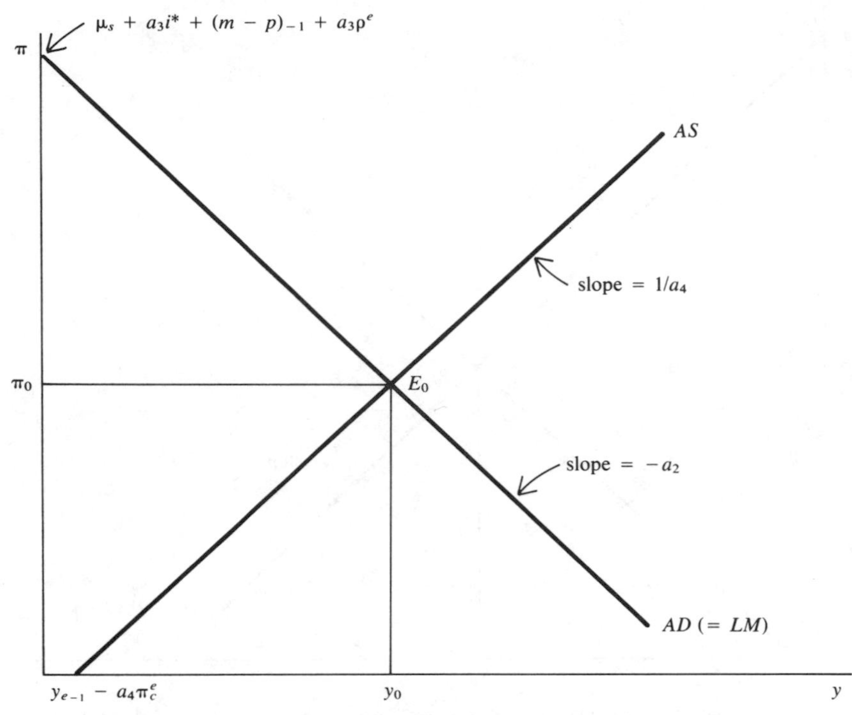

Figure 9-4 The *AD* and *AS* curves in an open economy with flexible exchange rates.

which has on the right side all the information needed to solve for ρ. All the other variables can then be calculated. For instance, t depends only on π, π^*, ρ, and t_{-1}; π_c needs π, π^*, and ρ; and so on. The balance of payments is automatically zero, and the growth rate of the money supply is limited to $s\mu_s$.

In conclusion, the flexible-exchange-rate macro model determines y, π, i, and ρ in the following sequence: (1) i^* and the exogenous ρ^e determine i through *IP*, (2) the *LM* and *AS* curves solve for y and π, and (3) the *IS* curve determines ρ.

9.5 LONG-RUN EQUILIBRIUM IN THE OPEN ECONOMY

In the closed economy, long-run equilibrium was defined as $AD = AS$ and $\pi^e = \pi$. For the open economy there are additional conditions that have to be satisfied. First there are two other expectational variables: ρ^e and π_c^e must equal their actual values or errors will have to be rectified. Second, constant terms of trade have to exist, which requires that $\pi =$

$\pi^* + \rho$; otherwise the *IS* curve would continue to shift over time. Third, the growth rate of the money supply must equal the inflation rate or the *LM* curve will keep shifting over time. This does not necessarily mean that the balance of payments must be zero, only that $(1 - s)\mu_r + s\mu_s = \pi$.

From these conditions we can derive other characteristics of long-run equilibrium. First, if $\pi = \pi^* + \rho$, then we have $\pi_c = \pi$ and also $\pi_c^e = \pi$, which means that $y = y_e$. Thus, for an open economy the *AS* curve is also vertical in the long run and output is determined strictly by equilibrium employment. Next, the other endogenous variables of the system can also be determined, but the process by which this is done depends on the exchange-rate regime. Consider first a system of fixed exchange rates. Here it is easy to see that i must be equal to the exogenous i^*. Together with y_e, the real money supply is determined, which requires that $\mu = \pi = s\mu_s + (1 - s)\mu_r$. Given μ_s, as determined by the central bank, we have $(1 - s)\mu_r = \mu - s\mu_s$. In other words, the supply of money is demand-determined; what the central bank does not provide willingly through open-market operations, it is forced to make available through foreign-exchange market intervention. In summary, the endogenous variables are y, i, π, and μ_r; they are determined sequentially: y by the *AS* curve, i by the interest parity condition, π by the foreign rate of inflation, and μ_r by the *LM* curve.

Now let us look at flexible exchange rates. Output is still supply-determined and equal to y_e. Also, to keep the real money supply constant, $\mu = s\mu_s = \pi$, but now π may diverge from π^* by the value of ρ and still keep the terms of trade constant; therefore $\rho = s\mu_s - \pi^*$. Since $\rho^e = \rho$, $i = i^* + \rho$ and the domestic interest rate can also deviate from the foreign rate by the value of ρ. Summing up again, the endogenous variables are now y, i, π, and ρ, with the important difference that π is determined solely by the policy variable μ_s, as it was in a closed economy.

Another result to note is that the real interest rates at home and abroad are equalized for both exchange-rate regimes. Since $i = i^* + \rho$ and $\rho = \pi - \pi^*$, we have $i - \pi = i^* - \pi^*$. For an open economy, therefore, an independent real interest rate is not a possibility in the long run; moreover independent nominal interest and inflation rates are impossible if the exchange rate is held constant.

Once we have these long-run characteristics in place we can conduct an interesting mental experiment, namely the effect on the home economy of a higher rate of inflation abroad. In fact, we can compare these effects under fixed and flexible exchange rates. In both cases we are considering only the long-run implications of this event, leaving until Chapter 10 a discussion of the short-run impact when anticipations are not necessarily fulfilled.

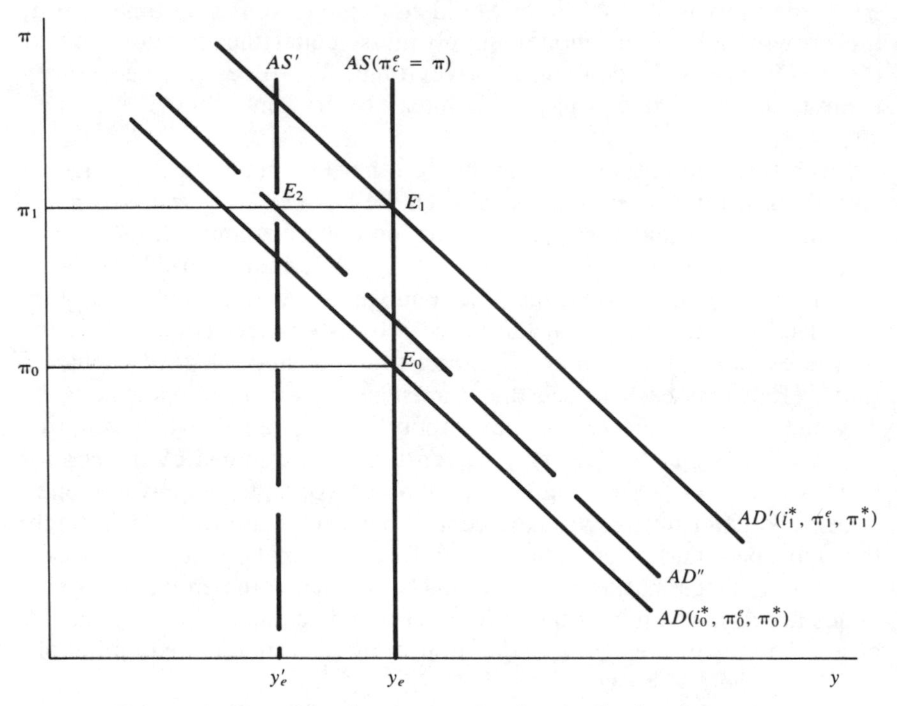

Figure 9-5 The effect of an increase in π^* under fixed exchange rates.

First consider an expansionary monetary policy in the rest of the world with the home country on a fixed exchange rate. From one long-run equilibrium to another, both π^* and i^* will increase to the same extent as the increase in the growth rate of the money supply. Furthermore, since domestic residents know that ultimately $\pi = \pi^*$ or the terms of trade would keep changing, they adjust π^e upward as well. From the *AD* intercept in Figure 9-3, the increase in i^* and π^e cancel each other to keep the real interest rate constant, but the increase in π^* is fully reflected in the vertical movement of the *AD* curve to *AD'* as shown in Figure 9-5. The *AS* curve is vertical, given the long-run assumption of $\pi_c^e = \pi$. Therefore, the economy moves from E_0 to E_1 with $\pi = \pi^*$ again at the higher rate, output is unchanged, the nominal interest rate is higher, and μ_r has increased, or a balance-of-payments surplus has appeared, to cope with the larger transactions balances that are needed in the home economy.

A fixed exchange rate forces the country to march in "lockstep" with the rest of the world. But before we jump to the conclusion that a regime of fixed exchange rates is therefore undesirable because of this feature, consider a *reduction* in π^* at a time when domestic inflation is considered to be unbearably high. Merely maintaining the existing exchange rate will cause π to follow π^* without the need for complicated monetary rules or incomes policies. Thus a fixed exchange rate can be an effective anti-inflation device, especially if there is political pressure on the central bank to follow an expansionary policy; the fixed rate allows the central bank to hide behind this "inescapable" commitment.

However, E_1 in Figure 9-5 is not the only possible outcome; there may be a permanent change in output. Although $\pi_c = \pi = \pi^*$ must hold both before and after the change, t need not be the same. For instance, if π is below π^* for part of the adjustment, then t will be lower.

EXAMPLE

> Initially $t = 0$ and $\pi = \pi^* = .10$. Then π^* rises to .12 and in the first period $t = -.02$. If, in the second period π rises to .11, then t becomes $-.03$. Finally, $\pi = \pi^* = .12$ in the third period, but t remains at $-.03$, so that the terms of trade have fallen 3% from beginning to end.

The AS curve would shift to the left as required by equation (9.14), and the end result could be E_2 on AS' with the same rate of inflation equal to π^* and a new AD curve, AD'', whose location is endogenously determined. But it is far from certain whether E_2 should be to the left of E_1 or to the right in all circumstances. The long-run version of the model does not provide us with the dynamics by which π is determined in each time period, and so the final outcome for t is ambiguous. However, it is now clear that in an open economy, even though the AS curve is still vertical, nominal variables such as π^* can have real effects on the economy because of their influence on an important relative price, the terms of trade.

Next, the experiment shifts to flexible exchange rates. The expansionary monetary policy in the rest of the world still increases π^* and i^*, but the transmission of these events to the home country differs from that shown above. In this case the AD curve does not shift at all. Since it is understood that the unchanged μ_s determines π and forces the exchange rate to absorb the difference between π^* and π, ρ^e falls by the same amount as i^* increases, canceling each other in the vertical intercept of the AD curve in Figure 9-4. For that reason there is only one AD curve in Figure 9-6 for both the initial situation and the one depicting the expansionary policy in the rest of the world. In the absence of a shift in the AS curve, the home economy's inflation rate and output are unaffected by this change. Instead, the exchange rate falls over time to keep t con-

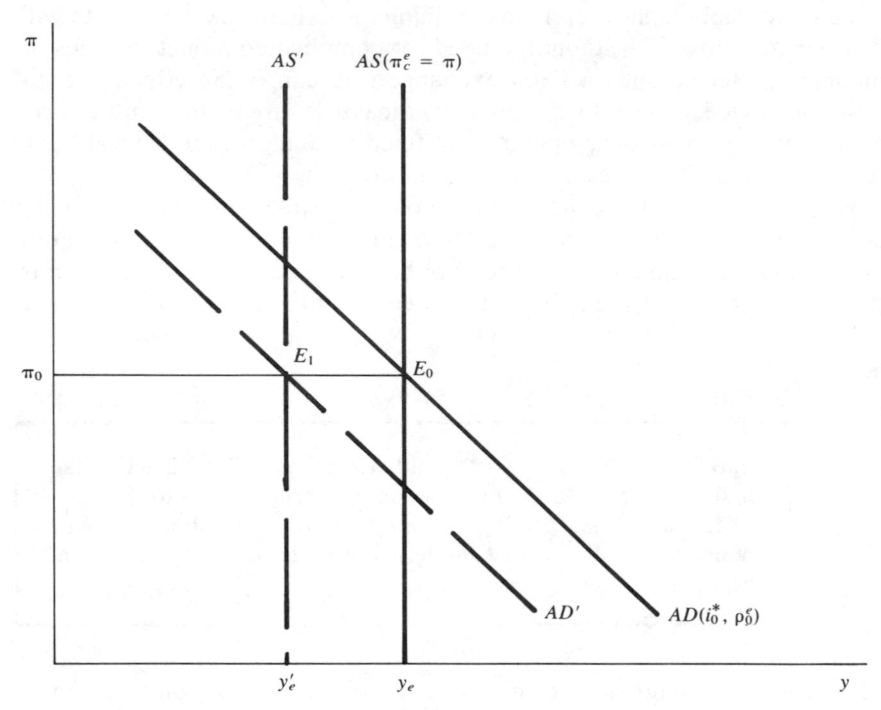

Figure 9-6 The effect of an increase in π^* under flexible exchange rates.

stant while $\pi < \pi^*$. In fact, we have $\rho = \pi - \pi^*$. Both the real and nominal interest rates remain unchanged; the increase in i^* is offset by the reduction in ρ^e, and therefore both i and π^e are constant.

Again, it is possible that the terms of trade did not remain constant throughout the adjustment period and y_e could be permanently altered. If, for instance, $\pi - \pi^* - \rho < 0$ for some time, t will be lower at the end and the AS curve will shift to the left as shown by AS' in Figure 9-6. At E_1, π_0 still prevails because the AD curve has to shift down to AD' as $(m - p)_{-1}$ falls when $\pi > s\mu_s$.

Although the domestic inflation rate is insulated from external events, we should again avoid drawing the conclusion that flexible exchange rates are superior to fixed rates because they allow us to maintain an independent monetary policy and inflation rate; in cases where there are strong political influences on monetary policy, this kind of independence may be illusory. In general, we do not want to draw any inferences about exchange-rate regimes from analysis of long-run equilibrium since no real policy issues arise in this context; income and output remain at the equilibrium level, all expectations are fulfilled, the terms of trade remain constant, and the rate of inflation has no welfare consequences in either case. A judgment about the best exchange-rate regime should be reserved until we deal with short-run policy problems, where the labor market is out of equilibrium, expectations are frustrated, the terms of trade are adjusting, and the inflation rate is rising or falling. Even here the choice is not between fixed and flexible exchange rates because an absolutely fixed rate could not be enforced in a world of divergent tolerances for inflation. Instead, the choice is between "clean" floating rates, in which case the central bank considers the exchange rate to be an irrelevant nominal variable, and "dirty" floating rates or "managed" rates, where the central bank manipulates the exchange rate to obtain desirable macroeconomic results. Which of these systems is better we will not try to decide until Chapter 10.

9.5.1 EMPIRICAL EVIDENCE ON LONG-RUN DETERMINATION OF EXCHANGE RATES

One of the predictions of the open-economy model is that over long periods, countries that choose to have high rates of inflation should have depreciating currencies in order to maintain their terms of trade; at the other end of the scale, countries with low rates of inflation should have appreciating currencies. By contrast, in a world of fixed exchange rates, inflation rates should be roughly the same in all countries. Since the early 1970s we have experienced much greater flexibility in exchange rates than was the case in the period 1945–70, when the Bretton Woods system was characterized by pegged exchange rates that were altered infrequently, usually in response to massive balance-of-payments deficits. Table 9-2 presents data for the 1970s for 10 countries of the Organization for Economic Cooperation and Development (OECD). The first column, indicating the average annual inflation rate for the decade, is repeated from Table 2-1. As we can see, there is a great variety of inflationary experience among these countries: Germany's inflation rate averaged 5%, while Italy's was over 15%, roughly three times as large. In the second column, the average rate of change of the exchange rate is listed for each of these countries. Since we are now dealing with a world of many countries, it would be misleading to look at the exchange rate as the price of *one* foreign currency in terms of the domestic currency, since each country trades with all other countries to some extent. Therefore, the International Monetary Fund has put together data on the *effective exchange rate,* which represents the price of a bundle of 17 foreign currencies, the weight of each currency in the bundle dictated by the importance of trade flows between the country and the home economy. The resulting index with a

Table 9-2. *Average annual inflation rates and rates of change of exchange rates: various countries, 1971–80 (%)*

Country	Inflation rate	Rate of change of effective exchange rate
Belgium	7.2	−1.9
Canada	9.3	2.3
France	9.8	0.0
Germany	4.9	−4.4
Italy	15.6	7.0
Japan	7.4	−4.2
Netherlands	8.1	−3.3
Switzerland	4.7	−6.8
United Kingdom	14.4	2.5
United States	7.1	2.1

Note: The effective exchange rate is an index (1975 = 100) of a weighted average of the price of a bundle of 17 currencies in terms of the home currency with the weights determined by trade flows. The index rises with reductions in this price, so the rate of change has the sign reversed to maintain symmetry with the definition of exchange rates used here.
Sources: Inflation rate, see Table 2-1; effective exchange rates, International Monetary Fund, *International Financial Statistics,* individual country pages, line amx.

base of 1975 = 100 rises when the price of this bundle falls. To keep the concept of the exchange rate the same as in our previous discussion, the rate of change reported in Table 9-2 has a minus sign for cases when the index rose from the beginning of the period to the end and a plus sign when it fell. For that reason, an appreciating currency shows a *reduction* in the effective exchange rate in Table 9-2. From the previous analysis we would expect that the countries with low inflation would have falling exchange rates, and, indeed, Germany and Switzerland had the highest rates of appreciation, except for Japan. Also, Italy, with the highest inflation, had the highest rate of depreciation at 7% per annum. But there are some anomalies: The United Kingdom and Italy had roughly similar experiences with their inflation rates, but the United Kingdom's effective exchange rate rose only about one-third of Italy's rate. Part of the explanation for this is that North Sea oil made the United Kingdom more attractive to investors, thus driving down the exchange rate. Another inconsistency relates to the United States. Its inflation rate was one of the lowest, yet its effective exchange rate rose, while that of Japan fell, even though its inflation rate was marginally higher. Here, at least part of the explanation relates to timing: In 1981 the U.S. dollar started to appreciate relative to most other currencies. Despite the need for additional explanations in some cases, the general proposition that high inflation rates and depreciating currencies go together in the long run seems to be borne out by the evidence for the decade of the 1970s.

9.6 SUMMARY

An open economy has markets not only for goods, assets, and factors, but also for foreign exchange through which all international transactions must pass. This requires that a model of the open economy explain not only output, inflation, and the interest rate, but also the exchange rate or the balance of payments, depending on the exchange-rate regime in existence.

In the open-economy version of the *IS–LM–AS* model, additional demand for home goods is incorporated into the *IS* curve, balance-of-payments effects on the money supply are included in the *LM* curve, and the difference between the worker's and the firm's real wage is featured in the *AS* curve. The open-economy macro model uses the *IS* and *AS* curves to determine inflation and output with fixed exchange rates and uses the *LM* curve and *AS* curve for flexible exchange rates. Other variables are determined after that.

The long-run characteristics of the open economy are very similar to those of a closed economy. The exchange-rate regime does make some difference: With fixed exchange rates it is not possible to have an independent monetary policy or inflation rate, but with flexible rates this can be achieved. Also, because of the role played by the terms of trade in the labor market, it is possible for changes in nominal variables to influence equilibrium output and employment.

Since the 1970s, countries have had widely different inflationary experiences. Countries with high rates of inflation have had depreciating currencies, while countries with low inflation have seen their currencies appreciate.

EXERCISES

1. Calculate Spearman's rank correlation coefficient for the data in Table 9-2. Is this coefficient significant at the 99% level?
2. Assume that $t_{-1} = 0$, $\pi = .12$, $\pi^* = .10$, $\rho = .03$, and $h = .7$.
   (a) What happens to t after one year? After five years?
   (b) Calculate π_c.
   (c) Why can this situation not last? What will happen to π and ρ in the long run under fixed and flexible exchange rates?

3. Consider the following open-economy version of the macro model:

$$y = 4 - 33.4(i - \pi^e) - .5t$$

$$(m - p) = .75y - .25i$$

$$y = y_{e-1} - 7(\pi_c^e - \pi)$$

$$i = i^* + \rho^e$$

plus all the other information provided in exercise 2, except information on π.

(a) Derive the *AD* equation [π = constant + (slope)y] for fixed exchange rates, given the additional information that $i^* = .15$ and $\pi^e = .12$.

(b) Derive the short-run *AS* curve for fixed exchange rates if $\pi^{*e} = .10$, and $y_{e-1} = 2.33$.

(c) Solve for y and π.

(d) Assume that a long-run equilibrium is established in the next period. Calculate y, π, and i.

4. (a) Derive the *AD* equation for flexible exchange rates if $\mu = .12$, $(m - p)_{-1} = 1.71$, $\rho^e = 0$.

(b) Using the same *AS* curve as for exercise 3(b), calculate y, π, and ρ.

(c) If $\mu = .12$, what are the long-run values of π, π_c, π_c^e, and ρ?

FURTHER READING

Dornbusch, R., S. Fischer, and G. Sparks, *Macroeconomics; Second Canadian Edition,* Toronto, McGraw-Hill Ryerson, 1985. Chapters 5, 6, and 18 deal with macroeconomics in a Canadian setting, treating both fixed and flexible exchange rates.

Turnovsky, S. J., *Macroeconomic Analysis and Stabilization Policy,* Cambridge, Cambridge University Press, 1977. Chapters 9–12 develop models of the open economy at a more advanced level.

CHAPTER 10

Managed exchange rates and monetary policy

10.1 INTRODUCTION

The purpose of this chapter is to extend the open-economy version of the *IS–LM–AS* model beyond its long-run characteristics to situations in which shocks occur, expectations are frustrated, and unemployment exists and to find the appropriate monetary mechanism in this environment. The transition here is very similar to the one between Chapter 2, which presented the structure of the model, and Chapters 3 and 4, which put that model into a policy context, and then Chapter 7, which investigated the optimal monetary mechanism for closed economics. To make that same transition for open economies, stochastic variables must be introduced, the choice of monetary policy instruments must be specified, and then the optimal monetary mechanism can be chosen. The choice will again depend on the types of shocks to which the economy is subjected, and therefore there is no universally optimal mechanism; it all depends on the circumstances. For that reason, most countries have chosen to operate with managed exchange rates instead of either fixed rates or flexible rates. At some times the monetary authorities allow the exchange rate to adjust to market forces, and at other times they resist market pressures strenuously. To understand this system of *managed exchange rates* we need to analyze the various shocks to which the economy is susceptible and their effect on the economy under alternative monetary mechanisms.

10.2 DOMESTIC AND FOREIGN SHOCKS

The first step is to reintroduce stochastic elements into the *IS–LM–AS* model, which now becomes

(10.1) $y = a_0 - a_1(i - \pi^e) - a_5 t + x_g$

(10.2) $\mu - \pi + x_m = a_2 y - a_3 i - (m - p)_{-1}$

(10.3) $y = y_{e_{-1}} - a_4[h\pi^e + (1 - h)(\pi^{*e} + \rho^e) - \pi - x_s] + x_s$

(10.4) $i = i^* + \rho^e + x_{i^*}$

(10.5) $t = \pi - \pi^* - x_{\pi^*} - \rho + t_{-1}$

Equation (10.1) is the *IS* curve, (10.2) is the *LM* curve, (10.3) is the *AS* curve, (10.4) is the interest parity condition, and (10.5) is a definitional equation for the terms of trade. All previously introduced variables have the same meaning as in Chapter 9. Here x_g, x_m, and x_s are domestic shocks to the goods market, money market, and labor market, respectively, as defined in Chapter 3. Their expected value is zero, but they may take on positive or negative values and therefore represent unexpected events to which the economy must react. In addition, x_{π^*} and x_{i^*} are foreign shocks that are transmitted to the home economy. A positive value for x_{π^*} should be thought of as an unanticipated increase in the foreign rate of inflation. It causes the *IS* curve to start shifting to the right as the terms of trade now fall and make home goods more attractive compared to foreign goods. The other foreign source of shocks is x_{i^*}, an unpredicted increase or decrease in the foreign interest rate, which now affects the interest parity condition.

There is a major difference between the domestic shocks, x_g, x_m, and x_s, and the foreign shocks, x_{π^*} and x_{i^*}. The former relate to specific markets and create excess demand or supply in those markets, but the latter group operate directly on foreign variables, which are themselves determined within a macroeconomic model of the rest of the world. For that reason we are not at liberty to conduct mental experiments in which x_{π^*} and x_{i^*} are changed independently of each other. The rest of the world is subject to random shocks, just as the closed economy was in Chapters 3 and 4. These shocks produce certain effects on the inflation rate and on the interest rate that are then transmitted to the home economy. But they do not come in isolation; they come in certain combinations. For example, an unexpected increase in government expenditures in the foreign country increases income, the inflation rate, and the interest rate. Therefore, for this experiment, both x_{π^*} and x_{i^*} must be positive. Alternatively, an unexpected increase in the growth rate of the money supply in the rest of the world increases income and the inflation rate but lowers the interest rate. Here, x_{π^*} is positive and x_{i^*} is negative. In short, foreign shocks come in pairs, and the appropriate combination can only be specified if the underlying event is identified.

Initially, foreign shocks are represented by nonzero values for x_{π^*} and

x_{i^*}. If the foreign event is a one-time shock to a particular market, π^* and i^* would remain unaffected and the foreign shock should then be treated as temporary; but if the event is permanent, it should be translated into changes in π^* and i^*. Again, to make this distinction it is important to indicate the precise nature of the experiment to be performed.

10.3 THE CHOICE OF POLICY INSTRUMENTS

In a closed economy, the central bank has the choice of controlling the money supply (subject to all the provisos discussed in Chapter 6) or the nominal interest rate. According to the analysis in Chapter 7, once that choice is made, it dictates a certain monetary mechanism that requires the central bank to respond automatically to any deviation of the control variable from its chosen value or path. There can only be one control variable or policy instrument: either the money supply or the interest rate, not both. If the monetary authorities are convinced that shocks are mainly of a monetary nature, interest-rate control has been found to be optimal; if, on the other hand, the shocks are likely to be in the goods market, controlling the money supply is the best strategy; if both types of shocks exist, the optimal mechanism involves a weighted average of money-supply and interest-rate control with the weights determined by the size of the variance of the two r's

In an open economy, the choice is not quite that simple, since the interest parity (*IP*) condition must be satisfied at all times in view of the perfect capital mobility that prevails between the home country and the rest of the world. In equation (10.4), given i^*, assuming that $x_{i^*} = 0$, and since ρ^e cannot change in the wake of disturbance to the system, there can be only one value of i that is consistent with *IP*. It is therefore not possible for the central bank to choose between control over the money supply and control over interest rates; instead, the choice is between the money supply and the exchange rate. In other words, in an open economy with perfect capital mobility, the authorities can allow a shock to be absorbed by exchange-rate adjustments while maintaining the existing growth rate of the money supply, or the balance of payments becomes the shock absorber with automatic effects on the money supply while the exchange rate is held to some predetermined value.

These choices and the direction in which variables are required to move when shocks occur can be analyzed in terms of Figure 10-1, which depicts the *IP* condition of equation (10.4). The *IP* line is horizontal in an *IS–LM* diagram. There is only one domestic interest rate that is consistent with equality of expected yields between domestic and foreign bonds regardless of the value of y. If the domestic interest rate happened to be

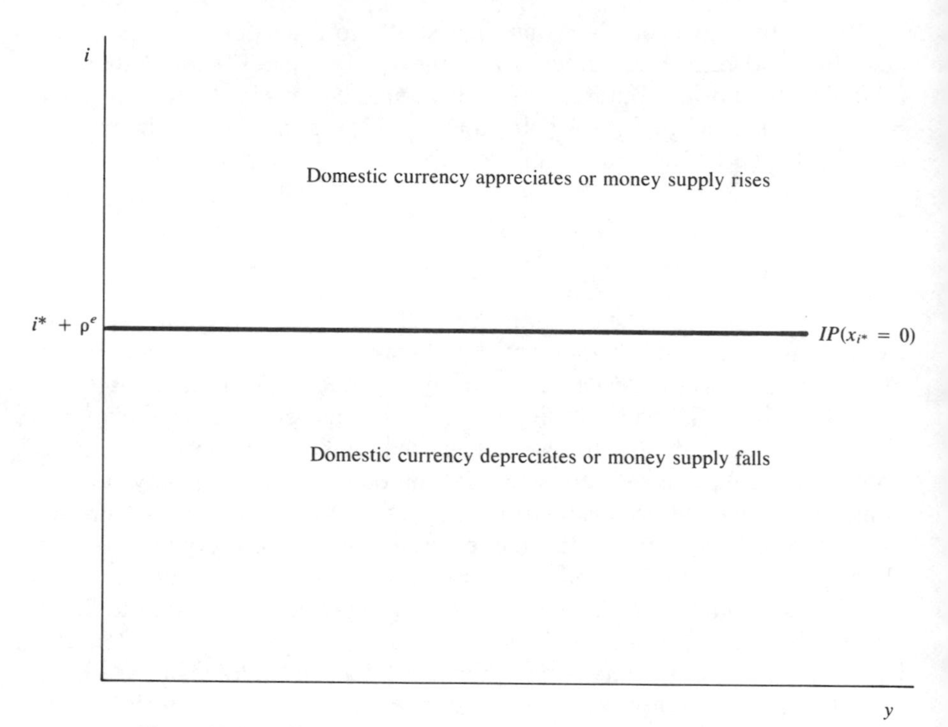

Figure 10-1 Effects of interest deviations from the *IP* condition.

above the *IP* line, then domestic bonds would become more attractive than foreign bonds, causing a capital inflow into the home country. If the exchange rate is allowed to be determined by market forces, it will fall or the domestic currency will appreciate, as there is excess supply of the foreign currency at the existing exchange rate. Alternatively, if the central bank holds the exchange rate constant or on its previous path, there will be a balance-of-payments surplus that forces the central bank to buy foreign assets in exchange for domestic assets, and in the process the monetary base and the money supply expand. In either case, the capital inflow creates excess demand for domestic bonds and forces their price upward or the interest rate downward until it reaches the *IP* line once more. Because of perfect capital mobility, the deviations of the domestic interest rate from the *IP* line are so short-lived that they are not actually observed, and any short-run equilibrium after a shock must be on the *IP* line. If the domestic interest rate is temporarily below the *IP* lines, there will be a capital outflow and either a depreciation of the domestic currency or a reduction in the money supply. The *IP* line itself can shift if x_{i^*} takes on a nonzero value or if i^* or ρ^e change for some reason.

Once the interest rate is determined by *IP*, the equilibrium level of output is derived from the intersection of *IP* with either the *LM* curve or the *IS* curve, depending on which monetary mechanism the central bank uses. If the monetary authorities maintain control over the growth rate of the money supply, then money-market equilibrium contained in the *LM* curve is relevant and it alone determines income; if they control the exchange rate, then the supply of money becomes demand-determined, the *LM* curve loses its importance, but the *IS* curve maintains goods-market equilibrium and determines income. This dichotomy between the roles played by the *IS* and *LM* curves is similar to the one in Chapter 9, where the *LM* curve became the aggregate-demand curve with flexible exchange rates while the *IS* curve was the *AD* curve when the exchange rate was fixed. In the short-run version of the model, the *IP–LM* curves are translated into the *AD* curve when the central bank controls the money supply and the *IP–IS* curves generate the *AD* curve when the exchange rate is controlled. The *IS* curve in the first instance then determines the path of the exchange rate, and the *LM* curve in the second instance allows us to calculate the endogenous growth rate of the money supply. In either case, the *AS* curve together with the *AD* curve solves for income and the inflation rate.

The question that we now want to investigate is which of the two monetary mechanisms is better in various circumstances. The aim of the investigation is the same as in Chapter 7. When the economy is subjected to random shocks, we want to choose the monetary mechanism that keeps y closest to y_e. Although in an open economy there are now many values of y_e that are consistent with equilibrium in the labor market because of the effect that the terms of trade have on the supply of labor and equilibrium output, it is still true that after a shock any deviation from the preexisting y_e signifies disequilibrium in the labor market, since the real wage from the workers' perspective will be altered after the optimal work–leisure choice has already been made. In that sense, the smaller the disequilibrium, the less involuntary unemployment or overtime work there is.

The initial *IS*, *LM*, and *IP* curves are drawn in Figure 10-2. In all three curves the x's are assumed to be zero to indicate a long-run equilibrium position for the economy. The curves intersect at E_0; there is only one combination of i and y that satisfies all the long-run equilibrium conditions discussed in Chapter 9. Here there is no distinction between controlling the money supply or controlling the exchange rate. In the long run, only one combination of μ and ρ is possible: $\mu = \pi$ and $\rho = \pi - \pi^*$. Once this starting position of the economy has been specified, four random events can be postulated: (1) a domestic monetary shock, (2) a domestic goods-market shock, (3) a foreign monetary shock, and (4) a supply shock.

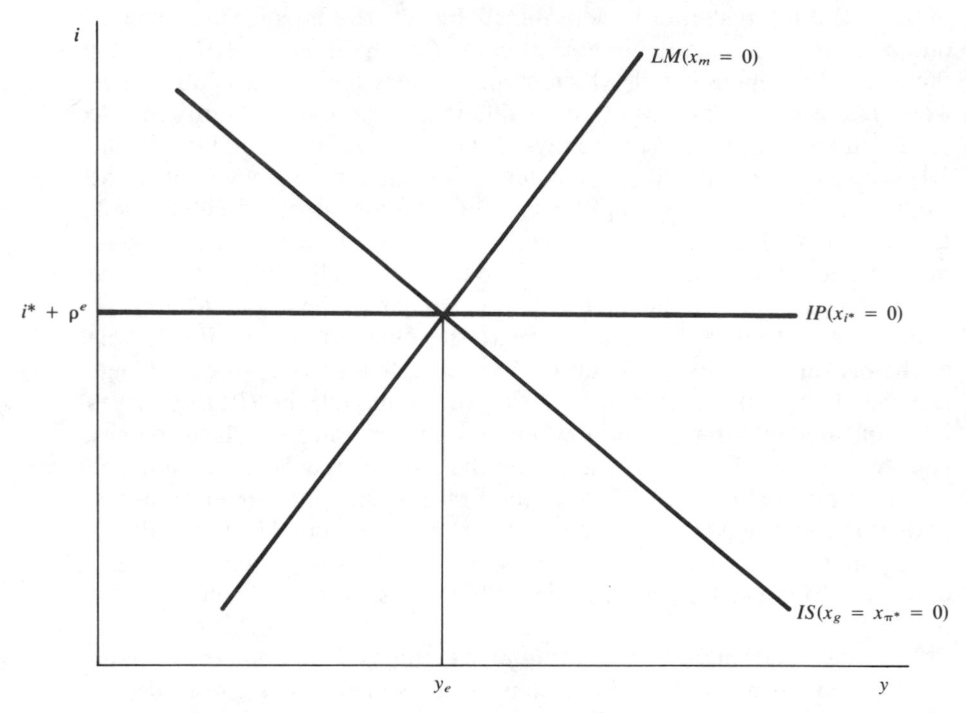

Figure 10-2 Initial long-run equilibrium of an open economy.

10.4 RANDOM SHOCKS AND THEIR EFFECTS

The previously listed stochastic events can now be imposed on this long-run equilibrium and the effect on output or employment compared for the two monetary mechanisms. The mechanism that leads to the smallest deviation of output from its equilibrium level is the best under these circumstances.

To make this decision we need to calculate $y_1 - y_0$ for $\mu_1 = \mu_0$ (i.e., money-supply control) and for $\rho_1 = \rho_0$ (i.e., exchange-rate control), where the subscript 0 refers to the value of the variable in the initial long-run equilibrium and the subscript 1 signifies the value of the variable at a new temporary equilibrium after the various x's take on positive or negative values. First, let us deal with money-supply control. Taking first differences of equation (10.2), but holding constant all variables that cannot change and setting $\mu_1 = \mu_0$, we obtain

$$(10.6) \quad y_1 - y_0 = [1/a_2][a_3(i_1 - i_0) - (\pi_1 - \pi_0) + x_m]$$

The last two terms provide us with the sources of a horizontal shift of the *LM* curve. Next, the horizontal shift of the *AD* curve is obtained by substituting $i_1 - i_0 = x_{i^*}$ from (10.4) into (10.6), namely

$$(10.7)\quad y_1 - y_0 = [1/a_2][a_3 x_{i^*} - (\pi_1 - \pi_0) + x_m]$$

Finally, the vertical shift of the *AS* curve is given by

$$(10.8)\quad \pi_1 - \pi_0 = [1/a_4][(y_1 - y_0) - (1 + a_4)x_s]$$

Substituting the *AS* curve into the *AD* curve gives the final effect of any shock on output. This is

$$(10.9)\quad y_1 - y_0 = \{a_4/(1 + a_2 a_4)\}\{x_m + a_3 x_{i^*} + [(1 + a_4)/a_4]x_s\}$$

which relates changes in y to the x's via the parameters of the system.

Now let us derive the same expression for exchange-rate control. The first difference of the *IS* curve is

$$(10.10)\quad y_1 - y_0 = -a_1(i_1 - i_0) - a_5(t_1 - t_0) + x_g$$

which gives $(t_1 - t_0)$ and x_g as the sources of the horizontal shift of that curve. Then, from equation (10.5),

$$(10.11)\quad t_1 - t_0 = \pi_1 - \pi_0 - x_{\pi^*}$$

where $\pi_1^* = \pi_0^*$, $\rho_1 = \rho_0$, and $t_0 = t_{-1}$. Substituting (10.11) into (10.10) shows the horizontal shift of the *AD* curve as

$$(10.12)\quad y_1 - y_0 = -a_1 x_{i^*} - a_5(\pi_1 - \pi_0 - x_{\pi^*}) + x_g$$

Together with the shift of the *AS* curve from (10.8), the overall effect of any shock on output is

$$(10.13)\quad y_1 - y_0 = \{a_4/(a_4 + a_5)\}\{x_g - a_1 x_{i^*} + a_5 x_{\pi^*} + [a_5(1 + a_4)/a_4]x_s\}$$

With these equations and the accompanying diagrams, we are now ready to consider each of the shocks in turn.

10.4.1 DOMESTIC MONETARY SHOCK

Consider first a monetary shock in the home economy that causes x_m to be positive. This event cannot be incorporated into anticipations of the future, and therefore all expectational variables remain constant. Also, all foreign variables and the other x's are unaffected. Only the *LM* curve begins to shift to the right as the real money supply starts to grow. Regardless of the monetary mechanism in place, there is a capital outflow as there is a tendency for the domestic interest rate to fall below the *IP* line. The remainder of the adjustment process depends on the actions of the monetary authorities.

If the central bank does not alter μ, then ρ will rise above its previous level to absorb the incipient deficit in the balance of payments. From equation (10.6), the *LM* curve shifts to *LM'* by the amount x_m/a_2. This is shown in Figure 10-3. Equation (10.7) dictates that the *AD* curve should shift to the right by the same amount. With the positively sloped *AS* curve, we find that both π and y rise to π_1 and y_1. The higher inflation in turn causes the real money supply to fall again, and the *LM* curve shifts back to *LM"*, whose location is dictated by the need for y_1 to be the same in the *IS–LM* diagram as in the *AD–AS* diagram. The final outcome is that y rises by $[a_4/(1 + a_2a_4)]x_m$, as indicated by equation (10.9). The extra output is sold to foreigners because the depreciation of the domestic currency is not completely offset by the higher domestic inflation; also, t falls, making home goods more attractive in international markets. This outcome is not desirable; workers find that their expectations of the real wage were wrong; π^e, π^{*e}, and ρ^e remained at their previous levels, but both π and ρ rose, resulting in a reduction in the ex post real wage and involuntary extra work effort.

As an alternative, the central bank could maintain the existing value of ρ and let the resulting balance-of-payments deficit automatically reduce the value of μ. In Figure 10-4, this is shown as *LM* shifting to the right to *LM'* and immediately returning to its original position as short-run equilibrium is determined by the intersection of *IP* and *IS*, neither of which is affected by the monetary shock. The economy is only observed at E_0. In other words, exchange-rate control provides a complete and automatic stabilizer to money-market instability in the form of positive or negative x_m's. The reason for this fortunate result is that the x_m is offset by $\mu_1 - \mu_0$ of equal value, but opposite sign, so that the sum of the expected and unexpected growth rates of the money supply remains constant. The fact that equation (10.13) does not contain x_m is extra proof that monetary shocks do not influence the *IS* curve when ρ is controlled.

From this comparison, it is possible to offer a fairly strong conclusion: If the open economy has an unstable *LM* curve, the existing equilibrium can be preserved by holding to the predetermined path of ρ when monetary shocks arrive. Any tendency of ρ to move away from its previous value should be resisted by letting the balance of payments move into surplus or deficit and forcing the growth rate of the money supply to be the shock absorber. This recommendation holds whether the shocks are transitory or persistent as long as they are monetary in nature and domestic in origin. The only difference between this conclusion and the one that is relevant for closed economies with unstable *LM* curves is that here the central bank should control the exchange rate and not the interest rate. The interest rate cannot be a control variable in the face of the *IP* condition, but control over the exchange rate accomplishes the same task.

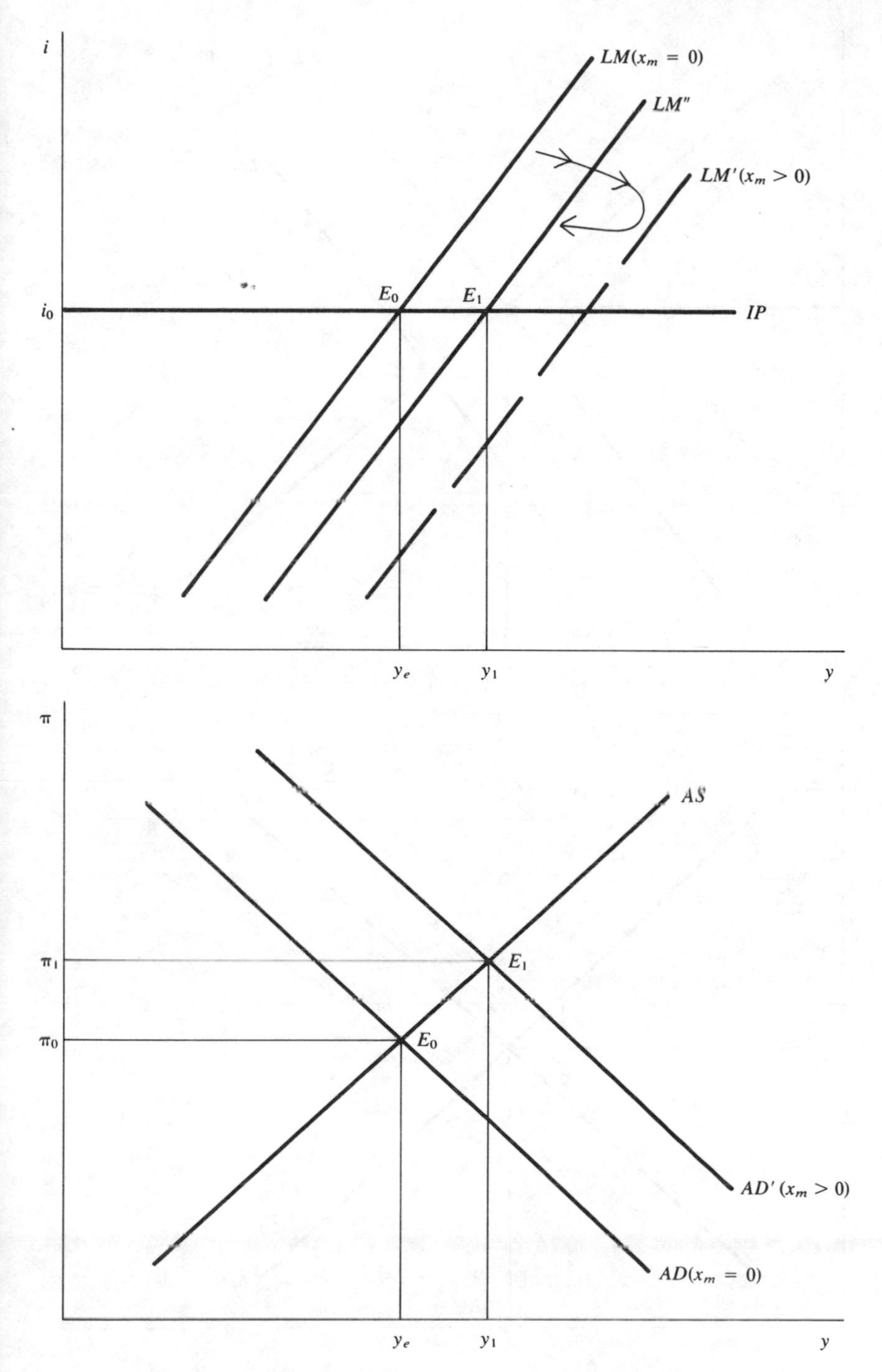

Figure 10-3 The effects of a domestic monetary shock when the central bank controls the money supply.

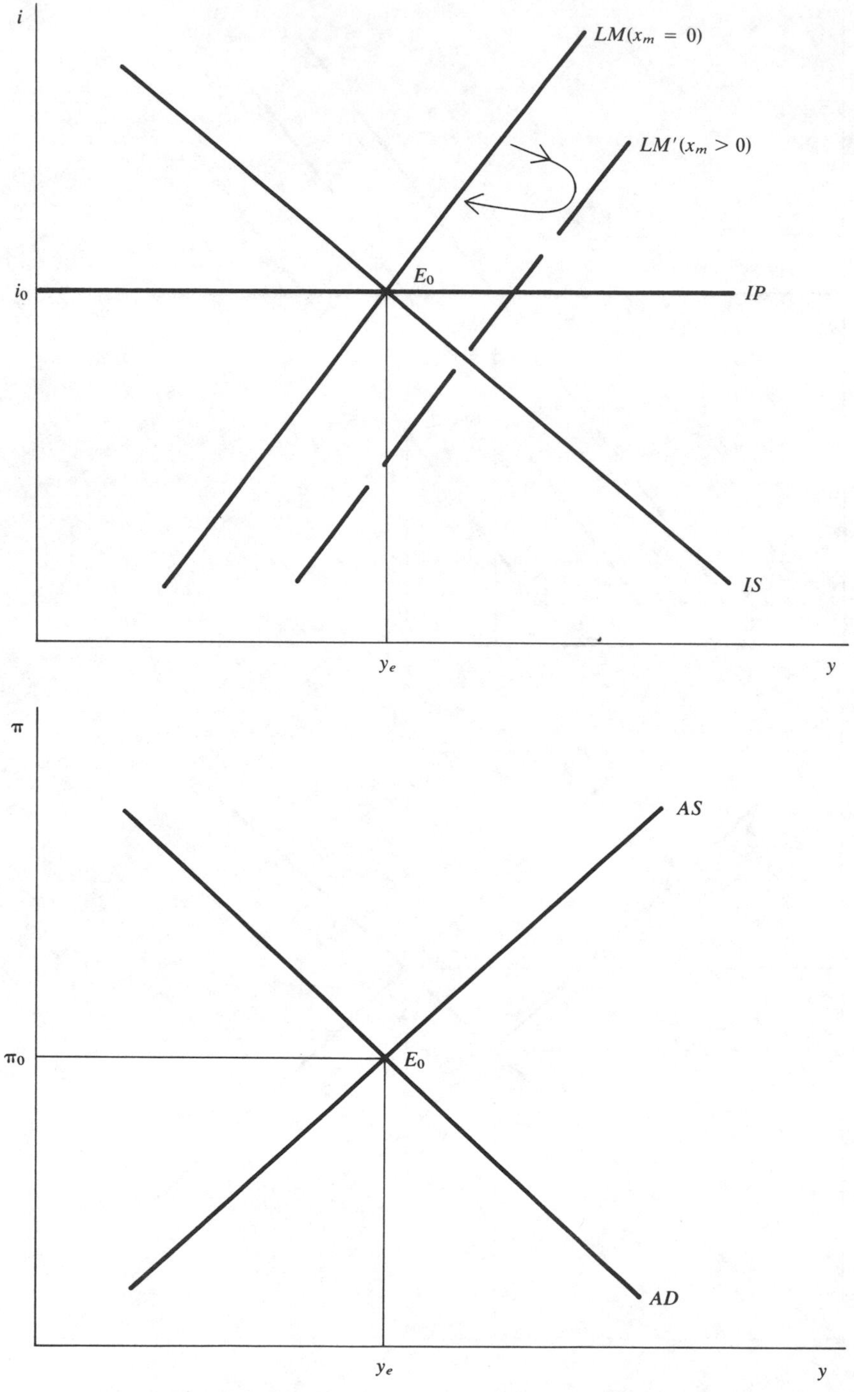

Figure 10-4 The effects of a domestic monetary shock when the central bank controls the exchange rate.

10.4.2 DOMESTIC GOODS-MARKET SHOCK

As a second experiment, suppose that x_g takes on a positive value as investment expenditures rise unexpectedly. This has a tendency to raise the domestic interest rate, which in turn causes a capital inflow. With money-supply control, this inflow is translated into an appreciation of the domestic currency or ρ falls. But this does not displace the *LM* curve, and equilibrium is maintained at E_0 in Figure 10-5. The *IS* curve initially shifts to the right to *IS'* because x_g is positive, but then reverses itself completely when ρ falls; the extra investment expenditures are offset by reduced sales to foreigners. Therefore, controlling the money supply insulates the economy from domestic goods-market shocks, as can be verified by the fact that x_g does not appear in equation (10.9).

For a country working with exchange-rate control, the result is quite different. In Figure 10-6 the *IS* curve still shifts to the right by the value of x_g. The *AD* curve also shifts to the right by this amount, and both π and y rise. Then the higher inflation causes the terms of trade to rise, and the *IS* curve shifts partially back again to *IS"*, whose location is again dictated by the change in y in the *AD–AS* part of the diagram. The end result is that y rises by $[a_4/(a_4 + a_5)]x_g$. In this case the extra investment expenditures are not completely displaced by a reduction in net foreign demand for home goods.

From this comparison of the two monetary mechanisms, it is easily seen that goods-market shocks are best accommodated by having a money-supply goal and sticking to it. This is exactly the same conclusion as for a closed economy. In fact, in an open economy this mechanism does better since it completely insulates the level of output because the interest rate does not have to adjust to absorb part of the shock; instead, the exchange rate shock absorber forces foreign demand to make room for the extra domestic demand.

After the analysis of these two shocks, the rationale for managed exchange rates begins to emerge. Since an open economy will be subjected to both money-market and goods-market shocks from time to time, it does not make sense for the monetary authorities to make an irrevocable and permanent commitment to fixed or to flexible exchange rates. From that perspective, managed exchange rates involve a compromise: Sometimes the authorities let the exchange rate yield to supply and demand conditions and maintain a target growth rate of the money supply, and at other times the exchange rate itself becomes a target and the money supply is demand-determined. If they choose the right mechanism at the right time they can overcome completely the effects of domestic money-market and goods-market shocks. But how do they know which of these mechanisms should be enforced at any one time since not even the central bank has advance

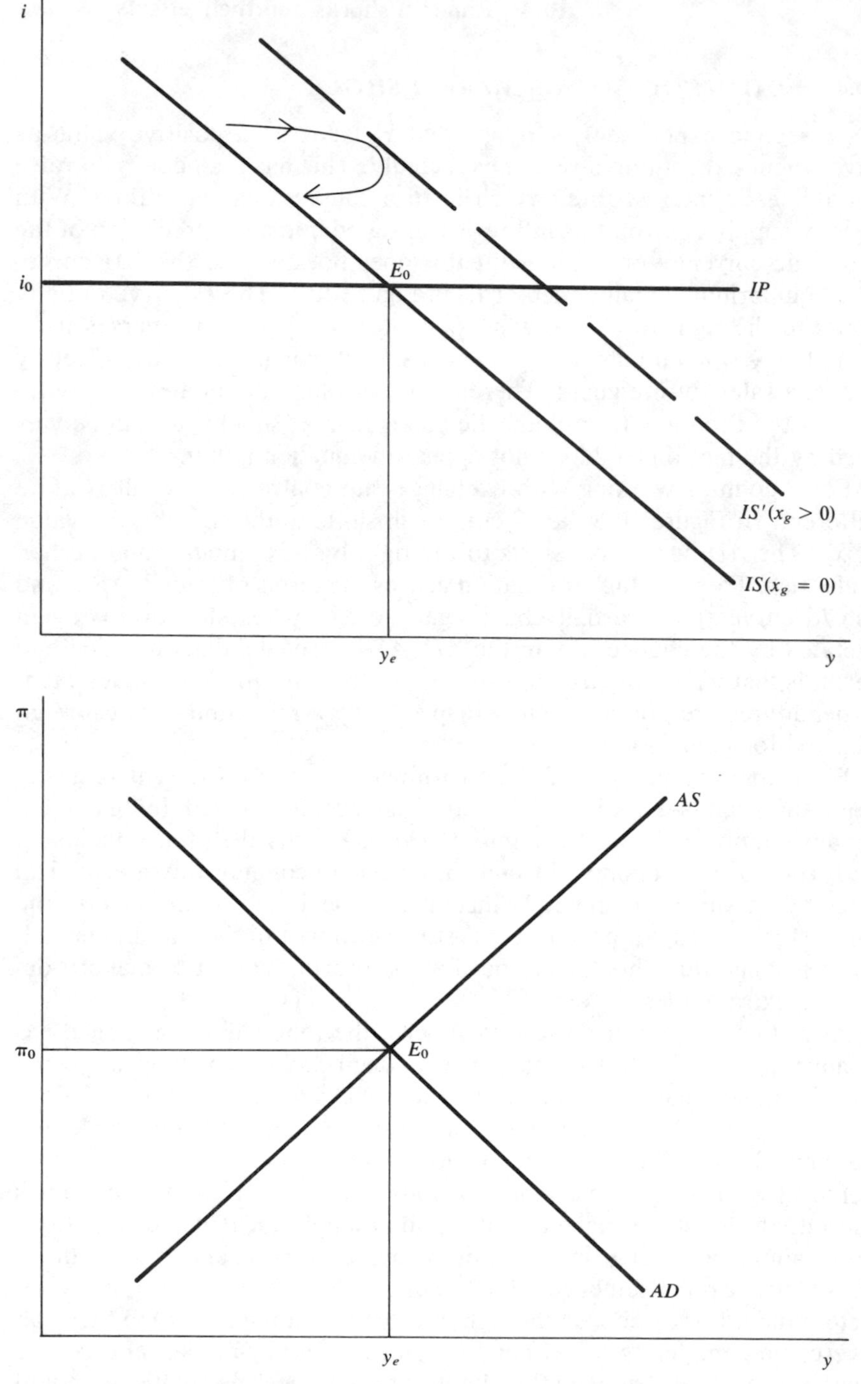

Figure 10-5 The effects of a domestic goods-market shock when the central bank controls the money supply.

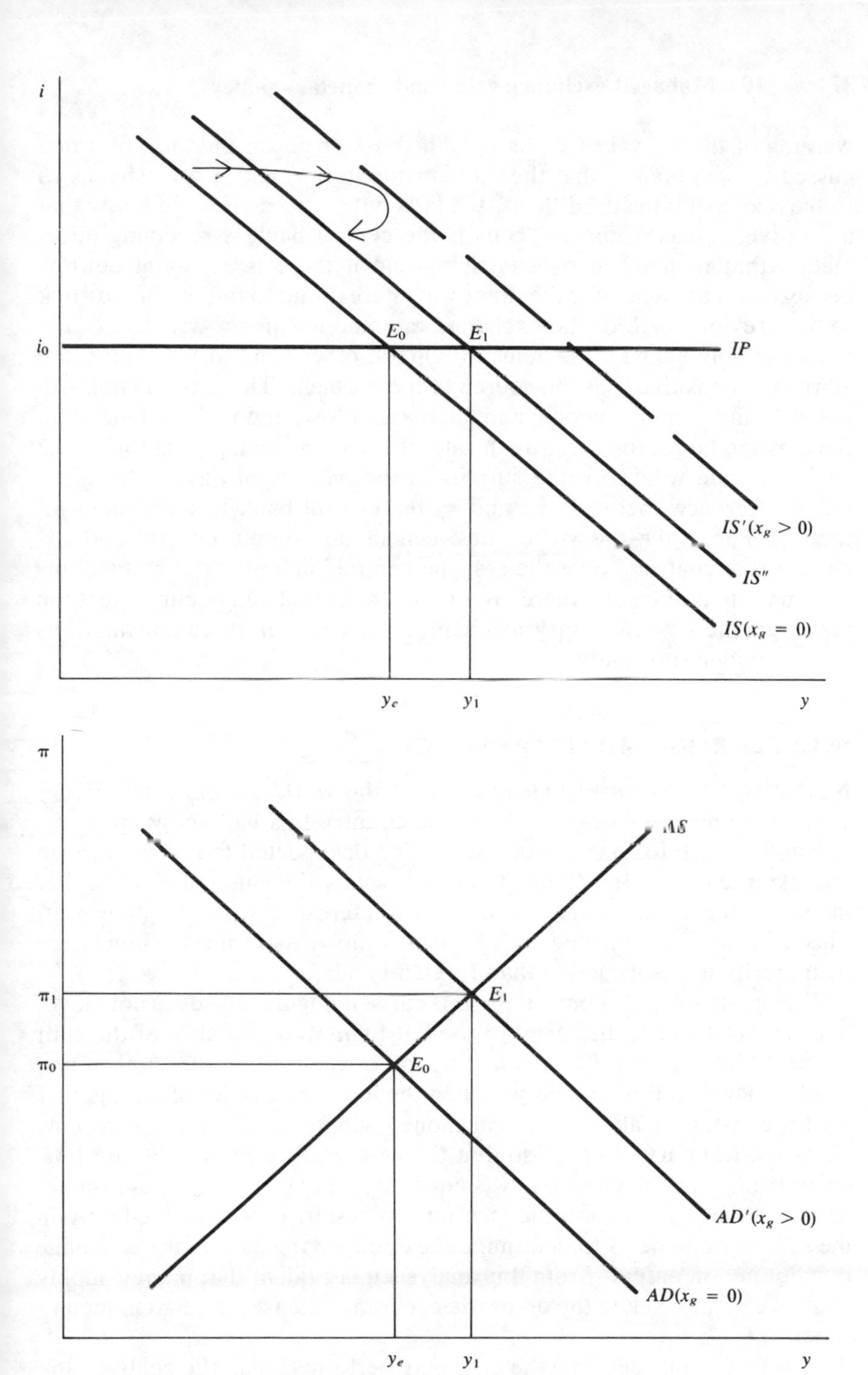

Figure 10-6 The effects of a domestic goods-market shock when the central bank controls the exchange rate.

warning of the arrival of x_m or x_g? The answer lies in the fact, first discussed in Section 3.2, that the movements in i, y, and π give signals as to the shocks that caused them. If i falls but y and π rise, we know that a positive x_m has occurred. Thus if the central bank is receiving information that nominal income is rising and if there is a capital outflow because of a tendency for the domestic interest rate to fall, it should stick to the previous path of the exchange rate and let the growth rate of the money supply adjust to its demand. On the other hand, if i, y, and π are all rising, a positive x_g is the source of the problem. The central bank will notice rising nominal income and a capital inflow, and it should maintain the existing target for the growth rate of the money supply, allowing the exchange rate to absorb the surplus in the balance of payments. From these differences between x_m and x_g the central bank has sufficient information to make the switch between money-supply control and exchange-rate control. Nevertheless, the central bank may not receive this information in time, and there are other shocks that can occur so that the choice of the best monetary mechanism becomes more complicated, as will be evident presently.

10.4.3 FOREIGN MONETARY SHOCK

Next it will be assumed that the rest of the world suffers a temporary positive monetary shock. In the home country this will show up as $x_{\pi^*} > 0$ and $x_{i^*} < 0$ for one period only.[1] The unexpected fall in the foreign interest rate causes the *IP* line to shift down by the value of x_{i^*} for either monetary mechanism, and the domestic interest rate must follow suit. This will be accomplished by a capital inflow, as domestic bonds are temporarily more attractive than foreign bonds.

With money-supply control, the *LM* curve in Figure 10-7 does not move, but the *AD* curve is displaced to the left by $a_3x_{i^*}/a_2$ because of the shift of the *IP* line. With *AD'* intersecting the original *AS* curve, both π and y fall to new levels at π_1 and y_1. Then the lower rate of inflation together with a constant μ allows the real money supply to expand, which now shifts the *LM* curve to *LM'* so that the new intersection of *IP'* and *LM'* occurs at i_1, y_1. The change in y is equal to $[a_3a_4/(1 + a_2a_4)]x_{i^*}$. It should be noted that x_{π^*} has no influence on this result. It is contained only in the *IS* curve and helps to determine the effect on the path of the exchange rate but not on output. From this analysis it is evident that money-supply control cannot insulate the domestic economy against a foreign monetary shock.

Now let us consider how the economy performs when the central bank controls the exchange rate. The *IS* curve shifts to the right by $a_5x_{\pi^*}$ to

[1] See Chapter 3 for the derivation of this result in a closed economy.

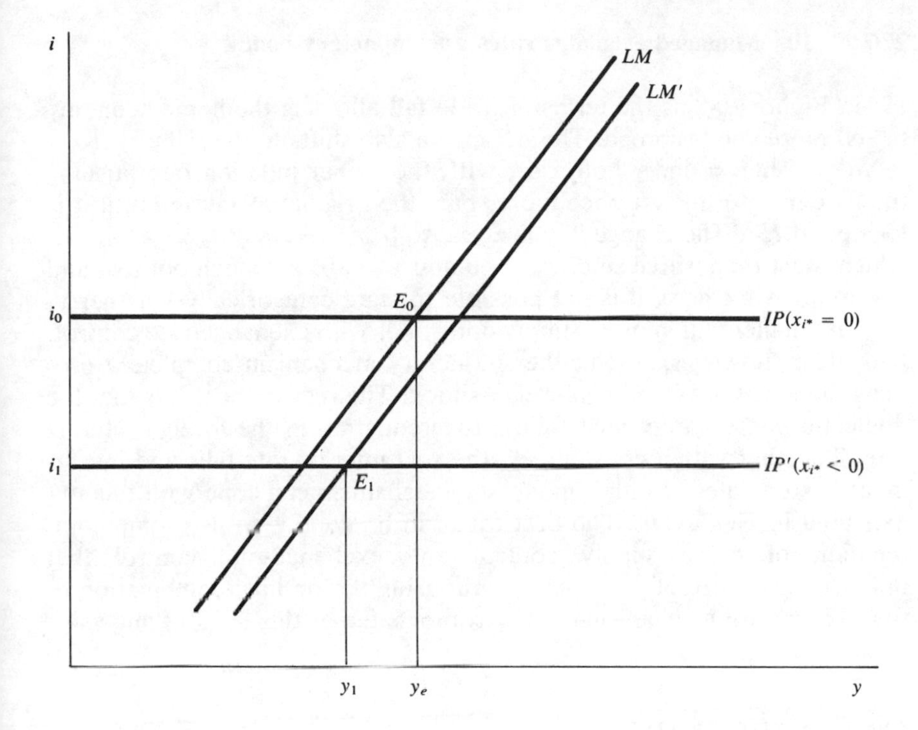

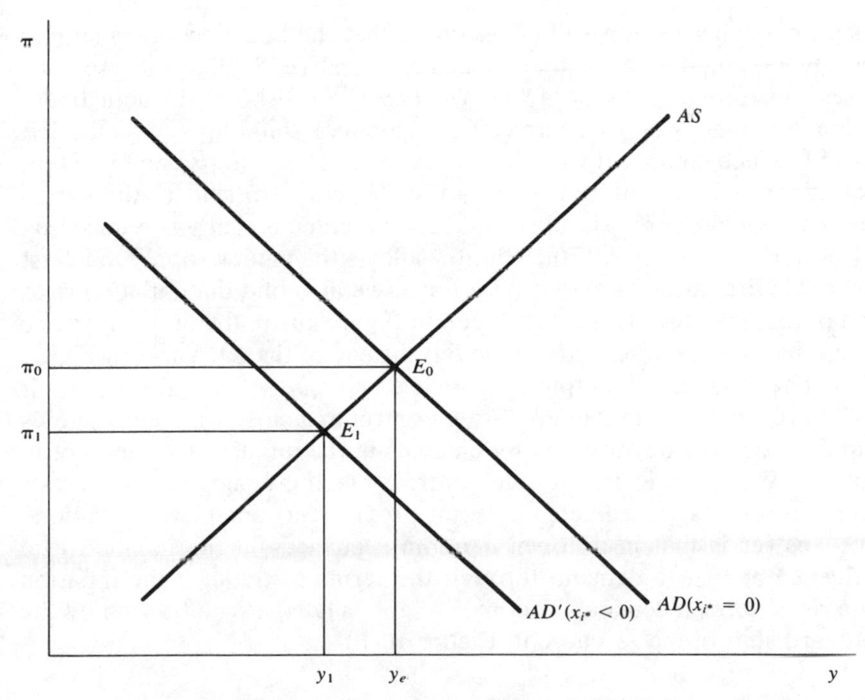

Figure 10-7 The effects of a foreign monetary shock when the central bank controls the money supply.

IS' in Figure 10-8 as the terms of trade fall allowing the home economy to sell more goods abroad. The *AD* curve also shifts to the right by $a_5 x_{\pi^*} - a_1 x_{i^*}$. Then π and y both rise, with the higher inflation rate pushing the *IS* curve to the left once more, past the original *IS* curve, until it is located at *IS"*. The change in y is equal to $[a_4/(a_4 + a_5)][a_5 x_{\pi^*} - a_1 x_{i^*}]$, which must be positive since $x_{\pi^*} > 0$ and $x_{i^*} < 0$. Although both x_{i^*} and x_{π^*} are at work here, it is not possible to state categorically whether $y_1 - y_0$ is smaller with money-supply control or with exchange-rate control. It is clear, however, that neither monetary mechanism completely protects the economy from this foreign shock. The reason for this is that the domestic interest rate must follow the reduction in the foreign interest rate. Together with a constant π^e, the real interest rate falls and investment is stimulated. Neither monetary mechanism can cope with this unexpected foreign event. The best that can be done is to use some combination of money-supply control and exchange-rate control that minimizes the size of $y_1 - y_0$, but choosing the optimal combination of the two control mechanisms is too complicated at this level of analysis.

10.4.4 A SUPPLY SHOCK

As a final experiment it will be assumed that the home economy suffers an adverse supply shock that makes x_s negative. Unlike the previous cases, this only affects the *AS* curve. Figure 10-9 shows the adjustment assuming money-supply control. The *AS* curve shifts up and to the left to *AS'*, which combined with the *AD* curve causes π to rise and y to fall. The increased inflation now causes the *LM* curve to shift to the left as the real money supply shrinks. The final outcome is that y is reduced by $[(1 + a_4)/(1 + a_2 a_4)]x_s$. If the country allows the money supply to adjust but holds firm to the previous path for ρ, we also find that inflation rises and output is reduced, as can be seen in Figure 10-10, the only difference being that the *IS* curve shifts to the left instead of the *LM* curve in Figure 10-9. The reduction in output in this case is $[(a_4 a_5 + a_5)/(a_4 + a_5)]x_s$. It will be remembered that interest-rate control in a closed economy allows supply shocks to be absorbed by changes in the inflation rate and not in output.[2] Why does exchange-rate control, which is analogous to interest-rate control in a closed economy, not provide this complete insulation? The answer is that in an open economy, changes in the inflation rate influence aggregate demand through the terms of trade; if the inflation rate rises, foreign demand for domestic goods falls, as can be seen by the leftward shift of the *IS* curve in Figure 10-10.

[2] See Chapter 8, especially the discussion for Figure 8-1.

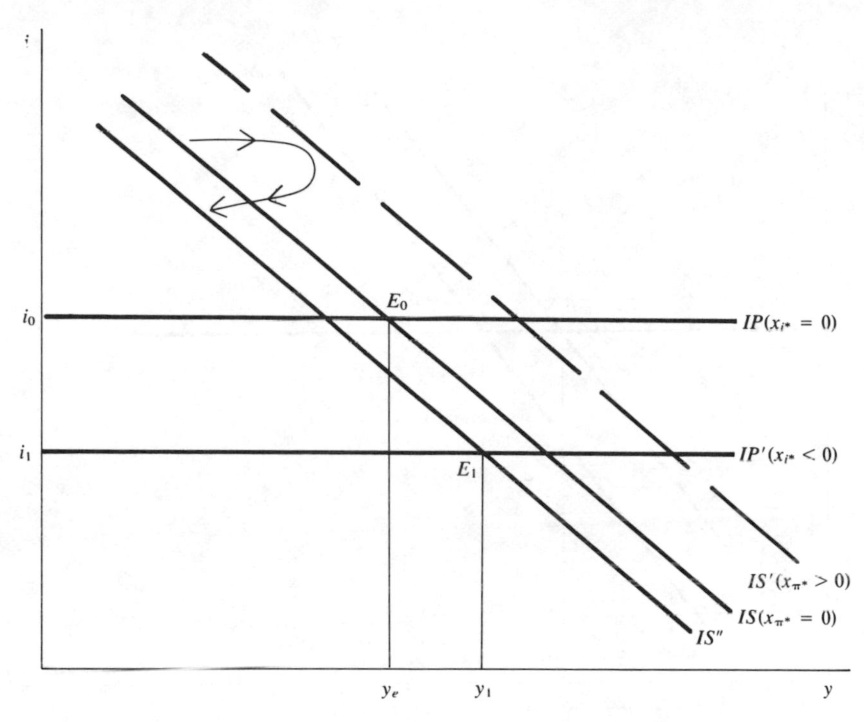

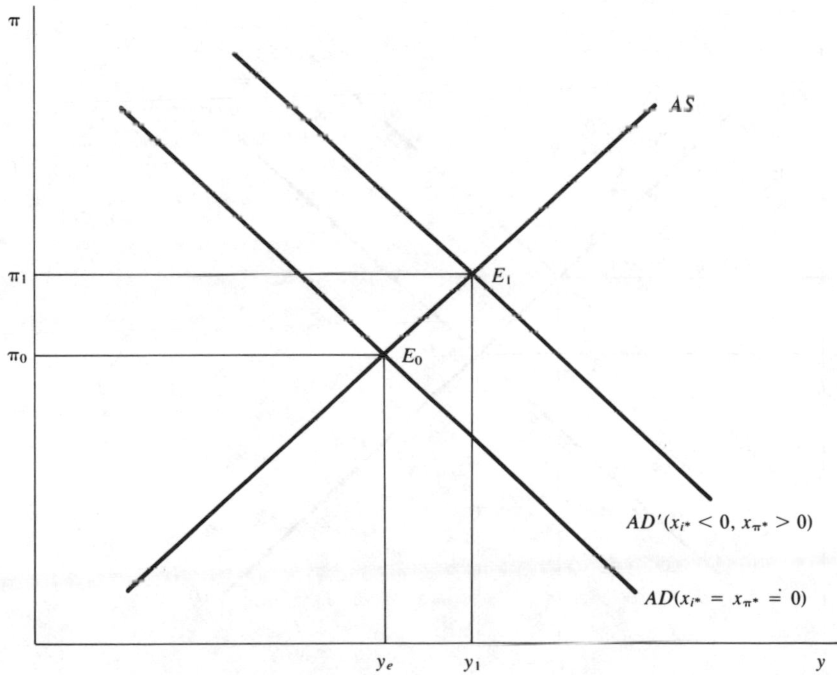

Figure 10-8 The effects of a foreign monetary shock when the central bank controls the exchange rate.

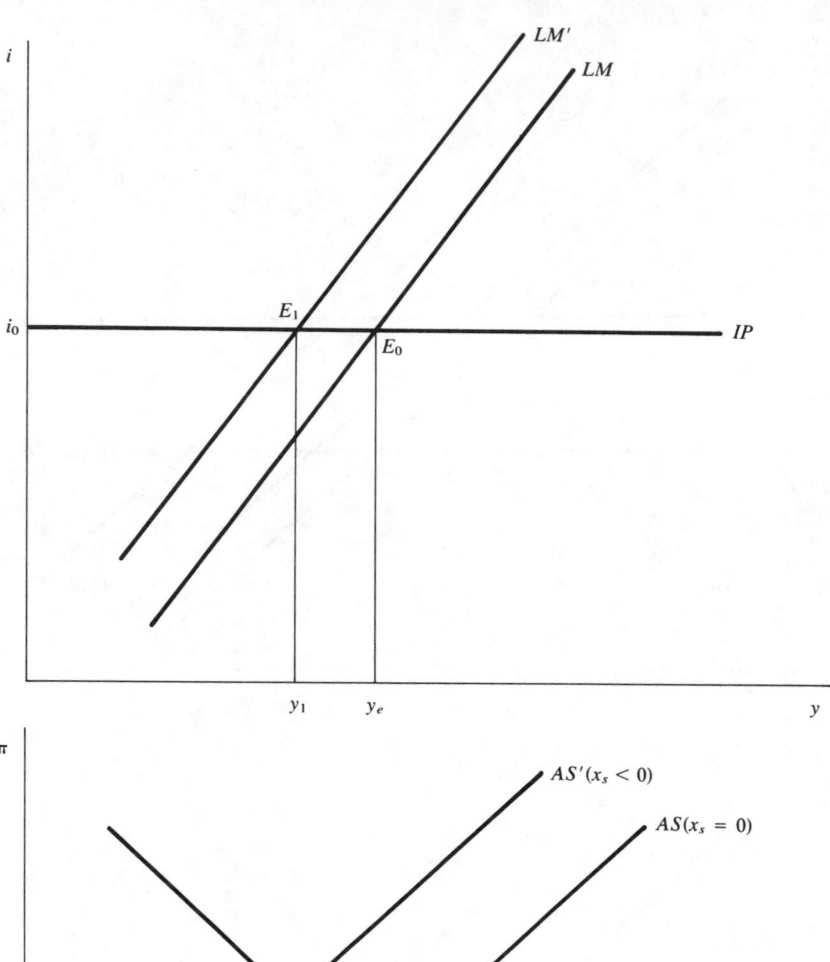

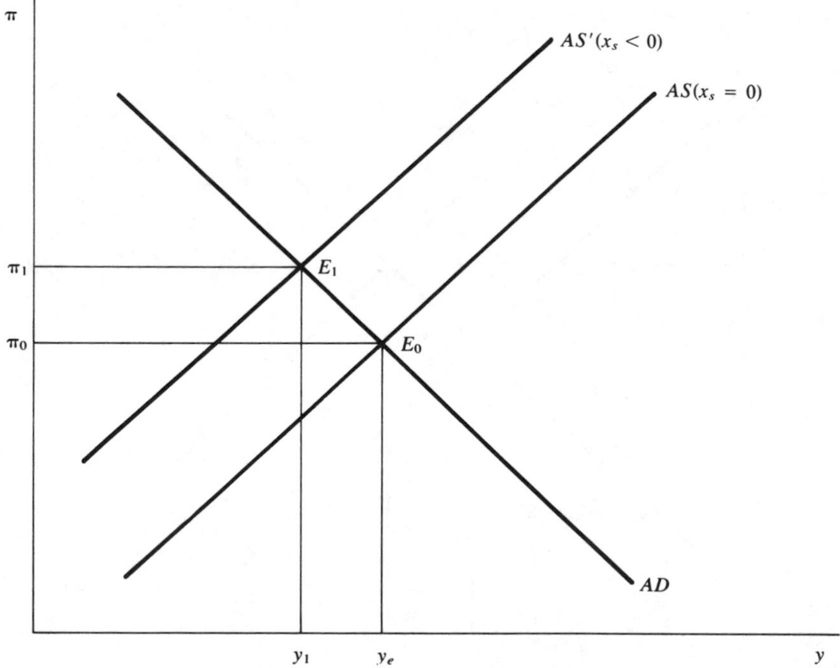

Figure 10-9 The effects of a supply shock when the central bank controls the money supply.

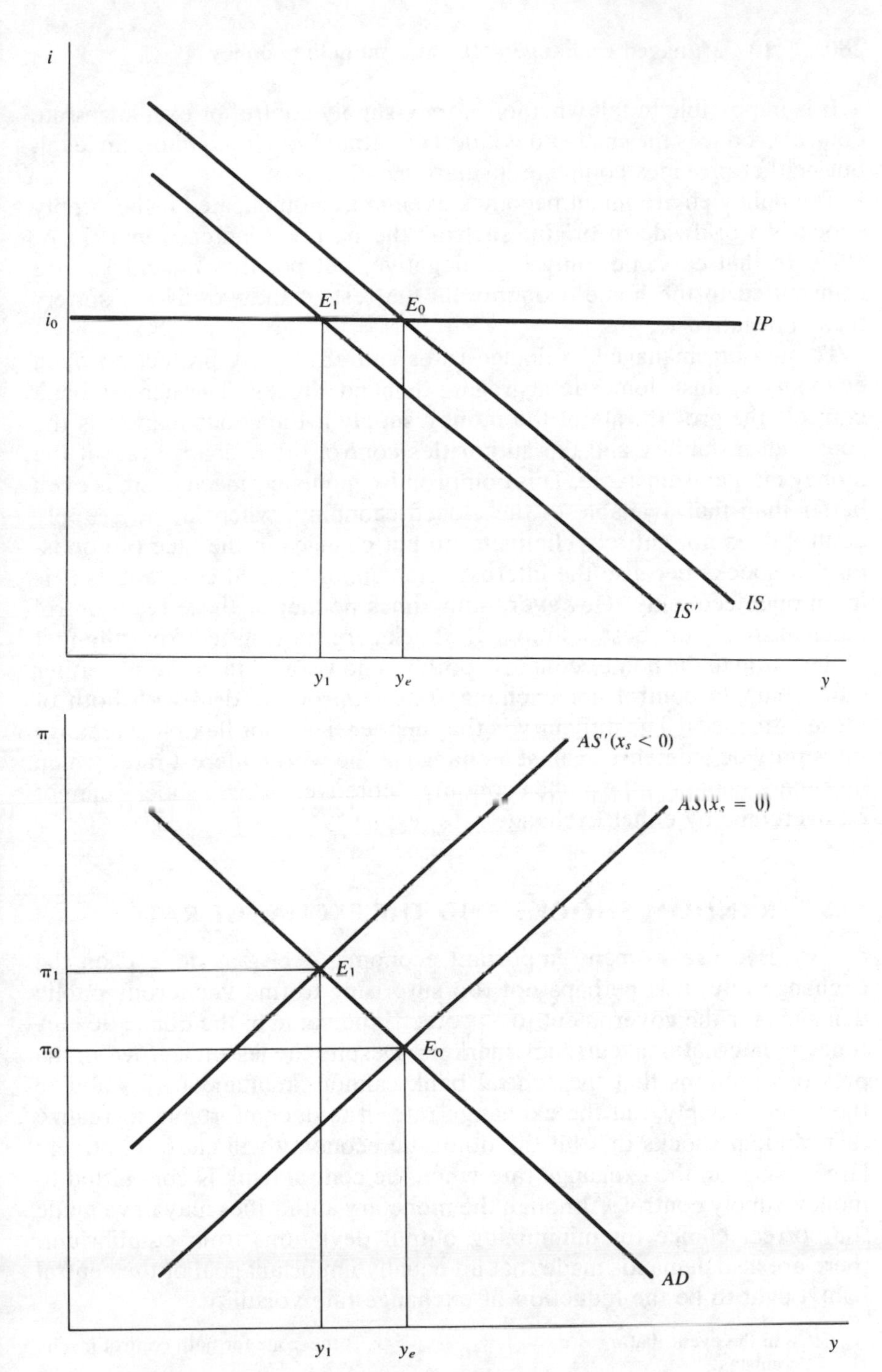

Figure 10-10 The effects of a supply shock when the central bank controls the exchange rate.

It is impossible to tell whether money-supply control or exchange-rate control produces the smaller deviation of output from its equilibrium level, but neither provides complete insulation.[3]

The policy environment becomes even more complicated if the supply shock is worldwide in origin, such as the oil-price increase in 1973 or 1979. In that case, not only is x_s negative, but positive x_{i*} and $x_{\pi*}$ are transmitted to the home economy as the rest of the world also suffers from a negative x_s.

To sum up, managed exchange rates can effectively protect an open economy against domestic aggregate-demand shocks: The central bank controls the growth rate of the money supply if the goods market is the source of instability and the authorities control the exchange rate if the money market is unstable. This compromise monetary mechanism is even better than that available to the closed economy, where money-supply control does not entirely eliminate output changes in the face of goods-market shocks because the interest rate cannot be held constant as it is in an open economy. However, sometimes neither of these two control mechanisms is the best solution. If shocks are transmitted from the rest of the world to the home economy, both x_{i*} and $x_{\pi*}$ are affected and neither money-supply control nor exchange-rate control can deal with both of these influences. The difficulty is that neither fixed nor flexible exchange rates provide a defense against a change in the world interest rate, which must be accepted in the home economy. Moreover, supply shocks cannot be overcome by either exchange-rate regime.[4]

10.5 RANDOM SHOCKS AND THE EXCHANGE RATE

Because so many important economic decisions depend on the exchange rate, it is perhaps not too surprising to find vociferous public demands for the government to "protect" the value of the domestic currency in international currency markets. Despite the lesson learned in the previous sections that the central bank cannot simultaneously stabilize the money supply and the exchange rate, it is uncomfortable to realize that random shocks that hit the domestic economy will cause relatively large swings in the exchange rate when the central bank is committed to money-supply control. Although the monetary authorities may have made the correct choice for minimizing output deviations from equilibrium, there are also demands made that an equally important goal of the central bank ought to be the reduction of exchange-rate volatility.

[3] In the event that $a_2 = a_5 = 1$, $y_1 - y_0 = x_s$ is the same for both control mechanisms.

[4] The exercises at the end of the chapter ask you to find an optimal combination of fixed and flexible rates or an optimal managed rate.

To determine the exchange-rate effects of stochastic variables we return to the *IS* curve of equation (10.1) which, together with the terms-of-trade equation (10.5), determine exchange-rate movements when the central bank controls the money supply. Taking first differences produces

$$(10.14)\quad \rho_1 - \rho_0 = (1/a_5)(y_1 - y_0) + (\pi_1 - \pi_0) + (a_1/a_5)x_{i^*} - x_{\pi^*} - (1/a_5)x_g$$

Substituting the *AS* curve for $(\pi_1 - \pi_0)$ and then equation (10.9) into (10.14) results in

$$(10.15)\quad \rho_1 - \rho_0 = [(a_4 + a_5)/(a_5 + a_2a_4a_5)]x_m - x_{\pi^*} - [1/a_5]x_g + [(a_1 + a_1a_2a_4 + a_3a_4 + a_3a_5)/(a_5 + a_2a_4a_5)]x_{i^*} + [(1 + a_4 - a_2a_5 - a_2a_4a_5)/(a_5 + a_2a_4a_5)]x_s$$

which links the exchange rate directly to the x's.

The first thing to note about this expression is that all three domestic shocks (x_g, x_m, and x_s) and both foreign shocks (x_{π^*} and x_{i^*}) have an effect on ρ. Second, some shocks have determinate results for ρ, but some combination of the x_{π^*}'s and x_{i^*}'s have indeterminate effects. For example, a positive x_{π^*} causes ρ to fall below its previous level by the value of x_{π^*}. This is a beneficial feature of the adjustment, since the exchange rate keeps the terms of trade constant. However, x_{π^*} cannot occur by itself; it comes with a certain value of x_{i^*}, depending on the nature of the foreign shock and therefore, it is most likely that the terms of trade will change in one direction or the other as both x_{π^*} and x_{i^*} have their combined effect. Only if x_{i^*} has the opposite sign of x_{π^*} will the total effect on ρ be determinate. Also, the term attached to x_s cannot be signed; it could be positive, negative, or zero. The ambiguity of the effect of a positive x_s on ρ arises from two conflicting influences on demand for domestic goods and services: On the one hand, the *AS* curve shifts down and reduces domestic inflation, which lowers the terms of trade and makes home goods more attractive to foreigners, and the resulting trade surplus puts downward pressure on ρ; on the other hand, the higher income raises domestic demand for home goods, leaving less available to foreigners and putting upward pressure on ρ.

A third feature of equation (10.15) that deserves attention is the reversal of short-run effects in the long run, or what is referred to in the literature as "overshooting" of the exchange rate. Consider as an example the adoption of an antiinflation policy in the foreign economy, starting from $\pi = \pi^*$ and $\rho = 0$. Although the policy may be announced in advance, let us assume that it is initially perceived as an unexpected monetary shock that produces $x_{\pi^*} < 0$ and $x_{i^*} > 0$. Of great importance is the fact that the foreign interest rate initially rises, although it will subsequently fall when the new policy is finally incorporated into everyone's expectations. From equation (10.15), $\rho_1 - \rho_0$ should be positive; in fact, the combination of $x_{\pi^*} < 0$ and $x_{i^*} > 0$ will make $\rho_1 - \rho_0$ larger than x_{π^*} and the terms of trade will fall initially. Then in the new final equilibrium when π^* and i^* have been reduced to the same extent as the growth rate of the foreign-money supply has been lowered, ρ will equal the difference between π and π^*, which is smaller than the short-run combined effect of x_{π^*} and x_{i^*}.

EXAMPLE

> Assume $\pi = \pi^* = 10\%$ initially. Then the foreign growth rate of the money supply is reduced from 10% to 5%, but being perceived as a monetary shock, the first effect is $x_{\pi^*} = -.04$ and $x_{i^*} = .02$. Also assume that the parameter attached to x_{i^*} in (10.15) is equal to 1.5. Then from (10.15), the first-round effect is $\rho_1 - \rho_0 = .04 + .03 = .07$ or 7% per period. In the final equilibrium, with $\pi = 10\%$ and $\pi^* = 5\%$, $\rho = 5\%$.

If the policy change had been credible in the first place, the unfavorable repercussions on the exchange rate could have been avoided. This is just another example of events that are similar in every other respect except for predictability, which makes an important difference to the results on macroeconomic variables; yet it is not easy to decide whether an event is temporary or permanent or whether a policy statement is a commitment or propaganda. In this situation, one can expect a great deal of political pressure on the central bank to intervene in the foreign exchange market in order to prevent such volatility of the exchange rate.

10.6 ONE MORE LOOK AT THE MONETARY MECHANISM IN CANADA

In the light of the analytical conclusions of the preceding two sections of this chapter we need to reassess the monetary mechanism employed by the Bank of Canada since 1975. First, the main points from the discussion of Chapter 7 will be reviewed. Between 1975 and 1982 the Bank of Canada followed a monetarist strategy by specifying and announcing target ranges for the growth rate of M1, and it used this strategy in its fight against inflation by lowering these target ranges from time to time. The Bank's monetary mechanism, however, did not involve day-to-day control of the money supply or the monetary base; instead, it manipulated the interest rate at the weekly Treasury bill auction and through its daily open-market operations in such a way as to keep the *demand* for money growing at a rate which was within the announced range. Both the strategy and the monetary mechanism were chosen in the belief that the money market was relatively unstable in the short run but rock-stable in the long run. Given that view and from the perspective of a closed economy, the Bank of Canada made the right decision in both areas. But Canada is decidedly an open economy, closely linked to other nations, especially to the United States. In an open-economy framework there are two new questions that have to be raised:

1. How does the Bank of Canada hope to manipulate the interest rate on a day-to-day basis when the interest parity condition dictates that the domestic interest rate in a small country be largely determined by foreign interest-rate developments?
2. Is there an inconsistency between the Bank's monetarist strategy and its espousal of an exchange-rate goal beginning in 1978?

Each of these questions requires an in-depth answer.

10.6.1 MANIPULATING THE INTEREST RATE IN AN OPEN ECONOMY

From Chapter 7 it will be remembered that the Bank of Canada solved the *LM* equation for the interest rate and obtained

$$(10.16)\quad i = [1/a_3][a_2 y + \pi - \mu - x_m - (m - p)_{-1}]$$

so that there is only one i that is consistent with projected values for y and π, with a targeted value for μ, with an assumption that $x_m = 0$ and with a known value for $(m - p)_{-1}$. If, as the Bank feared, x_m was not zero, $\mu + x_m$ could be held constant by maintaining the interest rate that it had previously calculated as the equilibrium interest rate. To the extent that there is a range for μ, there is also a range for the equilibrium interest rate. From the example in Chapter 7, in 1978 the growth rate for M1 was to be between 7% and 11%. With values for all the variables and parameters on the right side of equation (10.16), the Bank of Canada found that interest rates could range between 9.0% and 10.7%. But in an open economy, equation (10.4) stipulates that $i = i^* + r^e - r_{-1} + x_{i^*}$. Does the *IP* condition prevent the Bank of Canada from following its stated monetary mechanism? The answer is no. The escape from foreign domination of domestic interest rates involves allowing r to absorb some of the adjustment that allows for manipulation of i. For example, if μ is larger than the top of the announced range, i would have to be raised to bring μ back down again. In turn, interest parity is preserved if r falls, so that the higher domestic interest rate is offset by an expected depreciation of the domestic currency, with $r^e > r_{-1}$ or $\rho^e > 0$. Thus μ and r are supposed to move up and down together. As long as r was not an "important" variable to the Bank of Canada, it could dictate a specific range for i to achieve any desired target range for μ.

10.6.2 EXCHANGE-RATE GOALS

One of the benefits of a monetarist strategy is that even an open economy can adopt it as long as it is not concerned about its exchange rate; but the Bank of Canada *was* concerned about the exchange rate after 1978. In his *Annual Report* for that year the governor indicated the shifting emphasis of monetary policy. He wrote, "The Bank decided in the spring of 1978 to give increasing weight in the conduct of monetary policy to cushioning the rate of decline in [the value of] Canada's [currency]."[5] The governor's main concern was the inflationary pressure created by a depreciating currency, which forces import prices to rise while wage bargaining and automatic COLA clauses will attempt to overcome this downward pressure on the real wage. This concern was essentially an admission that the antiinflation policy begun in 1975 was not working as well as the Bank had hoped. A lower growth rate of the money supply which also brings down the rate of inflation, should have produced an appreciating Canadian dollar vis-à-vis those countries whose inflationary performance was worse.

Whatever the merits of the governor's case, could the Bank have both monetary and exchange-rate targets? Tom Courchene, a lucid critic of the Bank of Canada for many years, argues that it could not. He states, "If the Bank's response . . . is to fix interest rates, it cannot at the same time control either the money supply or the exchange rate."[6] What Courchene is asserting is that only *one* of the three variables (i.e., i, μ, or ρ) can be controlled at any one time. As seen above, a reduction in μ also forced a reduction in r and vice versa. However, it is possible, within limits, to achieve both monetary and exchange-rate targets by having a target *range* for monetary aggregates. As long as μ remains within this range, the central bank can manipulate i in order to achieve a particular level of r that the authorities wish to reach. It was precisely this kind of situation that faced the Bank of Canada in early 1978. In a press release dated March 8, the governor stated:

[5] *Annual Report of the Governor of the Bank of Canada*, Ottawa, 1978, p. 7.
[6] T. J. Courchene, *Money, Inflation, and the Bank of Canada*, vol. II, Montreal, C. D. Howe Research Institute, 1981, p. 92.

> The trend growth of the money supply to date was relatively strong, and was above the centre of the Bank's target range. In the Bank's judgment there was now room for some increase in short-term interest rates in Canada without prejudicing the achievement of an acceptable rate of monetary expansion. Some increase in short-term rates would moderate the downward pressure on the [Canadian dollar] and would contribute to more orderly conditions in the foreign exchange market in Canada.[7]

As another example, if the United States raises its own interest rate, but the Bank of Canada wishes to maintain the current exchange rate, the Bank must raise i quickly to prevent a capital outflow. It must also accept a slower growth of M1 in these circumstances as the opportunity cost of holding money balances rises and demand falls.

But there are definite problems if r and μ become inconsistent. By 1981, the growth rate of M1 was well below the bottom of the target range, as seen in Chart 7-1. Nevertheless, the Bank of Canada felt the need to raise interest rates to match those in the United States to protect the Canadian dollar from further depreciation. In 1981 the governor admitted that

> actions by the Bank to moderate excessive exchange rate or interest rate declines have on occasion caused M1 to move below its target range or to remain there somewhat longer than otherwise. However, these divergences from the target have been temporary and the Bank believes that this approach has been preferable to one of permitting inflationary pressures to build up before monetary policy responds.[8]

Moreover, as Courchene has noted, "Focusing on exchange rates *serves to politicize both exchange rates and interest rates*."[9] Since credibility is such an important ingredient of a monetarist antiinflation strategy, it is vital that the Bank not give any indication of vacillation in keeping money supply targets at the forefront of its long-term policy. At the same time, it can improve the short-term performance of the economy in the face of random shocks if it manages the exchange rate from time to time. The important point is to keep a clear distinction between the short run and the long run.

In summary, the Bank of Canada is operating in a complicated economic environment, and it finds any one strategy or monetary mechanism too simple to cope with all the macroeconomic problems that it tries to alleviate. Some critics of the Bank, particularly Courchene, argue that it should not try to deal with all of these inconsistent goals; instead, it should focus on one important and achievable goal, namely lowering inflation, and stick to it through all the temptations to change course. The Bank, although divorced from direct political pressures, is nevertheless ac-

[7] *Bank of Canada Review,* March 1978, p. 17.
[8] *Annual Report of the Governor of the Bank of Canada,* Ottawa, 1981, p. 30.
[9] Courchene, *Money, Inflation, and the Bank of Canada,* vol. II, p. 95; emphasis in the original.

countable to the government and to the public for its action and for its inaction. It therefore tends to adopt a somewhat shorter time horizon than economists are inclined to do and, as a result, interest rates, exchange rates, and the money supply all seem to take on equal importance. From that perspective, managed exchange rates are a very natural part of a broadly defined monetary strategy to lower the inflation rate.

10.7 SUMMARY

Monetary policy and the choice of a monetary mechanism in an open economy are more complicated than in a closed economy for a number of reasons:

1. The exchange rate can become either a target or an instrument.
2. Shocks are not only domestic in nature but can also be transmitted from abroad.
3. The central bank can lose control over the money supply if it follows a fixed exchange-rate policy.

A monetary mechanism is chosen to protect the existing equilibrium of an economy. The optimal mechanism depends on the source of the shock:

1. Unfavorable effects of domestic demand shocks can be avoided entirely by a managed exchange rate that involves controlling the path of the exchange rate when shocks are monetary in nature and controlling the growth rate of the money supply if shocks emanate from the goods market.
2. Foreign shocks and supply shocks cannot be overcome completely by either technique, and minimizing deviations from equilibrium output involves a combination of the two control procedures.

Canada was the first major country to abandon pegged exchange rates in 1970. It adopted a monetarist strategy in 1975 that required that the long-term path of the exchange rate absorb differences between domestic and foreign inflation. However, in the short run, the Bank was able to manipulate both the exchange rate and the money supply by controlling interest rates on a day-to-day basis. For the most part, it was not faced with inconsistent choices between the exchange rate and the money supply, partly because the Bank operated with a 4% tolerance in the growth rate of M1. But by 1981 it was clear that the exchange rate goal was more important than the monetary targets, and in 1982 targets for M1 growth were discarded. Alternative strategies facing the Bank of Canada at the end of 1982 were discussed in Chapter 7.

EXERCISES

Fixed and flexible exchange rates represent only two of many choices available to the central bank. To add to its potential ability to stabilize output, the monetary authorities could respond to a shock by letting the exchange rate *and* the money supply adjust, in which case there is neither money-supply control nor exchange-rate control but some combination of the two mechanisms. The point is to find the *optimal* combination of the two regimes that involves a managed exchange rate, now characterized by the exchange rate being partially fixed and partially flexible, instead of being sometimes fixed and sometimes flexible. If we denote the change in y arising from money-supply control in equation (10.9) as $y_1^m - y_0$ and the change in y using exchange-rate control in equation (10.13) as $y_1^r - y_0$, then we can write a linear combination of the two as follows:

$$y_1 - y_0 = \beta(y_1^m - y_0) + (1 - \beta)(y_1^r - y_0)$$

The idea is to find that value of β that minimizes $y_1 - y_0$ for any of the shocks that can affect an open economy. The parameter β is the choice variable for the central bank and indicates the exact mix of the two mechanisms. The closer β is to one, the greater is the emphasis on money-supply control and the less is the emphasis on exchange-rate control; at the other end of the spectrum, the closer β is to zero, the more the mechanism resembles exchange-rate control.

1. (a) Is it possible to find a value of β that *eliminates* the effect of a supply shock on output?
   (b) Using an *IS–LM* and *AS–AD* diagram, assume $x_s < 0$ and show the automatic responses of the various curves that would take place with this optimal mechanism.
   (c) Consider now a "permanent" supply shock. What is the optimal monetary mechanism if the central bank is aware of this permanence? What problems are created if the central bank does not recognize the permanence of the shock?
2. Assume that the central bank has continuous information on the domestic and foreign interest rates and inflation rates. On the basis of this information, how would it distinguish among the following?
   (a) A foreign goods-market shock and a domestic goods-market shock

(b) A domestic money-market shock and a domestic goods-market shock
(c) A domestic supply shock and a domestic goods-market shock
(d) A foreign goods-market shock and a foreign money-market shock

3. In the event of domestic goods-market shocks, it has been shown that flexible exchange rates are the best monetary mechanism. However, they also create a trade-off between output now and output in the future, through their effect on the terms of trade. Show how the terms of trade are affected by goods-market shocks with flexible rates and indicate how this affects output in the future.

FURTHER READING

Courchene, T. J., *Money, Inflation, and the Bank of Canada,* vol. II, Montreal, C. D. Howe Research Institute, 1981. Chapter 4 provides a detailed discussion and criticism of the attempt by the Bank of Canada to follow exchange-rate objectives.

Sparks, G. R., "The Choice of Monetary Policy Instruments in Canada," *Canadian Journal of Economics,* 12, November 1979, pp. 615–24. An open-economy version of the Poole analysis.

CHAPTER 11

Monetary policy in Canada and its macroeconomic consequences

11.1 INTRODUCTION

In this chapter the various threads that were developed in the preceding two chapters will be pulled together to show how monetary policy influenced the performance of the Canadian economy from 1975 to 1982. The purpose is to show how the *IS–LM–AS* model, especially the open-economy version, can be used to analyze real macroeconomic problems and policies. It runs parallel to Chapter 8, which dealt with the U.S. experience, but it does not necessarily emphasize the same issues; whereas Chapter 8 focused on supply shocks, this chapter will highlight the role played by monetary targets in the Canadian economy. However, although monetary events and policies receive pride of place in this account, other factors were also at work and their effects must be incorporated into the discussion of the period.

11.2 HIGHLIGHTS OF THE PERIOD

Supported by the data in Table 11-1, the following general observations can be made about macroeconomic developments in Canada between 1975 and 1982:

1. Throughout the period, Canada suffered from high and variable inflation. The growth rate of the GNE price deflator reached 15.3% in 1974; its low point for the whole period was 6.8%. The size of inflation makes accurate predictions desirable, but the variability of inflation makes these predictions very difficult.
2. Interest rates tended to move up and down with the inflation rate. Their high variability made it unattractive for both borrowers and lenders to enter into long-term contracts.

Table 11-1. *Important macroeconomic variables in the Canadian economy, 1972–82*

	π									
Year	GNE	CPI	i	$\mu 1$	$\mu 2$	u	y	y_e	r	t
1972	5.0	4.7	3.6	14.4	10.8	4.1	11.52	11.56	4.81	4.68
1973	9.1	7.7	5.4	14.5	14.7	3.4	11.59	11.62	4.78	4.71
1974	15.3	10.9	7.8	9.4	20.5	3.3	11.62	11.64	4.81	4.76
1975	10.8	10.8	7.4	14.0	15.2	4.3	11.64	11.70	4.77	4.72
1976	9.5	7.5	8.9	8.0	13.0	4.2	11.69	11.75	4.82	4.75
1977	7.1	7.9	7.4	8.5	14.3	4.9	11.71	11.80	4.74	4.68
1978	6.5	8.8	8.6	10.1	11.1	5.2	11.75	11.83	4.64	4.61
1979	10.3	11.6	11.6	6.9	15.7	4.5	11.77	11.86	4.61	4.61
1980	11.0	10.2	12.8	6.4	18.9	4.8	11.78	11.89	4.61	4.60
1981	10.1	12.5	17.8	4.0	15.2	4.9	11.81	11.92	4.61	4.61
1982	10.7	10.8	13.8	1.2	9.4	8.1	11.76	11.95	4.60	4.61

Sources: π(GNE), growth of GNE deflator, *Bank of Canada Review*, table 1, col. (14); π(CPI), growth rate of consumer price index, all items, ibid., col. (36); i, Treasury bill rate, ibid., col. (32); $\mu 1$, growth rate of M1 money supply, ibid., col. (1); $\mu 2$, growth rate of M2 money supply, ibid., col. (2); u, unemployment rate of males, 25 years and over, ibid., table 57 (D767657); y, natural log of real GNP in 1971 dollars, *Bank of Canada Review*, table 53 (D40593); y_e, natural log of potential output, J. Brox and M. Cluff, "Potential Output and the Real GNP Gap," *Canadian Statistical Review*, January 1979, pp. vi–xii, table II (fourth quarter × 4), for 1972–7, with 3% growth rate thereafter; r, natural log of index of effective exchange rate (1980–2 = 100), Morgan Guaranty Trust, *World Financial Markets*, August 1983, p. 10, table 7; t, natural log of index of real effective exchange rate (1980–2 = 100), ibid.

3. The Canadian economy underwent two major recessions, one in 1974–5 and then the most serious setback since the Depression of the 1930s occurred in 1981–2 when the unemployment rate reached "double-digit" figures.[1]
4. There was steady pressure on the Canadian dollar to depreciate against the U.S. dollar and other major currencies.[2] Also, the terms of trade, measured by the index of real effective exchange rates, fell quite steadily from 1976 onward, indicating the improved competitiveness of Canadian goods in world markets.
5. The Bank of Canada adopted a monetarist strategy to fight inflation in 1975 when it implemented target growth rates for M1 which were lowered from time to time and preannounced. At the same time, no target was set for M2, and it was allowed to grow at very high levels.

[1] The unemployment rate for adult males, shown in Table 11-1, remained below 10%, but the overall unemployment rate reached 11% in 1982.

[2] Because of its construction, the index of effective exchange rates *falls* when the currency depreciates.

These are the events that have to be explained by our model, and we now turn to a prediction of events following a monetarist antiinflation policy in an *IS–LM–AS* model.

11.3 PREDICTIONS FOR A MONETARIST STRATEGY

The principal aim of monetary policy after 1974 was to bring down the rate of inflation, gradually and steadily. By announcing target growth rates for M1 and lowering these targets about once a year, the Bank of Canada hoped to lower the rate of inflation at the same pace both directly through its contractionary effect on aggregate demand and indirectly through its effect on inflationary expectations in the aggregate-supply side of the economy. Combined, these policy effects should have succeeded in bringing down the rate of inflation, the nominal interest rate, and the rate of change of the exchange rate, but should have left the real side of the economy untouched, with full-employment output preserved at a constant real interest rate and unchanged terms of trade. These very strong predictions were previously analyzed in Chapter 3, but they can now be put into action to evaluate the Bank's policy.

From Chapter 9, in an economy operating with flexible exchange rates, the *AD* curve is the *LM* curve, which is written as

$$(11.1) \quad \pi = \mu + (m - p)_{-1} - a_2 y + a_3(i^* + \rho^e)$$

which is essentially the same as for a closed economy except that the domestic interest rate, i, is linked to the world interest rate, i^*, and expected changes in the exchange rate, ρ^e, via the interest parity condition. The other variables are the following: μ stands for the growth rate of the money supply, $(m - p)_{-1}$ is the log of the real money supply prevailing at the end of the previous period, and y is the log of real income or output. Given i^*, ρ^e, $(m - p)_{-1}$ and μ, equation (11.1) shows a negative relationship between π and y, which is drawn as the *AD* curve in Figure 11-1. The *AS* curve is given by

$$(11.2) \quad y = y_{e_{-1}} - a_4[h\pi^e + (1 - h)(\pi^{*e} + \rho^e) - \pi]$$

where $y_{e_{-1}}$ is the log of the previous level of equilibrium output and π^e and π^{*e} are the expected rates of inflation for domestic and world output, respectively. For any given π^e, π^{*e}, ρ^e, and $y_{e_{-1}}$, there is a positive relationship between π and y, shown in Figure 11-1 as the *AS* curve. In addition, the *IS* curve allows us to calculate the rate of change of the exchange rate according to

$$(11.3) \quad \rho = [1/a_5][y - a_0 + a_1(i^* + \rho^e - \pi^e)] + \pi - \pi^* + t_{-1}$$

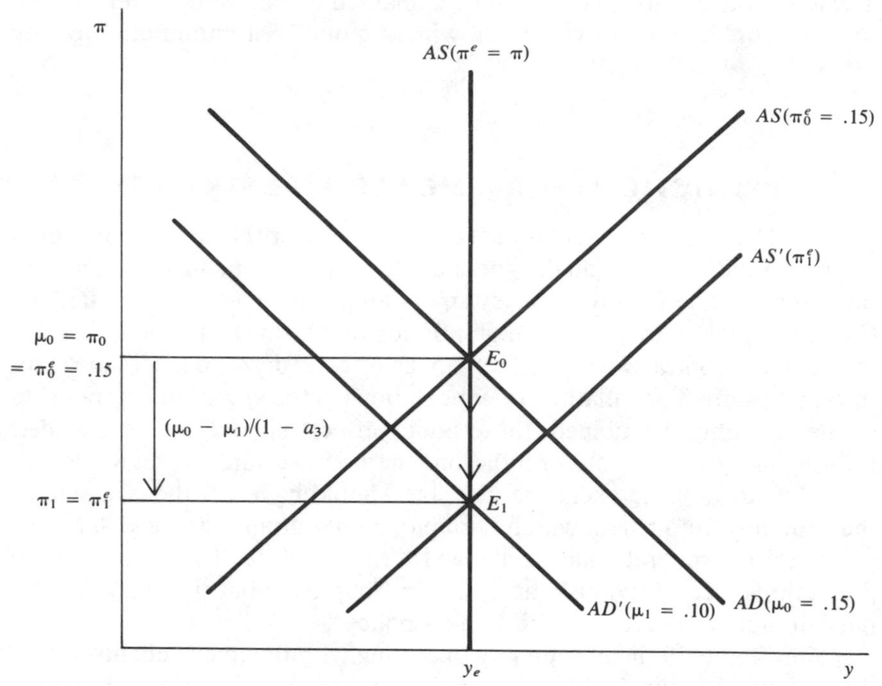

Figure 11-1 Predictions of a monetarist antiinflation policy in Canada, 1975–82.

where additional variables are the following: a_0 represents exogenous demand for home goods, including government demand; π^* is the actual rate of inflation abroad; and t_{-1} stands for the terms of trade at the end of the previous period. Once π and y are obtained from the AD–AS part of the model, ρ can be calculated from equation (11.3), given i^*, π^*, and t_{-1}. In none of these equations do the x's (i.e., stochastic shocks to the economy) appear because we are dealing with *predictable* monetary policy in this discussion.

Although it is unlikely that the year 1974 represented a situation of full equilibrium, where $\mu = \pi = \pi^e, y = y_{e-1}$, and $\rho = \pi - \pi^*$, it is necessary to specify some initial conditions to allow the analysis to proceed. Hence it will be assumed that actual and predicted inflation were equal to the growth rate of the money supply in the neighborhood of 15%; thus $\mu_0 = .15$. Also, the presumption is that output was near its full-employment level and that the terms of trade were constant.

Starting in 1975, the Bank of Canada announced target growth rates for M1. The initial range was 10–15% a year. In 1976, this was lowered to 8–12%. Let us use 10% as the working figure for μ_1 for the first year of the policy as a basis of comparison for the previous μ_0 of 15%. This reduction in μ of 5 percentage points has predictable effects on the important variables in the Canadian economy, and now we can look at these predictions in detail. In particular, we want to know what should happen to π, y, i, and ρ as a result of this new policy and then compare these predictions to what actually happened. We can follow a sequential procedure and start by looking at the effect on output, using the *AS* curve of equation (11.2). Since the policy was *predictable* and to the extent that there were no long-term contracts in the economy that prevented the incorporation of this new information in wage bargaining starting in 1975, both firms and union negotiators would have had a paramount interest in keeping the real wage constant in the absence of any changes in the marginal product of workers. This would require that nominal wage increases be lowered to the same extent as the new expectations about inflation or that contracts rely on complete wage indexation, which would have made ex post wage increases equal to ex post inflation. In equation (11.2), the aim is to keep π_c^e, the expected rate of inflation from the worker's point of view, equal to π. Since π_c is a weighted average of π and $\pi^* + \rho$, as shown in equation (11.2), this involves lowering π^e and ρ^e equally, as long as π^* is expected to remain constant, as it should unless new policies or shocks occur in the rest of the world. This allows both domestic goods and import goods to have the same lower rate of inflation, although we do not yet know what that rate is. Therefore, if π, π^e, and ρ^e all fall equally, $h\pi^e + (1 - h)(\pi^{*e} + \rho^e) - \pi$ remains zero.

EXAMPLE

> If π, π^e, and ρ^e drop from 15% to 10% while π^{*e} remains constant. $h(.15 - .10) + (1 - h)(.15 - .10) - (.15 - .10) = 0$ no matter what the value of h happens to be.

In that case y stays at y_{e-1} and the real side of the economy is insulated from the change in policy because the *AS* curve is vertical in these circumstances. In fact, it was this feature of the *AS* curve that caused the Bank to make the policy change as credible as possible. Even though it may not have succeeded in this, it certainly was not for lack of trying. Both a vertical *AS* curve where $\pi = \pi_c^e$ and a positively sloped *AS* curve where π_c^e remains constant are shown in Figure 11-1.

To determine the effect on π we turn to the *AD* curve in equation (11.1). The reduction in μ from 15% to 10% shifts the *AD* curve down by an equal amount. Also, ρ^e falls by the same amount as π or π^e. Now $(m - p)_{-1}$, y, and i^* remain constant, although $(m - p)$ will subsequently change until we get a new equilibrium level of real balances. It will be remembered from Chapter 3 that $(m - p)$ is the only real variable in the system that is affected by a nominal variable, namely the interest rate; as the interest rate falls so does the opportunity cost of holding money and real balances will rise. This requires that $\mu > \pi$ for some period of time although in the new equilibrium $\mu = \pi$.

In equation (11.2), π falls by the extent of the reduction in μ plus a_3 times the reduction in ρ^e, which as previously stated falls to the same extent as π. Thus

$$\pi_1 - \pi_0 = \mu_1 - \mu_0 + a_3(\rho_1^e - \rho_0^e)$$

or

$$(11.4) \quad \pi_1 - \pi_0 = [1/(1 - a_3)][\mu_1 - \mu_0]$$

In other words, π and ρ (as well as their expectations) initially fall by more than the decline in the growth rate of the money supply. This is what allows the real money supply to rise. These dynamics will continue with π and ρ rising and falling until they both settle at 10%. This is *not* a troublesome feature of the antiinflationary policy as long as everyone who is involved in forming expectations is aware of this process and can incorporate this information into π^e and ρ^e.

EXAMPLE

If $a_3 = .25$, π falls by $1/.75 \times 5\% = 6.7\%$ or from 15% to 8.3% in the first period. Then in the second period, π will rise above 10%, its final destination. From equation (3.14′) in Chapter 3, the change in π is equal to $-[a_3/(1 - a_3)^2][\mu_1 - \mu_0]$ or $-.25/.56 \times -5\% = 2.3\%$ and π rises from 8.3% to 10.6%. This process continues until changes disappear and π equals 10%.

Although we already know that ρ must move in line with π, we can check this result with equation (11.3). Since both ρ^e and π^e move together, they cancel out in the term attached to a_1, the real interest rate. The variables y, a_0, i^*, π^*, and t_{-1} are constant, and thus ρ adjusts to changes in π by equal amounts. Next we can see that the terms of trade should remain constant. Changes in t are given by

$$(11.5) \quad t - t_{-1} = \pi - \pi^* - \rho$$

With π^* constant and π and ρ both reduced to the same extent, we have $t = t_{-1}$. Also, it is easy to see that the Canadian real interest rate should remain constant and equal to the real interest rate abroad. Although inflationary expectations are now lower in Canada, so is the nominal interest rate. This does not violate the requirements of equal expected returns on domestic and foreign bonds since

$$(11.6) \quad i = i^* + \rho^e$$

is still satisfied when i and ρ^e fall by the same amount; however, ρ^e oscillates around its new value and so does i.

In the new final equilibrium, we should again observe $\mu = \pi = \pi^e$ at a new lower level of 10%; ρ should fall by 5 percentage points, as should i. At the same time, y should remain at y_e, $i - \pi^e$ should stay the same, and t should remain constant. However, since the target range for the growth of M1 was again reduced from 8–12% to 7–11% in 1977, there would be further reductions in π, ρ, and i, but the real variables would still remain unaffected since these changes were preannounced. In other words, we would observe the Canadian economy moving downward along a vertical AS curve from 1975 onward.

These are the detailed predictions of the effect of antiinflationary policy instituted by the Bank of Canada in late 1975. We must now check these predictions against the events that actually occurred after 1975.

11.4 WHAT ACTUALLY HAPPENED IN THE CANADIAN MACROECONOMY, 1975–82?

First, we should determine whether the Bank of Canada was indeed able to reduce the growth rate of the money supply as it had promised. Table 11-1 indicates that the growth rate of M1 fell from 14% in 1975, the last year of the old policy, to 8% in 1976, the first full year of the new policy. This appears to be an overachievement, but it must be remembered that the Bank had set a range of 8–12% and thus it was at the bottom of that range. A more useful way of comparing the performance of the Bank with its commitments is to look at the growth rate of M1 relative to the "target cones" as shown in Chart 7-1. Since the target ranges were not established at the beginning of each year and since the base for the growth rate was arbitrarily fixed at the actual average performance for recent months, the credibility of the Bank's statements is better analyzed in terms of these cones. It is readily apparent that except for the postal strike, which caused an upward "blip" in the path of the money supply, the Bank's performance tended to fall below the 8–12% cone. In the years thereafter, both Table 11-1 and Chart 7-1 clearly indicate that the Bank of Canada was able to reduce the growth rate of M1.

In fact by 1981, the growth of M1 had become negative for short periods, so that the path fell substantially below the bottom of the cone. At the same time M2 continued to grow at a rapid rate; but since the Bank of Canada explicitly excluded M2 from its target, we cannot argue that they were unable to deliver on their promise. Nevertheless, the financial innovations that began in the late 1970s and that caused people to shift out of M1 and into M2 as then defined may have made M1 the wrong target. This was discussed in Chapter 5 in great detail, and we will return to this theme again later in this chapter.

Next we can turn to an examination of the evidence on the macroeconomic variables that are likely to be affected by the reduction in the growth rate of M1. Whether we look at the GNE deflator or the Consumer Price Index, Table 11-1 shows the inflation rate falling from a peak in 1974–5 to 1978 and then rising again, staying at 10% and above until 1982. We definitely do not observe that π falls faster than μ as was predicted in the previous section, except for the years 1977–8. In fact, from 1979 to 1982, the growth rate of M1 was falling rapidly but the inflation rate remained above 10%. Furthermore, the interest rate generally rises throughout the period, reaching a peak of 18% in 1981, with some interest rates actually exceeding 20% for some period of time. These developments are again not consistent with the previous predictions.

Now we can look at output to see whether it remained close to its potential level throughout the period. In Table 11-1, data for both y and y_e are given. It should be noted that y_e is not a constant quantity throughout the period. The productive capacity of the economy and the equilibrium level of employment are expected to rise over time and therefore y_e is estimated from a production function that incorporates equilibrium in the labor market, but allows the factor inputs to vary over time. Unfortunately, the available estimate only takes us up to 1977; thereafter it was assumed that potential output grows by 3% per annum. The GNP gap can be measured by $y_e - y$. If $y_e - y$ is positive, there is excess supply in the labor market, since more workers were available at the going real wage who could have produced more output. Throughout the period $y_e - y$ is positive, implying that the economy was operating consistently below its potential or that the unemployment rate was above the natural rate, but what is perhaps even more important is the fact that the gap was widening for most of the period, reaching 19% by 1982. The unemployment rate for adult males also rises for much of the period. We do not have a direct measure of the natural rate of unemployment, but adult males are likely to have a fairly stable labor-market experience, and their natural rate should have remained relatively constant during the period; therefore movements in the adult male unemployment rate should give a fairly clear indication of demand-deficient unemployment.

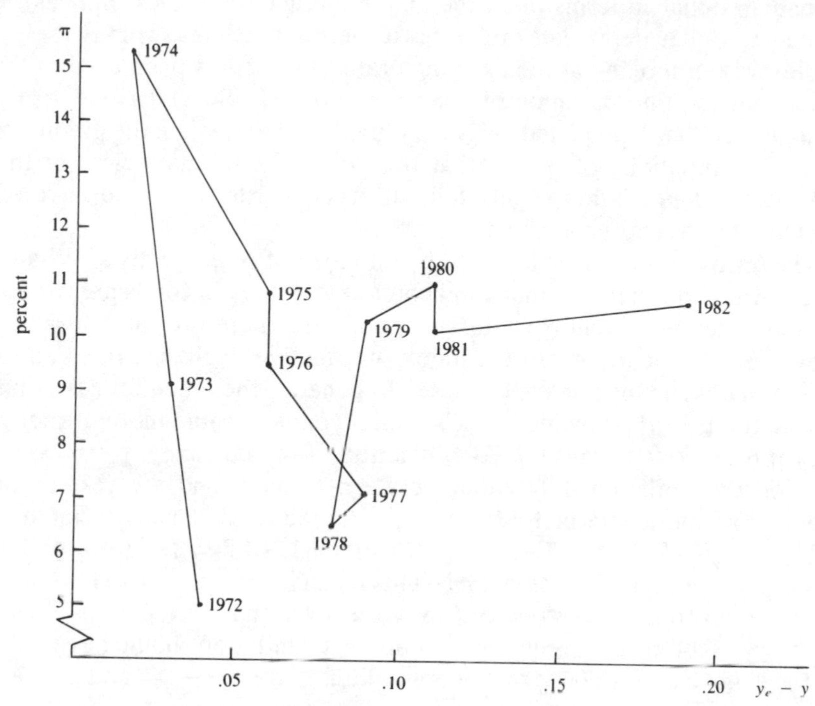

Chart 11-1 Canadian inflation and GNP gap, 1972–82. Source: Table 11-1.

EXAMPLE

> Assume that equilibrium unemployment for adult males is 3% and constant. In 1976 the actual unemployment rate was equal to 4.2%, indicating demand-deficient unemployment was equal to 1.2%.

Any way that we look at the output or employment performance of the Canadian economy from 1975 to 1982, it does not seem to be consistent with downward movement along a vertical *AS* curve. The actual relationship between π and y is shown in Chart 11-1, which plots the combinations of π and $y_e - y$ for the years 1972–82. If anything, the movement is much more horizontal than vertical. It would therefore appear that the brunt of the adjustment was taken by quantity changes and not by price changes, or put another way, there were substantial changes in the real economy but only minor ones in nominal variables.

Finally, the external variables can be examined. The index of effective exchange rates, which represents a weighted average of the value of the

Canadian dollar in terms of all the major foreign currencies, *falls* as the Canadian dollar depreciates relative to these currencies. This is the opposite way of looking at the exchange rate to what has been used in this book, but the interpretation of the r column in Table 11-1 is clear: The Canadian dollar depreciated fairly steadily after 1975, when the prediction of the antiinflation policy was that the dollar should appreciate or that the rate of depreciation should fall. In other words we would have expected r to have a rising value.

The terms of trade are measured by an index of *real* effective exchange rates. An increase in this index indicates that domestic goods are becoming more expensive relative to foreign goods and therefore t and this index move together, contrary to the index of effective exchange rates and r, where one is the inverse of the other. In general, the index for t is falling during the period, showing that Canadian goods became more attractive in world markets because the depreciation of the currency overpowered the positive inflation differential between Canada and the rest of the world. From the data in Table 11-1, the Canadian dollar depreciated by $4.77 - 4.60 = .17$ or 17% from 1975 to 1982, while t fell from 4.72 to 4.61, representing a decline of 11%. This means that prices rose in Canada by 6% more than in the rest of the world over that period. This is also contrary to the earlier prediction that domestic inflation should have fallen to the same extent as currency depreciation, that is; $\pi - \pi^*$ and ρ should have been the same.

To sum up, most of the evidence points to results that are contrary to the predictions of the antiinflation policy that the Bank of Canada adopted after 1975. We must now start the important task of analyzing the reasons why this monetarist approach to fighting inflation did not work the way it should have.

11.5 WHAT WENT WRONG?

There are a number of alternative explanations of what went wrong in the Canadian economy between 1975 and 1982. First, we can list the various explanations and then explore each one in greater detail:

1. The Bank of Canada had the wrong target in M1 – M2 would have been better.
2. The Bank's policy lacked credibility.
3. The Bank had the exchange rate as an additional target.
4. The oil-price shocks of 1974 and 1979 had independent effects.
5. External events had additional effects on the Canadian economy.
6. Fiscal policy in Canada also changed dramatically during this period.

11.5.1 CONTROLLING THE WRONG MONETARY AGGREGATE

The Bank of Canada specifically chose to control M1, defined as currency plus demand deposits, rather than some other monetary aggregate or some combination of aggregates, as was done by the Federal Reserve Board in the United States. Was this an important error? Before trying to answer that question we can quote Milton Friedman, the father of monetarist strategies against inflation. He wrote,

> I believe that a monetary total is the best currently available guide or criterion for monetary policy – and I believe that it matters much less which particular total is chosen than one be chosen.[3]

Also, Tom Courchene, a long-time critic of the Bank of Canada, has stated, "In most cases all common definitions of money generate similar policy signals."[4] This suggests that M1 was as good a choice as M2 or the monetary base, presumably because they were expected to move together during the fight against inflation. But as we have seen in Table 11-1, $\mu 2$ was consistently higher than $\mu 1$, so that reducing $\mu 1$ over time does not reduce $\mu 2$ automatically. In that case, it is important to choose the right monetary aggregate to control. In fact, Courchene has argued quite strenuously that M2 or the monetary base would have been better targets than M1.

It will be remembered from the discussion in Chapter 7 about the monetary mechanism that the Bank's choice of M1 was predicated on its use of the interest rate as its control mechanism, and since M1 is likely to be more interest-sensitive than M2 (i.e., a_3 is larger for M1 than for M2), this control mechanism is also going to be "stronger" for M1 than for M2. Courchene, on the other hand, argues in favor of direct control of the monetary aggregate and considers M2 to be a better candidate than M1 because it has a firmer relationship to nominal GNP. Then since real GNP is determined by the supply side of the economy, movements in nominal GNP reflect inflation directly. Thus the Bank thought of the relationship between interest rates and money as the most important, whereas Courchene focused on the relationship between money and inflation. Since the aim of the policy is to reduce inflation and since money is the policy instrument, Courchene's view seems to be more straightforward, but the matter cannot be decided that easily. In part, this controversy can be resolved by invoking the distinction between the short run and the long run. Both the Bank and its critics would agree that there is a strong relationship between money and inflation in the long run, but

[3] M. Friedman, "The Role of Monetary Policy," *American Economic Review*, 58, March 1968, p. 15.

[4] T. J. Courchene, *Money, Inflation, and the Bank of Canada*, vol. I, Montreal, C. D. Howe Research Institute, 1976, p. 109.

the Bank was also convinced that in the short run the supply of money was subject to many random events and could not be controlled completely. Thus it was trying to find a day-to-day operating procedure that had to rely on the strong relationship between interest rates and money. Since the long run is just a series of short runs, the Bank was forced to use M1 as its target. Difficulties arose, however, when the demand for M1 could no longer be accurately predicted by past relationships between money on the one hand and income and interest rates on the other, because of financial innovations that made assets in M2 virtually perfect substitutes for assets in M1. For that reason as well, Courchene argued that M2 was better than M1 as a target. Any shift among assets by the public (e.g., demand deposits to daily-interest accounts) are likely to be contained within M2 but not within M1; therefore, the demand for M2 is more stable, in a structural sense, then the demand for M1. But these financial innovations did not really take hold until 1980 or 1981, so this argument cannot be a complete explanation of the problem in the early part of the period.

In any case, it cannot be argued that the *uncontrolled* growth rate of M2 better explains the behavior of the Canadian economy after 1975 than does the *controlled* growth rate of M1. In Table 11-1, it is clear that $\mu 2 > \pi$ for most of the period, forcing real M2 balances to rise. This is inconsistent with a rising nominal interest rate. Even though some components of M2 pay interest, the opportunity cost of these balances still rises with the interest rate. Also, the growth of real income is not large enough to account for the higher M2 balances. Nominal M2 balances were \$50,118 million in 1975; in 1982 they had increased to \$127,718 million. The GNE deflator rose from 1.463 to 2.726. Real money balances therefore increased by 254% – 126% or 128%. Real GNP rose from \$113,005 million to \$128,057 million over the same time period, an increase of 13%. This would imply a value for a_2, the income elasticity of the demand for money, in excess of 9, but we know that a_2 is typically less than 1 if M2 represents only transactions balances. Even wealth effects should not raise a_2 that much.[5]

In summary, there is probably no clear answer to the question of whether M2 would have been better than M1 as a target for the Bank of Canada. Ex post, M1 was the wrong choice, because financial innovations made it less relevant as a monetary aggregate after 1980, but the decision had to be made ex ante, and in 1975 the evidence against M1 was not convincing. Perhaps the best course for the Bank would have been to shift to M2 or to redefine M1 in 1981, with a careful explanation of the reasons for the change so as to maintain credibility of the policy.

[5] See Section 5.8.

11.5.2 CREDIBILITY OF ANTIINFLATION POLICY

Throughout the postwar period, unemployment was always the more terrible specter than inflation.[6] In this environment, when faced with the choice between reducing inflation or unemployment, government policy tended to favor the latter. In terms of the *AD–AS* model, if the "target" level of unemployment is lower than the equilibrium level, there is a tendency to keep shifting the *AD* curve upward, but since output is ultimately determined by an unchanged vertical *AS* curve, the final effect is higher inflation and only temporary reductions in unemployment. This trade-off between higher inflation and temporary reductions in unemployment was acceptable until inflation became a serious problem in the 1970s. By 1975 the Bank had to address the issue directly, and it chose a monetarist strategy to reduce inflation. In the process it had to eschew a target employment goal. If the Bank was going to fight inflation, it could not try to alleviate an unemployment problem at the same time. In other words, the order of importance of these goals was now reversed. However, by announcing beforehand what policy was to be implemented, the Bank had in mind a way of reducing inflation *without* putting the economy "through the wringer." If all agents in the economy used the available information on μ and if the x's were all zero in the process, there would be no trade-off between inflation and unemployment. The Canadian economy could have both lower inflation and full employment. To achieve this result, however, it was vital that the policy have *credibility*.

Ironically, it is the lack of credibility that creates the unpleasant side effects of antiinflation policy. In 1975 the public was asked to believe a new regime, but they may have chosen to ignore it and to assume instead that the Bank would continue to create enough growth in the money supply to keep the economy at "full" employment without worrying about the inflationary consequences. Why was credibility so difficult to achieve? To answer this question, it must be remembered that expected inflation plays an important role in nominal wage determination for the next period. There are adverse consequences for choosing a real wage that is too high or too low. If nominal wage increases are 15% and inflation turns out to be 10%, firms will reduce the labor input to increase the marginal product of the remaining workers to allow for the 5% increase in the real wage. On the other hand if workers accept 10% increases in wages and inflation turns out to be 15%, they will have lost 5% in real wages and, in the bargain, they may work more than they want to. Past experience seemed to indicate that the Bank of Canada would be unable or unwilling to keep

[6] In Germany, where the hyperinflation of the 1920s is still relatively fresh in people's memory and where unemployment has been traditionally low, their relative importance is reversed.

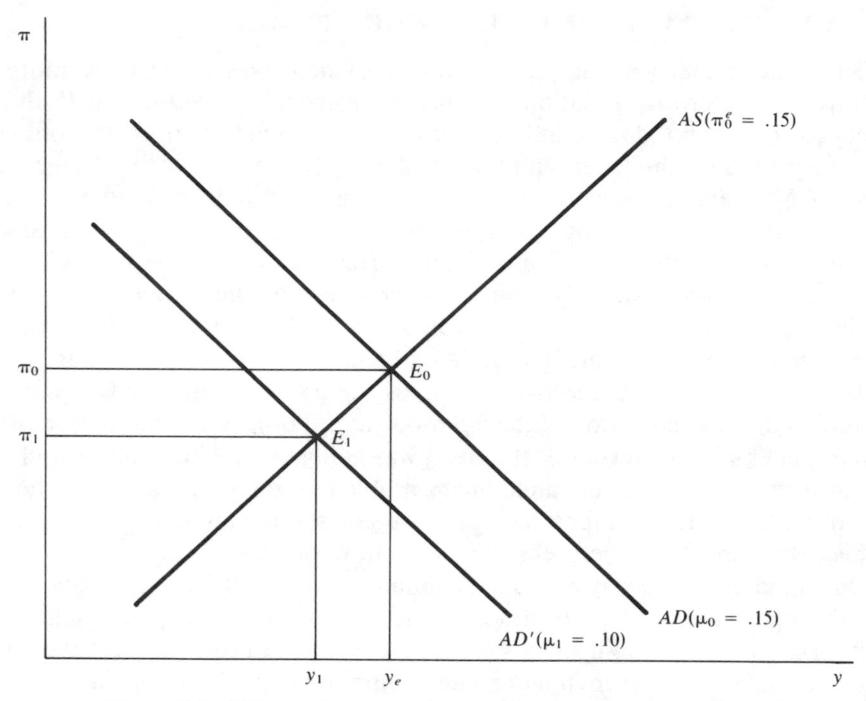

Figure 11-2 Effects of a monetarist antiinflation policy without credibility.

its promise of reducing the inflation rate after 1975 and instead would underwrite full employment by validating almost any wage increases. Thus it is safer to err on the high side (i.e., to expect 15% inflation rather than 10% inflation); the Bank will bail out the economy if $\omega > \pi$ but not if $\omega < \pi$. We cannot measure π^e directly, but we can assume that π^e remained at 15% and then see how the economy would react differently from what the Bank of Canada had in mind.

Consider again, as in Section 11.3, a reduction in the growth rate of the money supply from about 15% to 10%, but this time π^e will remain at 15% on the assumption that the policy change, although it is still predictable, is not credible. In this case, the *AD* curve in Figure 11-2 shifts down by the amount equal to $\mu_1 - \mu_0$, which is less than previously since ρ^e remains constant as well. The *AS* curve remains in place. Therefore, the new short-run equilibrium is established at E_1 to the left and below E_0, the original equilibrium, which is the same as in Figure 11-1. Now both output and inflation fall. In particular, it should be noted that the inflation rate falls by less than $\mu_1 - \mu_0$, compared to the analysis in Section 11.3, where it fell by more than this initially. The difference is that the *AS* curve did not shift down as it did previously. The prediction that y falls and π is reduced by less than the decrease in the growth rate of the money supply seems to be more in line with the data in Table 11-1 than does the constancy of y and π falling more than μ. For example, $\mu 1$ fell by 6 percentage points from 1975 to 1976, but the inflation rate as measured by the GNE deflator fell only by 1.3 percentage points, while the GNP gap opened from 4% to 6%. Hence, we have at least one acceptable explanation for the events after 1975: an antiinflation policy that forced the economy to go through the wringer because it lacked credibility.

An alternative explanation is based on the existence of overlapping labor contracts. There may have been credibility of the Bank's new policy, but workers with continuing contracts could not act on the basis of this new information. Consequently, the *AS* curve falls by less than the *AD* curve, y is reduced, and π falls by less than μ, which is qualitatively the same prediction as for the absence of credibility. They will differ quantitatively to the extent of the shift of the *AS* curve: The greater is credibility or the fewer workers that are locked in by old contracts, the greater is the downward shift of the *AS* curve. Governor Bouey recognized this difficulty: "All sorts of existing arrangements, including virtually all wage contracts, are based on the assumption of some continuing inflation."[7]

However, there are still some missing pieces to the puzzle that cannot be accounted for by the lack of credibility of the Bank's policy. Although credibility may have been the initial problem, it would take a particularly obtuse public to deny that the Bank was maintaining its new strategy after 1975. Therefore, after a learning period, the predictions outlined in Section 11.3 should be observed. Yet as late as 1979, Mr. Bouey was warning that "if Canadians effectively resist a gradual reduction in the size of price and income increases they will force a reduction in the growth of employment and output."[8] Also, right to the end of 1982, we find that π exceeded $\mu 1$ and the GNP gap continued to widen. To explain the poor performance of the Canadian economy after 1977 or 1978, other explanations are needed. Also, since the inflation rate did fall, one would expect movements in the exchange rate to reflect a new differential between domestic and foreign inflation rates. In other words, the domestic currency should appreciate more or depreciate less after 1975 than before, regardless of whether the policy had credibility or not. Instead, since the index of effective exchange rate generally falls throughout the period, the evidence is that the Canadian dollar tended to depreciate against the currencies of its major trading partners, perhaps at an even faster rate. For an explanation of this phenomenon, we need to look at external events.

[7] *Annual Report of the Governor of the Bank of Canada,* Ottawa, 1975, p. 10.
[8] *Annual Report of the Governor of the Bank of Canada,* Ottawa, 1979, p. 9.

11.5.3 EXCHANGE-RATE TARGETS

Once the Bank of Canada decided to establish and follow targets for monetary aggregates, it also had to abandon any target it might have had for the exchange rate. Therefore, one would expect the Bank to treat the exchange rate as an "irrelevant" variable after 1975. To the extent that Canadian inflation was lowered relative to that prevailing in the rest of the world, the Canadian dollar should have appreciated, but in fact there was almost steady pressure on the dollar to depreciate. By 1978 the Bank was trying to reverse that trend.[9] Although it may be possible to have short-run goals for the exchange rate *and* maintain the growth rate of the money supply within the target range, sooner or later there will be a conflict between the exchange rate and the money supply and the Bank will have to make a choice. It became clear that after 1978 more and more emphasis was placed on keeping the exchange rate from rising and less and less emphasis on keeping the money supply within its announced target range. More than any other action, this decision contributed to the continuing lack of credibility of the monetary strategy. Despite the governor's statement that "the firm commitment of the Bank of Canada to persist with the gradual reduction over time in the rate of monetary expansion is intended both to encourage and to justify confidence in declining inflation in the years ahead,"[10] the "politicization" of the exchange rate, as Courchene has argued, made inflation watchers in Canada pay more attention to the actions of the Federal Reserve Board than to those of the Bank of Canada.

If the Bank of Canada was so concerned with the exchange rate, would it not have been better to fix the exchange rate in 1975 than to have an independent monetarist strategy? The answer depends on whether the Bank thought it could pursue a more successful antiinflationary policy than the Federal Reserve, but the Bank's *Annual Reports* do not give us any clues to this question.

11.5.4 OIL-PRICE SHOCKS

Twice in the 1970s the world economy was rocked by substantial increases in the price of oil. Unique among the industrial countries, Canada was fortunate to have enough oil resources to provide for a large part of its domestic needs and share the burden of the shock between consumers and producers. It thus was able to mitigate but not escape the effects of

[9] See Section 10.6.2.
[10] *Annual Report of the Governor of the Bank of Canada*, Ottawa, 1979, p. 8.

these price increases. In 1973, imported oil was priced at $3.95 a barrel, while Alberta oil was $3.48. In 1974, the former rose to $11.29, while the latter increased to $5.83. Then, between 1978 and 1980 the imported price rose from $16.28 to $36.96, while Alberta oil rose from $12.25 to $15.58. Although perhaps not as large as in other countries, severe disruptions were suffered in Canada because of these two events. They can be thought of as supply shocks in terms of the *IS–LM–AS* model. As was previously argued in Section 3.5 and discussed in relation to U.S. macroeconomic events in Chapter 8, increasing the price of oil, an intermediate input into the production process, destroys some of the existing capital stock that is no longer "energy-efficient." In turn, this reduces the marginal product of labor and shifts the demand curve in the labor market downward, reducing equilibrium employment and the real wage. In the product market, one can think of this as a negative x_s, which is later translated into a permanent reduction in y_e.

What are the effects of these shocks on the Canadian macroeconomy, and could they frustrate the intent of the Bank's policy to reduce inflation? To answer these questions it is assumed that the Canadian economy was in equilibrium prior to the oil-price increase of 1973 and then allow x_s to take on a negative value. In Figure 11-3, the initial equilibrium at E_0 is disturbed by a leftward shift of an *AS* curve, for which π^e is fixed, by the amount $(1 + a_4)x_s$. In the absence of any other event, a new short-run equilibrium will be established at E_1, where inflation is higher and output falls, but by less than $(1 + a_4)x_s$. If the event is temporary, the economy will move back to E_0 in subsequent periods. In 1974 it was not known whether the increase in the price of oil was temporary; only later did it become apparent that oil prices would not come down to their previous levels. The permanence of the event is thus translated into a shift of a vertical *AS* curve, along which $\pi = \pi^e$, by the same amount $(1 + a_4)x_s$. Thus, at the final equilibrium of E_2, output falls more in the long run to y_2, but since the growth rate of the money supply has not been changed in response to this event, π will fall again until it is equal to μ once more, so that *AD* must shift down again because real money balances will be reduced while $\mu < \pi$. Of course, in the *very* long run, the inefficient capital can be replaced and y_e can increase once more, but that time horizon does not concern us here.

Over a shorter time period, the oil-price shock is predicted to reduce output "permanently" and to raise inflation temporarily. The evidence in Table 11-1 is certainly consistent with these predictions. A permanent reduction in output and an increase in the unemployment rate are evident after 1974. This is also seen in Chart 11-1, where the GNP gap closed between 1972 and 1974 but then opened between 1974 and 1975. Also, the inflation rate, measured either by the GNE deflator or the CPI, rose

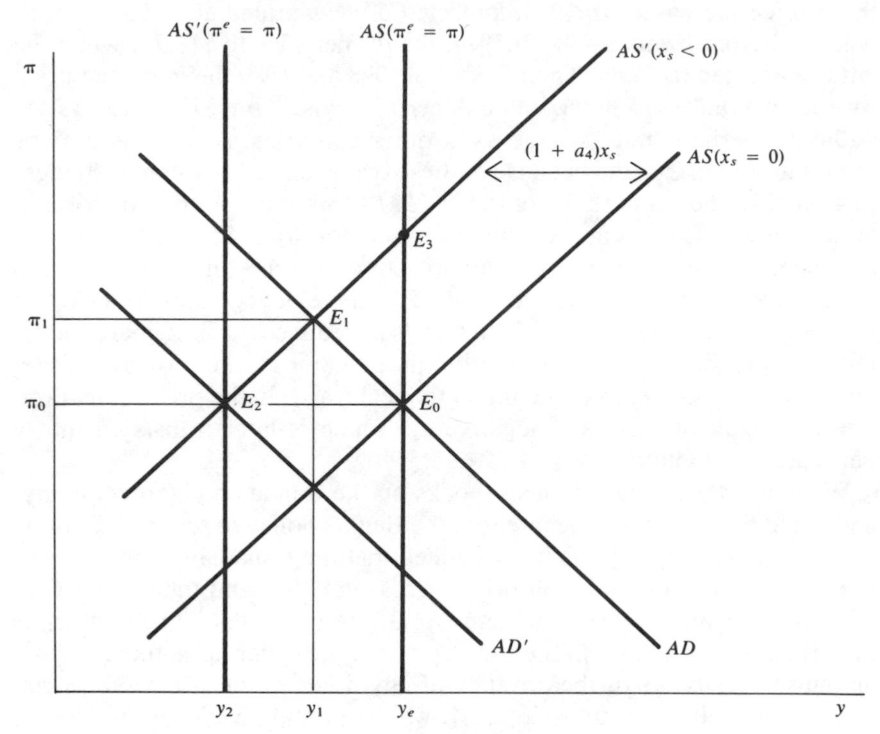

Figure 11-3 Long-run and short-run effects of the oil-price increase.

between 1973 and 1974 and then started to fall again in 1975, but not to the neighborhood of 5%, the value of π in 1972. It appeared that a high-inflation environment had been created by the oil-price increase, even though it was a once-and-for-all event, and it was in response to this development that the Bank of Canada put primary emphasis on fighting inflation in its policy decisions after 1975. The oil-price shock of 1979 had similar effects: a temporary increase in the rate of inflation and a permanent reduction in output.

When these effects on the Canadian macroeconomy are combined with those of a predictable and even credible antiinflation policy, it is perhaps not surprising that the economy did not behave as would be predicted for the antiinflation policy alone; the oil-price shock had significant independent effects on the economy that have to be included in the analysis. From that perspective, all that can be asked of the Bank's actions is that inflation be reduced in the long run, recognizing that in the short run, oil-price shocks can cause temporary increases in π. Also, the reduction in output or increase in unemployment cannot be entirely blamed on the Bank's policy if y_e is falling due to two substantial adverse events that affected the productive capacity of the Canadian economy. Probably the success of the Bank's policy cannot be measured, but it may consist of preventing hyperinflation, a situation described by a rising π, or prices rising at an ever-increasing rate. In the absence of an antiinflation policy, inflation may have risen to 20% after 1975 and then to 25% or 30% after the 1979 oil shock. Once hyperinflation gets a start it is a difficult process to reverse, as those countries with "triple-digit" inflation know.

It can also be asked whether monetary policy should have been altered to try to overcome the effects of the oil-price shock on output and employment. In general, the answer is no: A supply shock that turns out to be permanent cannot be eliminated by aggregate-demand policies. The initial level of output, y_e in Figure 11-3, could be maintained temporarily if the AD curve were moved up to intersect with AS' at E_3, but since the shock was initially unexpected, stabilization-policy instruments cannot be changed in time to reach such a point. If there are long-term labor contracts, in subsequent periods a role for stabilization policy does exist since the adjustment to the new equilibrium would take longer than in the absence of such contracts. This is an example of the kinds of policy problems discussed in relation to the institutionalist model of the macroeconomy in Chapter 4.

In any event, the oil-price shock does not help us to explain the severity of the recession in 1981–2, by which time the worst should have been over. For this period we need to look at developments in the rest of the world.

11.5.5 EXTERNAL EFFECTS ON THE CANADIAN ECONOMY

Throughout the period that has been reviewed the rest of the world did not stand still, and for that reason it is not possible to assess the effects of domestic policies without allowing for international events and policies. This is especially true for a country like Canada because of its high degree of "openness." In that light, we must review briefly the important macroeconomic events in the rest of the world, particularly in the United States, after 1979–80.

The most important influence on the Canadian economy after the oil-price shock of 1979 was the rising real interest rate, which was largely imported from the United States. Table 11-2 presents data on nominal interest rates, expected inflation rates, and real interest rates for both the United States and Canada for the years 1975–82.[11] Because it is important to measure the effect on investment expenditures, the prime bank lending

[11] Earlier data contained in Table 7-1.

Table 11-2. *Real interest rates in the United States and Canada, 1975–82*

	United States			Canada		
Year	i^*	π^{*e}	$i - \pi^{*e}$	i	π^e	$i - \pi^e$
1975	7.7	6.9	.8	9.4	11.3	−1.9
1976	6.8	8.4	−1.6	10.0	11.6	−1.6
1977	6.9	7.0	− .1	8.5	10.7	−2.2
1978	9.2	6.3	2.9	9.7	8.8	.9
1979	12.8	6.7	6.1	12.9	7.3	5.6
1980	15.4	7.7	7.8	14.3	8.6	5.7
1981	18.8	8.6	10.1	19.3	9.9	9.4
1982	14.7	9.2	5.5	15.8	10.2	5.6

*Sources: i, i**, prime bank lending rate in the United States and Canada, *Economic Review,* April 1983, reference table 88; π^e, π^{*e}, calculated from the previous four π values with weights .5, .3, .15, and .05.

rate in both countries is used here instead of the Treasury bill rate. Expected inflation rates are calculated according to a formula that depends on actual past inflation rates for the previous four years. The rationale for this procedure is that data for current μ are not available or that announcements by the central bank may not be credible.

In both countries, real interest rates were low or even negative in the first three years. Thereafter, they rose until they reached the neighborhood of 10% in 1981. These figures may be compared to the historical average of around 3%. During that period, both i and π^e were generally rising, but obviously i more than π^e. The maximum effect of the high real interest rates on investment expenditures in Canada occurred in 1982, when business investment expenditures fell by 11.5% and housing expenditures dropped by 23.5%. These represent substantial reductions in aggregate demand, which were not overcome by the fact that government current expenditures rose by .7%. Thus, the economy was not faced by government demand crowding out private demand; total demand for goods and services fell. Other categories are the following: Consumption expenditures down by 2.5% and exports down by 1.5%, but imports were also lower by 10.4%. As a result, output fell by 4.8% in real terms, and the unemployment rate for adult males rose from 4.9% in 1981 to 8.1% in 1982. There are two questions about these events that have to be answered:

1. How did real interest rates in the United States get so high?
2. How were these developments transmitted to Canada?

The real interest rate for a closed economy such as the United States is determined according to

(11.7) $i - \pi^e = (a_0 - y)/a_1$

In Chapter 8, it was pointed out that increases in budget deficits, which are represented by increases in a_0, contributed to the higher real interest rate at this time. Also, contractionary monetary policy, which was not necessarily credible, raised the nominal interest rate without lowering the expected rate of inflation, thus adding to the upward pressure on real interest rates. It was believed that the Fed could not possibly continue its antiinflation policy in the face of the unprecedented deficits and the worsening recession and that it would succumb to the pressure to ease its policy stance, which in turn would fuel inflation. In these circumstances, it may have been wise to keep π^e high. One offsetting development was the reduction in income and output by 1.8% between 1981 and 1982, which had a tendency to reduce the real interest rate.

Foreign events are transmitted to the Canadian economy by certain values of x_{i^*} and x_{π^*} if the events are unexpected or through i^* and π^* if they can be anticipated. The events just described seem to fit the former category more than the latter. The contractionary but not credible monetary policy would cause x_{i^*} to be positive and x_{π^*} to be negative. The budget deficits would also generate a positive x_{i^*} but have the opposite influence on x_{π^*}. Since in fact, U.S. inflation fell from 8.6% in 1979 to 6.0% in 1982, x_{π^*} will be taken to be negative.

The effect of these impulses on the Canadian economy depends on the monetary mechanism in force at this time. It was concluded in Chapter 10 that the central bank should either practice exchange-rate control or money-supply control, depending on what it perceived would be the dominant shocks to the economy. In general, after 1978 the Bank of Canada paid more and more attention to exchange-rate targets and less and less to monetary targets, presumably because of its belief that increases in the exchange rate exacerbated inflationary expectations. Therefore, it will be assumed that in the period 1981–2, the Bank attempted to protect the existing exchange rate.

In this environment we can analyze the effect of these external shocks using essentially the framework developed in Section 10.4.3 and Figure 10-8. The initial starting point, taken to be somewhere around 1980, is shown as E_0 in both parts of Figure 11-4. It is not possible to be too precise about the timing of x_{i^*} and x_{π^*}, but our main aim is to explain the deep recession in 1981–2. In the top portion of Figure 11-4, i and y are determined by the intersection of the *IP* line, which represents the requirements of interest parity, and the *IS* curve. The location of the *LM* curve is determined residually, since the Bank of Canada allows the

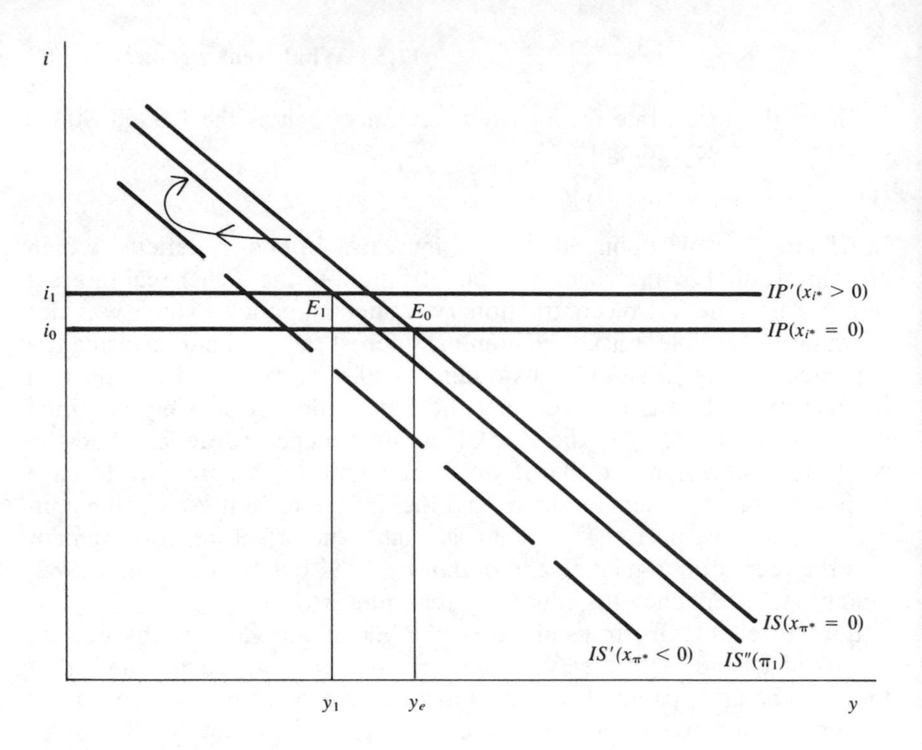

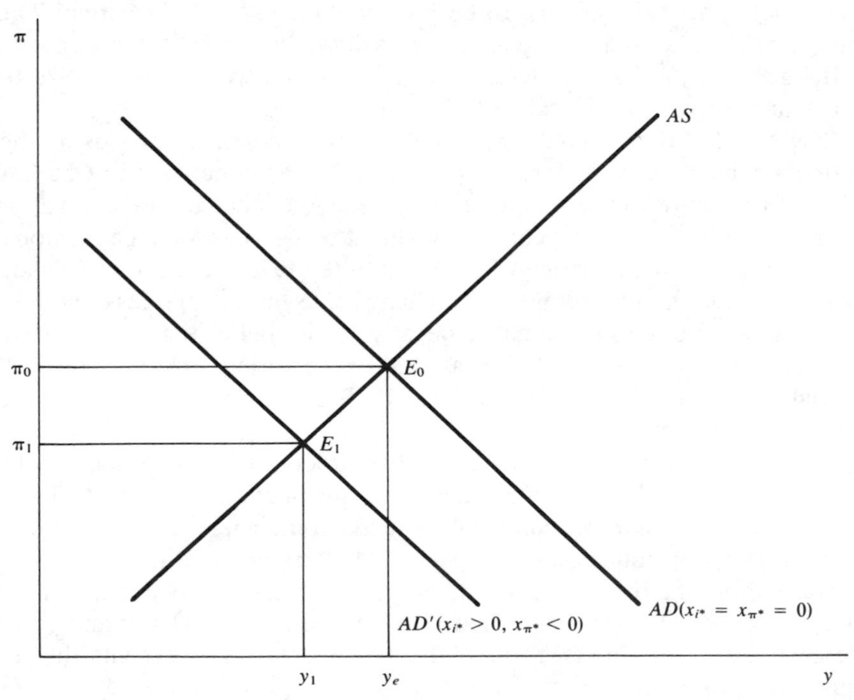

Figure 11-4 Effects of U.S. policy on the Canadian economy.

growth rate of the money supply to be demand-determined. In the bottom portion of the diagram, π and y are determined. Of course, y has to be the same in both places. The initial values of y, π, and i are not necessarily full-equilibrium quantities, as would be required by $y = y_e$, $\pi = \pi^e$, and so forth. It is better to think of the Canadian economy operating at subpar performance, as it continued to adjust to past events, particularly the 1979 oil-price increase. Nevertheless, E_0 is a short-run equilibrium. Then x_{i^*} becomes positive and x_{π^*} takes on a negative value.

The first of these shocks causes the *IP* line to shift up by the value of x_{i^*}; therefore, the Canadian interest rate must follow suit, rising from i_0 to i_1 in Figure 11-4. Also, the *IS* curve shifts down and to the left because of the lower inflation in the United States. Furthermore, the *AD* curve shifts to the left for both reasons by the value of $-a_1 x_{i^*} + a_5 x_{\pi^*}$. The *AS* curve, on the other hand, is unaffected by these events, since they are assumed not to be incorporated into expectations about future inflation. A new temporary equilibrium is established at E_1 in the bottom part of the diagram at the intersection of *AS* and *AD'*. The same level of income is required in the *IS–LM* diagram; this means that the *IS* curve must shift to the right once more because of the reduction in domestic inflation from π_0 to π_1, which allows the terms of trade to fall and encourage demand for Canadian goods. At E_1 there is a reduction in income compared to E_0, π has also fallen, but i has increased. The data in Table 11-1 for the years 1980–2 are consistent with these predictions, except that the reduction in π does not become noticeable until 1983. For that reason, the "import" of high real interest rates from the United States may offer the best single explanation of the Canadian recession of 1981–2.

It is interesting to note that the less-than-credible U.S. monetary policy created results in Canada that are very similar to those that would have been produced by a less-than-credible Canadian monetary policy. In essence, Canada suffered twice from contractionary monetary policy that lacked credibility: once in 1975–6, when π^e did not adjust to the new antiinflation policy begun in 1975, and the second time in 1980–2, when the Fed's continuation of its antiinflation policy was in doubt. The lack of credibility in these two situations stems from different sources but the results are the same: Inflation was reduced, but only by putting the economy through the wringer.

It is worth commenting on the Bank's choice of exchange-rate control as the monetary mechanism in these circumstances. Would it have been better if the Bank had chosen money-supply control? Aside from the problem of instability of the demand for M1 beginning in 1980, it cannot be argued that money-supply control would have insulated the Canadian economy against the increase in real interest rates that became the major source of the recession. The optimal monetary mechanism in this case would have involved watching the real interest rate and attempting to keep it constant. However, in Section 7.6, it was found that not only is the real interest rate difficult to measure, but also that it is not amenable to manipulation by monetary policy. Thus the Bank of Canada was powerless to adopt a monetary mechanism that would have protected the Canadian economy from the adverse effects of U.S. policies.

11.5.6 DOMESTIC FISCAL POLICY

The major problem in the Canadian economy in 1981–2 was a large-scale reduction in aggregate demand, triggered by the increase in real interest rates in the United States starting in the late 1970s. Although it would appear that domestic monetary policy was not in a position to combat the recession, we can ask whether fiscal policy made a contribution to solving this problem. In a closed economy, a reduction in government expenditures or an increase in taxes will lower the real interest rate, but adopting such a policy in Canada during this period would have been precisely the wrong one. In an open economy, the domestic real interest rate is largely determined by what happens in the rest of the world. Substituting the *IP* condition into $i - \pi^e$ produces $i^* + \rho^e - \pi^e$, with i^* exogenous and either $\rho^e = 0$ in a system of fixed exchange rates or $\rho^e = \pi^e - \pi^{*e}$ in the case of flexible rates, with π^e determined by μ and π^{*e} again exogenous. In either case, $i - \pi^e = i^* - \pi^{*e}$, and fiscal policy cannot change that fact. Table 11-2 indicates quite clearly that the Canadian real interest rate moved in line with the real interest rate in the United States, although the two are not exactly equal because of possible mismeasurement of π^e in the two countries, differences in risk factors or tax treatment, or other relatively minor causes. Therefore, the focus of fiscal policy should be to replace the missing investment expenditures and not try to restore them. In 1981–2 fiscal policy should have been expansionary.

In this light we can look at the stance taken by the federal government to see if it followed a countercyclical strategy in its budget. The actual budget balance depends not only on the decisions of the government of the day to spend and to tax, but also on the state of the economy, which dictates the size of tax revenues and entitlement programs. A cyclically adjusted budget balance captures only the former, since it presumes that the economy is operating at its full potential. Both balances are shown in Chart 11-2 for the years 1972–82. It is this latter budget balance that measures the government's strategy. The general trend is to larger and larger deficits after 1974, even though the economy was near equilibrium, as evidenced by the fact that the two lines are quite close to each other until 1978. Then in 1978, the government seemed to make a conscious

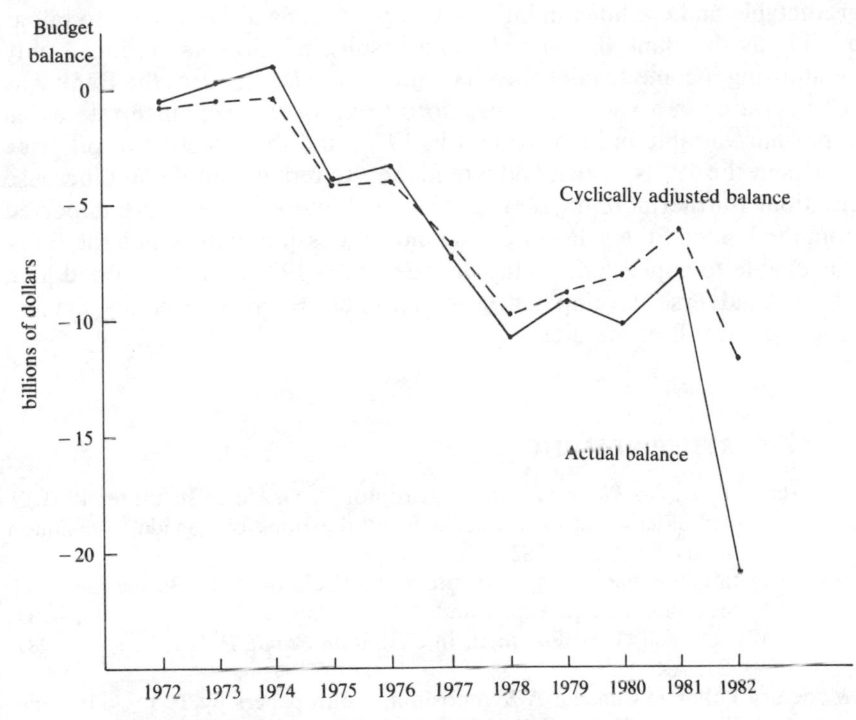

Chart 11-2 Canadian federal government budget balances, 1972–82. *Source: Economic Review,* April 1983, reference table 54.

decision to reduce the deficits. In 1982 it moved substantially toward an expansionary stance. This appears to be appropriate in the circumstances, but the government should also have been running surpluses during the earlier period so that the budget is balanced over the entire business cycle.

It is perhaps the cumulative deficit of the last few years that creates the greatest dangers to the independence of monetary policy. In Section 6.10, it was pointed out that fiscal policy could influence the money supply if the monetary authorities can be forced to "monetize" the government debt generated by the deficits. Although this does not appear to have happened as of 1984, fears of the erosion of monetary independence may have contributed to higher expected inflation than would occur otherwise.

11.6 SUMMARY

The Bank of Canada adopted a monetarist strategy in the fight against inflation in 1975. Despite every effort to make the new policy predictable and credible, inflationary expectations did not seem to fall as quickly as the Bank had hoped. As a result, inflation was reduced only by allowing income to fall below its equilibrium level. Also, the Bank was not operating in a vacuum. It began to think of the exchange rate as an important variable in its own right in 1978, and there were two oil-price shocks in the 1970s, which had a tendency to reduce output and increase inflation. Furthermore, in 1981–2, high real interest rates were imported from the United States, leading to a major recession, with which the Bank was unable to cope. Perhaps the decade of the 1970s was full of bad luck with one adverse development after another. Even wise policy makers need a good roll of the dice!

FURTHER READING

Courchene, T. J., *No Place to Stand?* Toronto, C. D. Howe Institute, 1983. A critical assessment of the decision by the Bank of Canada to abandon monetary targets in 1982.

"Has Monetarism Failed?" a symposium with papers by C. L. Barber and J. C. P. McCallum, D. D. Peters and A. W. Donner, T. J. Courchene, R. G. Warick, and G. E. Freeman, in *Canadian Public Policy,* 7, April 1981, pp. 215–64.

"Monetary Policy in Canada: A Symposium," with papers by T. J. Courchene, P. Fortin, G. R. Sparks, and W. R. White, in *Canadian Journal of Economics,* 12, November 1979, pp. 590–646.

CHAPTER 12

Improving the monetary policy apparatus

12.1 INTRODUCTION

In this closing chapter we need to look at some larger issues concerning monetary policy, issues that go beyond a critical assessment of the decisions made by the chairman of the Federal Reserve or by the governor of the Bank of Canada during the turbulent decade of the 1970s. We have already discussed at great length whether, in retrospect, the central banks in Canada and in the United States performed well in the various circumstances that they faced. We looked at questions such as Did they choose the right target? and Did they choose the best monetary mechanism? On the whole, it is easy to be critical of policy mistakes with the benefit of hindsight. To counter this temptation, we must be reminded that central banks were making decisions in an uncertain environment and facing new situations. Once we realize that very few critics could consistently outperform those in charge of the central bank, we obtain a better perspective from which to make reasonable judgments.

No matter what those judgments are, we now want to focus on a more fundamental issue of whether the central bank can *ever* be successful in achieving its macroeconomic objectives. The overriding problem may be that there is an inevitable incompatibility between *public* policy and *private* maximizing behavior and that the latter will always prevail.

Economic policy involves regulation of economic behavior. In a Stalinist command economy, this might be achieved through detailed "orders" on what must and must not be done, with heavy penalties for lack of obedience to these orders. In a more democratic society, instead of relying on fear, it is customary to use economic incentives and disincentives to modify the outcome of individuals acting in their own interests when they maximize utility or profits. But can an increase in the money supply "persuade" people to work more, to save less, and to hold larger real money balances? From our *IS–LM–AS* model of the macroeconomy we think we know the answer to that question: Decisions in the labor, goods, and money markets would not be affected by predictable changes in the money supply; only unpredictable monetary shocks can force people to alter their decisions. As important as the notion of predictability is, it does not capture fully the essence of policy effectiveness. All economic regulations will have some adverse effects on some individuals, and we should not be too surprised to find that they will make efforts to escape these regulations rather than passively accept them.

12.2 THE RESPONSE OF MAXIMIZING INDIVIDUALS TO GOVERNMENT REGULATION

It is normal to conceive of economic policy as imposing a constraint on behavior, with individuals then maximizing their utility functions subject to that constraint. But it is just as likely that they will try to escape that constraint. For example, if the government imposes a tax on commodity A, we would argue that the quantity purchased would decrease and the price paid by consumers would increase. But since this action reduces the profits of the producers of A, we might more likely see these firms try to convince the government that what they now produce is really B (a nontaxed item) while simultaneously persuading consumers that what they are still selling is A. If successful, the result would be the status quo ante, which makes the tax completely ineffective.

While this is an abstract example of no immediate consequence, we can find similar responses in a macroeconomic context where public policy and self-interest collide. Two such cases will be considered, one operating in the money market and the other in the labor market.

12.2.1 CONFLICT BETWEEN THE CENTRAL BANK AND COMMERCIAL BANKS

Consider an economy in which the central bank can control M1, the narrowly defined monetary aggregate composed of currency and demand deposits. It engages in open-market operations to keep M1 exactly on its predetermined and preannounced path. In this same economy, commercial banks, which actually provide the bulk of M1 through their deposit liabilities, are profit-maximizing institutions. As such, they attempt to keep marginal revenue equal to marginal cost in their operations. Revenue is derived from making loans or other investments and costs are incurred for personnel, buildings, computers, and other costs of servicing their

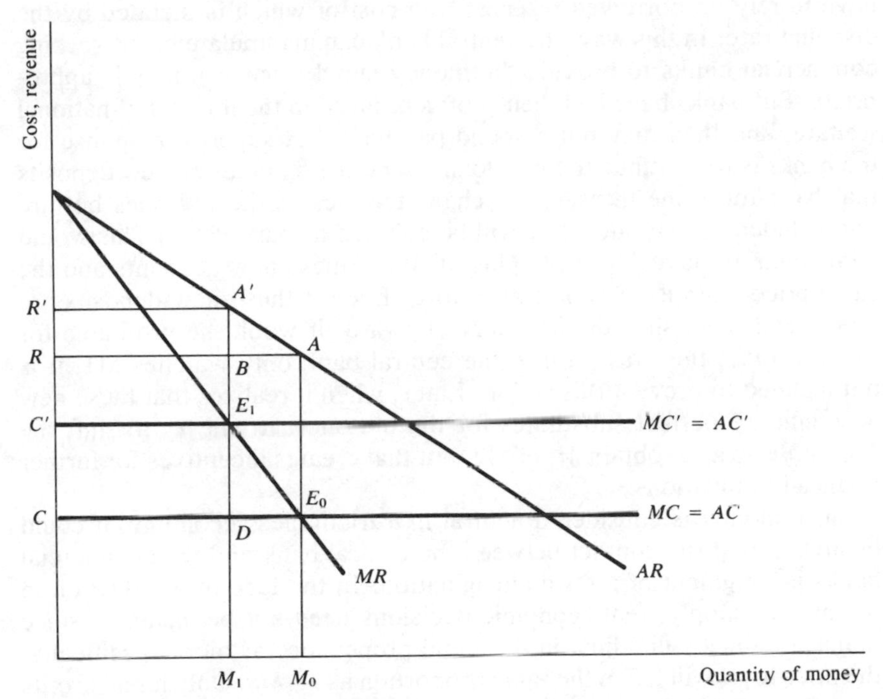

Figure 12-1 Bank profits after a reduction in the money supply.

customers. The banking system faces a downward-sloping demand curve for loans, shown as *AR* in Figure 12-1. As long as *AR* is a straight line, *MR* (marginal revenue) will slope down twice as fast. It is also assumed that the banking industry displays constant costs, hence $MC = AC$ is a horizontal line in the diagram. The horizontal axis measures the "size" of the banking system, which is almost synonymous with M1. The profit-maximizing point is E_0, with a money supply equal to M_0. Initial profits are equal to RAE_0C.

Now assume that the central bank believes that a lower money supply, at M_1, would improve the performance of the macroeconomy. To resolve the conflict between these two views of the "optimal" money supply in its favor, the central bank would have to raise the *MC* curve to *MC'* to cut through E_1. The central bank does not operate directly on all the costs that commercial banks face; instead it concentrates on the cost of reserves through a combination of open-market operations and adjustments to the discount rate. To move to *MC'*, the central bank would sell bonds out of its portfolio, which has the effect of reducing the owned reserves of the commercial banks and increasing their opportunity cost. Then, if the banks were still reluctant to eliminate some of their loans, they would have to rely on borrowed reserves, the cost of which is dictated by the discount rate. In this way, the central bank can manipulate profit-seeking commercial banks to provide the money supply that it thinks is appropriate. But banks have had their profits reduced in the interest of national welfare, and they may not respond passively.[1] A superior response for the banks is to continue to make loans as before by creating new deposits that have the same transactions characteristics as the old ones but are not included in M1; later they will be counted as part of M2. This would allow them to have M_1 of M1 plus M_1M_0 of these new accounts and the same price-quantity outcome as before. Even if these new deposits are more costly and shift the MC curve upward, it would be profitable for them to react this way.[2] Since the central bank only watches M1, it is not inclined to prevent this action. Later, when it realizes that these new accounts are perfect substitutes for the old ones, it will try to shift the MC curve so as to obtain M_1 of M2, but that creates incentives for further financial innovations.

Since money is considered neutral in a frictionless economy, it could be argued that the conflict between the central bank and the commercial banks is a figment of a fertile imagination. In the face of a reduction in the money supply, real economic decisions need not be changed, since nominal values will adjust in the same proportion, or more specifically, the price level will fall in the same proportion as M_1M_0. Only if real profits are affected will the banks have an incentive to alter their current behavior. In Figure 12-1, if nominal profits fell to $RBDC$, real profits would have remained constant, since BAE_0D represents only a price reduction. Instead, profits fell to $R'A'E_1C'$. The difference is $C'E_1DC$ versus $R'A'BR$, with the former being larger since $E_1D > A'B$. Consider the triangles E_1DE_0 and $A'BA$, which have equal bases, but since MR is steeper than AR, E_1D must be larger than $A'B$.[3] Hence real profits are reduced by the action of the monetary authorities. In other words, banks are being "squeezed" from two directions: (1) the quantity of their services and (2) their markup, that is, the gap between AR and AC. If the markup remained constant and only the quantity of loans and deposits were affected by the central bank's open-market operations, then indeed neutrality would prevail even for bank profits and decisions.

Both the Canadian and American banking systems experienced such financial innovations in the past decade, precisely because it was profitable for banks to undertake them. These innovations occurred during

[1] Here $R'A'E_1C' < RAE_0C$: $C'E_1 < CE_0$ because $M_1 < M_0$ and $A'E_1 < AE_0$ because the vertical distance between the MR and AR curves shrinks as M falls.

[2] Any point on MR below E_1 generates larger profits than E_1 itself.

[3] If there are increasing costs, the same conclusion prevails as long as AR rises faster than AC falls as M is reduced.

periods of monetary restraint. The particular circumstances were that nominal interest rates were rising, increasing the revenue available from a given quantity of loans. Costs rose as well, but less than they would have without the introduction of NOW and daily-interest accounts. Although banks paid interest on these accounts and not on demand deposits, these extra costs were more than offset by easing the constraint on required reserves. These new deposits had, at that time, lower reserve requirements and allowed existing reserves to support a larger volume of total deposits and loans.

EXAMPLE

> Assume demand deposits have a reserve requirement of 10% while the new, interest-earning deposits have a reserve requirement of only 5%; if total reserves are $100, the money supply is $1,000 if only demand deposits exist, but rises to $1,500 if half are shifted to the new deposit.

12.2.2 CONFLICT IN THE LABOR MARKET

In Chapter 2, two important characteristics of the labor market were specified:

1. The wage rate is set in advance.
2. In periods of disequilibrium, the quantity transacted would be observed on the demand curve.

These were institutional features of the labor market that distinguished it from "spot" markets and from markets where the "short" side dominates during disequilibrium. It is now time to consider two additional characteristics:

3. The labor market is not composed of identical individuals, but instead workers differ by their susceptibility to unemployment, which can usually be measured by years of seniority: The more years on the job, the less the likelihood of being laid off or "forced" to work overtime.
4. The wage rate is set by majority voting of those in a firm or industry and not by the individual worker at the margin of unemployment. In other words, it is considered "unfair" and therefore unacceptable for an individual who is unemployed to offer to do the same job as an employed worker for a lower wage; not

even those unemployed workers who are desperate for a job seem to violate this rule of labor solidarity.

In this new environment, let us consider an announced and credible reduction in the growth rate of the money supply. From our previous analysis we would argue that increases in nominal wages would be reduced to match the new rate of inflation to keep the labor market in equilibrium. However, it may be in the interest of a majority of workers to *pretend* that they do not believe the central bank and to negotiate wage increases based on the old rate of inflation. When inflation does in fact fall, the real wage will rise, unemployment will occur, but those who remain employed are better off with a higher real wage. Therefore, the burden of unemployment is not shared equally; a rate of unemployment above the natural rate makes workers with high seniority better off and workers with low seniority worse off. Even in a severe recession, only about 10–15% of workers need to fear unemployment, and therefore the median voter, who is in the middle of the seniority roster, will have a tendency to demand wage increases that are too high to maintain full employment. If a majority vote is needed to decide the issue, the median voter is the only important one, and he or she will not have full employment in mind, but instead self-interest. Only in cases where the firm is faced with bankruptcy will senior workers feel intimidated. Such circumstances can explain the wage concessions made in the 1982 recession when many companies threatened to close down altogether.

In this experiment, there has again been a conflict between public policy and private interest. Presumably the central bank wanted to reduce the growth rate of the money supply to decrease the inflation rate, but by making the policy credible, it had hoped to eliminate any real side effects, including an increase in the unemployment rate beyond the natural rate that prevails in equilibrium. The private interest of the marginal worker is not in conflict with this aim, but it is not in the best interests of the median worker. The marginal worker knows that any increase in the real wage will leave him or her unemployed with a major reduction in economic welfare, but the median worker can safely demand a higher real wage without much fear of unemployment.

It may be argued that the median worker can take advantage of this privileged position in such an institutional setting at any time, not just when an antiinflation policy is being pursued. However, this argument would neglect the frailty of the institution of labor solidarity. If it meant that 49.9% of workers would *always* be unemployed because 50.1% got a higher real wage as a result, it is highly probable that the majority-vote rule would be replaced by another institution that removed some of the power enjoyed by the median worker and give more to the marginal

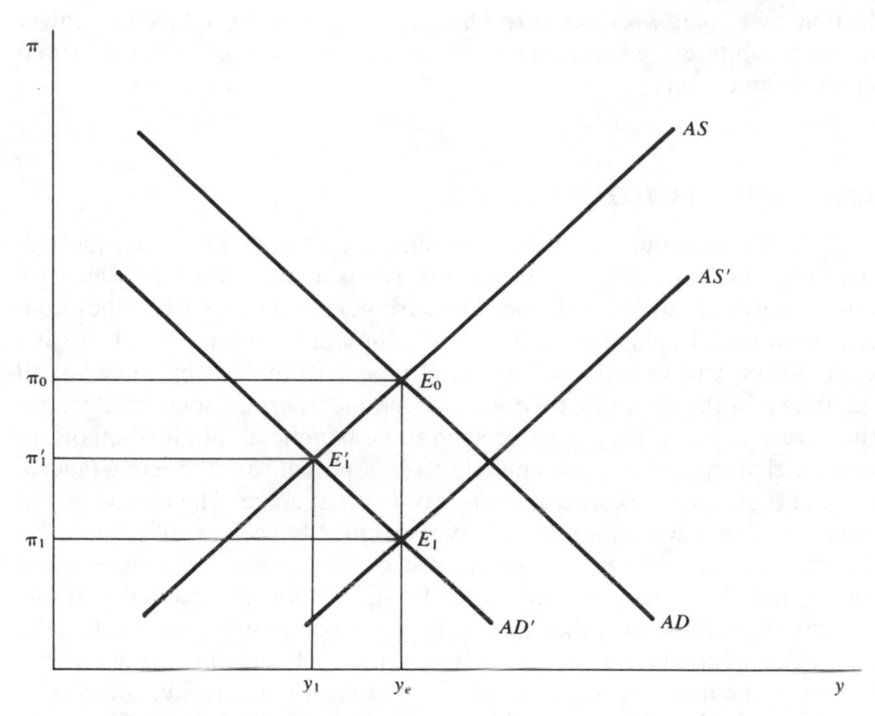

Figure 12-2 Antiinflation policy with conflict in the labor market.

worker. But in a period of policy change, it pays median workers to use the power that they have. They can argue that the new policy will not go into effect and that *all* workers will suffer a decline in the real wage if they accept a smaller increase in nominal wages when the inflation rate remains unchanged. In fact, by taking this position they will turn out to be at least partially correct, even if the central bank does try to deliver on its promise. From Chapter 3 it will be remembered that a reduction in the growth rate of the money supply will shift the AD curve down to AD', as shown in Figure 12-2. If the policy is credible, the AS curve will also shift down to the same extent to AS'. At E_1, y_e is preserved and π falls to π_1. If, however, inflationary expectations do not adjust downward, the AS curve remains in place and a new equilibrium is established at E'_1, with output falling to y_1 and the inflation rate dropping to π'_1, which is less than originally predicted, allowing the median voter to cite this evidence against the dependability of the central bank.

The discussion of these conflicting priorities has pointed to the possibility that macroeconomic policies can never be successful as long as some group's interest suffers and that group has sufficient power in the current institutional setting to prevent the achievement of national aims.

In that case, is it worthwhile to change institutions to reduce the power of special-interest groups and improve our chances of success in macroeconomic goals?

12.3 INSTITUTIONAL REFORM

An institution is a voluntarily imposed constraint on our individual behavior. Therefore, an institution is a social contract in which we collectively acknowledge the need to curb personal rights when they conflict with social obligations. Sometimes they are "enforced" by custom or tradition, and sometimes they are "imposed" by law, but they are all voluntary in the sense that we want to be members of society. Because they are voluntary, they must be seen to be beneficial, but it is important to note that institutions are unlikely to be optimal for all circumstances; instead they can be expected to work only on average. The reason is that we cannot have institutions that serve specifically each set of conditions. Institutions are difficult to change, not because people are necessarily hidebound, but because institutional reform involves irreducible transactions costs. Rewriting the social contract involves time, interpreting the new rules of conduct involves costly errors, and adjusting economic behavior to the new environment involves, at least temporarily, some extra resources. In this light, although we want to change policies as frequently as new problems arise, we want to take a somewhat longer perspective when we deal with institutional reform. An analogy to the difference between laws and constitutions is illuminating: We may want to change laws as quickly as necessary, but when it comes to changing constitutions, we should be forced to be deliberate, careful, and slow.

For example, consider the institution of wage indexation. The economic consequences of cost-of-living allowances (COLAs) in labor contracts were discussed in Section 4.7. Not surprisingly, whenever inflation becomes high and variable, demands for compulsory wage indexation become louder and more widespread. If these demands were met, negotiations would be in terms of real wages instead of nominal wages as is mostly the case now. Legislation could be passed requiring that COLA clauses be included in all union contracts. However, it may be unwise to make such an institutional change even in times when inflation is highly unpredictable. First, it will be remembered from the analysis in Chapter 4 that only in cases of demand-side instability do fully indexed wages provide the optimal solution; in cases of supply shocks, partial indexation would be optimal. Therefore, unpredictability of inflation by itself is not a criterion for choosing indexation; instead, it is the source of the shock that leads to inflation being variable that dictates the optimal degree of indexation. Second, even if monetary shocks are currently the dominant source of instability, they may not be in the future, and it is not always easy to change the existing legislation quickly enough to abrogate the requirement of complete indexation.

Therefore, we should be reluctant to change institutions unless it is obvious that current arrangements do not work in a majority of cases. Nevertheless, there are recurrent demands for institutional reform that promise to improve the performance of the macroeconomy, and it is important that we evaluate these proposals. It is not possible to cover all the reforms that have been suggested, so we will concentrate on those that deal with the money market and monetary policy. More specifically, we want to ask the question: How can we improve the mechanism that would ensure the "optimal" amount of money in the economy? In answering this question, we should not limit ourselves to investigating proposals that would *increase* central bank control over the money supply; it may be that reducing or even eliminating the role of the central bank in the money-supply process may be a superior alternative, especially if the monetary authorities react more to political pressures than to economic requirements. In fact, it is difficult to point to any serious proposals for institutional reform in recent times that would give greater power to the central bank than it currently enjoys; most of the suggestions now go in the other direction.[4] We will now consider three proposals: one that enhances the role of the central bank in the money market and two that would reduce the discretionary power of the central bank.

12.3.1 CENTRAL BANK MONOPOLY

The money market is characterized neither by perfect competition nor by monopoly; it is somewhere between these two extreme positions, with the central bank and commercial banks sharing the ability to "produce" money. In Canada, there are far fewer commercial banks (only 70 in 1982) than there are in the United States (well over 10,000), but the competitive conditions in the two countries are probably not much different. We want to look at proposals that would make the central bank more powerful and the commercial banks less powerful in the determination of the money

[4] Two influential documents of the 1950s and 1960s worried about the lack of central bank control over "credit conditions": *The Report of the Commission on Money and Credit* (Englewood Cliffs, N.J., Prentice-Hall, 1961) in the United States and *The Report of the Committee on the Working of the Monetary System* (London, Her Majesty's Stationery Office, 1959) in the United Kingdom. In Canada, *The Report of the Royal Commission on Banking and Finance* (Ottawa, Queen's Printer, 1964), on balance, wanted to reduce the unilateral power of the Bank of Canada in the wake of the "Coyne affair," discussed below.

supply, essentially making the central bank a monopolist in the money market. This does not involve either the simplistic solution of forcing all transactions to be made with coins and currency only and outlawing the use of checks for any payment or an attempt to legislate a lasting definition of money. Such a law could not possibly be enforced when assets with moneylike characteristics are being created every day, and it is therefore not worth further consideration. Instead, new legislation could require the following changes in banking practices:

1. All transactions balances, whether at banks, at savings and loans, or at trust companies, would be subject to a uniform reserve requirement.
2. Neither banks nor any of the near-banks would be allowed to borrow reserves from the central bank, except perhaps for emergency cases at severe penalty rates.

By making reserve requirements equal for all transactions accounts, the link between the monetary base and any of the definitions of the money supply would be strengthened. This link is the money multiplier and the discussion in Chapter 6 suggested that in the current situation, a shift of funds from one type of deposit to another could change the value of the multiplier if the two types of accounts had different reserve requirements. With reserve requirements being the same for all deposits, the multiplier would no longer be subject to such random disturbances. Also, by eliminating commercial-bank borrowing from the central bank, the monetary base would be completely under the control of the monetary authorities. Again in Chapter 6 we saw that the monetary base was the sum of various central bank assets, which could be changed through sales or purchases of government securities and through loans to the commercial banks. By eliminating the latter category, the central bank can dictate the size of the monetary base, almost to the last dollar. Since the money supply is equal to the monetary base times the money multiplier, reducing the unpredictable or uncontrollable elements of the base and of the multiplier has similar effects on the money supply. According to this view, although the banks would continue to be the source of most of the money in the economy, they would be on a much tighter rein held by the central bank. The advantage of these reforms for the macroeconomy would be that the central bank would be better able to deliver on its promise to keep the money supply growing at preannounced target ranges if some of the "noise" in the *LM* curve can be eliminated. In turn, the improved credibility of the monetary authorities in the eyes of the public would make calculations of expectational variables easier and allow the economy to stay closer to equilibrium output.

However, there are a number of counterarguments to such a proposal.

First, there are constitutional complications that may not be easily overcome. Both in Canada and in the United States, the federal government does not have unilateral legislative jurisdiction over banks. In the United States, state governments control the actions of state banks and other nonbank financial intermediaries, whereas in Canada, trust companies and other deposit-taking institutions are chartered by the provincial governments. In this setting it would be difficult to force all banks and near-banks to observe minimum reserve requirements dictated by the federal government. Legislative coordination between the two levels of government would be necessary but not easily acquired, as each side jealously guards its prerogatives in this area.

Second, it is probably not possible to list completely all the various transactions balances that would be covered by the uniform reserve requirement, and financial innovations would make any list out of date almost as soon as it was published. Therefore, if a bank introduced a new type of deposit, it would take time to determine whether it was being used primarily as a savings deposit or for transactions purposes, something the bank could not control; meanwhile, it may be subject to no reserve requirement because it is not on any list. One way to get around this problem is to require banks to obtain prior permission from the monetary authorities to introduce a new type of deposit.

Third, the existence and variability of *excess* reserves would still be under the control of the commercial banks, and they are another source of instability of the multiplier. Beyond paying interest on these excess reserves to make them more predictable – a proposal discussed in Chapter 6 – there is very little that the central bank could do; it certainly could not prohibit banks from having excess reserves.

Fourth, eliminating the discount window at the central bank may not improve central bank control over the money supply. In the Canadian banking system, borrowing by chartered banks from the Bank of Canada is not significant; instead they borrow indirectly, using investment dealers as middlemen.[5] This example suggests that legislation prohibiting borrowing would have to try to specify all the techniques for getting access to the discount window, both direct and indirect, and it should not be impossible for commercial banks to find ways around these restrictions and regain some of their lost control over the monetary base through "creative accounting."

Fifth, even if all these objections could be overcome, it should not be taken for granted that the central bank would always use this power wisely, and it may be that the current system which incorporates some checks and balances may in fact be better. In cases where the best course

[5] See Section 6.5 for details.

of action is in some dispute, it may be dangerous to give the central bank an all-powerful position in the money market. For example, during the late 1950s, James Coyne, the governor of the Bank of Canada, maintained very tight monetary conditions, despite heavy criticism not only from the public and the economics profession, but from the minister of finance himself. When Coyne refused to resign, it appeared that he could dictate singlehandedly any monetary policy that he chose. Special legislation to declare the post of governor vacant was introduced but failed to pass. Only then did Coyne resign his office. To prevent the recurrence of the "Coyne affair," the new governor, Louis Rasminsky, acknowledged in an exchange of letters with the minister of finance, that the government of the day was ultimately responsible for monetary policy and that the governor could be forced to resign in cases of strong disagreement.

In summary, one of the reasons that the macroeconomy does not remain in equilibrium is the existence of money-market shocks, random events that prevent the money supply from being what was previously predicted. In an attempt to reduce or even eliminate these shocks, the reforms discussed in this section are meant to give the central bank greater control over the money-supply process. However, it is not clear that legislative action by itself can overcome all of these shocks or that a banking system that puts all power in the hands of one person or agency can be supported in a democratic society.

12.3.2 FREE BANKING

At the other end of the spectrum of institutional reform is the possibility of removing almost all of the power of the central bank and allowing commercial banks much greater latitude in deciding the optimal stock of money. This approach is called "free banking" or the "real-bills" doctrine of banking. The basic idea involved in this doctrine is that the amount of money in existence at any one time would be demand-determined, unlike the present system where it is largely, but not completely, supply-determined. Instead of making the monetary base determined exclusively by the central bank, as in the previously discussed proposal, the monetary authorities would make available to the commercial banks any reserves that they needed to discount any "real bills" that were presented to them. Real bills are demands for loans by producers of goods, with the goods themselves being offered as collateral for the loan. If all businesses relied on real bills, they would represent the nominal value of production or income, but even if only a certain fraction of goods is financed by real bills, income and the volume of such loans would move together in the same proportion. Then, because loans made by the commercial banks also appear as deposits of the public, economic activity and the amount of money in the economy are strongly linked together, with causality going from the former to the latter in this instance.

For example, consider an increase in production by a particular firm. To finance this new activity, the firm would borrow from its bank, and the central bank would automatically increase the reserves of the commercial banks either through open-market operations or by allowing the commercial banks easy access to the discount window. Since the money supply increased to the same extent as output or income, inflation and interest rates would remain constant. If, instead, the central bank maintained a constant monetary base in the face of increased output, excess demand would appear in the money market, interest rates would have to rise, and other adjustments would follow. Thus the real-bills doctrine of banking was considered by some to be a better monetary mechanism than any other system.[6] The automatic feature of reserve provision by the central bank is often stressed by those who are concerned that the central bank cannot escape political influence without imposing some institutional constraint because the real-bills doctrine allows very little discretionary power to the central bank.

These proposals for "free banking" must not be confused with suggestions for free competition in banking. In Chapter 1, the dangers of a competitive banking system with free entry were discussed: Since printing money uses virtually no resources, there is a great temptation to be a banker instead of a worker; as a result, competition would lead to too much money and not enough goods being produced. Because of these undesirable incentives, banks must be coerced into having sufficient capitalization to force shareholders to absorb any losses instead of customers. In other words, one must have a certain amount of "money" to be allowed to become a banker, and free banking does not imply "wildcat" banking.[7] Thus government must still play a role in a free-banking regime: enforcing rules for minimum capitalization. But the real-bills doctrine did not worry about this very much because losses on loans were excluded by assumption, since there were always "real" goods backing each loan. If for any reason a firm could not repay its loan, the bank could confiscate the goods and sell them on the open market. However, even if banks avoided "speculative" loans and restricted themselves to "productive" loans, they were still subject to risk of default. It must be remembered that *real* bills were issued in terms of the *nominal* value of goods. If, for instance, prices were

[6] In terms of the discussion in Chapter 7, this is similar to interest-rate control, which is the optimal mechanism in case of goods-market shocks.

[7] Wildcat banks were established on the frontier in the nineteenth century. They often had very little capital and made highly speculative loans. They frequently went bankrupt, leaving holders of their banknotes with worthless pieces of paper.

expected to increase, existing inventories would have a higher value, the real bills used to finance them would reflect this, and the money supply would rise automatically. Thus the real-bills doctrine would validate the expected inflation. In fact, an inflationary spiral could take place, since the larger money supply after the first round would trigger a further increase in expected prices and again raise the value of real bills. Ultimately, the central bank would have to stop increasing reserves automatically, the expectations process would reverse itself, prices would begin to fall, but banks would be holding assets with deteriorating values and the danger of bankruptcy would become palpable. In other words, the automatic feature of free banking may not always be best for the macroeconomy because it is unable to distinguish between increased output and increased prices; money, being a *nominal* variable, cannot guarantee, by itself, a predictable "split" between *real* and *nominal* influences.

Despite these dangers, two well-known monetarists, Thomas Sargent and Neil Wallace, have tried to rehabilitate the real-bills doctrine. From their analysis they conclude that a real-bills regime would lead to a Pareto-optimal allocation of resources, whereas other regimes that involve some restrictions on the activities of banks would be less desirable.[8] However, they are forced to admit that their model also leads to possible price instability and perhaps even to a complete absence of monetary equilibrium. Nevertheless, in a world of perfect foresight that they assume, this has no undesirable welfare consequences, and therefore they conclude that a real-bills approach to money is better than the quantity theory, which requires central bank control over the money supply. In reply, David Laidler asserts that price stability must be an important feature of any real-world banking system where future events are at best imperfectly anticipated; otherwise people would not be willing to make contracts denominated in money and we would be back to the inefficiencies of barter trade, first discussed in Chapter 1.[9] Furthermore, Sargent and Wallace assume that real bills are "evidences of indebtedness which . . . are safe or free from default risk" and then suggest that "no government regulations ought to restrict the scope of such intermediation."[10] But who is to enforce the requirement that these loans be default-free when there is every incentive for individuals and firms to present a biased view of their worth, especially when asking for a loan? It is probably impossible to specify a loan that is absolutely safe, and consideration of such practical

[8] "The Real-Bills Doctrine versus the Quantity Theory: A Reconsideration," *Journal of Political Economy,* 90, December 1982, pp. 1212–36.

[9] "Misconceptions about the Real-Bills Doctrine: A Comment on Sargent and Wallace," *Journal of Political Economy,* 92, February 1984, pp. 149–55.

[10] Sargent and Wallace, "The Real-Bills Doctrine," pp. 1212–13.

issues forces us to admit that an unrestricted real-bills approach to banking is not viable.

12.3.3 RULES VERSUS DISCRETION

An alternative to the implementation of the real-bills doctrine that would also take away much of the discretionary power of the central bank is a set of rules that the monetary authorities *must* follow. One such rule is to force the money supply to grow at a prestated rate, say 5%, regardless of current conditions or predictions about future performance. Economists have long debated the question: Would it be better from the point of view of the optimal money supply to restrain the central bank with rules or to allow it to use its discretion in making policy? On the surface, the answer seems simple: Discretion is better than a rule because a policy that uses all the available information must be superior to a policy that deliberately avoids using some information. For example, in Chapter 4, an economy with overlapping contracts in the labor market and suffering from a pervasive shock can be returned to equilibrium faster and with less pain by a policy that consciously counters the shock. The central bank uses the information that the shock will continue and that nominal wages are rigid in the short run to decide that a temporary deviation from the previous long-run growth rate of the money supply is an optimal response in these circumstances. However, reacting to such shocks may have some costs attached to it. In a rational-expectations framework, decisions of economic agents depend on expectations, especially about the inflation rate, which in turn depend on current and future policies. If the central bank is forced to follow a rule about the money supply process, then future policies will be known with certainty and inflationary expectations will not be in error on that account. Alternatively, if the central bank reacts to the current situation, the money supply becomes more "noisy" and less predictable, so that expectations about future inflation also become less precise, with resulting disequilibrium effects on the labor market and the need for even more central-bank intervention. This is a problem of *time inconsistency*: A policy based on discretionary power of the central bank may be optimal at a point in time, but it may be suboptimal over time; on the contrary, a rigidly specified rule may lead to some macroeconomic disequilibrium when shocks occur, but the extra information provided by the central bank may avoid the kind of disequilibrium associated with policy-induced errors in expectations.

This trade-off between rules and discretion takes us back to an issue first raised in Section 8.6.2 concerning the provision and use of information. With rules, the central bank provides information to the public but does not use any itself; with discretionary policy, the authorities use information emanating from the economy but provide little or none in return. The debate is therefore about the comparative advantage of the authorities and the public in these two activities. However, it may be possible to combine the best features of the two systems and improve the information process in the bargain. The rule for the money supply growth rate could be breached by the central bank at its discretion if it provided to the public the information as to what it did and why. In that way, expectations about the inflation rate would continue to be based on the rule because deviations from the rule would be known to be temporary.

Whatever one's view in this debate, there are some practical problems of establishing monetary rules that need to be discussed. The primary impetus for establishing rules for the rate of growth of the money supply came from Milton Friedman, who suggested that the growth rate be set equal to the long-run growth rate of the economy's productive capacity times the income elasticity of the demand for money. This would ensure that long-run inflation is zero. From the *LM* curve of the macro model,

$$m - p = a_2 y - a_3 i \tag{12.1}$$

where m is the natural log of the nominal money supply, p is ln of the price level, y is ln of income, and i is the interest rate. From one period to the next, equilibrium in the money market is maintained if

$$\mu - \pi = a_2(y_1 - y_0) - a_3(i_1 - i_0) \tag{12.2}$$

where $\mu = m_1 - m_0$ is the growth rate of the money supply and $\pi = p_1 - p_0$ is the inflation rate. If μ is set equal to the known $a_2(y_1 - y_0)$, the inflation rate is zero and the interest rate is constant.

EXAMPLE

> If $a_2 = .75$ and $y_1 - y_0 = 5\%$, μ should be set equal to 3.75%.

In the short run, as the economy goes through a business cycle, this growth rate of the money supply may lead to inflation that is greater or less than zero, with consequent errors in expectations, but Friedman thought that this result was still better than "tinkering" with the growth rate every time the central bank thinks it can improve on the situation. Even if this point is granted, however, there is still a serious difficulty with such a rule. What should be done if there is a secular change in the growth rate of the economy, from say 5% to 3%, or if there is a decrease in a_2 as a result of financial innovations that increase the velocity of the narrow monetary aggregates? At the old rule of $\mu = 3.75\%$, there will now be an inflationary bias.

EXAMPLE CONTINUES

> If $\mu = 3.75\%$ and $y_1 - y_0$ is now 3%, $\pi = 1.5\%$; if a_2 falls from .75 to .5 while $y_1 - y_0$ remains at 5%, $\pi = 1.25\%$.

The temptation is to change the rule in either of these cases, but if one yields to this temptation, one will yield to many others. So even with rules there is some discretion required.

In evaluating the three proposals for institutional reform in the relationship between the central bank and commercial banks it is important to remember that there will always be a certain amount of tension between the governors and the governed. A fundamental disagreement concerns the appropriate degree of legislative restriction placed on individual behavior. In the money market, that translates into arguments about the optimal amount of money and who should make that determination. The proposals considered here have tended to take extreme positions in this debate, but this has helped us to understand both the deficiencies of the current system and the fact that these deficiencies are not nearly as crippling as the critics would have us believe. The middle of the road may not be a perfectly smooth path, but it avoids the dangers of falling in the gutter!

12.4 SUMMARY

This final chapter has attempted to go beyond a critical assessment of macroeconomic policy errors in the past decade to a consideration of reforming the institutions, especially those relevant to monetary policy, that seem to stand in the way of successful policy implementation in the future. But there will always be a conflict over what represents success in macroeconomic performance, since some people gain while others lose when any policy is adopted. A macroeconomy is not just an aggregation of identical microeconomic units. Banks are not like other businesses because they are likely to have their real profits reduced when the central bank imposes a reduction in the money supply. Also, workers are not all alike because some have more seniority than others, so that a reduction in the demand for labor imposes costs of unemployment unevenly.

We then looked at three proposals for reform of the monetary policy apparatus. The first dealt with increased central bank control over the money supply, whereas the second, labeled "free banking," suggested that demand determination of the money supply would improve the operation of the macroeconomy; the third proposal involved tying the hands of the central bank by insisting on a monetary rule that would be optimal over a longer period of time. Although these conflicting proposals have some merit, significant critical arguments can be mounted to make them less than compulsively attractive. In the end, the present system, with its checks and balances as characterized by the active participation of all groups – the public, the commercial banks, the central bank, and the government of the day – in the determination of the money supply may not be best in all circumstances, but it works in enough diverse situations to be able to survive.

FURTHER READING

Fama, E., "Banking in the Theory of Finance," *Journal of Monetary Economics,* 6, January 1980, pp. 39–57. Deals with some fundamental issues about the regulation of banks and the operation of a monetary system.

Friedman, M., and A. Schwartz, *A Monetary History of the United States, 1867–1960,* Princeton, N.J., Princeton University Press, 1963. A classic account of monetary events since the Civil War.

Kydland, F. E., and E. C. Prescott, "Rules Rather Than Discretion: The Inconsistency of Optimal Plans," *Journal of Political Economy,* 85, June 1977, pp. 473–91. Takes the position that "tinkering" with the economy results in suboptimal planning.

Mints, L. W., *A History of Banking Theory in Great Britain and the United States,* Chicago, University of Chicago Press, 1945. Contains a critical assessment of the earlier expressions of the real-bills doctrine.

Index